Athenian Legacies

To Anna [signature] Sept 28 2004

Athenian Legacies

Essays on the Politics of Going On Together

Josiah Ober

PRINCETON UNIVERSITY PRESS

PRINCETON AND OXFORD

Copyright © 2005 by Princeton University Press

Published by Princeton University Press, 41 William Street, Princeton, New Jersey 08540

In the United Kingdom: Princeton University Press, 3 Market Place, Woodstock, Oxfordshire OX20 1SY

All Rights Reserved

Library of Congress Cataloging-in-Publication Data

Ober, Josiah.
    Athenian legacies : essays on the politics of going on together / Josiah Ober.
        p. cm.
    Includes bibliographical references and index.
    ISBN 0-691-12095-1 (cloth : alk. paper)
    1. Democracy—Greece—Athens—History—To 1500.   I. Title.

    JC75.D36O235 2005
    320.938'5—dc22   2004066027

British Library Cataloging-in-Publication Data is available

This book has been composed in Sabon.

Printed on acid-free paper. ∞

pup.princeton.edu

Printed in the United States of America

10 9 8 7 6 5 4 3 2 1

For my students, my teachers

Contents

Abbreviations

For abbreviations of classical authors and works, see the *Oxford Classical Dictionary*, 3d edition. Oxford: Oxford University Press, 1996.

Ath. Pol. *Athēnaiōn Politeia*

CAH *Cambridge Ancient History.* 1st edition 1923–39; 2d edition 1961–. Cambridge: Cambridge University Press.

DK *Die Fragmente der Vorsokratiker.* Ed. Hermann Diels and Walther Kranz. 6th ed. Berlin: Weidmann, 1966–67.

F Fragment (of a lost work by an ancient author)

GHI *A selection of Greek historical inscriptions.* Ed. Marcus N. Tod. 2 vols. Oxford: Clarendon Press, 1962.

HCT Gomme, A.W. (with Antony Andrewes and Kenneth J. Dover). *A Historical Commentary on Thucydides.* 5 vols. Oxford: Clarendon Press, 1945–81.

IG *Inscriptiones Graecae.* Berlin, 1873–

Loeb Loeb Classical Library. Cambridge, Mass., and London: Harvard University Press.

LSJ *A Greek-English Lexicon*, compiled by Henry George Liddell and Robert Scott, revised and augmented throughout by Sir Henry Stuart Jones, 9th ed., with supplement. Oxford: Oxford University Press, 1968.

OCT Oxford Classical Texts. Oxford: Clarendon Press.

OGIS *Orientis Graeci Inscriptiones Selectae.* Ed. W. Dittenberger. 2 vols. Leipzig: Hirzel, 1903.

RO *Greek Historical Inscriptions 404–323 B.C.* Ed. P. J. Rhodes and Robin Osborne. Oxford: Oxford University Press, 2003.

SEG *Supplementum Epigraphicum Graecum.* 1923–

SIG *Sylloge Inscriptionum Graecarum.* Ed. W. Dittenberger. 3d edition. 4 vols. Leipzig: Hirzel, 1915–24.

Teubner B. G. Teubner Velangsgesellschaft. Leipzig.

West Martin L. West, *Iambi et elegi graeci*, 2d ed. 2 vols. Oxford: Clarendon Press, 1991–92.

Preface

THE TERM "LEGACY" is not always used in a positive sense: Modern organizations struggle to free themselves from the constraints of legacy systems (like antiquated proprietary software), and social comedians have long mocked legacy hunters for fawning upon those they despise. The phrase "historical legacy" is quite frequently used in a negative sense as well, as in "legacies of Nazism" or "colonial legacies" (see, for example, Adelman 1999 on "the problem of persistence" in Latin American history). But "historical legacy" can also be employed in a positive sense, and is often associated with value terms like "rich" and "vital." Negative historical legacies threaten to constrain us from going forward or even to drag us back into an unhappy past; they are useful only as warnings of what we must work to overcome or avoid. Positive legacies, by contrast, are resources that we may call on to further progressive goals. As rightly valued resources that make the past useful in desirable ways, positive legacies are worthy of our esteem and should be preserved.

Coming to grips with the positive as well as the negative legacies offered to us by the past—including the deep cultural past—is essential if the members of human communities (whether they are nation-states or other purposeful organizations) are to find a way to go on together into a better future. This book is devoted to defining those conditions under which the project of going on as a community might come to be regarded (as I believe it should be) as a fundamental human good for the political animals we are. It is meant to show how the complex historical legacy of classical Athens could be a valuable resource in furthering that project. This is not an entirely new undertaking. An unexpected pleasure of working on this book was coming to realize how often I had been anticipated, in the concerns that animate these essays and in some of their conclusions about Athens and democratic politics, by one of the fathers of modern liberalism, J. S. Mill (see, in detail, Urbinati 2002).

The essays offered here were composed under diverse circumstances, and published in a wide variety of venues. Yet each seeks to answer a question set by Sheldon Wolin, in the course of a late-night conversation at a conference on ancient and modern democracy. Wolin's question may be formulated as follows: "How can the historical experience of democracy (especially Athenian democracy) become a positive legacy for subsequent generations of political theorists and historical actors *while remaining true to its revolutionary origins*?" Wolin worried that as soon as a revolutionary moment is domesticated as a "useful legacy from the past" it loses its power to challenge and potentially to overthrow the complacent and ultimately oppressively constraining order of things that constitutes "ordinary political life." Because I believe that the interest and value of Athenian democracy lies in the conjunction of its revolutionary character and its capacity to provide us with "legacy resources" for our own theory building, I felt that Wolin's question demanded an extended answer.

The essays presented here were written with multiple audiences in mind: political theorists, moral philosophers, classicists, and students of cultural studies. I have translated all unfamiliar Greek terms, and have kept use of the Greek alphabet to a minimum. Those without much previous knowledge of Athenian political history may find the short primer on Athenian political development, offered in chapter 5, helpful prior to reading chapters 6 through 10. The last two chapters introduce categories of evidence (archaeology, epigraphy, iconography) that may be less familiar to some readers than are classical Greek texts, but I hope these chapters will be no less interesting for that. Eight of the chapters were previously published; I have revised each of them slightly for this collection, but I have not systematically updated the references to secondary literature.

I wrote these pieces as a member of the faculty of Princeton University's Department of Classics and Center for Human Values; each essay bears the stamp of Princeton's distinctive and extraordinary intellectual environment. Yet I also spent time as a visitor in Cambridge University (Clare Hall), at the Université de Paris (I: Sorbonne, Centre George Glotz), and at the University of California at Irvine (Department of Classics and College of Humanities); and the final editing was done at the Center for Advanced Study in the Behavioral Sciences in Stanford; so I like to think that there are Cambridgian, Parisian, and Californian traces as well. My thanks to the many people in each of those very different places who helped to make my visits productive and enjoyable. Earlier versions of these essays were presented as lectures at a number of universities and colleges. I thank the organizers of those events and the audiences, respondents, and correspondents who prompted me to refine my grasp of the issues addressed here.

My faculty colleagues in Princeton and elsewhere have been a constant source of inspiration; a number of them are thanked by name in the notes. But this book is dedicated to those who have been my students (albeit many now hold faculty positions). They have, through their writing and their conversation, their substantive comments and their critical queries, helped me to think through my own projects. I cannot hope to acknowledge each student with whom I have worked and from whom I have learned something of value, but several of them deserve special thanks: Danielle Allen, Kasia Hagemajer Allen, Ryan Balot, Sean Corner, Katharine Derderian, Sarah Ferrario, Kyle Fingerson, Sara Forsdyke, Sarah Harrell, Zena Hitz, Peter Hunt, Jennifer Jordan, Andromache Karanika, Kiki Karoglou, Benjamin King, Cynthia Kosso, Susan Lape, Tom Lytle, John Ma, Emily Mackil, Sarah Monoson, Charles Pazdernik, Nadya Popov, Joshua Reynolds, Nick Rynearson, David Rosenbloom, Robert Sobak, David Teegarden, Peter Turner, Gonda Van Steen, Deirdre von Dornum, James Woolard, and Nancy Worman.

Danielle Allen and an anoymous reader for Princeton Press read through a draft of the manuscript and made profoundly helpful suggestions for improvement. My editor at Princeton Press, Chuck Myers, helped me to see how a collection of essays could turn into a book with a strong central theme; Jonathan Munk's careful copyediting and Barbara Mayor's proofreading caught many a slip. Adrienne Mayor was and is my companion and best reader. We have been going on together for quite a while now, and for reasons that have nothing to do with politics.

CHAPTER ONE

Introduction: Climbing the Hill of Ares

THIS COLLECTION OF ESSAYS on Athenian political culture is a sequel to my previous collection, *The Athenian Revolution* (1996), in a very specific sense: Those earlier essays centered on democracy's revolutionary origins; these concern what must come after a revolution if the diverse members of a political community are to go on together. Both the energies inherent in revolutionary moments and the techniques of collective "going on" must be taken into account by any theory of democracy that claims to take history and culture seriously. Both revolution and going on are historical and cultural processes. While I take the human propensity to culture making as a natural endowment, particular cultures are the products of history, and history is made by willful agents. Political culture includes the values, structures, and practices of a community, along with the evolving social and political identities from which it is constituted. Ancient Athens becomes more valuable for us as modern history-making agents and for democratic theory building when we recognize it as a particular, historically unique polis with a distinctive political culture—rather than categorizing it, generically, as "the polis." Historical Athens was much more diverse and much more conflicted than the generic and idealized polis often imagined by political theorists (from Aristotle to Arendt and beyond). Because it is concerned with diversity and conflict as well as solidarity, the study of Athenian politics can contribute, not only to discussions about democracy's original potential, but also to democracy's possible future.[1]

The approach to Athens offered here rejects backwards-looking "polis nostalgia." It seeks to specify what is admirable in Athenian political culture, while never forgetting the evils permitted and promoted by the structural injustices of Athenian slavery, imperialism, and exclusion of women from active citizenship. The Athenian failure to generalize access to the freedom, equality, and security characteristic of participatory citizenship was a profound moral failure. But acknowledging that failure of moral imagination need not, in and of itself, lead to a general indictment of the

---

[1] Recent political theoretical work drawing upon Athenian critical theory and democratic practice includes books by D. Allen, Balot, Euben, Farrar, Lane, Monoson, Saxonhouse, Villa, and Wallach (see bibliography). Use of Athens for political theorizing need not be "positive." Lape 2004, for example, concludes that apparent Athenian democratic resilience proved false in that it was grounded on an incapacity to acknowledge the political agency of anyone other than native males.

values and practices typical of Athenian democratic self-governance. A historically disciplined account of politics that addresses normative concerns should allow the experience of an ancient city-state to interrogate and challenge, rather than simply to reify our modern intuitions about the possibilities of political life.[2] The practice of democracy in Athens is in some ways different from all contemporary versions of democracy (e.g., parliamentary, constitutional, deliberative, strong). But after all, it makes little sense to ask modern readers to grapple with Greek antiquity unless doing so will yield understandings not readily available in more familiar places.

GOING ON TOGETHER

At the heart of each of these essays is the attempt solve a mystery. How did the Athenians manage to go on together as an internally diverse and democratically governed community, one that sought (if never altogether successfully) to promote conditions of justice, in the face of so many circumstances that made going on so very difficult? We can sharpen that question by personalizing it: Why did Socrates choose to live in the city of Athens and obey its laws, despite his belief that other places were better governed (see chapter 7)? Why did Athenian resident foreigners and slaves risk their lives in joining the pro-democracy uprising against an oligarchic government in 404 B.C. (see chapter 8)? Why did so many Athenians choose to subordinate their individual and sectarian group interests in favor of working to maintain a community, even though that meant living and working with persons and groups who were very different from themselves?

The "going-on-together" question thus has descriptive and analytical dimensions, but it is also has normative force: Going on together under (always imperfect) conditions of democracy and justice should be valued in much the same way that we value the more familiar political goods of liberty and equality. Going on together implies these political goods and like them it is a condition of human flourishing. To pose the historical question of how going on together was possible for the Athenians, without assuming that "false consciousness" provides an easy answer, is to assert the moral equality and capacity for agency of people who were constrained in their choices (even the juridically unfree).[3] It denies that "plurality" and

---

[2] My use of Athenian history for theory building was recently the subject of a sustained critique by a leading ancient Greek historian of the positivist school (Rhodes 2003). I am pleased that in the course of his extended normative argument about why historical positivists ought not approach history in the way I do, Rhodes does not find factual errors in my work; see chapter 8, below.

[3] This formulation assumes that even slaves had some capacity to choose to work to build or to undermine a given community: see chapters 4 and 8, below.

"diversity" are distinctively modern political concerns. It acknowledges humans as political animals who will truly flourish only in sustainable communities, but regards every human community as an artifact of historical circumstances. Moreover, it supposes that socially experienced difference among people is produced in large part by revisable human judgments and willful actions. Unless we are willing to regard cultural differences as objective "facts of nature," we have no warrant for simply assuming, a priori, that Athens was in fact more culturally homogeneous than a modern nation-state.[4] If going on together is intrinsically valuable, then we should also value the processes by which the Athenians achieved that choiceworthy end and did so without resorting to forms of homogeneity that denied the value of personal freedom and without confusing equality with sameness.

The Athenians *chose* to go on together, chose it as something of value, in the face of experienced difference and periodic conflict. That choice was not foreordained: In the course of classical Greek history many poleis degenerated into a sustained civil strife that ran roughshod over written law and social convention, and ultimately extinguished the possibility of a sustained civic community: Thucydides (3.70–85) sketches a famously harrowing portrait of the dissolution of the once-great polis of Corcyra, and notes grimly that this was only one example of a pattern of collapse that affected many communities. The historical record bears him out; in the century following the Corcyrean civil war catastrophic intra-polis conflict was a frequent occurrence in the Greek world. For Thucydides' younger contemporary, Plato, and for Plato's student, Aristotle, the problem of political conflict within the city was the central problem of Greek political theory.[5]

In the *Republic* Plato employs the conflicted polis as a way to address the problems of moral psychology: His use of the polis as a model of the human soul means that solving the problem of justice, by instituting a proper system of civic education and thereby ending conflict in the city, entails an end to troublesome internal conflict within the soul of the individual. Although modern democratic theory necessarily approaches the question of

[4] While classical Greek antiquity was admittedly unfamiliar with the non-negotiable religious beliefs associated with fundamentalist versions of revelation-based monotheism, the ancient Mediterranean-western Asian world was extremely diverse in terms of religious practices, just as it was diverse in terms of language, ethnicity, dress, eating habits, and so on. Many of the horrors and benefits of modernity (colonialism, imperialism, ethnic cleansing and forced migrations of ethnic groups, mixed economies, "globalized" trade networks, etc.) have recognizable counterparts in the Mediterranean-western Asian world that was the context of ancient Athenian political culture. While we must not overlook the differences (e.g., in technology and scale), we must not allow "ancient v. modern" to do more explanatory work than it can bear.

[5] For a catalogue of Greek civil conflicts, see Gehrke 1985. For an introduction to civil conflict as a key problem in Greek history and political thought, see Ober 2000.

"politics as soulcraft" quite differently, Plato's central insight—linking the political life of the community to the moral-political psychology of individuals—remains extremely powerful. In hopes of making Plato's insight relevant to democracy, the second half of this introductory essay looks at some of the political choices made by a particular Athenian individual in the course of a lifelong civic education.

The answers to the problem of civic conflict offered by Greek philosophers centered on eliminating the very possibility of strife by carefully managing diversity within the community at large, and by eliminating diversity within the the body of active, participatory citizens. The solutions (notably Callipolis of Plato's *Republic* and the "polis of our prayers" of Aristotle's *Politics*) focused variously on reifying and naturalizing social and psychological differences (Plato's gold- silver- bronze- and iron-souled classes in the *Republic*; Aristotle's notorious theory of natural slavery) and on strong forms of civic education that intentionally left no room for resistance to the dominant culture or the development of alternative personal identities. Arlene Saxonhouse has rightly pointed to the "fear of diversity" that underlay these radical theoretical solutions to the problem of conflict.[6]

It is tempting to extrapolate from these *philosophical* responses to the imagined threat of intracommunity strife by Athens-based writers to the *historical* response of the Athenian polis to the actual fact of conflict. Yet that temptation must be resisted because the historical Athenian response was actually substantially different. While determined to find and celebrate commonalities among Athenians (some, like "autochthony," were exclusivist, exclusionary, and expressly fictive), the polis also frankly acknowledged that the umbrella term "Athenian" covered a highly diverse range of social identities. Although it is certainly true that the polis publicly promoted an ideology of "proper Athenian-ness" (e.g., in the "All Athens" Panathenaic Festival) and periodically presented its members with an idealized conception of the Athenian past (e.g., in the ritualized funeral orations over the war dead), it is also clear that these expressions of ideological coherence were countered by frank acknowledgments of diversity and conflict—notably in Athenian drama, legal process, and religious ritual.[7] The Athenians were historically familiar with internecine strife (see chapters 3, 8, 10). Yet time and again they managed to pull themselves out of the

[6] Saxonhouse 1992.

[7] A good deal of work by Hellenists in the last twenty years has sought to explain Athenian culture either as an "hegemonic" expression of coherence or as a "subversive" expression of diversity. The fact that both sides in this debate have been able to muster considerable evidence for their divergent position points, I believe, to an emerging consensus in favor of a "both-and" explanation (see Manville 1997) that acknowledges the role of culture in both reification of coherence and its subversion. See, recently, Wilson 2000, Hesk 2000, Wohl 2002, Lape 2004.

degenerative cycle of retributive violence that shattered Corcyra and so many other classical Greek poleis. They did so, not by retreating from the challenges of change and difference into a fantasy of sameness and change-lessness, but by finding democratic means by which to meet political challenges. It is in exploring those means that contemporary theorists may learn something of value from the Athenian experience of politics.

These essays were written in a millennium-spanning decade, 1995–2004. Some of my earlier work on Athenian political practice was written in the previous half-decade, 1989–1994, a historical moment of boundless democratic optimism. Democracy was the catchword of that era, and celebrating democracy's Athenian origins suited the festive atmosphere of the time.[8] But it was not entirely clear, in the years immediately following the collapse of the Soviet Empire, why political theorists should bother to learn much about ancient history in building their models of democracy. At a moment sometimes proclaimed the "end of history," the modern world seemed to be doing very well with the models readily at hand.

Since 1994 history has resumed with a vengeance. We survey a world in which the question, What conditions might allow the members of a deeply divided community to go on together under something approximating conditions of justice? is posed with increasing urgency. And we are more than ever aware that the failure to answer that question entails profound human suffering. Under such circumstances nondemocratic approaches to politics, posing as solutions that are realistic in that they put good ends (constitutional order) ahead of fallible means (democratic process), may come to seem increasingly attractive (see chapter 5). I believe that people who promote such approaches are wrong, but they rightly point to the need to think more seriously about democracy's costs. This book's "imagined ideal reader" has been sobered by the limited applicability of the standard models of democracy to the challenges of group identity and violent conflict, yet remains willing to believe that an always-imperfect democracy might ultimately be preferable to even the most benevolent autocracy. For such a reader, learning something of Athenian political history may seem worth the effort.

Each of these essays draws attention, from different angles, to tensions within the Athenian democratic political community and within Athenian political identities. And each essay suggests that these tensions were in a strong sense productive rather than destructive: The solution to the mystery of going on together is not to be sought, I argue, in construing Athenian democracy as a neutral space in which tensions arising from diversity and inequality are finally resolved. Rather the solution lies in recognizing in democracy a sophisticated means for transforming into productivity the

---

[8] See, for example, Ober and Hedrick 1993; Morris and Raaflaub 1998.

potential divisiveness arising from diversity. That transformation is effected through an ongoing discursive acknowledgment of difference, and
through a willingness to make and carry out public decisions in the face
of unresolved tensions. As Danielle Allen reminds us, at any given moment in history the processes of what I am calling "democracy as diversity
management" will require sacrifices by some people, and these processes
necessarily leave certain individuals and groups in a position of loss and
disappointment. But, by the same token, the democratic process holds out
the promise that the ledger will be balanced over time and that today's los-
ers will be tomorrow's winners.[9] A careful historical account of democratic
politics should be able to answer the essential question of how well that
promise was kept. This may not yet be the most familiar way of looking at
democracy and political culture, but it can explain a lot about politics in
classical Athens and, I would argue, about the still unrealized potential of
modern political life.

Contemporary democratic theory, in its dominant communitarian and
liberal versions, is, of course, very concerned with identities, difference,
and tension arising from pluralism within political communities (understood primarily as nation-states). In modern political theory there is a
tendency to emphasize two primary sites of tension: between the state
and the individual as "rights-holder," and between the state and groups
within it that lay claim to special rights or recognition (see chapter 4).
The persistence of state-individual and state-group tensions may be regarded as inevitable, but it is not ordinarily regarded as productive. The
challenge of democratic politics is thus typically understood as finding
ways to enable the state to achieve public purposes without doing undue
damage to individuals or groups and distributing public goods as fairly as
possible among them. The appropriate way of dealing with tensions between the state's purposes and its constituent groups and individuals is
addressed variously in communitarian and liberal accounts. In the communitarian story the state is responsible for promoting civic values and
the common good; democracy is the means by which the reified will of a
fundamentally homogeneous citizenry is publicly expressed. In the standard liberal account, the state is responsible for maintaining the rule of
law and for fair distribution of valued resources. Democracy ensures that
individuals have the opportunity to define and express their own wants,
but democracy is possible only because the rule of law provides a secure
place (inaccessible to majoritarian pressure) for expertise and thereby
prevents selfish group interests from devolving into competitive interest-
based majoritarianism.

[9] Importance of democratic fairness as achievable only over time: Allen 2004.

Much of the energy of recent political theorizing has been generated by attempts to accommodate individual and group identities, and to find a way past the reductive "either-or" choice of regarding either the good of the individual, of groups, or of the community at large as the indispensable starting point of politics.[10] Proponents of deliberative democracy seek to replace the conception of democratic decision making as a zero-sum contest among interests with a conception of decision making as a cooperative reciprocity-based process of seeking the best answer. Neorepublican accounts attempt to replace Benjamin Constant's and Isaiah Berlin's negative conception of liberty as noninterference with a more positively inflected conception of liberty as noncoercion. Various postmodernist approaches to political theorizing seek to take into account the ways in which the identities of individuals and groups have been constructed by historically contingent (and hence contestable and revisable) relationships of power. Each of these approaches seems to me promising, yet none can yet be regarded as definitive. And so there remains room for other models of democratic politics to be considered as complementary alternatives—including a model based in part on the political culture of classical Athens.[11]

In the pages that follow, I will have some things to say about standard liberal and communitarian conceptions of politics and political identity. I will argue that Athens is in some conceptually relevant ways less "thick" (i.e., homogeneous and unified) in terms of its political culture (its *politeia*, a term that embraces much more than institutional structure) than enthusiastic communitarians and suspicious liberals alike have often supposed it to be. I will argue that Athenian identities were considerably more diverse than would be tolerable in a genuinely thick culture, and by the same token that much more valuable for contemporary theorizing. Among the primary goals of this book is to develop a historically sensitive line of investigation within democracy studies, by expanding the standard accounts of the formative tensions that have given rise to what Michael Sandel calls "democracy's discontent."[12] This means unpacking the familiar box of the structuring tensions of democratic political life in some unexpected, and (I hope) productively unsettling ways.

At the heart of the tensions that defined Athenian political life, and thus the lives and moral-political psychologies of individual Athenians, was the contrast between an outwards-looking "centrifugal" push toward social diversity and an inwards-looking "centripetal" pull towards political coherence. Rather than expending vain effort in an attempt to finally

[10] See, for example, Gutmann 2003.

[11] Deliberative: Dryzek 2000; Gutmann and Thompson 1996. Republican: Skinner 1998; Pettit 1997. Postmodern: Brown 1995; Butler 1997.

[12] Sandel 1996.

resolve that dichotomy through strong homogeneity or "once-and-for-all" constitutional enactment, Athenian politics existed, and flourished, through a refusal to give up robust commitments to both diversity and coherence. Although one might (with Plato) suggest that the inability to choose between coherence and diversity is, in and of itself, evidence for conceptual incoherence, it is clear that the Athenians did not see matters that way.

The essays in this collection explore several particular aspects of the general "diversity-coherence" theme, looking at issues that emerge from the interplay of commitments to diversity and coherence within Athenian political culture and within Athenian "souls." Prominent among these issues are the following:

- *Boundaries.* The tension between an orientation to dynamic, experimental, future-oriented expansionism on the one hand and a concern for consistency in judgment, respect for the legacies of the past, and acknowledgment of established limits on the other (esp. chapter 9).
- *Identities.* The interplay between the senses of self that are given by prepolitical "private" associations (e.g., the family), or created by individual effort (e.g., Plato's Socrates), or gained through participation in the institutions and practices of democratic self-governance (esp. chapter 4).
- *Knowledge.* The simultaneous recognition of the political value of rewarding merit and technical expertise and a conviction that "rule by experienced amateurs" promotes the resilience of the community by educating citizens, and by allowing for the aggregation of what is known and thereby promoting innovation (esp. chapter 2).
- *Persistence.* The recognition of the contingency and thus fragility of any existing political order (including democracy), and an acknowledgment of the losses that make possible both its continued ordinary existence and its recovery from crisis (esp. chapter 10).

Although my contention is that the tensions intrinsic to boundaries, identities, knowledge, and persistence are essential and indeed structural components of Athenian political culture, it is tempting to seek to resolve these tensions by one of two strategies. The first strategy draws a neat separation between ideas and practices. Thus, in terms of boundaries, it might seem possible to claim that mainstream Athenian political culture was expansive, but that conservative Athenian intellectuals urged an acknowledgment of limits. Likewise, one might define a strong sense of "citizen identity," a devotion to amateurism, and confidence in resilience as typical of Athenian democratic political culture. Conversely, one might see a concern for "personal identity," an attachment to expertise, and a recognition of contingency and fragility as typical of the thinking of democracy's critics—among others, Plato. In the *Republic*, Plato seemingly set himself staunchly against Athenian-style diversity (which he characterizes as "many hued-ness"—*poikilia*). He famously suggested that an ideal-type well-ordered political community (a "best polis" or "polis constructed in words") might provide a model of an integrated human soul and thus a means to construct a new moral psychology, a fully grounded personal identity. Plato characterized the "democratic soul," by contrast, as a chaotic hodgepodge of ungrounded desires—and thus as incapable of consistently formulating morally relevant projects either for good or evil. I will offer a very different account of the diverse "democratic soul" at the end this chapter.[13]

In both the *Republic* and the *Laws* Plato develops a vision of an ideal political community that is limited in size, ruled by experts, resistant to variation, and very durable—although ultimately doomed (like all human communities) to catastrophic change. Thucydides, Aristotle, and Isocrates (among others) might likewise be made into staunch proponents of consistency, who rejected the inherent diversity and mutability of Athenian political culture. But any attempt to situate "critics and their ideas" on one side of the diversity-coherence question and "Athens and its practices" on the other leads to dangerous oversimplification. We should not forget that the citizens of Magnesia (the polis of Plato's *Laws*) are periodically to send out explorers who will seek to discover useful innovations.[14] Although the give and take between Athens' political culture and Athenian critical intellectuals is indeed an essential part of my story, and the debate between the political culture and its intellectuals was fierce and sustained, the relationship between political culture and political theory in Athens was productively recursive: It is reductive and misleading to resolve the tension between diversity and coherence by splitting ideal theory off from democratic practices (see chapters 6, 10).

An alternative strategy to resolving the various contrasting tendencies that emerge from the urges toward diversity and coherence is the resort to an explanation based on diachronic historical change: Thus, one might posit that the dynamic expansionism of the imperial fifth century B.C. yields to a chastened acceptance of limits in the postimperial fourth century B.C. According to this view the community orientation of the fifth century devolves into the individualism of the fourth, and the amateurism characteristic of the fifth century is replaced by the political domination of

[13] My thanks to Zena Hitz, whose Princeton University dissertation (2004) has clarified for me Plato's account of the democratic soul (among other problems).

[14] Among the major developments in modern Platonic political theory has been taking the later political dialogues, *Statesman* and *Laws*, seriously. See, for example, Bobonich 2002.

experts in the fourth. In sum, fifth-century confidence and optimism might be regarded as transmogrifying into a fourth-century pessimistic recognition of political ephemerality. Once again, that story is reductive and historically indefensible.

We should indeed acknowledge that things *did* change in substantial and relevant ways over the course of time in democratic Athens. Few historians these days are likely to disagree with the assertion that paying careful attention to diachronic change is essential to the historical enterprise. But allowing diachronic change to provide a causal explanation powerful enough simply to dissolve the tensions of democratic Athens is to fall into a mode of analysis which necessarily ignores salient historical continuities and thereby evacuates much of the value of the long-term historical case to the project of rethinking democratic theory. In the end, neither the strategy of splitting off the ideas of intellectuals from the culture in which they lived nor leaning on historical change can resolve the structuring tensions within Athenian political culture. And so we are left with the more interesting and demanding task of seeking to understand democracy through paying close attention to how enduring tensions sustained it.

ENTER THEOGENES

I have suggested above that the structured tension between coherence and diversity was part of what allowed citizens of Athens to find a workable course through a confusing world. That world presented a never-ending series of sharp challenges. The temptation was always present to answer those challenges by recourse to a fixed set of unquestionable cultural verities—such as a thick and unitary tradition about the past. Athenian democracy is worthy of our attention because the Athenians by and large resisted that temptation but nonetheless found ways to go on together as a community.

In order to make the political and psychological concerns about boundaries, identities, knowledge, and persistence that motivate this book more accessible and transparent, it may be helpful to consider a particular citizen, interacting with others in his city, and at two particular moments in Athenian history. The first moment, described in this section, occurs around the middle of the fourth century B.C. The date cannot be precisely determined but the events are documented and (on the whole) credible. The second moment, described in the following section, is a historical fiction—a product of my own imagination but grounded in the relatively full historical record for Athens in 335 B.C. Both moments, the chronologically uncertain real one and the chronologically precise fictive one, center around the doings of a historical individual: Theogenes of the deme (township) Erchia.[15]

Our knowledge of Theogenes' life is almost entirely limited to what we are told by the wealthy and litigious Athenian politician, Apollodorus, in *Against Neaera*, a legal speech of prosecution preserved in the extensive corpus of Demosthenes' dicanic (i.e., courtroom) orations. Some time in the 340s B.C. Apollodorus addressed a court of Athenian judges, speaking in support of a younger brother-in-law. The two men sought to secure the conviction of a woman named Neaera on the charge of falsely presenting herself and her daughter, Phano, as native Athenians and thereby breaking the laws governing legitimate marriage and the procreation of citizens, and potentially corrupting the Athenian citizen body.[16]

The issue of political identity is immediately to the fore in this courtroom drama: Apollodorus was himself the son of a manumitted slave, Pasion, who had been naturalized as an Athenian citizen. The issue of how to define and patrol the boundaries between "we, who are the Athenians" and "those residents of Athens who are not Athenian citizens" is a framing concern of the speech. Knowledge is also an issue: just how is anyone to know who among the residents of Athens is a citizen, and who is not? Apollodorus repeatedly argues that the persistence of Athens, as a social and political community defined by Athenian identity, was riding on the answer to that question, which he personalized as, who *is* Neaera, really? The identity issue underlying the Neaera question is, he suggests, *the* sociopolitical challenge confronting the Athenians. In the course of his prosecution speech, Apollodorus lays bare tensions about how Athenian identities are established and the role of popular and expert knowledge in the sociopolitical project of boundary setting. He claims that the survival of the democratic community depends upon getting the answer—and thus the court's verdict—right. A wrong verdict would, he argues, result in a collapse of the requirement that citizen men marry only native-born women and thus in the collapse of the rules of social intercourse—inter alia, nice Athenian girls will choose to become prostitutes. The wrong answer to the Neaera question will, in short, fatally violate the boundaries that sustain the existence of the polis as a community of citizens.

Yet, as Apollodorus readily admits in the course of his speech, the woman Neaera herself was merely a target of convenience. The real object of his legal attack is Neaera's consort (or perhaps husband), Stephanus,

[15] Theogenes may possibly have belonged to the deme Kothokidai (cf. *SEG* 28.149.7) but he was more likely of the deme Erchia (cf. Kroll 1972, 163). He is described in [Demosthenes] 59.72, 80–84. The speech, included in the corpus of Demosthenes was probably delivered in the 340s B.C.

[16] Editions and commentaries on the speech: Carey 1992; Kapparis 1999. Victor Bers (2003) offers a lively new translation. Career of Apollodorus: Trevett 1992.

an Athenian citizen who was a current political enemy (and former legal opponent) of Apollodorus. The speech is an exercise in using the legal process for conjoined personal and political ends by exposing the "private lives of public enemies."[17] *Against Neaera* offers a vivid portrait of Athens as a highly diverse community, in which adults and children, citizens and foreigners, free and slave, neighbors and strangers, men and women, worked and played, fought and loved, formed and broke alliances (political, marital, and otherwise), all the while negotiating complex personal identities that were deeply informed by the democratic political culture of the city that they co-inhabited. Underlying the prosecution's case is an abiding Athenian concern with "coherence as nativity," which was put under considerable pressure by the self-evident fact of Athenian social diversity, made manifest for the jurors in the non-native ancestry of Apollodorus himself. It was sharpened by the fact that no individual Athenian actually knew a large proportion of his fellow citizens by face or name. Under such circumstances, "social knowledge," and thus trust and social capital, was necessarily constructed out of multiple overlapping networks of association, friendship, kinship, and collegiality.

Theogenes enters Apollodorus' story because he was chosen, by lottery, to serve a year's term as Basileus—one of the nine annually appointed archons, public magistrates charged with important ritual, legal, and civic duties. Upon being chosen Basileus, Theogenes appointed Stephanus to be his assessor (*paredros*). He also married Phano; that is, he took her as his legitimate wife, with the intention of producing children who would be Athenian citizens. Phano was presented to him as the daughter of Stephanus and his Athenian wife. Theogenes is introduced by Apollodorus (59.72) as "a man of good birth (*eugenēs*), but poor (*penēs*) and without experience in affairs (*apeiros pragmatōn*)." Each term in this rhetorical tricolon helped to build a clear picture of Theogenes in the minds of the Athenian jurymen, yet each is susceptible to misinterpretation by modern readers.

Far from implying that Theogenes was an impoverished aristocrat innocent of Athenian political culture, Apollodorus sketches for the jury an Athenian Everyman. Theogenes was "well born" because he was a native Athenian, "poor" because he worked for a living, and "inexperienced in affairs" in that he trusted his fellow citizen, Stephanus, too readily. In Apollodorus' narrative, Theogenes' inexperience became dangerous when he appointed an unscrupulous political hack as his *paredros*, and then took at face value Stephanus' claims regarding Phano's lineage. This proved to be a near-fatal error. It is central to Apollodorus' case that Stephanus lied

[17] Cf. Wallace 1994.

about Phano's parentage, that in fact he was Phano's pimp rather than her father. In Apollodorus' story Phano is depicted as a luxury-loving prostitute—and as Neaera's daughter by some unknown father. Neaera herself was, Apollodorus claims, a scheming foreign-born prostitute being kept as a mistress and partner in crime by Stephanus and falsely passed off as his legitimate Athenian-born wife. Thus the contrast is drawn and the contest engaged: Athenian Everyman Theogenes, on his own, is no match for the wiles of the corrupt household of Stephanus; he mistakes a schemer for a friend and prostitutes for citizen women, and so falls easily into their trap. Apollodorus' implied lesson for the jurors is clear: Without the legal apparatus of the democratic state, the ordinary Athenian could never guard the boundaries of legitimate identity against devious outsiders who sought to insinuate their way, as free-riders and worse, into the community and who would just as surely abandon it when it collapsed.[18]

As wife of the Basileus, Phano was required to perform certain important, community-sustaining ritual functions on behalf of the Athenian polis. As with all aspects of polis religion, it was regarded as vitally important to the persistence of the Athenian community that these rituals be properly carried out.[19] Apollodorus waxes eloquent on the subject of the grotesque impropriety of a foreign-born prostitute (herself the daughter of a foreign-born prostitute) being permitted to officiate at such an exalted and intimate level in religious rituals essential to the ongoing welfare of the Athenian people. In the process Apollodorus demonstrates his own expert mastery of Athenian religious practice; his pride in his mastery recalls Socrates' interlocutor, Euthyphro, in the eponymous Platonic dialogue. Apollodorus' expertise helps him to make his case. But it is also essential to Apollodorus' story that the Athenian community itself possessed nonexpert but reliable knowledge resources adequate to detect and expose "identity-frauds" that threatened the community. Stephanus' plot unravels within a year of the marriage, at a formal scrutiny following Theogenes' term as Basileus. The scrutiny was conducted by the Areopagus Council, a public body composed of former archons.

According to Apollodorus (80–83), "the Areopagus Council which in other cases also is of great value to the polis in matters pertaining to piety, then undertook an inquiry as to who this wife of Theogenes was and established the truth." In order to explain the seriousness of the crime and thus the depth of the Areopagites' horror upon finding out the truth (and thereby to stimulate a similarly horrified response among the jurors), Apollodorus digresses at length upon the ancient Athenian tradition regarding

[18] A similar scenario is sketched by Plato's Socrates in the *Gorgias*: as non-Athenians Gorgias and Polus have no stake in the society that their rhetorical practice helps to corrupt.

[19] On Athenian religion in general and role of the Basileus in particular, see Parker 1996, esp. 7–8.

the institutionalized role played by the Basileus' wife (73–79): Among other improprieties, Phano "conducted on the city's behalf the rites which our fathers handed down for the service of the gods, rites many and solemn and not to be named." There is an obvious tension here: If the rites are ancestral and unnameable, how is the non-native Apollodorus to speak of them—or even know of them? Apollodorus does not seek to cover up the tension; indeed he makes fine dramatic use of it. He expands upon the hoary antiquity of the rites, claiming that they dated back to before the distant time that King Theseus settled the Athenians in a single city and "established the democracy." This nice mythohistorical detail makes Stephanus' deception a threat to a deeply ancestral democratic constitution. And yet the story of "Theseus, founder of democracy," far from having the status of unquestionable tradition, competed in fourth-century B.C. Athens with several other "democratic foundation stories," variously featuring Solon, Cleisthenes, and the Athenian people themselves.[20] To prove the truth of his contentions about the sacred rites, Apollodorus cites an extremely obscure law: He claims (76) the law was written on a stone stele in a sanctuary of Dionysus of the Marshes, in archaic "Attic letters" now almost illegible due to age. Moreover, the stele was, he says, accessible for inspection only on one day each year. With this extraordinary citation of a barely legible and barely public monument, Apollodorus establishes his own bona fides as an expert in sacred law, worthy of instructing the jurors on their own Athenian traditions.

Upon discovering the awful truth about Phano, the Areopagus Council was at first inclined to impose a stiff fine upon Theogenes. But, Apollodorus notes, the Areopagites realized that the fine would have to be imposed "in secret and with due regard for appearances; for they are not in possession of the authority do just as they please" (80). Apollodorus' narrative points to a tension between the Council's ancient authority, its deep and righteous anger, and its concern for public appearances in a democratic community highly protective of individual immunities (see chapter 5).

This tension led to productive discussions (*logoi*) between the council and Theogenes. The latter protested his innocence: He had married Phano in the sincere belief that she was an Athenian woman, and it was because of his own inexperience in affairs and the guilelessness of his character that "he had made Stephanus his assessor to attend to the business of his office; for he considered him a friend, and on that account had become his son-in-law" (81). In the course of his discussions with the

---

[20] Competing democratic foundation–ancestral constitution narratives are evident in the Aristotelian *Athēnaiōn Politeia*. See, recently, Morris and Raaflaub 1998, and Anderson 2003 for discussion.

council Theogenes agreed to divorce Phano and dismiss Stephanus. And so it came to pass:

> Theogenes, immediately on coming down from the hill of Ares, cast out of his house the woman, the daughter of this Neaera, and expelled from the board of magistrates this man, Stephanus, who had deceived him. Thus it was that the members of the Areopagus desisted from their action against Theogenes and from their anger against him; for they forgave him, because he had been deceived. (81)

And so, with the end of a household, of a friendship, and of righteous anger, we come to the end of the story of Theogenes the Basileus. Apollodorus' tale boldly underlines the painful personal losses that attended the persistence of a community founded on jealously guarding the boundaries of citizen identity.[21]

Without worrying over much about the unanswerable question of the accuracy of Apollodorus' charges against Neaera, the story he tells about Theogenes brings to the surface a variety of structured tensions between private and public, individual and community. In Theogenes' Athens citizens "ruled and were ruled over in turn," but this was clearly not an Aristotelian "face-to-face" community in which each citizen knew each other's character and virtues and was able to judge and act accordingly. We do not know how Theogenes first came to befriend Stephanus, but the archon evidently did not know a lot about his *paredros*' private life. Yet Theogenes trusted Stephanus, and depended upon his superior experience of Athenian magisterial service. Public life (the relationship between archon and *paredros*) merged seamlessly (up to a point) with private life, resulting in the marriage of Theogenes and Phano.

In Apollodorus' narrative this seemingly proper but actually disastrous relationship between Stephanus and Theogenes, between more experienced and less experienced citizens, is detected and quickly corrected by the public-spirited Areopagus Council. The council employs its collective social knowledge to discover the truth (perhaps aided by the self-interested offer of information on the part of Stephanus' enemies, although we are not told that). Caught out by a public body, "inexperienced" Theogenes is not, however, without resources of his own. The council lacks unlimited discretionary power of punishment and is clearly not eager to put its own moral authority at risk by pressing the issue (see chapter 3). And so there are "discussions" aimed at finding a negotiated solution to the problem. The outcome of these negotiations is Theogenes' break with Stephanus

---

[21] On the central role of anger in Athenian judicial practice, see Allen 2000b.

and Phano: the dissolution of both their private connection (the marriage) and their public connection (the *paredria*).

As a result of his year as Basileus and its dramatic denouement, Theogenes became considerably more "experienced in affairs"—in the complexities of Athenian identity and the formal and informal practices that sustained the political community. But he was not the only one to learn from his experience. In listening to Apollodorus' story (as well as the defense offered by Stephanus on behalf of his household, sadly lost to us), and then formulating a judgment upon the entire matter, the Athenian jurors were educated as well (see chapter 6). Apollodorus' speech is a rhetorical masterpiece. It is wickedly salacious in depicting the lifestyles of Neaera and her daughter. But it is also filled with allusions to informal legal precedents, to recent and deep Athenian history, and to public procedure. Apollodorus, who was himself the son of a former slave and thus a citizen only through a public act of naturalization, can lay claim to having the deepest personal stake in the laws that limit the extension of citizenship to formal acts of the plenary citizen assembly. He reviews Athenian naturalization procedure and the history of the Athenian practice of naturalization at length (88–106), revealing in the process that the Athenian citizen body could be regarded as a community of "earth-born natives" only by a willing suspension of commonly available knowledge about Athenian history. And thereby Apollodorus exposes one more of the key tensions underpinning Athenian political identity. He offers himself, the adopted son of Athens, to the jurors (legal amateurs and mostly "born natives") as the antithesis of the wicked Stephanus: as a model "experienced citizen" who uses his hard-won special knowledge of public affairs (Athenian law, religion, and magisterial practice) only to promote the public good—and thereby the persistence of the community that had given him his own Athenian identity.

We have no idea of what actually happened to Theogenes after he divorced his wife and deposed his assessor. But it appears that he passed his formal scrutiny after his year as Basileus (Apollodorus says the Areopagus Council forgave him), and thus he would have become a member of the very council that had threatened to fine him for his improper marriage to a noncitizen. The internal evidence offered by Apollodorus suggests that Theogenes' year as Basileus was in ca. 352 B.C. The imagined scenario that follows postulates that Theogenes was born in 397 B.C. and had in the course of his life, before and after his service as Basileus, joined the ordinary sorts of associations and performed the ordinary sorts of duties expected of the Athenian Everyman portrayed by Apollodorus. Like Socrates (see chapter 7), the imagined Theogenes portrayed in the next section was neither wealthy nor politically ambitious, yet deeply concerned with his personal dignity and that of his community. He was eager to earn the esteem of his fellows, but not obsessed with personal honor. He was neither overeager to put himself forward nor a free-rider. We resume the story of Theogenes on a day some seventeen years after his year as Basileus, three years after Athenian independence in foreign policy was lost at the Battle of Chaeronea.

Approaching the Hill of Ares

Imagine a member of Athens' Areopagus Council in the year 335 B.C., walking to the city from his home in Oinoe, a fortified village some twenty miles from the city, on Athens' northwestern border. Oinoe is not Theogenes' deme, not the "ancestral" village assigned according his family's place of residence in 507 B.C. But, like many Athenian families, Theogenes' family had changed its primary residence periodically over the years—relocating to places within and even (in the imperial era of the fifth century) beyond the confines of the Athenian homeland. As a result, Theogenes' ancestral deme of Erchia was only one aspect of his "regional" Athenian identity.[22]

Theogenes' ultimate destination is the hill of Ares, one of several low limestone outcroppings west of the Acropolis that give natural definition to the southern side of the Agora—the central Athenian public square. Theogenes plans to climb up the hill of Ares, which is where the Areopagus Council sits and from whence it received its name. There he will join his fellow Areopagites in the conduct of some item of Athenian public business—perhaps a homicide trial or an investigation of a charge of treasonous activity.[23] It was a long walk from Oinoe to Ares' hill, but Theogenes had ample opportunity to visit with friends, kinsmen, and acquaintances along the way. They were a diverse lot, rich men and poor, variously employed: they included fellow Eleusinian initiates, colleagues from the various public offices he had held over the years, tribal messmates from his years of military training and service, along with blood-relatives and old friends of the family.

Theogenes approaches the city along the road between Athens and Eleusis known as the Sacred Way. As he nears the city and enters the neighborhood of Kerameikos ("potters quarter") his route is flanked by funerary monuments, some erected by the polis, others marking the graves of prominent individuals. As always, Theogenes' eye is caught by the impressive cenotaph of the cavalryman Dexileos—and as always he feels at once attracted and repelled by the depiction of the horseman skewering a naked

[22] Demes and ancestry: Whitehead 1986. Athenians move about within Attica: Hansen, Bjertrup et al. 1990.
[23] Areopagus Council and its duties: Wallace 1989.

fallen warrior whose sword arm is cocked behind his head in a last futile gesture of defiance (see chapter 10).

Now it is the massive fortifications of the city that command his attention: stone and brick walls, just recently rebuilt in order to meet the threat of new siege technologies. Passing through the great Dipylon Gate he is very conscious of having passed an important boundary: he has left the *chōra* and entered the *asty*, the walled city that, a century before, Pericles had exhorted his fellow Athenians to regard as an island (Thuc. 1.143.5). Yet as a farmer struggling to make a living on tiny holdings diversified across the territories of several villages, Theogenes was committed to regarding all Attica as worthy of defense—and very glad of the massive border fortresses that had been built and rebuilt during the course of his life—for him, *asty* and *chōra* were intimately conjoined: the mighty city walls were only the last of several lines of defense against enemy incursions.[24] Theogenes wondered if the defenses would be enough to stop a Macedonian army if it came to that—the faint smell of smoke from Alexander's sack of the once-mighty city of Thebes still hung in the ordinarily clear air of Oinoe and was a constant reminder that stone walls were no longer a secure boundary between Athens and the dangers and opportunities of the outside world.

Inside the city, Theogenes walks along a wide street, thinking of the great Panathenaic procession that annually used this route on the way up to the Acropolis. It was a brilliant spectacle of "All-Athens on parade": citizens in military garb, women in their finest, and the resident foreigners unmistakable in their scarlet cloaks.[25] He passes the unassuming external façade of a large private house that he knows well—as a boy he had spent months in its richly appointed interior, a guest of the house's wealthy owner—the *chorēgos* who had voluntarily taken on the expensive liturgy of "boy's chorus producer" for the tribe of Aigeis. Inside those walls, Theogenes had been trained in singing and close-order dancing as a member of Aigeis' fifty-boy chorus, a group that had gone on to win in the City Dionysia— much to his delight and that of his tribesmen. It had been Theogenes' first personal experience of how wealthy citizens lived, and his first deep experience of his tribal identity. Boys from different parts of Attica, and from various walks of life lived under the chorus-producer's roof, ate his food, dressed in the splendid costumes he provided. Used to a farmer's simpler circumstances, Theogenes had not been altogether comfortable in such surroundings, but he cherished the experience of being bonded into a tight-knit group under the supervision of a expert chorus-trainer.

Years later, Theogenes had sat on a jury in a civil dispute; by chance the chorus-producer's son, one of his old chorus-mates, had been a defendant

---

[24] Pericles: Thucydides books 1 and 2; city-walls: Camp 2000; border fortifications: Ober 1985 and chapter 9. Diversified holdings: Osborne 1985; Gallant 1991.

[25] Panathenaia: Neils 1992.

and had alluded in his defense speech to his father's choregic tripod monument, erected in celebration of Theogenes' chorus' victory.[26] Theogenes had been more than willing to give his old chorus-mate the benefit of the doubt; indeed he had joined in the *thorubos*—the jeering outburst of other jurors when the prosecutor sought to depict the producer's son as an arrogant and selfish rich man, who cared only for his luxurious lifestyle and not at all for the common good.[27]

Within a few minutes Theogenes had arrived at the outskirts of the public square. Here he is confronted by a formal boundary-marker: a *horos* that informs him that this is indeed the beginning of the Agora (see chapter 9). The *horos* thereby implicitly warns him to proceed only if he is among those permitted to do so; if he is a murderer or otherwise polluted, he is forbidden to go further. Dipping his hand into a shallow basin of water, Theogenes performs the required lustration and continues on his way, passing into the Agora square with its surrounding public buildings. Some of these had only recently been completed, in the course of a great program of civic construction, associated with by Lycurgus of Boutadai, who held the newly created elective office of "city manager." Lycurgus' building program, which included a new theater, stadium, and arsenal, was already rivaling that associated with Pericles, a century before. Theogenes was proud of all the new construction: It showed that Athens was still a great city even after the battle of Chaeronea.

The loss at Chaeronea meant that the Athenians had been forced to join the Macedonian-led League of Corinth, and sign on to a grand "expedition of revenge" that the Macedonian King had announced against the Persian Empire. The loss of true independence had been a blow to Athenian pride. Some of Theogenes' friends argued that pride might be regained by joining the Macedonians in avenging Persian crimes committed during the Greco-Persian wars, now a century and a half past. But Theogenes himself had no particular animus against barbarians. He was well aware that the new public building in the city was matched by a similar construction boom in the Athenian port town of Piraeus—the center of the transit trade that had fueled Athens' recent prosperity. Piraeus, and indeed the polis as a whole, was home to many barbarians—non-Greek foreigners who came from places around the Mediterranean and deep into the Persian empire. Along with their trade goods, they had brought their gods to the polis and these were duly recognized by the democracy. Like Socrates before him (Plato, *Republic* 327a), Theogenes had attended festivities associated with these new cults and had found nothing to

[26] The only bit of evidence for Theogenes' life other than [Demosthenes] 59 is a juror's "allotment plate." See note 15, above.

[27] Chorus-production and training: Wilson 2000. Citation of liturgies in legal speeches: Ober 1989. Jurors' *thorubos*: Bers 1985.

despise. There were Greek-speaking barbarians, men and women, free people and slaves, among his fellow Eleusinian initiates. Theogenes was sensitive to the special bond he shared with them: Sacred knowledge that was kept strictly secret from all those who had not been initiated, including some of his fellow citizens. Like other Athenians, Theogenes remembered that the Persians had once burned Athenian temples and he was stirred by tales of ancestral Athenian courage and self-sacrifice in the wars of the distant past. But he lived in a present in which Greeks and barbarians were in constant contact; he was left cold by the empty rhetoric of "revenge against the ancestral enemy."[28]

Among the first buildings Theogenes passes as he enters the Agora is the Stoa of the Basileus. Theogenes notes it with mixed emotions: It was his office during the eventful year that culminated in his divorce from Phano. Even before its dramatic denouement, the year's service had been by turns frightening, demanding, and exciting. He had been responsible for preliminary hearings on some difficult legal cases—and he was very aware that a couple of years before his own birth a Basileus had sent the philosopher Socrates off to the trial that the Athenians had never managed to forget.

Beyond the Stoa of the Basileus were many other monuments to distract Theogenes' attention: statues of illustrious military figures, tribal heroes, and heroically naked tyrant-killers, sacred altars, innumerable public inscriptions, fountain houses, law courts, public offices, and temporary shops where men and women sold all manner of goods. Like the Stoa of the Basileus, some of the buildings had strong personal associations for Theogenes: He passes the Bouleuterion where he sat for a year as a member of the advisory council of 500 citizens, the Tholos where he ate and slept with other members of his fifty-man tribal team (*prytanis*) for a tenth part of that year, and the temple of Hephaestus where he and his sister each gave evidence in a privately arbitrated dispute with some of his cousins. There are courtrooms in which he sat as a juror. And there is the public office where two years ago he had spent a mandatory year (as did all Athenian citizens upon reaching the age of sixty) as a public legal arbitrator, seeking to resolve legal disputes delegated to him by other magistrates. In each public capacity he had come to know a diverse array of people and had learned to work with them. In the process he had become reasonably expert in some of the manifold ways in which the democratic system judged, categorized, and negotiated the differences between people (see chapter 2).[29]

Passing out of the Agora at its southwestern boundary, marked by more boundary-stones, Theogenes has neared his destination. To his left

[28] Positive Athenian attitudes towards barbarians: K. H. Allen 2003a, 2003b.

[29] Agora monuments: Camp 1992 and chapter 9. Activities in the Agora: Millett 1998. Public and private arbitration: Hunter 1994.

looms the awe-inspiring limestone massif of the Acropolis, with its famous marble temples and treasuries—along with the inscribed public records showing that they had been built by mixed work-teams composed of citizens, foreigners, and slaves. To his right is the hill of the Pnyx—the meeting-place of the Athenian demos, which had recently been given a substantial renovation—allowing many more citizens to attend each open-air meeting in relative comfort. And directly before him is his destination: the hill of Ares itself.[30]

As Theogenes prepares to climb the hill, he is confronted with an inscription (RO 79): a tall marble stele, about his own height, crowned by a relief sculpture of a draped female figure he knew to be Demokratia crowning a seated man, Demos (see chapter 10). The lower part of the stele recorded a law (nomos) recently passed by the Athenian lawmakers (nomothetai). Theogenes had seen dozens of more or less similar inscriptions on his walk in from Oinoe—Athens was justly famous for its habit of publicly displaying the official acts of its public bodies and parts of the city now resembled a forest of stelai. But this inscription had particular relevance for him, as an Areopagite. The law, passed the year before (337–336 B.C.) on the motion of a certain Eukrates, regulated when it was and when it was not allowable for an Areopagite to climb the hill of Ares. Specifically, Theogenes and his fellow Areopagites were forbidden by Eukrates' nomos from ascending the hill if and when "the demos and the democracy were overthrown." Should Theogenes choose to mount the hill in such circumstances, he would be declared an outlaw: Anyone who subsequently killed him was declared free from charges arising from committing an act that would in other circumstances be regarded as impious and a heinous crime against the public order. By demanding that Theogenes consider the legality of fulfilling his intention of joining his colleagues upon the Hill of Ares, the inscription served as a sort of boundary-marker— it was in relevant ways analogous to the horoi of the Agora he had passed upon entering and leaving the public square: in both cases the inscription indicated that proceeding into public space was only allowed under specific circumstances. But whereas the Agora horoi implicitly forbade entry to those who had committed specific acts, the Eukrates nomos forbids entry to state officials under specific political conditions.

If we imagine that Theogenes is in a thoughtful mood, we may picture him pausing at the stele recording the Eukrates nomos to ponder its significance for the relationship between the democracy and himself, as citizen and magistrate. The law explicitly acknowledges the possibility of political conflict in the community, conflict that could lead to the revolutionary overthrow of the democracy and thus the suspension of the

[30] Mixed work-teams: Randall 1953; Pnyx rebuilding: Camp 2001, 153–54, 266.

political authority of the demos. One might suppose that if the democracy were overthrown, its laws would be nullified and that they would thereby lose (inter alia) their capacity to allow or forbid Theogenes to climb the hill. And yet Eukrates' law specifically asserts its authority over Athenian magistrates in the (anticipated) condition of the democracy being overthrown. And thus democratic Athenian law claims a persistent moral authority that transcends the institutional authority of the demos itself (see chapter 3). Yet by so doing, Eukrates' law also points directly to the adamant linkage between democracy and the daily practice of citizens: If Athenian magistrates (and other citizens) respect the law's restriction upon their participation in nondemocratic regimes, those regimes will be denied both the appearance of legitimacy and the expertise necessary to sustain themselves. And so antidemocratic interludes will be correspondingly ephemeral: short detours on the long democratic road.

The Eukrates law ties the capacity of democratic culture to persist in the face of a nondemocratic government to Theogenes' willed choice as an Athenian magistrate, and thus the political community to the moral-political psychology of the individual: If Theogenes (inter alios) chooses to obey the law, democracy will survive—*even if overthrown*. But the law also seeks to constrain Theogenes' individual choice by declaring him an outlaw—subject to arbitrary killing—if he does not obey. Simply by noticing the stele, Theogenes is required to ask himself, *Is* the democracy and the demos now overthrown? Depending on his answer, Theogenes' act of continuing up the Hill of Ares either asserts the current persistence of democracy, or he willingly declares himself an outlaw, or he denies the authority of the law to designate his status or constrain his actions.

In any event, the law's physical presence (or even its remembered presence) thus makes a magistrate's simple act of climbing a hill into a highly charged public performance. Theogenes' trudge up a slope to meet his fellow magistrates on what might be a dull administrative matter becomes a politically significant mini-procession, a cultural practice with profound implications for the individual and his relationship with the political community. By going on up the hill or by turning back, Theogenes makes a choice that is directly relevant to the democratic community's chances of going on together into an always uncertain future.

If Theogenes is not merely politically thoughtful, but possessed of a historical and mythopoetic turn of mind, a whole series of ideas might flit through his head as he completes his journey. He might begin by musing on the strangeness of having a hill sacred to the god of war and strife located in the political and sacred center of the city.[31] And indeed, the Hill

---

[31] Ares in the city: Loraux 2002, 35–39, 111–20.

of Ares lived up to its name in Athenian myth and history: Theogenes would have heard over and again how the fierce woman warriors, the Amazons, occupied most of Attica and made their camp upon the Hill of Ares before being pushed back by the ancestral heroes mustered on the Acropolis. In historical time (480 B.C.), the invading Persians used the Hill of Ares as a staging ground for their successful assault on the Acropolis, leading to the eradication of the last Athenian defenders of the homeland. Yet the invaders' victory proved hollow because most Athenians had been willing to abandon their homeland in advance of the Persian arrival, and willing to risk their collective future on a military plan that gave Athens' poorest citizens a military role equal to that of the heavily armed infantrymen.

It was the Areopagites who had coordinated the orderly withdrawal of the population from Attica in advance of the Persian invasion, but less than two decades later (462 B.C.) the council's powers were limited by democratic enactment. The constitutional change was not accomplished without bloodshed: Ephialtes, the proposer of the change, was murdered.[32] It was in the aftermath of these events that Aeschylus presented his tragedy *Eumenides*, which is set on the Hill of Ares and celebrates the creation of the Areopagus Council as a court for judging acts of homicide. Ares himself does not figure as a character in the play, but his presence is felt when Athena exhorts the Furies of the chorus not to shatter Athenian society by unleashing the horrors of an "intra-kindred (*emphulios*) Ares" (lines 861–66).

Theogenes might compare this mythic account to his recognition that it was in response to a historical threat of *stasis*, in the aftermath of an unsuccessful bid for tyranny in the late seventh century, that Drakon set down the earliest Athenian written law on homicide. From the moment of its beginnings (in history and myth) the council that met on the Hill of Ares was involved with the gnarly problem of conjoining a legal standard with the aggregated capacity for wise judgment of its members, for the purpose of managing conflict in a diverse and divided community. Before Ephialtes' reforms, the council had been charged with a generalized "guardianship of the laws." In the era of Theogenes, the council was still regarded by most Athenians as an important bastion of legal authority, and a reliable source of justice. Areopagites had long been among the most important interpreters of Athenian law.

Theogenes the Areopagite is reminded by Eukrates' law that he is not only a judge responsible for interpreting law, but is himself, like every other Athenian, subject to the laws. That subjection might, as the law's projection of its own authority into a "postdemocratic" future suggests, be regarded

[32] Murder of Ephialtes and Athenian memory: Ibid., 71–75.

as uncontestable. The law urges him, in a sense, to take the model of Socrates to heart in choosing to "go home" rather than to collaborate with a new nondemocratic political and legal regime: When the democracy had been overthrown by the Spartans and the Thirty Tyrants in 404 B.C., Socrates had refused to obey the legal order of an oligarchic magistrate to arrest Leon of Salamis. Yet in contrast to his willingness to disobey an unjust order issued by an oligarchic magistrate, Socrates (of Plato's *Crito*) was completely obedient to an unjust order of an Athenian jury mandating his own execution. The key difference for Socrates was that the Athenian jury's order was procedurally correct and issued under the authority of the democratic laws under which he had been born, raised, and educated. Those laws, so he supposed, continued in effect through the oligarchic interlude, and Socrates' refusal to cooperate with the oligarchs had helped insure that it was only an interlude (see chapter 7).

Like the reified "laws of Athens" to which Socrates attends in the *Crito*, Theogenes is urged by the law of Eukrates to regard democratic laws as part of a political culture to which he owes profound loyalty and allegiance, rather than simply the rules of the moment, suited to and maintained by a historically contingent structure of power, which might be replaced by other rules when some other structure is put in its place.

DEMOCRATIC SOULS

The apparent absoluteness of the demand for citizen loyalty to the legal order of the community, to the point of Socrates choosing to accept capital punishment resulting from a substantively flawed legal judgment, has seemed to many modern political philosophers more than any regime should demand of its members. Socrates and Theogenes were encouraged by the laws of Athens to regard their individual choices and actions as directly relevant to the survival of the political community. They were expected to interrogate themselves about the public consequences of their individual actions and to hold themselves personally responsible for the consequences of those actions. They knew, moreover, that the law actively exhorted their fellow citizens to take responsibility for enforcing the law—up to the point of treating the lawbreaker as an outlaw who might be killed with impunity. The alternative, as Plato's Socrates points out in the *Crito*, is that the laws have no force and thus, by very strong implication, that "going on together" as a community will no longer be possible.

And so we return to the question of how thick and how constraining political culture must be in order for a democratic community to persist over time. As I noted above, the "standard Greek polis" is often taken, by liberals and communitarians alike, as a very thick community, deeply grounded in tradition and situated commitments. Among the motivating ideas of this collection of essays is that Athens is actually considerably less tradition-bound than is often supposed (see esp. chapter 4). Athens allowed, I will argue, many (though not all) of its people to authorize their own histories, to define for themselves a variety of goods, and it provided many of them with resources adequate to pursuing a variety of diverse ends. And so Athenian political coherence remained thin enough to be consistent with the demands of political theorizing that must engage with the real conditions of multicultural modernity. If this is right, the Athenian polis (unlike the "standard-ideal polis" of much political writing) need not be relegated to the projects of celebrating and castigating the homogeneous cultural order of an imaginary past. Attending to the high level of personal responsibility assumed by Plato's Socrates and my Theogenes, however, brings us face to face with the difference between the "democratic soul" (the moral-political psychology) of the Athenian citizen and the attitude toward the political sphere that is fostered by modern political culture.

The Athenian's democratic soul was admittedly not the autonomous result of the sort of reflective individual self-fashioning demanded of a Kantian subject. But neither was it the conditioned result of a coercively hegemonic political culture. It was indeed formed in part by a regime of personal and collective obligations. But meanwhile rights, or perhaps better "quasi rights" (see chapter 5), provided space for plural identities, for individuals and groups to participate in defining themselves and their desires. These vital immunities were in turn understood as being secured by the responsible choices, the ongoing willed behavior, of the citizens. They were enshrined in the law, but the Athenians realized that in the absence of the consistently chosen activity of a citizenry, immunities could never be guaranteed by the authority of a written document.

The understanding of Athenian democracy offered in the following pages is based on a vision of political space as a common good that variously asks for voluntary self-sacrifice, defers the pursuit of personal happiness, and denies the possibility of absolute justice for all of the people all of the time. It acknowledges the existence of social boundaries. It recognizes transnational responsibilities, but also respects the special value of honoring obligations to those relatively close by. And it admits that what is owed locally may be in some ways different in nature from what is owed to those further away. Athenian political culture was undeniably demanding and nonperfectionist. It is disruptive to any fond hope that conflict can be eliminated while diversity is preserved. The acceptance of the tragic inevitability of conflict, loss, and the incompleteness of all political solutions is one of the two legs upon which an Athens-inspired democratic theory must stand. Its other leg is a historically justified optimism about the potential of a diverse community of citizens, of men and women who have constructed appropriately democratic souls for themselves, to choose to go on together in the face of that tragic acceptance.

CHAPTER TWO

Classical Athenian Democracy and Democracy Today

This essay was originally presented at Bristol University, under the sponsorship of the British Academy, as one of nine public lectures offered at universities across the United Kingdom in celebration of the academy's Centenary.* The rather challenging assignment was to write a paper that would be accessible to a broad audience, would speak to the history of a substantial field of scholarship within classical studies, and would point to both promising research trends and the relevance of classical scholarship to contemporary society. I chose as my topic a question that has been in the center of my work for some time, Why did Athenian democratic political culture work as well as it did in producing a variety of goods, at surprisingly high levels, for the members of the Athenian community?

Here I approach that basic question historically, by asking how the Athenians managed to make the difficult transition from a moment of violent revolution to a political regime capable of confronting immediate challenges and of sustaining itself in the long run. I suggest that part of the answer to these questions is to be found in the most conventional of places (in terms of answers offered by Greek historians of the twentieth century): In the creation of new political institutions, notably an advisory Council of 500 citizens. The essay breaks with conventional historical interpretation, however, by arguing that the council should be understood as a way of creating a polis-wide master network of useful knowledge, and as a vital element of Athenian civic education. Understood as such, Athenian political practice becomes relevant for thinking about modern organizations—not so much the nation-state, but purposeful nongovernmental organizations, including for-profit businesses. This essay borrows from insights gained in the course of working with Brook Manville on a book aimed at a modern business readership (Manville and Ober 2003).

Looking at Athenian political institutions in this way may seem radical, when judged by the standards of twentieth-century scholarship in ancient history. I suggest, however, that it may actually be a return to

---

* This essay was first published in J. Morrill, ed., *The Promotion of Knowledge: Essays to Mark the Centenary of the British Academy, 1902–2002,* in *Proceedings of the British Academy* 122 (2004): 145–61. Reprinted with permission of the British Academy.

the understanding of ancient Athenian political practice offered in the mid-nineteenth century by John Stuart Mill. Among the serendipitous events of my recent scholarly career was the appearance of Nadia Urbinati's fine book on Mill and Athens (Urbinati 2002) shortly before the original public presentation of this essay.

• • •

THE YEAR 2002 WAS not only the British Academy's Centenary, it also marked the semicentennial of the publication of Charles Hignett's influential study of the *History of the Athenian Constitution*.[1] Hignett's book is primarily concerned with political institutions as nodes of formal authority and with the distinction between "moderate" and "radical" forms of ancient democracy—the latter marked by the active participation by ordinary working men in the processes of government. I first read Hignett as a student in the 1970s, but a quarter-century later I find it is still frequently included on university course syllabi—I counted 150 Google hits at a recent check.

The issues raised in this essay are especially important in light of the enduring, indeed apparently growing, popularity of Greek democracy as a topic in school and university curricula.[2] How, a half-century after Hignett's *History*, should teachers explain to their students the nature and meaning of ancient Athenian democracy? Are questions about institutions as formal nodes of authority and about the development of "radicalism" what we should be focusing upon? Might the potential of modern (or even postmodern) democracy be reassessed in light of new approaches to studying the history of ancient Athens? These are pressing questions in the early twenty-first century, but they are not new ones. As Nadia Urbinati's *Mill on Democracy: From the Athenian Polis to Representative Government* has demonstrated, the most influential British liberal of the nineteenth century was convinced that Athenian democracy might be an important and useful model for designing a modern democratic regime.[3] The portrait of Athens offered here is much closer to John Stuart Mill's mid-nineteenth-century reading of Athenian political culture than it is to Hignett's mid-twentieth-century study of the Athenian constitution.

J. S. Mill did not write Greek history for historians. He deployed his conception of Athens to defend democracy against French revolutionaries who

---

[1] Hignett 1952.

[2] There are currently at least three collections of essays on Athenian democracy, designed for course use, recently published or in press (Rhodes 2004, Robinson 2004, K. Raaflaub et al. in press), which suggests that textbook publishers see the topic as a growing market. See also note 5, below.

[3] Urbinati 2002.

had found in "the ancient Greeks" (i.e., Sparta) a model of republicanism that delegitimated deliberation and individual rights, and also against British conservatives like William Mitford who used a tendentious interpretation of Athenian history in an attempt to show that democracy was both immoral and unworkable. Today, some of Mill's battles have been won and so there is less need to spend time on the question of whether we should value democracy as such. "Democracy" is now enrolled in the pantheon of approbative political terms—along with justice, freedom, equality, and human rights. Yet unlike those other highly favored value terms, democracy describes a political regime: a potentially comprehensive way of organizing legitimate public authority within an established collectivity. The regime described by democracy is comprehensive in that it offers a system for institutionalizing the moral intuitions and public practices that are implied by various other favored political terms.

Moreover, the system on offer is more than a utopian ideal, it has the potential of existing in practice. Democracy is a powerful concept in part because democracy renders it possible to imagine actually living our own lives, here and now, according to principles of justice, freedom, equality, and human rights. Indeed, it is indicative of the success of democracy as an idea that living such lives has (in much of the world) become an expectation, if not yet a consistently experienced reality. The gap between our current political regimes and the preferred democratic alternative is still perceptible, but that gap is now more likely to provoke impatience and demands for change than wistful utopian longing.

Democracy does all of this conceptual work under the (etymological) sign of power (*kratos*), a power that is wielded by "the people" (*dēmos*). So it seems obvious enough to ask: What sort of power are we talking about when we say "democracy"—and what sort of "people"? But those are not the questions usually asked by either classicists or political theorists seeking to analyze how democracy works in practice. Instead, the usual approach is still to ask, with Hignett, What are the appropriate institutions of governance? And how is institutional authority distributed? In the United States (and many other modern nations) it is quite easy to describe the basic framework of institutional authority and governance, because those matters are detailed in a self-consciously foundational document, a written constitution. But of course, the act of writing a constitution is never the end of the story. The very existence of a formal constitution in a system predicated on free speech and equal votes means that there will be a great deal of debate about how to interpret the language of the foundational document. Much academic political philosophy in the United States is therefore devoted to problems of constitutional interpretation, with special reference to Supreme Court decisions, past and future (see chapter 3).

Debates about those decisions require confronting genuinely complex issues of institutional authority. The denouement of the U.S. presidential election of autumn 2000 provides a well-known example of an outcome that presented a strange spectacle for students of democracy. In the end, the will of the "people" (in the guise of the popular vote) was overridden by a constitutionally established but ordinarily invisible elite of supervoters (in the guise of the Electoral College), whereas the authority of each state to settle disputes about elections (in the guise of superior court judges in Florida) was overridden by the national Supreme Court. Of course there has been a lot of academic ink spilled about the implications of the 2000 election for matters of formal constitutional authority.[4] I have brought up an admittedly peculiar, and peculiarly American example, but mutatis mutandis, I dare say that the bulk of European academic work on democracy (and Canadian, Australian, etc.) also tends to focus on problems of elections, governance, and distribution of institutional authority.

The modern penchant for reading the meaning of democracy through the lens of "the authoritative institutions of government" has had a substantial impact on the way ancient Greek democracy has been understood. An obvious example of this "modern-to-ancient" interpretive approach is the habit of translating the Greek term *politeia* as "constitution." Beginning students of antiquity, when they are first confronted with the polemical late fifth-century pamphlet entitled *The Constitution of the Athenians* (*Athēnaiōn Politeia*), written by an anonymous Athenian sometimes called "The Old Oligarch," are likely to be deeply confused when they discover that, instead of a coherent account of government authority, they are confronted with an slyly ironic analysis of the cultural, material, and ideological means by which the "despicable many" maintain their political power and prevent the rightful assumption of power by the "excellent few." Obviously, in this text, *politeia* has little (if anything) to do with a formal "constitution."

Nevertheless, leaning heavily on parts of the other surviving text that goes under the name *The Constitution of the Athenians* (that is, the *Athēnaiōn Politeia* written in the later fourth century B.C. by a student of Aristotle), a great deal of twentieth-century scholarly effort was devoted to explaining ancient Athenian democracy in explicitly institutional and even constitutional terms. Hignett's *History of the Athenian Constitution to the End of the Fifth Century B.C.* is a distinguished example of the genre, as well as an example of the tendency—almost universal among

---

[4] Posner 2001, Gillman 2001, Sunstein and Epstein 2001, and Dworkin 2002 offer different interpretations.

Anglophone specialists in Greek democracy until the late 1970s—to privilege the relatively ill-documented fifth century over the relatively well-documented fourth century. Even today, the academic preference for the democracy of the fifth century is evident in school and university curricula.[5]

Of course a great deal can be learned (and has been learned in the half-century since Hignett's opus) about the institutional structure of Athenian government. But much has also been learned about the culture of Athenian democracy: About political ideology and discourse, social contestation and negotiation, and the public and private practices by which Athenian citizens came to understand themselves collectively as "we, the demos." I have argued elsewhere and at length that a cultural-ideological approach has more to tell us about ancient Athenian democracy per se than does a "constitutional" approach.[6] But here, my main point is that looking at Athenian democracy as political culture rather than as a constitution will have more to tell us about the potential for us as moderns to learn something meaningful for our own situation.

Not that political institutions are ever unimportant for democracies. Indeed, much of this essay concerns Athenian institutions. But I want to suggest that when we study democratic institutions we should augment our concern with institutions as "discrete bureaucratic nodes of formal authority" by looking at institutions as "inter-connected nodes of knowledge exchange, of civic learning, and of public teaching." Once we move to the level of culture, we see that the system of democracy (in antiquity and potentially today) is less predicated on the formal specification and separation of institutionalized powers than it is on the aggregation and distribution of knowledge in the service of collective power. So I propose that we reverse the usual approach. Instead of domesticating Athenian democracy by reading it through the lens of modern constitutional governance, we should focus on ancient Athenian democracy as a culture and as a way of knowing, and one that was genuinely radical ab intitio. Approached as a political culture, Athens begins to look genuinely startling, and might actually prove useful for rethinking the potential place of democracy in our own lives.

But useful *where* in our lives? I do not intend to argue here that the political culture of ancient Athens provides a particularly useful model for the modern nation-state. Despite the possibilities of what is sometimes called "teledemocracy" (i.e., employing modern communications technology to foster deliberation and voting on issues by large populations), despite

---

[5] The continuing sway of the fifth century is marked by the publication by the London Association of Classical Teachers in 1998 of a teaching manual entitled *Athenian Radical Democracy, 461–404 BC.*

[6] Ober 1989.

remarkable and ongoing technological advances, I am not convinced that the problem of political scale can readily be solved. For the time being, I think, the Athenian model is likely to be more useful for thinking about groups consisting of thousands of individuals than it is for groups numbering in the millions.[7] Nor, despite the optimism of communitarian theorists, am I yet convinced that the highly participatory political culture typical of an ancient city would actually be able to guarantee what most people now agree are essential human rights.

Even if we do *not* regard slavery or the political exclusion of women as necessary *prerequisites* for democracy in the Athenian style (as I do not), we may still doubt that an Athenian-style democracy would ever be *as* deeply committed to the rights of individuals or of minorities as modern liberals will demand of any respectable nation-state.[8] But the nation-state is only one of the sites at which modern people come together as purposeful collectivities, only one of the many sorts of organization that might be structured more or less democratically. If we assume the persistence of a regime of nation-states, committed to providing an enduring "umbrella" guarantee of fundamental human rights, we are free to imagine how various other sorts of organization might become more fully participatory, more "Athens-like," in adopting more strongly democratic cultures of self-governance "by their people." The potential democracies I have in mind include voluntary and not-for-profit organizations, but also for-profit business firms. I would offer the Athenian model as a practical, time-tested alternative to anyone dissatisfied with organizations governed as oligarchies or tyrannies, as a resource to anyone interested in the potential of strongly democratic self-governance at (say) her own place of work.[9] This sort of thinking is very much in the spirit of J. S. Mill, who, as Urbinati points out, "proposed to reconfigure the family and the workplace according to the principles of equal partnership and mutual responsibility so as to make them a school of democracy for the moderns."[10]

My ideal and imagined interlocutor in the enterprise of thinking about "what democracy could mean in our lives today" knows that there was a spate of work in the mid-1970s to mid-1980s on "democratic workplaces," believes that it never achieved its full potential, and wants to know more about Athenian democratic political culture. She will look in vain for useful answers as she turns to Hignett's *History of the Athenian Constitution*. But I think ancient Greek historians can offer her something worthwhile by specifying the relevant and defining features of

[7] Compare, for example, Slaton 1992.
[8] See, further, chapter 5.
[9] This section of the paper draws upon Manville and Ober 2003.
[10] Urbinati 2002, 26.

Athenian democratic political culture. First was a set of core values concerned with the individual: that is to say, a cultural commitment to valuing the freedom, equality, and security of each citizen. Next, was a commitment to the notion that "the people qua citizenry both *constitute* the polis (as an organization) and are (collectively and directly) its rightful rulers." And finally, there was a commitment to the idea that it is nothing other than participation by the citizens in the day-to-day practice of self-governance that makes the core values real (that is, renders people free, equal, and secure in fact). It is participation in democratic practices that teaches people to "become what they are"—that is, citizens of a democratic polity. Each of these commitments was predicated on an expansive (although far from universalistic) definition of citizenship: In Athens the citizen was ordinarily defined as "a native adult male who had been formally acknowledged as such by his fellow citizens." Democratic citizenship can be best understood, I believe, not as a constitutionally guaranteed status, but as a sort of "social knowledge." And it is a distinctive pattern of circulation of knowledge (social knowledge and technical knowledge alike), encouraged by democratic culture, that makes the Athenian model particularly worthy of our contemporary attention. If that claim sounds both grandiose and peculiar, let me again have recourse to Mill, who focused on the importance of both a widely distributed "deliberative capacity" and specialized "technical knowledge" for modern democracy. For Mill, "democracy was a legal system of communicative interaction in which knowledge was passed 'from one citizen to another' and made each a protagonist of social and political life, willing to revise opinions and adapt to new circumstances."[11] Yet, unlike the now unproblematic notion that democracy is desirable, reconceiving democracy in terms of the exchange of social knowledge still, 150 years after Mill, requires some explanation.

This is in part because our standard modern way of thinking about knowledge tends to privilege the technical at the expense of the deliberative. As such it bears some similarities to Platonic epistemology: not in that dominant modern epistemologies are committed to Plato's Theory of Forms, but we are (for the most part) committed to expertise and to segregating the realm of "true knowledge" from that of "social practice." As a result, in modern pedagogy, knowledge is gained from communion with appropriate experts, and it is seen as something different from the political skills which might be learnt through participation in the processes of self-governance.[12]

Academics are likely to have a substantial investment in technical expertise. The entire modern academic enterprise concerns the proper

[11] Ibid., 62, citing Mill.

[12] On the distinction between social learning and the dominant learning paradigm, see Wenger 1998.

transmission of knowledge from experts to students, and issuing the appropriate credentials (e.g., university degrees, professorships) only to those who have demonstrably achieved the right level of knowledgability. That surely makes lots of sense in many domains. I certainly want the people who design the airplanes in which I fly to be certified experts, and ditto medical doctors, architects, and so forth. But should we follow Plato in supposing that expert knowledge must play an equally central role in the realm of politics?

The Athenians did respect technical expertise in various spheres and sought it out when making collective decisions about technical matters (as Plato freely acknowledges in his dialogue *Protagoras*), but they remained unconvinced that governance was a realm in which technical expertise should be dominant. And thus, for example (and scandalously from where Plato sat), they decided matters of justice in the People's courts without recourse to anyone even vaguely resembling a legal expert. And they decided major policy in the citizen Assembly by majority vote among whosoever of the citizens showed up for a given meeting. Moreover, any citizen could be a magistrate if his name were chosen in a lottery.

Each of these Athenian institutions (judicial, legislative, and executive) was structured around the active participation of "knowledgeable amateurs"—that is, people who were assumed to bring to their political service a useful body of nonspecialized knowledge; who were assumed, moreover, to be engaged in an active and ongoing process of knowledge exchange in the course of their participation, and whose decisions and actions as participants in the system would help to educate others. This recursive relationship between "knowing and (political) doing" appeared a patent absurdity to Plato, but it was essential to the functioning of the democratic system. Except for certain age requirements for specific forms of service (e.g., assemblymen had to be 18; jurors 30; public arbitrators 60), there was no privileged entry-point into the system: a citizen taught others as he himself learned. There was no knowledge-certification, no expert direction, no automatic disqualification for inadequate knowledgability.

How could it possibly have worked? Notably, Plato's objections to democracy are moral rather than practical. He freely acknowledges (e.g., in the *Gorgias*) the success of the democratic system in providing the city with the trappings of wealth and power. Plato's concerns centered on the capacity of democracy to corrupt the individual soul, especially by its celebration of ill-managed diversity. But my imagined interlocutor, interested in exploring the potential of Athenian-style self-governance for improving her workplace, does not regard diversity as requiring expert management or as inherently corrupting. She is interested instead in whether Athenian-style democracy might actually promote an organizational environment in which she (and her fellow workers) could operate as free, equal, and secure persons; she wants her organization (whatever it is) to flourish as an internally self-governing community. Familiar with the standard arguments for the essential role of specialized experts in the effective governance of any complex organization, she is not concerned that democratic diversity poses a danger to her soul, but she is worried about the danger that participatory democracy (with its reliance on knowledgeable amateurs) might pose to the capacity of her organization to achieve its goals.

What does a modern organization require in order to flourish in today's highly competitive environment? This "managerial" question may seem to take us a very long way from ancient Athens, but at least part of the answer is straightforward and directly relevant to the concerns raised here. Whatever else they require, modern purposeful organizations certainly require quick, effective access to "relevant knowledge" if they are to achieve their goals. As a mass of contemporary business-management literature asserts, effective use of knowledge is a key differentiator between failure and success in the highly competitive markets in which today's organizations (both for-profit and not-for-profit) typically operate.

Not too long ago, "superior technology" (the Internet, local intranets, information banks, teleconferencing, and so forth) was being trumpeted by business gurus as *the* answer to the "problem of knowledge." Many companies built elaborate and expensive databases, only to find that they were seldom actually used. The problem is, as the Athenians realized, that organizations depend heavily on the "tacit" knowledge that exists largely inside people's heads. Databases (e.g., written lawcodes) are indeed necessary as adjuncts, but knowledge is only valuable *in use*, and people will only choose to access databases in the context of an appropriate organizational culture, one that allows ready interplay between the tacit knowledge people already have in their heads and what they suppose they might find in some database. So the management mantra became "human capital"—leveraging the social knowledge about people and practical know-how that is typically embedded in the processes and practices of people working together and solving problems together over time. Yet as the mordantly amusing Dilbert cartoon strip points out, "people" are not necessarily ready to be "rebranded" as "human capital" and tacit knowledge has proved to be extremely hard to codify. The dilemma is famously summed up in the lament, attributed Lew Platt, chief executive of Hewlett Packard Corporation in the 1990s, "If only HP knew what HP knows, we would be three times as productive."

So the big issue in any complex organization is how to get what "we (collectively) know" to the right place at the right time—how to focus all of the relevant knowledge of the organization's people on a given problem? If the answer is not "technology," neither is it "knowledge management" (another largely defunct business slogan). Command-and-control managerial approaches to knowledge are counterproductive in a culture in which people value freedom and equality. Under the hierarchical systems of patronage and cronyism that still characterize many modern organizations, knowledge is hoarded rather than freely shared. "Knowledge is power," as we all know, but the problem that hierarchies face is that private, local knowledge is used to gain and keep private, local power: that is, to build and defend personal fiefdoms within the organization. And as a result the organization's overall capacity to perform effectively is substantially lessened.

What organizations need, then, is a culture of voluntary sharing of knowledge, effective knowledge circulation, and constant mutual instruction. Which brings us back to democracy in the Athenian style. I will not attempt, here, to analyze the entirety of the Athenian democratic system in terms of its capacity to integrate core values with effective public practices, and thereby to solve the problem of organizational knowledge. Instead, and more modestly, I will look at just one "institutional node," a favorite of Hignett and other specialists in Athenian democracy: the Council of 500, established in the aftermath of the epochal revolution of 508–507, through the leadership of Cleisthenes.

After the revolution, the Athenians designated (presumably through vote of the citizen Assembly) 139 existing villages and urban neighborhoods as self-governing communities (demes). Those 139 districts covered almost the entirety of Athenian territory.[13] Every Athenian would belong to one of these demes, and, for purposes of local self-governance, he would regard his neighbors as "fellow-demesmen." The business of the deme would be carried out in public, through public assemblies at which all the demesmen could gather to debate and decide upon issues of local concern.

These relatively small assemblies (most demes would not have a population of more than 200–300 adult men) immediately began to serve vital functions. The demes became the key institutional nodes for making decisions about Athenian citizenship. Among the primary duties of the deme assemblies was inducting new members, judging the legitimacy of the claim of each local boy to become a full member of the deme (that is, born to an Athenian father who had contracted a legitimate marriage), and thereby a citizen of Athens. Next, the deme assembly would take care of essential local business, including the appointment of local magistrates.

---

[13] There are a couple of exceptions, notably the island of Salamis. For the deme system, see Whitehead 1986.

Yet most important of all was the *educational* role of the deme assembly. Carrying out the public business of the deme, in cooperation with his fellow demesmen, taught each Athenian the political habits of participatory decision making and follow-through.

Once the demes had been designated, the next organizational step was more challenging: How to seamlessly integrate the many diverse local networks (the demes) into the *master network* that was the total citizenry of Athens.[14] This step required, of course, the prior step of re-envisioning the citizen body as constituting a "master network" of human relationships and then of imagining that master network as having a sort of architectural form: as consisting of a large number of smaller, self-governing networks. Those steps required a huge leap of imagination and a bold implementation plan. But the anticipated benefits were immense: the specialized knowledge resources possessed by the members of each local network, each deme, would potentially be made available to the polis as a whole. And, by the same token, that which was learned in any part of the polis could potentially be distributed throughout the organization. Once again, I am here treading in the footsteps of Mill, who argued that modern democracy required "the growth of an intermediary network of communication that would both prevent the representatives from becoming a new oligarchy and unite the whole country 'simultaneously into one *agora*.'"[15]

A dynamic and well integrated "master network of local networks" would preserve the autonomy and specificity of local knowledge in cases where that knowledge was uniquely valuable within a local framework. Each local network, each deme, remained free to respond to local needs and local emergencies by deploying local resources and locally developed expertise—but now with the added assurance that the diverse and vastly greater resources and expertise of the entire polis were available as a "backup" in cases where local solutions proved inadequate. So, for example, demes located near border-zones, faced with incursions of foreign raiders from across the frontier, could potentially call upon the military might of the entire citizenry-in-arms.

The conviction that the many self-governing divisional networks could in principle be quickly and seamlessly integrated into a master network was translated into practice through an elegant institutional design. Each deme was made responsible, each year, for appointing one or more of its citizen-members (depending on the deme's population) to the national Council of 500. The 500 annual appointees to this all-Athenian council

---

[14] Note that this "master network" was also a "virtual network" in that it was not in any way tangible to the senses. And yet, like modern virtual networks it had the possibility of doing real work in the world, the possibility of making things happen.

[15] Urbinati 2002, 9.

would, therefore, represent all of the territorial "parts" of Athens. The council, physically located in the city-center, was responsible for much of the day-to-day administration of the city. But its primary responsibility was setting an agenda and preparing legislative recommendations for each meeting of the polis-wide citizen Assembly, which might be attended (at least in the fourth century) by as many as 6,000–8,000 men, each an active, participatory citizen, each expecting to exercise his equal vote and, perhaps, his equal right of public speech.

The Council of 500 did *not* function as a "representative legislative body": the members of the council were not legislators (legislation was left to the Assembly) and councilors were not expected to serve the interests of their "local constituencies."[16] Rather, the 500 councilors chosen each year by their fellow demesmen were the human embodiment of the *knowledge resources* of the entire Athenian polis. Their duty as councilors was to bring local knowledge to the center—to participate in open discussions, bringing to bear all the relevant information they possessed, in order to best serve the needs of Athens as an independent city-state. Moreover, working together with their fellow councilors built knowledge—it served as a deep education of each councilor in the functioning organization as a whole. And the newly educated councilors were in turn teachers. Upon return to his home deme, a councilor became a local source of knowledge about how Athenian governance worked at a macro level. And thus, for each Athenian the "virtual" became real and tangible through the presence of a man (and in time many men) who had participated directly in the processes of what I am calling the "master network."

It must have been clear from the beginning that the many self-governing local networks would only work effectively as a master network if Athenians from diverse territorial regions worked closely together with other Athenians from all parts of the polis. On the council there would be a natural tendency for councilors who lived in coastal demes, for example, to gravitate towards other councilors from the coast, who would share more experiences with them than with the men from the inland districts or from the urban center. If the work of the council came to be dominated by conflicting regional interests, the goal of creating a genuinely integrated network would be lost, and the overall goal of creating a workable system of self-governance would never be realized. In order to achieve a more thorough integration, the new council structure would have to ensure that councilors would work, day by day, with men from very different parts of

[16] Of course Mill saw modern nation-state democracy as based on representation. But note that (as Urbinati 2002 shows in detail) Mill himself regarded a properly constituted democracy to be about the development and maintenance of "political culture" and not about the promotion of pre-existing interests.

the polis. The Athenians effected this by arranging for much of the work of the council to be carried out by fifty-member teams (*prytaneis*). Each team was made up of the councilmen from one of ten newly created tribes (*phylai*).

Part of the innovation of the new governance system was that, while the demes were, in a sense, *natural units*—pre-existing villages and neighborhoods—the ten new "tribes" were *blatantly artificial* units. Each tribe was composed of a number of demes from distinctly different parts of Athenian territory: Roughly one third of each tribe's population hailed from coastal districts, another third from inland regions, and a final third from urban areas. Each tribe thus included natives of coastal villages specializing in (say) fishing and trade, farmers from the agricultural inland, and craftsmen from neighborhoods of the urban center. Each "tribal team" was, therefore, made up of a diverse cross-section of men from across Athenian territory, men with different backgrounds, different skill-sets, as well as different networks based on kinship, friendship, and neighborhood.

Just as the Council of 500 as a whole represented in human form the "knowledge base" of the entire polis-organization, so each fifty-man "tribal team" embodied a microcosm of that same organization-wide body of shared and "sharable" technical and social knowledge. When he began his year of service on the council, each councilor knew that he would be working closely with the other men from his tribal team—he would be talking constantly with them, and for part of the year, eating and sleeping in the same room with his team-members from diverse parts of Athens. He would get to know these men intimately. The success of the council as an institution depended directly on his capacity to work effectively with his teammates—to share what he knew when it was relevant, and to defer to others when they had more relevant knowledge to offer. In short, the council as an institution depended on the councilors' capacity to deliberate. Each councilor learned the value of working intensively and cooperatively on a team. He learned to place his trust in men from very different parts of the polis: a trust based on developing a personal knowledge of them as individuals, and on a shared dedication to the flourishing of the organization to which they all belonged. Furthermore, the ten tribal teams had to learn, in turn, to work together. As they dealt with the daily business of Athens, and with the recurrent task of designing an agenda for the meetings of the Assembly, the 500 councilors learned how to move from the relatively intimate society of their tribal teams to the much larger bodies of the full council and, ultimately, to the vast citizen Assembly itself.

Each councilor returned to his deme, after a year's service, with an expanded "rolodex"—a personal network of men he knew well. His contacts were no longer just local folks—they were now "organization-wide." He knew, from personal experience, how the polis-organization was run at virtually every level. He had participated in making tough decisions that might affect the future of the polis as a whole. He had been among the first to receive the reports of generals, ambassadors, and foreign embassies. He had helped to conduct elections and votes in the huge citizen Assembly. He had scrutinized the accounts submitted by magistrates. In brief, he had sat at the very hub of the public business of the city, participating actively in all the manifold business that allowed the citizens to govern themselves. It was an immensely useful education: it taught him, in detail and through his own day-to-day practice, how self-governance really worked.

The valuable experience of a year's service on the council was not limited to a small elite of influential and wealthy citizens. Terms of service on the council were only for one year. Although a citizen might serve a second (nonconsecutive) year some time in his life, it appears that few Athenians actually did so. And by law no one could serve a third term. And so, there was a constant turnover among councilors. As a result, there was little tendency for the development of constraining institutional traditions, and no place for the elaboration of complex parliamentary procedures that would allow expert "government insiders" to control the system. There were no experts as such, this was governance by dedicated amateurs. A very high percentage of all Athenians over age thirty (the minimum legal age for councilors) spent a year on the council.[17] The system ensured that the extraordinary experience of a full year's work as a member of a tribal team, seeking to further the interests of the entire community, was a common one for adult Athenians—and thus that the educational benefit of council service was widely diversified throughout the citizenry. At any moment in Athenian history, a high percentage of Athenians had been councilors, and virtually everyone could count a number of former councilors among his intimates.

The institutionalization of the master network of local networks through the workings of the Council of 500 facilitated the practical integration of very widely diversified knowledge resources, beginning at the workable face-to-face level of the fifty-man "tribal team." The knowledge-work of the teams was quickly leveraged at the higher level of the discussions and decisions of the entire Council of 500. And the work of the council was immediately leveraged at the level of the organization-wide Assembly, through the agendas formulated by the council and through the council's recommendations on legislative items that came before the Assembly. The

---

[17] Scholarly estimates vary (see, for example, Hansen 1986), but at least one-third of all Athenians over thirty, and in some periods perhaps virtually all of them, served a year on the council. It is worth noting that the philosopher Socrates, who claimed that he avoided most forms of participation in governance, duly served his year on the council.

result was that a vast body of highly diverse local knowledge—technical and social—was effectively aggregated and made practically available to the polis-organization as a whole. This helps to explain how legislative decision making by a mass of 6,000 or more participatory citizens, which sounds initially like a recipe for chaos and disaster, quickly became an effective method of governance for a complex organization constantly faced with new and difficult challenges.

The core governance principles of equality, networks, and self governance immediately proved applicable across the polis. In every area of organized endeavor, the Athenians sought to exploit the synergies that arose within networks of people who regarded one another as equals. On juries, on boards of magistrates, and in the armed forces, just as on the Council of 500, the Athenian system combined men with diverse but compatible skill-sets into teams (large and small), teams that both served the needs of the organization and, in the process, furthered the education of each individual.[18] Service to the polis in the capacity of councilor, magistrate, juror, or soldier provided a chance to develop a sense of trust in a broad cross-section of fellow Athenians, men who might come from very different social backgrounds and who had quite different personal and local interests. That trust was developed both on the basis of personal knowledge of individual character, and on a recognition of a common loyalty, a shared commitment to advancing the common good of the entire organization.

As a result, although Athens was never actually a "face-to-face society," it had the feel of a face-to-face society. Although no Athenian actually knew more than a small percentage of his fellow Athenians, virtually every Athenian had access to a network of personal contacts that was based in part on local residence, and in part on knowing a cross-section of Athenians from distant parts of the territory. Because the system of governance and the public life of the city actively encouraged this networking, every Athenian was connected to every other Athenian by only one or two "degrees of separation." And this in turn had profound consequences for knowledge sharing. If one Athenian needed access to specialized knowledge held by some other Athenian, there was a very good chance that he could work through his local-national network to identify the right person, and that he would be able to establish the conditions of mutuality and trust which would facilitate the sharing of relevant knowledge.

The new governance system worked right away because it was based on the deeply felt commitment of the ordinary people of Athens to the idea of Athens as an independent, self-governing organization. They were committed to the idea that Athens should continue to exist as an independent

---

[18] The value of focused work-teams in the performance of modern organizations is the theme of the classic study of Katzenbach and Smith 1993.

polis not subject to Sparta or any other outside entity. And they were committed to the idea that Athens should be ruled by the consensus of the citizenry, not by a few aristocrats or by a single tyrant. They backed their commitments with a willingness to offer a substantial part of their time, their wealth, and, if necessary, their lives. The new system of self-governance allowed those deeply felt convictions, which had first been made manifest in the revolution of 508 B.C., to be translated into actual policy. The system allowed timely and binding decisions to be made on the relevant questions, and facilitated carrying out the specific practical steps demanded by those decisions. All of this was possible because the system of democratic self-governance facilitated the working of the polis-organization as an effective network of people, of knowledge, and of trust.

A very considerable conceptual leap is required if we are to move from thinking about democracy as a "constitution," suited primarily to nation-states, to thinking of democracy as a "political culture," suited to purposeful nonstate organizations. But a similar conceptual leap had already been made by J. S. Mill in the mid-nineteenth century. And the leap is surely no greater than that made by the Athenians in the late sixth century B.C. In Athens extraordinary payoffs followed from making the leap of re-envisioning their community as a master network of local knowledge networks. Whether we moderns are ready to make a similarly bold conceptual leap remains to be seen. But in any event, our leap would not be into the dark—as J. S. Mill realized 150 years ago when he argued that a proper understanding of the history of Athenian political culture could illuminate the way to a more democratic future.

CHAPTER THREE

Historical Legacies: Moral Authority
and the Useable Past

This essay, which has not been previously published, originated as an oc-
casional piece, delivered at a conference on "the moral authority of the
past," held in November 2002 in honor of W. Robert Connor, upon his re-
tirement as Director of the National Humanities Center. Each participant
was asked by Connor, who took the lead in setting the conference's intel-
lectual agenda, to reflect upon the phrase "the moral authority of the past"
and what it might actually mean. I took the opportunity as an invitation to
make explicit the conjunction of normative and historical concerns that
have informed my work for some time. Given that "historicism" is often
regarded as a primary sin among political philosophers and "essential-
ism" as an equally unforgivable sin among historians, this conjunction is
not an especially easy one to achieve—which is, I take it, precisely why
Connor set us the task of thinking about it.

I attempt to show that the concerns of liberals who suppose that it is
undesirable for the past to have moral authority for the members of a
contemporary political community are misplaced, as are the concerns
of traditionalists who regard the conditions of modernity as having de-
stroyed the very possibility of deriving moral authority from the past.
Historical legacies can and should have moral authority for people liv-
ing in a culturally diverse constitutional democracy. Moreover, I suggest
that borrowing moral authority from the past should be valued because
it furthers the normatively valuable capacity of the members of a com-
munity to go on together. The burden of the essay is specifying the con-
ditions under which moral authority may be borrowed from the past
within a "thinly coherent" community like ancient Athens or modern
America.

Partly in honor of Connor's fundamental work on Thucydides, the
essay concludes with a consideration of moral authority in Thucydides'
History. *This section also allows me to be specific about the ways in which*
a historian's account of the past might participate in the process of mak-
ing particular sorts of historical legacies available to a community, and
helping the community resist the temptation to forget inconvenient parts
of the real past in favor of a fictionalized narrative. Connor's topic proved
an extremely challenging one and I have consequently rewritten this essay
many times. Its current incarnation owes a great deal to the participants

in the original conference, to audiences at several university venues, and especially to the Fellows Seminar of Princeton University's Center for Human Values.

• • •

UNDER WHAT CIRCUMSTANCES MIGHT WE, as members of a democratic community, accept a historical legacy as having moral authority for us? The question is at once normative and descriptive. Moral authority and the utility of the past have been much debated by historians and moral philosophers in the United States in the late twentieth and early twenty-first centuries, as indeed they were in classical Athens of the fifth and fourth centuries B.C.[1] These debates are not merely academic. Like contemporary Americans, if for different reasons, ancient Athenians confronted times when institutional resources seemed inadequate to maintain a coherent political community in the face of internal discord and external challenges. Athenians and Americans alike found that reference to historical legacies helped to bridge the gap.

This essay's argument rests on a normative claim and an empirical claim. The normative claim is that going on together under conditions of democracy and justice (even if those conditions are always imperfectly realized) is valuable—and thus that we should value and seek to promote practices, like borrowing moral authority from the past, that enable it. The empirical claim (argued in more detail in chapter 4) is that, when compared to more tradition-centered communities, the democratic societies of the modern United States and ancient Athens are relevantly similar in that each manifests a relatively thin but resilient cultural coherence.[2] In such "thinly coherent" societies, just as in more traditional communities,

---

[1] This chapter was originally prepared for a symposium on "The Moral Authority of the Past," organized by W. Robert Connor and held at the National Humanities Center in November 2002. My thanks to Bob Connor and the other participants in that symposium. I have benefited substantially from insightful critiques when versions were offered subsequently to the Princeton University Human Values Fellows Seminar; a USC-UCLA Greek Seminar on Authority and Resistance; the Rutgers University Classics Department; a Yale University Conference on the Use and Abuse of Ancient History; Columbia University's Political Philosophy Colloquium; and Ohio State University's Classics Department. Special thanks to Danielle Allen, Lowell Edmunds, Chris Eisgruber, Peter Euben, Bruce Hitchner, Susan Lape, Adrienne Mayor, and Jerry Schneewind, who offered valuable comments on earlier drafts.

[2] See chapter 4, below. I adapt the concept of thin coherence from William Sewell's discussion of culture as manifesting "real but thin coherence that is continually put at risk in practice [by human agents] and [is] therefore subject to transformation": Sewell 1999, 52. I do not claim that ancient Athenian cultural coherence is just as thin as that of modern America, only that both look relatively thin in comparison with more traditional societies, ancient and modern.

borrowing authority from the past in support of judgments in the present is an important social practice because it contributes to going on in ways that institutional authority cannot.

Historical legacies may be either positive or negative in their moral force. *Negative* legacies are frequently cited in situations of judgment; they may concern past actions that are immoral in themselves (genocide, slavery),[3] or they may point to a combination of immorality and imprudence (the Athenian invasion of Sicily). Negative legacies have been much discussed (e.g., in the huge literatures on the Holocaust and American slavery) and they have an obvious and important role to play in present judgment. Yet because negative use of the past's moral authority (i.e., citing history in order to avoid repeating it) seems, as a practice, relatively unthreatening to thinly coherent societies, I focus here on the potentially more troubling case of the positive use of the past—on the practice of citing a past judgment or action because it is thought to be a positive legacy and thus worthy of respect.

Successfully borrowing moral authority from a historical legacy does not require the intervention of moral or historical experts. It does, however, demand that a public make a moral judgment regarding *fairness* and a historical judgment regarding *suitability*, that is, about the appropriateness of the fit between a reference to the past and current circumstances. Judgments about moral authority require both historical and moral thoughtfulness. I suppose, therefore, that a philosophical historian, concerned with public judgment and the moral authority of the past should have something to say on this topic. And so I conclude this chapter with a reconsideration of how the past was rendered useable by Thucydides, who wrote a didactic history in and about a period in which Athens' coherence was stretched to its breaking point. Thucydides' older contemporary, Herodotus ("The Father of History"), had stated that his purpose in writing history was the preservation of memory, "so that things done by men not be forgotten in time, and that great and remarkable deeds . . . not lose their glory."[4] Like Herodotus, Thucydides was intensely aware of his own role in the cultural process of preserving the past. But Thucydides was also explicitly concerned with teaching his readers how they might use the past for judgment in their own present. Asking how the history that Thucydides recorded might provide a reader (ancient or modern) with a morally relevant historical legacy tests the approach to using the past developed in the first parts of this essay.

---

[3] The "Princeton Principles on Universal Jurisdiction" (Macedo 2001) list as "serious crimes": piracy, slavery, war crimes, crimes against peace, crimes against humanity, genocide, torture—this list offers a starting point for thinking about actions that are unambiguously immoral in themselves.

[4] Herodotus 1.1.

WHAT'S AT STAKE

Citation of external sources of moral authority is a familiar social practice, a quotidian feature of the discourse of speakers who hold the institutional-ized authority to make decisions with substantial public consequences.[5] Think, for example, of the appeal for God's blessing at the conclusion of policy speeches by American presidents. But when formal institutional authority is in doubt, the practice of appealing to external sources of moral authority may be more than a banal rhetorical trope. At such times, a speaker may seek to borrow moral authority in order to create or regain a sociocultural coherence that seems beyond the reach of institutional means alone.

Achieving coherence (in the sense of going on together as a democratic community under conditions of justice) need not imply "maintaining the existing order" or "returning to a status quo ante." Achieving coherence will sometimes demand radical, even revolutionary, change. Examples of American public speakers borrowing authority from historical legacies, during a period in which institutional authority was in doubt, and with the explicit aim of achieving long term sociocultural coherence, include, for example, John Hancock's invocation of the Boston Massacre of 1770 in his oration of March 5, 1774; Abraham Lincoln's citation of the American Revolution of 1776 in his address at Gettysburg on November 19, 1863; and Martin Luther King's reference to Lincoln's Emancipation Proclama-tion of 1863, in his "I Have a Dream" speech delivered on the steps of the Lincoln Memorial on August 28, 1963.

Successfully borrowing authority from a historical legacy may ultimately allow coherence (and thus a community's capacity to go on) to trump other considerations—including the ordinarily compelling considerations of the free pursuit of individual happiness and absolute justice in the here and now. Achieving the outcome of coherence sometimes requires a decision (e.g., a declaration of war, an act of civil disobedience, or the declaration of a general amnesty) that may defer the possibility of happiness or justice for some individuals or groups.[6] Yet if we have reason to believe that loss of coherence will entail protracted suffering, injustice, or other evils, even those who do not regard the persistence of a community as a good in itself

---

[5] By "external" I mean external to the expressed will of the people, whether it is expressed in a historical constitution, by a democratic assembly, or through the legislative, executive, and judicial acts of officials ultimately accountable to the people. By "transcendental" (below) I mean, in the first instance, God or nature.

[6] On the ways in which acceptance of some injustice and some personal sacrifice of hap-piness may facilitate the chance of long-term social coherence, and on the fundamental im-portance of ensuring that it is not the same persons or groups who are always asked to accept injustice or to sacrifice happiness, see Allen 2001 and 2004.

may accept that the act of "trumping" led to the right outcome. Thus appealing to the past can limit, in salutary ways, the purchase of morality as such upon complex (all things considered) judgments. On the other hand, authority gained by invoking the past (e.g., Nazi citations of "Aryan history," American slaveholders' appeal to Greece and Rome) can also contribute to violations of justice that are sufficiently horrendous as to render the maintenance of sociocultural coherence abhorrent. So it is essential to find criteria that can limit how and when we allow the past to gain cultural purchase. Taking fairness and suitability as primary criteria limits the purchase of "the past as such" upon complex judgments. Under such constrained circumstances, in which neither morality nor history is granted final sway, moral authority borrowed from the past may contribute in genuinely valuable ways to the resilience of democratic communities.

The relative thinness of the shared culture underwriting "national" coherence in classical Athens or the modern United States allows for the flourishing of social diversity and for substantive political debate. But by the same token, the thinness of cultural coherence makes it more difficult for a community to augment institutional authority by reference to external sources. Cultural conservatives, ancient and modern, have tended to regard that difficulty as signaling a crisis of moral authority. This crisis, they suggest, can only be addressed by re-establishment of transcendental sources of authority (God or nature) or by "rethickening" cultural coherence through restoration of a comprehensive tradition about the past as the once and future order of political life.[7] In this, they seem wrong to me. It is true that by legitimizing very substantial disagreement about the meaning of the past, thin coherence makes it more difficult to appeal in a generally compelling way to a comprehensive inherited tradition. People living under conditions of thin coherence do have less reliable access to the rich and integrated thesaurus of past precedents and historical exempla that might otherwise (as argued, for example, by Edmund Burke and Thucydides' contemporary, Isocrates) offer them guidance as they confront troubled times and difficult decisions.[8] It is my contention, however, that historical legacies can nonetheless remain an important cultural resource.

If conservatives tend to overstate threats to moral authority, liberals tend to be oversuspicious about any remnant of it. One liberal response is to deny that the appeal to moral authority can ever be a valid part of democratic deliberation. This involves defining moral authority as "authoritative moral expertise" and then showing that a liberal democratic

---

[7] This argument is implicit in many of the Internet sites discussed below.

[8] Burke, and the conception of tradition as source of moral authority: Stout 2004, 208–17. Isocrates on the moral authority of the past: Ober 1998, 277–86.

society has no place for authoritative moral experts.[9] But moral authority (in the sense I employ here) is not to be equated with authoritative moral expertise: If moral authority is based on publicly accessible conceptions of fairness, one need not *be* a moral authority in order to appeal *to* moral authority. Liberals are wrong to reject the potential value of deriving moral authority from the past because the desirable social and political goal of going on together as a democratic community is furthered by agreement that some elements of the past can be made provisionally relevant to moral judgment in the present.

SOCIAL FACTS AND BORROWED AUTHORITY

In late 1999, the public affairs television network C-SPAN conducted two polls, asking viewers (1,145 responded) and prominent historians (58 responded) to rank all U.S. presidents on a "moral authority" scale. High and low scores in the two polls were similar and predictable: presidents with the most moral authority were Lincoln, Washington, and Theodore Roosevelt; those with the least were Harding, Nixon, and Clinton. The fact that the polls were not scientific (the response group was self-selecting) does not matter for my purposes. The very fact that there *are* polls about "the moral authority of presidents" (as opposed to polls about "the physical heights of presidents") makes an important if obvious point: the moral authority of a person or an institution (like their popularity but unlike their physical properties) is a social fact rather than a brute fact of nature.[10] Social facts, unlike natural facts, depend on what the people constituting a given public think, what they say, and how they act.

Social facts are real, important, and come in many varieties: money, marriage, and popularity are all social facts, but not identical kinds of social fact. Understanding moral authority depends on specifying what kind of social fact it is. As a social fact, the moral authority of a person is not inherent in that person. It is not the same as character, virtue, or moral expertise. Rather it is a product of what people think about, what they say about, and how they act toward a person (or an institution).[11] Because

---

[9] My thanks to Jerry Schneewind for raising this point. See also notes 12, 16, and 19, below.

[10] Polls: http://www.americanpresidents.org/survey/historians/moral.asp; http://www.nwaonline.net/pdfarchive/2000/February/22/D5.pdf. Social facts versus brute facts: Searle 1995. I am not concerned here with the defense of realism in the latter chapters of that book.

[11] This is not to say that a person's character or virtue has nothing to do with her moral authority; rather it is to say that these are not *identical to* her moral authority. See note 17, below.

moral authority depends on opinion, the moral authority of person or institution X cannot be directly equated to X's objective moral standing.[12] Measuring the degree of correlation between "the objective morality of X" and "the moral authority of X" might be an interesting task for a moral realist interested in the relationship between moral facts and social facts, but it is outside of the scope of this essay. What matters here is that moral authority and objective morality are not the same thing.

All forms of authority are social facts, but different forms of authority are different kinds of social facts. Unlike legal authority, moral authority is not an institutional social fact—that is, it is not a constitutive property of an institution. As president, Bill Clinton possessed legal authority as a function of the office he held. His legal authority was a constitutive property of his office because absent legal authority he would not have been president. For as long as he remained president, Bill Clinton held legal authority regardless of what people thought about his moral authority.[13] For at least part of his presidency he possessed relatively little moral authority precisely because most people refused to attribute it to him.[14] Yet, absent substantial moral authority, he remained president. Moral authority is more vulnerable to shifts in reputation than is legal authority. Because moral authority is both valued and fragile, individuals and institutions are constantly seeking to borrow it from external sources—including the past. In sum, moral authority is not the same thing as character, moral expertise, or objective morality, nor is it another name for or an aspect of established institutional authority.

[12] Unless the people in question are true moral experts or have formed their opinions strictly in accordance with the recommendations of moral experts. I am not making an argument here about whether there are or could be moral experts. Nor am I asserting that objective morality actually exists (in any sense that is more comprehensive than the baseline commitment to fairness). The point is that if it does exist, objective morality cannot be just a function of other people's opinion, and moral authority is just a function of opinion. Thus objective morality is nonidentical to moral authority.

[13] Of course there is much constitutional debate about the precise scope of presidential legal authority (e.g., on issues of executive privilege). And a president's capacity to use his legal authority effectively—to achieve his ends—is not a simple matter of institutional authority in and of itself. Possessing or failing to possess moral authority will have a lot of effect on how legal authority is used—that is, whether the president seeks to move his agenda through Congress or accomplishes his ends via executive orders. And furthermore, a sufficiently catastrophic loss in moral authority might lead to a loss of legal authority: for example, to impeachment or (conceivably) revolution.

[14] Moral authority should not be confused with "favorable regard" (e.g., popularity, public sympathy, or ratings of job effectiveness). Clinton stayed popular (especially among African-Americans); his impeachment evoked considerable sympathy; and his effectiveness rating remained quite high. But these indicators do not mean that he retained a high level of moral authority, either among the general population or among those demographic segments which otherwise regarded him favorably.

So what sort of social fact is moral authority? That question can be answered by looking at the term in use—and it is indeed much used. "Moral authority" is a pervasive expression, tightly woven into the fabric of modern American discourse. A Google search (May 2003) for the phrase "moral authority" came up with about 72,000 hits: fewer than "legal" or "legislative" authority—but more than "political," "executive," "divine," "parental," "congressional," or "presidential" authority.[15] The list of entities to which moral authority is ascribed (or denied) in this Internet material is extremely diverse; It includes religion, the United Nations, the United States, leaders, parents, the Catholic Church, trolls, the family, medicine, *Penthouse Magazine*, bishops, and teachers. Perhaps unsurprisingly, moral authority seems to be most often characterized by its absence: Many of the references have to do with moral authority that was lacking, lost, squandered, or in decline. Concomitantly, some of the references emphasized the need to regain it and recommended how to restore it. The baseline meaning of moral authority that emerges from this diverse material is "justified moral esteem in respect to judgment." That seems a reasonable enough definition so long as we acknowledge that in a thinly coherent society there will not be a consensus on who or what institution has in fact earned "our" esteem.

The primary difference between the conception that lies behind most of the Internet material I surveyed and the position I develop here lies in the source of moral authority rather than in the process by which it is gained. The Internet discussions seem typically to assume that there must be an ultimate and transcendent source of moral authority, a source that stands outside of ordinary human judgment—God, nature, tradition, or some combination thereof.[16] According to this view, individuals or institutions can earn other people's esteem by properly associating themselves with the ultimate source. Unlike the ultimate source, individuals and institutions possess moral authority only provisionally—it is "borrowed" by them from the source rather than "owned" as an inalienable possession. The loss of moral authority deplored by many Internet sites was not attributed to a failure on the part of the source. Rather the fault was on the part of human beings or institutions that were demonstably unworthy of the moral authority they had provisionally borrowed. Because the

---

[15] Google hit numbers (in thousands) for various other forms of authority: "legal" 289, "legislative" 88.3, "political" 50.1, "executive" 45, "divine" 38.5, "parental" 28.4, "congressional" 10.3, "presidential" 7.3. Google search: May 7, 2003.

[16] One might add as a fourth "inaccessible, undebatable" source the opinion of moral experts. The Platonic version of this is the true philosopher's knowledge of the Form of the good. Another version, familiar from the Islamic tradition, is "the consensus of certified experts in Koranic interpretation." This source is different from the others in not being "external" in the same sense. I owe this point to John Kelsay.

borrowers came to be regarded as unworthy, the loan was voided. So the social fact of moral authority emerges from a three-way relationship: an external source, an individual or institutional borrower, and the public that determines whether or not the loan is valid.

My concern here is with democratic political communities and with historical legacies as a source of moral authority for them. Like "ultimate, transcendental-source" conceptions of moral authority, I imagine "the moral authority of the past" as emerging from a three-way relationship between source, borrower, and public. The difference is that the source with which I am concerned, the historical legacy, is a nontranscendent artifact of culture and amenable to human judgment.[17] So how does the past become useable—in the sense of "borrowable by someone seeking moral authority"? How does a public decide what constitutes an appropriate past judgment or past action, such that citation by an agent will lend that agent moral authority? I imagine three possible scenarios; only the third fulfills democratic purposes.

In the first, "totalizing" (fundamentally undemocratic) scenario, the past is reified as authoritative tradition and the meaning of that tradition is not open to debate. And so, there is no real decision to be made by individuals: the decision has already been made by the tradition. Under such circumstances the process of borrowing is *utterly reliable* and the moral authority of the past is, by the same token, utterly oppressive.

In the second, "comprehensive" scenario, tradition is very important, but it is not reified as transcendental authority and so the process of borrowing moral authority from the past need not entail the oppressive requirement of blind adherence to tradition. Such Burkean or Isocratean conceptions of tradition as rich and thick, as comprehensive and yet not totalizing, are understandably attractive to conservative political theorists. Comprehensive conceptions of tradition allow the process of borrowing

---

[17] The notion of borrowing moral authority and the role of opinion in determining the validity of the loan helps explain why moral authority is not the same thing as virtue. An agent's chances of successfully borrowing moral authority from an external source are enhanced by, but not a simple function of, her pre-existing reputation for virtue. An individual with a pre-existing reputation for virtue may persuade others that some overlooked aspect of the past is a valid source of moral authority. Yet the same individual may fail in her attempt to borrow moral authority from a past action or past judgment if that action or judgment is regarded by others as inappropriate. By the same token, even an individual with a poor reputation for virtue may succeed in borrowing moral authority by citing a past judgment or action that is regarded as appropriate. A successful act of borrowing in itself enhances the reputation of the borrower—that is, increases her moral authority. The relationship between the moral authority of human agents and the past source of moral authority is thus reflexive: Things from the past may come to be regarded as sources of moral authority through association with virtuous "borrowers," whereas borrowers in turn gain in moral authority by their successful citation of the past.

moral authority from the past to be *generally reliable,* but they allow relatively limited scope for individual judgment.

The third scenario, which is the assumed context for the rest of this essay, concerns diverse and "thinly coherent" democratic societies. In such societies important decisions must be made and defended without reference to either totalizing or comprehensive past traditions. Reference to the past does not reliably decide issues on which there is substantial disagreement. The weight of the past no longer lies "like a nightmare on the brain of the living," and tradition no longer does much heavy lifting. Yet the past remains an important *provisional* source of authority that may be borrowed by judging agents under specifiable conditions. In a thinly coherent society, the public decision on what constitutes an appropriate citation of the past is made by reference to the criteria of fairness and suitability. The sections that follow consider three types of historical legacy: an agent's record of past judgments, the appeal to precedent, and the past action as exemplum and legacy-gift.

LEGACY I: RECORD OF PAST JUDGMENTS

Authority in a democratic society may be minimally defined as "the right granted to me, under specified conditions, to make a judgment with (potential) consequences for others."[18] Determining whether my judgment carries *legal authority* will depend on an implicit public judgment regarding the legitimacy of the institutional conditions under which my judgment takes place. If my judgment does have legal authority, its consequences for others may include reward or punishment. Those consequences do not depend upon either the objective morality of my judgment or upon public opinion regarding my moral authority.[19] Saying that my judgment carries *moral authority* is different: In this case the consequences of my judgment for others do not emerge from the legitimacy of institutional conditions. Rather its consequences have to do with the perceived moral force ascribed to my judgments.

To say that someone's judgment carries moral authority does not mean that everyone agrees with it. For example, suppose I am a fellow at a research center, and I propose to Bob, the center's director and a man

[18] One might want to flesh out the minimal definition to include ". . . or perform an action"—but I am supposing that in order to perform an action I must first make a judgment, and so the authority to act in some way presupposes the authority to make a judgment regarding the propriety of the contemplated action. Of course, much richer definitions of authority are available and are necessary for any fully fleshed-out analysis of the operations of institutional and cultural power.

[19] The idea that legal authority does not depend upon the objective morality of legal judgment is a central principle of legal positivism; see Hart 1958.

whose moral authority I acknowledge, that my fellowship be indefinitely extended in order to allow me to pursue my promising line of research. Bob denies my request. I may disagree with Bob's decision, while still respecting his moral authority. The mark of my respect is not just that I accept that Bob has the power to make the decision, but that I accept that his decision probably has moral force for me. As a result of my acceptance I should think more carefully about how my proposal may violate principles of fairness: given scarce resources, extending my fellowship would deny others a chance to develop their own projects. To speak of "my acknowledgment of Bob's moral authority" is to say that I give Bob's judgments the benefit of the doubt in respect to their likely moral content. I accept that his judgments are likely to have moral force—even if I disagree with them, and even if my disagreement survives sustained reflection. I may still think Bob decided wrongly but that does not lessen my respect for his moral authority, which is based in this case on his earned reputation for fairness: he has made many fair judgments in the past.[20] That record of fair judgment constitutes one sort of historical legacy.

Moral authority is gained and maintained in *practice*; in Bob's case it is borrowed (inter alia) from the fair judgments he has made in the past and it gives added weight to the judgments he makes in the present. Under certain circumstances that added weight may prove decisively important and entail great consequences for others. Take the example of the United States Supreme Court, an institution that possesses certain legal powers as a result of constitutional enactment. In the ordinary course of events, the consequences for others of the Court's judgments appear to emerge directly from its legal authority. But the Supreme Court has also accrued considerable moral authority over time. That moral authority is, in part, a historical legacy, a product of the American public's beliefs about the Court and its record of judgment. The Court enjoys its moral authority because the public believes that the Court is justifiably esteemed in respect to judgment, because it has judged well over time.[21] The noninstitutional social fact of moral authority does not require that the Supreme Court *actually* have a sterling record of fair judgment, but that it is widely *perceived* to have such a record.

[20] Bob's judgment is not based merely on his expert knowledge of (for example) the available resources for fellowship support, but on a moral principle (in this case, both substantive and procedural fairness).

[21] The Supreme Court consistently ranks high (in polls by Gallup and Harris) among institutions in which Americans report high levels of confidence—consistently above Congress and often above the presidency. The fact that the public's confidence resides in the Court as an institution that has persisted over time, rather than in any of its current members, is suggested by the relative stability of the Court's public confidence ratings and the fact that two-thirds of Americans cannot identify a single Supreme Court judge (source: http://www.pollingreport.com).

A court's moral authority becomes decisively important when the extent of its legal authority is unclear. Take, for example, the legal struggle over race and civil rights in the mid- to late-1950s, beginning with *Brown v. Board of Education* (1954) and culminating in *Cooper v. Aaron* (1958). In the *Brown* case, the Supreme Court found that race-based segregation violated the Equal Protection clause of the Fourteenth Amendment to the U.S. Constitution. The Court subsequently (in "*Brown II*") ordered southern states to desegregate public schools with "all deliberate speed." Matters came violently to a head in 1957, in Little Rock, Arkansas, when the governor and white mobs sought to block black students from entering formerly all-white schools. In *Cooper v. Aaron*, the state of Arkansas argued that it was not compelled to obey the Court's desegregation order because it was not a party to the *Brown* case, and furthermore that a state governor had as much right to interpret the Constitution as did the Supreme Court. In a unanimous decision, the Court bluntly asserted its own final authority: Expanding upon Chief Justice John Marshall's opinion in *Marbury v. Madison* (1803), the Court stated that "the basic principle that the federal judiciary is supreme in the exposition of the law of the Constitution . . . [is] a permanent and indispensable feature of our constitutional system." Moreover, it was not simply the Constitution, but "the interpretation of the Fourteenth Amendment enunciated by this Court," that was "the supreme law of the land." Thus the Court's interpretation was declared to be authoritative for both federal and state officials, whether or not they were parties to a particular case.[22]

As subsequent legal commentators have noted, the superiority principle asserted by the Court was far from indisputable.[23] Yet the outcome of the case was clear: All relevant parties did, even if reluctantly, obey the Court's order. The constitutional question settled (at least for the time being) by *Cooper v. Aaron* concerned nothing less than the ultimate institutional locus of decision-making authority in the United States: In cases of fundamental dispute among government institutions about interpretive authority, does the legal principle of judicial review or the democratic principle of majority rule hold sway? The long jurisprudential debate on that question suggests that it is not in the nature of constitutional democracy for it ever to be definitively answered.[24] Given the absence of any ultimate locus of supreme institutional authority in a constitutional democracy, and given the fact that the Court has no financial or military means to effect its will, it was pretty clearly the Court's *moral* authority

[22] *Cooper v. Aaron* 358 U.S. 1 (1958). For discussion, see Eisgruber 1994 and 1995 with literature cited.
[23] See Eisgruber 1995, Devins and Fisher 1998, Friedman 2002.
[24] See Eisgruber 2001, with literature cited.

that, in 1958, decided the outcome. The Court prevailed in asserting its own interpretive superiority, not because it rested its case on unimpeachable legal principle, but because of its deep reserve of moral authority. That moral authority derived both from its long record of past decisions and because the Court defended the moral high ground (equal protection as an aspect of fairness) and pointed the way to going on together as a national community at a moment when the violent conflict in Little Rock represented a grave danger to the coherence of the national community. The role of moral authority in deciding the outcome "filled the gap" between the principles of judical review and democratic majoritarianism, in that it ensured that the Court's decision rested at least in part upon values embraced by the public.[25]

The social fact of moral authority therefore *can* sometimes be of decisive importance in determining the outcome of disputes and effect of decisions—even in the case of institutions that already possess substantial legal authority. The U.S. Supreme Court is just one institution whose perceived record of past judgments bears on its moral authority. Mutatis mutandis, similar sorts of considerations explain the moral authority of (for example) parents, teachers, political leaders, legislative bodies, and directors of research centers. In each case the moral authority of the judging agent is either gained or lost over time by the opinion of those affected (offspring, students, citizens, Fellows) regarding the fairness of past judgments.

Legacy II: Precedent

The Supreme Court example suggests that even established legal authorities may at times borrow from a historical legacy in order to achieve their ends within a democratic community. The process of borrowing depends on fairness and suitabilty. In the cases we considered above, concerning an agent's record of past judgments, the criterion of suitability does little work: But other sorts of historical legacy put more stress on suitability. Suppose that, in the course of turning down my request for ongoing fellowship support, Bob cited the Athenian victory

---

[25] The Court's landmark 1992 decision in *Planned Parenthood v. Casey* (112 S.Ct. 2791, 2816 [1992]) claimed that the American people's "belief in themselves as [a people who aspire to live according to the rule of law] is not readily separable from their understanding of the Court invested with the authority to . . . speak before all others for their constitutional ideals." If so, the inverse (the Court's authority is not readily separable from the American people's beliefs about the Court) is equally true, and it is the belief held by the public (i.e., their "democratic knowledge"), not the objective correctness of the belief, that does the work.

at Marathon in 490 B.C.,[26] or, alternatively, the Athenian court's conviction of Socrates in 399 B.C.[27] Under the right circumstances, Bob's reference to a historical legacy completely unrelated to Bob's own record of past judgment may help to persuade me to regard Bob's decision as having moral content and force for me. If so, then Bob has successfully borrowed from the moral authority that seems somehow to inhere in the historical legacy itself. Bob successfully borrows moral authority from a historical legacy when his audience values that legacy and when the audience grasps the fit between the legacy and their current circumstances.

Precedent plays an obvious role in establishing a relationship between judgments made by others in the past and a given agent's moral authority. When someone cites a precedent as the basis of her judgment, she is making an implicit suitability argument, claiming that "someone else's past judgment has direct bearing on the decision that I must now make." The concept of precedent (qua *stare decisis*) is, of course, the basis of English common law. But it is extremely important in other legal systems (like those of classical Athens) in which prior judicial decisions do not legally constrain the scope of subsequent judgments.[28] Citation of precedents is also a common practice outside of the realm of legal judgment: precedents are constantly invoked by parents, teachers, administrators, and so on because they are valued legacies.

Judgments that seem to violate established precedent are likely to lead to objections by those affected. For example, having been denied permission to play with a snake, young Sally may object to her father, "That's not fair; Mom let Johnny play with a snake!" The moral force of Sally's appeal to past precedent is derived from a simple belief about fairness: the conviction that relevantly similar cases should be treated in a similar manner.[29] The strength of that conviction about "fairness as consistency" is, I suppose, one of the primary reasons that we grant "the past" its moral authority. But there remains the question of suitability. Outside of the tidy realm of English common law, the fairness criterion leaves open the question of *where* in the past one may legitimately seek precedents, and *what counts* as a valid precedent and what does not. Sally's father may answer her objection about playing with snakes by rejecting the

[26] Perhaps suggesting that "if each of the men fighting there believed his life projects deserved special treatment, the Athenian army would not have been capable of the coherence necessary for the task of defeating the enemy."

[27] Perhaps suggesting that "the jury's failure to transcend procedural fairness by considering all of the relevant moral issues in the case led to a bad decision with deleterious consequences."

[28] Precedent-based reasoning in Athenian law: Lanni 2004; Rubinstein forthcoming.

[29] Similarity of relevant cases is of course only one part of fairness and ought not to be equated with fairness as such; see further, below, on fairness as reciprocity.

validity of her precedent, on a variety of suitability grounds that Sally will find more or less convincing: For example, he may remind Sally that "Johnny was older when he was granted permission" (grounds she may have reason to accept); or "in our family, girls have never played with snakes" (grounds I do not suppose she should accept without argument); or he may point out that the snake Johnny played with was harmless whereas Sally wishes to play with a cobra (grounds that Sally almost surely should accept).

The point is that although our commitment to fairness renders precedent a powerful concept, the circumstances surrounding judgments made in the past are never *identical* to the circumstances for judgment in the present. So, in a diverse democratic society, there will be lots of room for debate about suitability, about what actually counts as a relevant historical precedent with moral force to lend in a given context of judgment. Lots of room, but not infinite room: if we assume a common commitment to fairness, and that a thinly coherent culture may be thick enough to sustain some agreed-upon standards of relevance, we can reasonably hope for some level of agreement (if not full consensus) about which historical precedents bear upon the present case. If so, those elements of the past become a legacy; they may augment the moral authority of a judging agent, and do so without reference to a thickly coherent cultural tradition.

LEGACY III: ACTION AS EXEMPLUM AND LEGACY-GIFT

Precedent and "fairness as consistency" help to explain why past *judgments* made by others have moral authority to lend. But how might citation of a past *action*, like Bob's citation of the Athenian victory at the battle of Marathon, lend moral weight to a judging agent? Thinking about what Bob could have meant, I might regard it as a warning against (Persian-like) over-reaching or a recommendation of (Athenian-like) tempering of boldness with restraint. But is my acceptance of that warning or recommendation a product of its *moral* force? Some part of the force of citing a past action is based on prudence: "It worked (or failed) then, so it will probably work (or fail) again." And some of its force is emotive: invoking Marathon may make Johnny's heart leap up with gladness or calm Sally's impetuousness. In real life decision making it is seldom possible to distinguish sharply between the relative weight of moral, prudential, and emotive elements in achieving persuasion. But the role played by citing past actions is not entirely a matter of prudence or appeals to the emotions. Citation of a past action as a historical exemplum may, under the right circumstances, allow an agent to borrow moral authority from the past in a way that is analogous to, but distinct from, the citation of a past judgment as a historical precedent.

The past action–exemplum borrows moral authority from the past through the concept of legacy as gift and our commitment to "fairness as reciprocity." That is, we believe that we owe something in return if we believe that an action in the past gave us something, if it passed down to us something of value.[30] J. S. Mill once asserted that the Athenian victory at Marathon was more important, as an event in *English* history, than the battle of Hastings. Mill presumably supposed that one could borrow moral authority from the Athenian victory because his audience believed that the future course of Western civilization was determined at Marathon. The citation assumes that the audience believes that some positive circumstances of their lives can be attributed to the past action. Western civilization becomes, according to Mill's story, a sort of "legacy-gift" from the Athenian warriors at Marathon in the fifth century B.C. to the British public in the nineteenth century of our era.[31]

If we acknowledge that we have indeed received something of substantial benefit as a result of the legacy-gift (in Mill's citation, if we believe that we do benefit from Western civilization and if it is a legacy of Marathon), we reciprocally owe something in return, and the only coin available to us to pay back the debt is that of our esteem—our willingness to treat the action as an exemplum and our commitment to seeking to pass the legacy on to the future. Under the right conditions, our esteem can be cashed out as moral authority. For example, Johnny's parents make their continued payment of his college fees contingent upon his academic performance. They justify this by citing the sacrifice his grandparents long ago made to provide him with a good education.[32] The respect Johnny grants to the exemplum in exchange for the legacy-gift generates moral authority that can be borrowed by his parents, because the exemplum of his grandparents' sacrifice is something Johnny feels compelled, on grounds of reciprocal fairness, to "live up

---

[30] This may seem somewhat mysterious, since we usually speak of owing something to a living person or institution. But it is based on an ordinary sense of owing respect to the memory of persons who accomplished worthy things while alive—which is presumably one reason (although not the only reason) we set up war memorials and why we are outraged by desecration of graves.

[31] Mill's claim about Marathon as a "European inheritance" was made in his review of the first two volumes of George Grotes' great *History of Greece* (published in the *Edinburgh Review*, 1846). For the context, see Urbinati 2002.

[32] We can strengthen the example by supposing that the parents are making a choice between paying Johnny's college fees and contributing to a charity strongly endorsed by the grandparents.

to."[33] Johnny works harder in college than he would otherwise be inclined to do, not only because he prudently fears the cutoff of funds, but also because he feels a reciprocal obligation based on acknowledged benefits received as a result of his grandparents' past sacrifice. And so the exemplum may be said to have actual *moral* force, above and beyond its prudential and emotive force.

When we move from "past judgment as precedent" to "past action as exemplum," the suitability criterion becomes weightier. In order for the exemplum to gain moral force, through the operation of our commitment to "fairness as reciprocity," there must be some minimal level of agreement on the "relevant past"—that is, on what aspects of the past we accept as genuine and valuable legacies. Today, most Americans might regard as bizarre a claim that the battle of Marathon was a centrally important event in *American* history.[34] Under the cultural conditions of thin coherence, once we step out of the realms of legal or parental judgment, we are less likely to be sure about "which past" contains the relevant universe of potential exempla. When making judgments about foreign policy, for example, where should American leaders and citizens be looking for exempla? In the ancient Greek past? In the past as defined by recent American diplomatic history? In European, Asian, or African social or religious history? As our conception of "the past" comes to be not only global in its potential scope, but also inflected (as, in a diverse and pluralistic community, it must) by considerations of race, gender, class, and ethnicity, we may ask whether *any* legacy from the past can gain the widespread esteem that would lend substantial moral weight to the decisions of those with a right to judge.

Judging agents in democratic societies are motivated to invoke historical legacies because they recognize the fragility of their own moral authority. Yet the difficulty of gaining a general agreement about which past in a diverse community renders the process of borrowing moral authority by invoking legacies less reliable, more provisional. The simultaneous

---

[33] We may feel a reciprocal obligation even if we did not *ask* for a legacy because we have tacitly *accepted* it by remaining members of our community (and benefiting accordingly); compare Socrates' argument in Plato's *Crito*, regarding what he owed to the *nomoi* on the basis of having received his birth, upbringing, and education—none of which he actually asked for, but all of which he believed himself to have benefited by and which he accepted by the act or remaining in Athens (see chapter 7). Of course the concept of the legacy of past events can also be rhetorically deployed negatively as justification for brutality: for example, the battle of Kosovo as a justification for Serbian atrocities; the execution of Jesus of Nazareth as justification for persecution of Jews; the Holocaust as justification for killing Palestinian civilians. The point is that both the value of a legacy (see below), and the reciprocal actions that its acceptance might reasonably entail, require critical moral judgment.

[34] Such claims are, however, made: Hanson 1999.

recognition (by politicians as well as by theorists) that even under cultural conditions of thin coherence the past *does* have moral authority to lend, but that the loan can be cashed out *only* once we agree that a legacy is valuable, raises the stakes in debates about history. This was as true in classical Athens as in the "culture wars" of the late twentieth- and early twenty-first century United States: Thinking about what it takes to borrow moral authority from the past can help us to understand (for instance) the project of the Athenian orator Lycurgus as exemplified in his speech of 330 B.C., *Against Leocrates*, just as it can help explain the debate in the 1990s over "national standards for United States History."[35]

Some of the ferocity of the ancient Athenian and modern American "culture wars" is based on the erroneous assumption (by conservatives and liberals alike) that borrowing moral authority from the past requires a pre-established comprehensive tradition and a thickly coherent culture. But if we can agree that historical precedents and exempla can become legacies, and thus sources of moral authority, with reference to nothing thicker than a shared commitment to fairness, we may also hope to seek some level of agreement (if never consensus) on suitability—on what constitute the positive circumstances of our lives and what actions in the past contributed to those circumstances. That demands some historical thoughtfulness, attention to how historians develop causal arguments, and a recognition that the historian's arguments are different from the causal arguments of the natural scientist. It requires recognizing the distinction between social and natural facts. But it does not demand professional expertise, nor does it imply that legacy-claims be predicated on a comprehensive tradition about the past, or a thick culture to which all must subscribe. Looking at the form, content, and purposes of Thucydides' history of the Peloponnesian War, in the context of attempts by his fellow Athenians to recover a useable past after an era of intense civic conflict, offers a case in point.

THUCYDIDES' *HISTORY* AND POLITICAL CONFLICT

During and after the long Peloponnesian War (431–404 B.C.) the Athenians struggled with their relationship to their own past. The war had exacerbated sociopolitical conflict in Athens, leading to a temporary overthrow of democracy in 411 B.C. Democracy was restored but Athens still lost the war. The victorious Spartans then imposed an oligarchic government; Athens was placed under the control of a band of thirty antidemocratic Athenians. The months of oligarchic rule featured arbitrary confiscations, expulsions, and killing; it was later dubbed by the Athenians the era of

---

[35] On the controversy, see Foster 1998.

the "Thirty Tyrants." Yet democracy was soon restored. The starkly immoral behavior of the ruling Thirty contributed to the rise of an armed democratic resistance. Within a year the democrats had won the civil war and deposed the Thirty. In the aftermath the restored democracy of Athens announced an amnesty, declaring that past actions, performed under the government of the Thirty, could not be the basis for legal prosecution.[36]

Political amnesty represents a judgment that going on together under long-term conditions of justice must take precedence over achieving strict justice in the here and now. As such it limits the purchase of absolute morality in decisions that may be decisively important to a society's persistence. In light of the fragility of restored institutionalized authority, the Athenian attempt to end an era of civil conflict by declaring an amnesty necessarily drew upon moral as well as legal authority: The uncertainty of legal norms under the Thirty and the erosion of social capital meant that people responsible for making judgments with public consequences were in dire need of moral authority borrowed from external sources—including the past. Yet, ironically, the declaration of an amnesty could also be thought of as setting a limit on the historical field in which precedents and legacies might legitimately be sought.

For the Athenians to declare a general amnesty was, in the most literal sense, to say that some range of past judgment–precedents and some range of past action–exempla were disallowed as legacies relevant to the process of judgment in their current situation. Amnesty, literally "not-remembering," demands that we wipe out some parts of our past, not by actual forgetting, but by declaring those parts to be irrelevant. Because it limits the past universe from which we may legitimately seek to find legacies, declaring an amnesty is a revolutionary political act. In the *Social Contract* Rousseau rejects the notion that there can be *any* past precedent or fundamental law which binds the "general will." The extreme presentism of Rousseau's conception of the general will links it to the radical antihistoricism of the later phases of the French Revolution.[37]

[36] On the Athenian amnesty, see Loening 1987, Loraux 1997 (English trans. 2002), Wolpert 2002.

[37] Compare Carla Hesse's paper at the Moral Authority of the Past Symposium (National Humanities Center, November 2002), on the key moment (in 1793–94) in which the French Revolution turned to a strong form of presentism. Hesse suggests that this moment constitutes a rejection of the "corruption" associated with "historically conditioned" behavior, and so a rejection of the sort of critical-empirical history associated with Voltaire in favor of a "conjectural history," based on appeals to nature and first principles, associated with Rousseau. It is worth noting that Rousseau's use of "Sparta" as a model for the imagined community of the *Social Contract* required dehistoricizing Sparta: a willful forgetting of the fundamental basis of Spartan society in the oppression of helots. Modern communitarian embrace of Rousseau: Barber 1984.

The political act of "wiping out" a part of the past, by declaring it off limits for current legal judgment, might seem to risk a general collapse of respect for the past. In the wake of an amnesty, and the prior horrors which precipitated the need for an amnesty, some people may be tempted to agree with Henry Ford that "history is bunk": They may suppose that the past is dispensable, and embrace the notion that it is our moral duty to create the world anew, from first principles. Plato's revolutionary community of Callipolis, the "city based on arguments" sketched in the *Republic*, might, therefore, be seen as motivated by the amnesty of 403 B.C., as well as by the trial of Socrates four years later.

As I have argued elsewhere, the emergence of democracy depends upon revolutionary action and breaking with certain past social practices.[38] But just as achieving coherence sometimes requires radical change, utterly abandoning the past as a resource for moral judgment in a postrevolutionary era, and depending on revolutionary principles alone, make it less likely that we will go on together under conditions of justice. When asked in the mid-1960s what comes after the revolution, the French filmmaker Jean-Luc Godard reportedly replied, "Revolution, revolution, and more revolution." But then Mao Zedong's Cultural Revolution demonstrated what continuous revolution entailed in practice.

Revolution and civil conflict sharpen perceptions about *negative* precedents and exempla. But in the aftermath of revolution and counter-revolution, the community may also feel a need to gain agreement about *positive* legacies. And so, civil strife, even when followed by amnesty, may be a spur to the practice of seeking to reconstruct a useable past. The late fifth-century B.C. era of civic strife in Athens and its aftermath fueled a great deal of work on the part of Athenian historians and politicians seeking to recreate a useable past for Athens. Given the troubles of the recent past, the deep past appeared a safer source to many of them. Athenian political writers became obsessively concerned with recovering the *patrios politeia*—the ancestral constitution of the deep Athenian past.[39] The debate about the ancestral constitution emerged as a central feature of Athenian public discourse—a means of debating the essential question of what elements of the past would have moral purchase upon contemporary Athenian judgment.

But the debate on the ancestral constitution was only part of the Athenian struggle to define a useable past. Thucydides' *History of the Peloponnesian War*, like much Athenian ancestral constitution literature, can best be understood as a "conflict-era historical project." Thucydides' *History* provides a good example of how an expert historian presents a

---

[38] Ober 1996.

[39] *Patrios politeia*: Ostwald 1986. For an illuminating discussion of the moral authority of the deep past in post-Soviet Mongolia, see Humphrey 1992.

past, recent to himself, as a permanent resource for judgment in his readers' present—no matter how distant from himself that present might be.
Thucydides' *History* has indeed been a rich source of borrowed moral
authority in modernity.[40] It may, therefore, serve as a test case for assessing the relevance of the criteria developed here to the problem of borrowing moral authority from a past very distant to ourselves.

We know from his own statements in the *History* (e.g., 2.65) that
Thucydides was still at work after the Spartan military victory of 404 B.C.
Which means, that unless Thucydides died during the civil strife of the
next year (and we would expect to hear about it in the ancient biographies
if he had), he lived to see the reign of the Thirty, the democratic restoration, and the amnesty of 403.[41] If he was still working on his *History*
during the era of the Thirty and after the declaration of amnesty, what relationship might that period of revolutionary strife and amnesty have had
to the *History* as it has come down to us? In the wake of Robert Connor's
important work on Thucydidean historiography, classicists have learned
to pay careful attention to Thucydides' text's relationship with its imagined reader. So what might we say about Thucydides' hypothetical reader
in, say, 402, someone who had survived Athenian civil war, lived under
the terms of the amnesty, and now confronted the text of Thucydides'
History?[42]

To that imagined reader, Thucydides' historical project must have appeared quite extraordinary. Think, for example, of reading Pericles' Funeral
Oration (Thuc. 2.35–46) in 402. At the beginning of Pericles' speech, as reported by Thucydides, the issue is explicitly "what events in the universe of
the Athenian past constitute positive legacies for the current generation?"
Thucydides' Pericles boldly breaks with Athenian oratorical tradition by

---

[40] Roberts 1994, index s.v. Thucydides, on the long history of appropriation of
Thucydides for political purposes. Recent examples include Kagan 2003 and the pre-
script to the preamble of the proposed constitution of the European Union (proposed by
Valéry Giscard d'Estaing in May 2003) which cites Thucydides 2.37, on the definition of
democracy.

[41] Indeed, the biographical tradition claims that he returned to Athens as a result of the
amnesty. Classical scholarship has ultimately proved unable to solve the question of exactly when and in what order various parts of the history were written and revised (see
Rawlings 1981). Munn 2000 offers an ultimately unpersuasive argument to the effect that
the *History* was written in its entirety in the mid-390s. We cannot suppose that the whole
of Thucydides' *History* was conceived and written in the wake of the amnesty, without vi-
olating what Thucydides himself says in his introduction (1.1) about the beginnings of his
project.

[42] Connor 1984. I am not making a substantive claim that Thucydides' text, as we now
have it, would have been available for reading in 402; the point is rather that Thucydides
must have been aware of the impact that his text (whether in progress or recently completed) would have upon a contemporary reader, and that awareness is relevant in thinking
about the text's intended force.

refusing to spend much time on the distant past: The reader learns nothing about the standard deep-past exempla—sacrifices of earth-born Kings, or ancestral battles against Amazons, or about the victories at Marathon and Salamis.[43] Instead, Pericles briefly lauds the empire-building generation of "our fathers," and then quickly turns to "our own" great accomplishments of the very recent past. The traditional moral authority of deep Athenian history—the primary concern of all those Athenian *patrios politeia* writers who were busy writing and circulating their texts—is explicitly rejected: Thucydides' Pericles proclaims that "we now have no need of a Homer." The legacy Pericles speaks of is not received from the deep past. Rather it is a product of recent and anticipated actions and it is offered *to the future*: future generations will, he predicts, live in awe of what we have accomplished. They will owe us their esteem, our own accomplishments will be a source of moral authority for them. Twenty-eight years later, in the face of the amnesty and the desperate Athenian need to recover a useable past, this sort of talk must have cut to the quick: The Athenians of 402 certainly *cannot* say, with Thucydides' Pericles, that "we ourselves" in our own generation have, by our own splendid efforts, rendered the moral authority of deep history simply meaningless.

And it is not just a matter of the Funeral Oration: Thucydides' entire *History* is a radical departure from the still-nascent genre of historiography in that it focuses primarily (although, significantly, not entirely) on very recent history, on events that took place during the author's own lifetime. In the spirit of Pericles' emphasis in the Funeral Oration on "my generation," Thucydides' *History* turns its back on the deep past as the primary center of attention, in favor of a focus on recent events. Thucydides' *History* is a didactic text, one that implicitly promises to produce in its reader a level of expertise adequate to judge historical legacies. And at the center of "what must be learned" is an extraordinarily detailed, careful, and artfully presented record of the recent past. For Athenian readers in 402, Thucydides' *History* offered a very difficult lesson indeed. It requires that "we" learn from what has happened in our own time: that we look first to our own collective experience as a suitable source of the precedents and exempla we need to make moral judgments.

In 402, this sort of demand might be read as an indirect challenge to the spirit of the amnesty. I do not mean by this that Thucydides risked actual censorship; the legal constraints imposed by the amnesty did not cover the activity of historywriting. I mean, instead, that by decreeing that actions done in the recent past were not liable to legal prosecution, the amnesty bracketed certain parts of the past. The historical zone that

---

[43] On the ways in which Thucydides' Pericles conforms to and breaks with the traditional topoi of the Athenian funeral oration, see Ziolkowski 1981, Loraux 1986.

was specifically interdicted was the immediate past of the civil war and the actions were those of the oligarchic government and its sympathizers. But in the aftermath of the Peloponnesian War and its terrible hardships, the interdiction might have seemed to extend to all that had led up to the era of the "Thirty Tyrants." This (in the postwar Athenian imagination) included the extraordinary arrogance, the bold spirit of presentism, that had led the Athenians of Thucydides' generation to ignore the moral considerations that sometimes constrained Greek behavior.[44] In 402, it was quite easy to suppose that abandoning traditional sources of moral authority had led to the over-reaching that ultimately fed the fires of civil war and so required an amnesty. Perhaps it was better, as the writers of *patrios politeia* literature implied, to forget the events of the last generation and rebuild a useable past from a deeper and less painful historical repository. Thucydides' *History* bluntly opposes such thinking. Like the South African Truth and Reconciliation Commission, it declares, no amnesty without a full account of what really happened, despite all of the pain that minutely accurate remembering must entail.

What, our imagined reader, sitting in the rubble of Athens in 402, might ask, is the *use* of such remembering? One obvious answer can be formulated in terms of negative legacies: Thucydides' text offers abundant material for anyone looking to the past for detailed examples of bad (because both immoral and imprudent) decisions and unsuccessful actions, not least on the part of the Athenian democracy. And indeed, the recent past was taken up as a source of negative historical legacy by Athenian democrats in the years after 403: as we have seen, the Athenians came to describe the short-lived oligarchic government of 404 as a collective tyranny. Reference to the wicked deeds of the "Thirty Tyrants" helped to vindicate the unique legitimacy of democratic government (see chapter 10). Yet, some moments in the recent past also offered Athenian democrats positive *exempla*: the actions of the "men of Phyle"—the handful of democratic freedom fighters who began the armed resistance to the oligarchs—came to symbolize the brave willingness of Athenian democrats to offer their lives in the attempt to win back democracy.[45]

Is there anything in Thucydides' account of the recent past that could serve a postamnesty reader seeking a useable past in the public judgments and official actions of an established democratic Athenian government? Could Thucydides' text have helped the Athenians after 403 (or members of any subsequent thinly coherent society) to go on together as a democratic society, by allowing them to borrow moral authority from a democratic

---

[44] On those moral considerations and the question of whether they had any bearing outside of the community of the polis, see Balot 2001.

[45] See Wolpert 2002 for the carefully limited honors offered the men of Phyle.

Athenian past? I suggested above that there is reason to suppose that Thucydides lived to see the amnesty, and thus that he had to confront the question of what a reader in ca. 402 might think about his historical project in light of the amnesty and the events that required it. And I'd like to think that Thucydides had an answer for the reader who sought suitable positive as well as negative legacies in Athens' own recent democratic past. The answer might go something like this:

> There is more to my history than an account of how Athens lost the war; there is also an image of the extraordinary quality of what was lost: If you read the Funeral Oration of Pericles (and related passages) with care, you will get some sense of that. If you read my history attentively, you may come to the conclusion that it is *not* the case that everything was lost after all. You may come to realize what a remarkably sustained legacy has been left you, even in the sad rubble of the present, by the sound judgments and the glorious actions that went into the portrait that Pericles, *my* Pericles, paints of our city. And when you grasp the fact of the continuity of that true legacy, a legacy which survives when all the marble and gold and all the gilded material bric-a-brac that dazzled people's eyes back then is gone, you will realize the extent of your own indebtedness. And so indeed, *that* past has true moral authority to lend, and if you fairly recognize your reciprocal obligations, you will in turn grant moral authority to those who appropriately cite those past judgments and actions.[46]

That imagined response brings the work of politically engaged history writing directly into the realm of political theory and moral philosophy. It conjoins the offer of a legacy with the historical tools necessary for judging its value—and thus offers a paradigm for Thucydides' successors in the project of philosophical historiography. But Thucydides' actual "textual voice" is never so explicit or so loquacious.

I conclude with a speculation: that Thucydides *did* live to see the amnesty, and that, however else he may or may not have changed his *History* as a consequence, he *did* add a brief passage which encapsulates the sentiments I have attributed to him: The passage is among the most famous in the *History*, because it is the most explicit about the author's purpose in writing: it explains to the reader what reading the *History* was good for. I cite a slightly emended version of the Crawley translation:

> The absence of romance in my history will, I fear, detract somewhat from its interest; but if it be judged useful by those inquirers who desire an exact knowledge of the past as an aid to the interpretation of the future, which in

---

[46] I emphasize that this passage is my own creation: meant to be in the spirit of what I think Thucydides might have said but in no sense an independent source for Thucydides' thought.

the course of human things it must resemble if it does not reflect it, I shall be content. In sum, I have written my work, not as an essay which is to win the applause of the moment, but as a legacy-gift for all time (Greek: *ktēma es aiei*).[47]

The legacy that Thucydides refers to is not only the text of his *History*, but also its subject matter and the methodological lessons necessary to judge it. Its subject is not only a depressing cautionary tale about mistakes made in the past and best avoided in the future, but it is also Thucydides' own vision of a human community that was, if only for a while, truly extraordinary: that vision is of a democratic community that managed, under the leadership of Pericles, to leverage a thin cultural coherence to achieve a common purpose, and thus to do some admirable as well as some terrible deeds. Thucydides regarded Athenian excellence as having been squandered after the passing of Pericles, but his reference to his text as a legacy-gift suggests that something like it might be regained, perhaps in some other place and some other time.[48]

Thucydides' text teaches historical judgment by demonstrating that the past is complicated. It tempers a primary focus on the recent past with occasional soundings into the deep past (e.g., the "Archaeology" of book 1 and the "Sicilian Antiquities" of book 6), and the attentive reader comes to realize that these deep soundings are essential to a proper understanding of more recent events. Thucydides' *History* urges us to be cautious consumers of historical narratives, warns us to be suspicious of the too-easy appropriation and the partisan agenda—and thereby encourages us to develop defensible criteria for selecting past precedents and exempla. Thucydides' own criteria may not be identical to ours. My point is not that we should accept his criteria, but that reading his *History*, in light of considerations about fairness and suitability, can help us become better participants in the public debate about the useable past.

As we consider the possible utility of the Greek past presented by Thucydides for moral judgment in our present, we may disagree, with one another and with Thucydides, about whether particular Athenian deeds and judgments were admirable or not. I do not suggest that we should accept the legacy Thucydides offers us uncritically or as a package. We certainly need not accept Thucydides' implicit claim that his readers are *uniquely* capable of understanding the past or that real

---

[47] Thucydides 1.22.4. There is a large classical bibliography on this passage. For *ktēma* as "heirloom," see LSJ s.v. (2), citing Homer, *Iliad* 9.382 and *Odyssey* 4.127; Moles 1999 argues that Thucydides 1.22.4 self-consciously references these Homeric passages. See Hornblower 1991 for further discussion.

[48] Ober 1998, chap. 2, offers a critical assessment of Thucydides' emphasis on Periclean leadership and his implicit argument that the post-Periclean democracy was doomed to self-destruction.

democracy (as opposed to democracy in name only) will fail under the hard conditions of a sustained war.[49] But on the other hand we should not reject the utility of the legacy of classical Athenian history on the false grounds that Athenian political culture was based on a thickly comprehensive traditionalism incompatible with modernity: Thucydides' *History* helps us to recognize the ways in which classical Athenian culture was thinly coherent; and the history of Athenian democracy after 404 B.C. shows that thinness can be compatible with persistence.

If we, as modern democrats, are concerned with moral judgment and have developed the level of historical thoughfulness available to Thucydides' readers (which does not require that we be expert historians, or even that we read Thucydides), we will reject grandiose attempts to borrow moral authority from history. We will pay careful attention to the recent past of our own societies. And yet we should also accept that some legacies of the deep past could, under the right circumstances, help us to confront the moral and political dilemmas that attend our distinctive (if not quite unique) modern condition.

---

[49] Thucydides, who wrote in an era in which full literacy was limited, and in a Greek idiom that was almost perversely difficult, surely did not intend for his *History* to be available as a resource for "the many." But in this sense, at least, the writer's intentions are simply irrelevant. The conditions of modernity make historical expertise (via Thucydides' text in translation, and via a wide array of other sophisticated historical work) potentially available to every citizen. Whether that potential is realized depends, of course, on educational policy and how it is implemented.

CHAPTER FOUR

Culture, Thin Coherence, and the Persistence of Politics

In the summer of 2002 Carol Dougherty and Leslie Kurke invited me to add a postscript to a collection of essays on the topic of "the cultures within Greek culture.* The new volume was intended as a sequel to their influential Cultural Poetics of Ancient Greece *of 1993, the collection in which the title essay of my own* Athenian Revolution *had originally appeared. The shared intellectual concern of the classicists contributing to* The Cultures within Greek Culture *was the role of cultural practices in the formation and persistence of individual and group identities—a matter that is also of considerable importance for recent writing by political theorists on ethics and citizenship (e.g., Kymlicka 1995, Gutmann 2003, Allen 2004). A key point in much of the new work on ethical citizenship is that individuals gain and create their identities from multiple and overlapping group memberships. By contrast, much earlier political theory had held that (especially in the strong form of citizenship identified with the polis) the citizen must identify intensely and exclusively with his "state citizenship," and thus that the political community (through its cultural resources) "gives" him an identity that is homogeneous and identical to that given to every other citizen. This is the vision of citizenship advanced by Rousseau in the* Social Contract, *based on an ahistorical idealization of ancient Sparta. It is also, mutatis mutandis, the frightening ideal of various modern totalitarians who appeal to ancient Greece, and therefore the reason that "polis nostalgia" can rightly be regarded as not merely silly but pernicious.*

One popular philosophical alternative to oppresive forms of "locality-oriented" national citizenship is cosmopolitanism—a condition in which the individual might be thought of as free to design her identity at will, from a wide variety of cultural resources. The moral cosmopolitan grounds her conception of duty on universal criteria rather than local attachments—and thus can become a fully responsible "citizen of the world." Yet the cosmopolitan ideal risks freeing elites with less highly developed moral intuitions from any sort of shared identity–based responsibility for improving their fellows, while simultaneously denying

---

* This essay was first published in C. Dougherty and L. Kurke, eds., *The Cultures within Greek Culture* (Cambridge: Cambridge University Press, 2003), 237–55. Reprinted with permission of Cambridge University Press.

citizens the political means of democratically determining their own collective destiny. Strong cosmopolitanism, for all its undoubted attractions, potentially deprives people of the human good of living in communities as participative "political animals," while unwittingly offering ungenerous elites a cover for abandoning local ties in favor of a world of diverse multicultural pleasures, free from constraining politically enforced responsibilities. A key part of the capacity of complex communities to go on together is the maintenance of political institutions and modes of public communication that compel privileged elites to attend to their disadvantaged fellow citizens; this was the core argument of Ober 1989.

This essay employs an anthopological definition of culture as "thinly coherent," and the model of Athens as a "thinly coherent political community," in order to argue for thin coherence as a normatively desirable middle way: Thin coherence offers an alternative both to oppressively "thick" versions of community, based on a deep array of shared history and cultural traditions, and to a depoliticized, fully cosmopolitan world in which people are left with no resources for going on together other than a hoped-for universal commitment to objective moral duty.

• • •

THE TERM "CULTURE" is asked to do a lot of work in the recent scholarship of many fields, including classical history and political theory. But culture is an inherently fuzzy term—it means very different things to different people, even in the same field. The anthropologist William Sewell has sought to bring some clarity to the situation by distinguishing between two of the primary senses of culture in use today: First, in the classical anthropology associated with Ruth Benedict, a culture is understood descriptively as constitutive of society, as "a concrete and bounded world of beliefs and practices." We may organize this first sense of culture along a spectrum, ranging from umbrella cultures or broad cultural zones ("Hellenic culture"), through clearly defined societies or communities ("Athenian culture"), to subsocietal groups or microcommunities ("Athenian citizen culture"). Within this spectrum, contemporary political theorists have been particularly concerned with the middle term, the so-called societal culture. The societal culture may or may not be coextensive with a sovereign state. It is defined by Will Kymlicka as "a culture which provides its members with meaningful ways of life across the full range of human activities . . . encompassing both public and private spheres . . . territorially concentrated and based on a shared language." Sewell's second sense of culture is "a theoretically defined category or aspect of social life." Sewell notes,

quite rightly, that a lack of attention to the fundamental distinction between culture-as-society and culture-as-theory causes confusion as the term
is borrowed from anthropology by other disciplines.[1]

Sewell concentrates on culture-as-theory, insisting upon its autonomy
from other forms of social analysis (e.g., politics or economics) and noting
that it can in turn be subdivided into two primary analytic approaches. The
first of these, associated with Clifford Geertz, maps quite easily onto the
descriptive concept of "societal culture." This Geertzian approach emphasizes the ways in which people create and maintain a distinct "world of
meaning." It assumes relatively high levels of *coherence* and consequently
emphasizes the connectedness of individuals who fall within a cultural
sphere. While sympathetic to some aspects of the Geertzian approach,
Sewell himself leans toward a second approach to culture-as-theory, associated with Pierre Bourdieu, which de-emphasizes coherence to focus on
how people employ social practices for purposes of cultural *contestation*.
Sewell's own preferred definition of culture-as-theory juxtaposes meaning and practice, coherence and contestation: "A dialectic of system and
practice, . . . a dimension of social life autonomous from other such dimensions [e.g., politics or economics] both in its logic and in its spatial
configuration . . . a system of symbols *possessing a real but thin coherence* that is continually put at risk in practice [by human agents] and
therefore subject to transformation" (emphasis added).[2]

The "thinness" of coherence in Sewell's definition is especially important to the project of thinking about Greek culture, resistance, and politics. A recent collection of essays entitled *The Cultures within Greek
Culture* (Dougherty and Kurke 2003) demonstrates that Greek culture is
amenable to a "Sewellian thin-coherence" analysis. This in turn suggests
that theorizing predicated on an assumption that the coherence of Greek
culture must be extraordinarily thick is likely to be misleading. Rousseau
and Hannah Arendt are prominent examples of influential theorists who
based their arguments on the thickness of Greek culture. But even more relevant here, contemporary communitarians and their liberal critics have
made very similar interpretive assumptions. The recognition that a given
Greek societal culture (e.g., Athens) is best understood as only thinly coherent, continually at risk in practice, and subject to transformation, provides grounds for rejecting appropriations of "the Greeks" by those who
seek to deploy an illusory "thick-culture Greece" for illiberal and anti-
modernist political projects. By the same token, "thinly coherent Greek

[1] Sewell 1999, quotes: 39. Kymlicka 1995, quote: 76. Kymlicka, following Gellner 1983,
supposes that societal cultures are unique products of modernization. But the concept of
societal culture, as he uses it, applies readily to the world of the Greek poleis.

[2] Sewell 1999, quotes: 52.

cultures" become newly available to very different sorts of theoretical projects. Freed from the baggage of thick coherence, Greek historical experience is relevant to those who embrace modernity, yet struggle with its dilemmas. And so Greek cultures could (as I hope to show below) come to play a very different role in contemporary debates on normative issues.[3]

Each of the contrasting ways of conceiving "culture" discussed by Sewell—as bounded society and bounded microcommunity, as coherent system of meaning and as contestatory system of practice—does some real work in describing the world as we know it, and none of them is easily abandoned. Given the persistence of these several conceptions of culture, once we have identified a variety of culture-worlds that coexist within any broad culture-zone—that is, "the cultures within Greek culture"—we may then assess each microcommunity, each societal culture, and each culture-zone in terms of Sewell's practice-meaning and coherence-contestation dialectic. And then we may assess the interaction *between* microcommunities, societal cultures, and culture zones in terms of the same dialectical tensions. Analysis along multiple axes (culture-world/cultural theory; microcommunity/societal culture/culture-zone; practice/meaning; coherence/contestation) is analytically challenging and normatively valuable. As I suggested above, in reference to "thin coherence," the normative significance of Greek culture emerges with much greater clarity only after a substantial amount of hard descriptive work has been done.

The field of classics is one in which there has been much attention to careful description. *The Cultures within Greek Culture*, and other recent work by classical scholars, points the way to an interdisciplinary dialogue between explicitly normative political theory and implicitly normative cultural studies. That dialogue could benefit both disciplines by supplying each with a richer conceptual vocabulary. In brief, political theorists concerned with problems of "multicultural justice" would benefit from a more nuanced vocabulary for addressing culture. Practitioners of cultural studies in turn would gain a vocabulary for making their implicit normative critique of power and inequality clearer and more explicit.[4]

---

[3] Holmes 1979 is a good example of a dedicated liberal's claim, on the grounds of the presumptive thickness of the polis and its appropriation by illiberal thinkers, that the polis is meaningless for contemporary political thinking. Communitarian fascination with the model of the polis (and their tendency to conflate Aristotle's ideal state in *Politics*, book 7, with Athens): Phillips 1993, esp. 122–48. On Arendt and the Greeks, see, recently, Euben 2000, Waldron 2000.

[4] I am assuming that some political theorists do embrace "nuance," and that some cultural studies practitioners do embrace "clarity," as desirable attributes.

Yet this is not an easy conversation to get going, given the divergent styles of argument typical of the two disciplines.[5] Despite the tendency of both political theory and cultural studies to privilege modernity as such, ancient Greece may be a particularly good place to begin. Once we have dispensed with the fiction of the preternatually thickly coherent polis, the field of classical studies becomes an apt space for opening such a conversation because classics, as an academic field, embraces the study of both political thought (e.g., Plato) and cultural studies (e.g., Herodotus) without supposing that there is anything peculiar about the conjunction. It is not news to classicists that paying attention to culture is important when reading Plato (the dramatic setting of the *Republic* is Piraeus, Athens's most multicultural deme), or that Herodotus explores problems of political theory (e.g., the "Persian Debate over Constitutions").

The interdisciplinary dialogue need not take place uniquely *within* the field of classics, as I will attempt to show by juxtaposing passages from two articles—one by a prominent student of cultural studies (Sewell) and the other by a prominent political theorist (Jeremy Waldron). Although developed as arguments within the context of specific intradisciplinary debates, each article is ultimately concerned with similar issues of culture and politics. Moreover that common concern with culture and politics is motivated by a common normative worry about the constraints associated with thick cultural coherence.

The essays that constitute *The Cultures within Greek Culture* reveal a diverse spectrum of cultural communities of meaning and practice within Hellas. Sewell's multiple definitions of culture allow us to think more clearly about large-scale culture-zones (e.g., "Hellas," "Inuit," or "Islam"). Such umbrella cultures are defined by widely shared attributes—in the Greek case, these include a common language, an orientation toward certain sacred places and their attendant rituals (Delphi), and an attachment to certain narratives and their attendant genres (Homeric epic). At the other end of the spectrum are microcommunities (e.g., professional musicians), whose members share in more arcane and specialized sets of attributes, for example the mastery of demanding and abstruse artistic techniques. In between these poles lie societal cultures, including states—communities whose members are bonded to one another by (inter alia) explicitly political ties: In Greece, these prominently

---

[5] The potential for that dialogue to be fruitful, as well as the difficulties of bringing it about were brought home to me by participation in Princeton's University Center for Human Values Fellows' Seminar in the academic year 2001–2002, which brought together cultural studies theorists and political theorists. This essay was first presented to that seminar, and it owes much to each of the seminar's participants.

include the *poleis*.[6] The demonstration that "cultural communities" are extremely diverse in their scope and defining attributes, and that the term "culture" is *not* usefully limited to societal cultures, is normatively important because it exposes with great clarity the error of robust forms of cultural *relativism*: if "Nazi officialdom" and "Doctors without Borders" (in a simple case) can both be described as "cultural communities of meaning and practice," manifesting a certain semiotic logic and coherence, then it is patently absurd to claim that all cultural communities are equally deserving of respect or disdain.

But there is a second, more challenging set of evaluative questions that is also, if again only implicitly, raised by recent work on the internal diversity of classical Greek culture: Does a vulnerable cultural community (at whatever scale) have an intrinsic right to persist, a valid collective claim to defense against hegemonic intrusion by states or intrusive umbrella cultures?[7] Alternatively, should we regard the potential access to "cultural variety" (that is, access to cultures and cultural products beyond those into which we are born) as a fundamental good? Should we regard it as a basic human entitlement comparable to or perhaps part of individual freedom or autonomy? If so, does free individual access to cultural variety require and deserve legal protection against hegemonic cultural demands of a particular community—whether those demands are made by a nation-state, some other societal culture, or even a microcommunity seeking to maintain coherence among the meanings accepted by its members? Something like that normative position is argued by cosmopolitan liberal political theorists like Waldron, who (as an expert in constitutional law) regards formal immunities guaranteed by legislative statutes and legal arguments as especially appropriate methods for protecting free access to cultural diversity.[8]

For Sewell, working with the concept of culture-as-theory, it is an important proof of the autonomy of culture that "the meaning of a symbol always transcends any particular context." Hence, meanings deployed in

---

[6] I say "prominently include" rather than "are" in recognition of the variety of non-polis political structures, notably *koina* ("federal leagues"; see Mackil 2004) that also existed in the Greek world. Note, too, that some "societal cultures" may exist as "microcommunities" within states: indeed much of the political theoretical work on societal cultures has focused on the rights such communities can claim against the state; see further, below.

[7] This, in respect to societal cultures, is the central claim of Kymlicka 1995. In the Greek case, this question is probably best addressed within the context of the *koinon*, rather than the polis.

[8] Waldron 1992; see further, below. It is important to distinguish Waldron's cosmopolitan concern for free access to diverse cultural resources from Kymlicka's preservationist concern for protecting existing indigenous and minority cultures from external encroachment or dilution.

the social context of any particular set of relations are invariably influenced or affected by other contexts in which meanings are determined.
The normative point is that this potential for "cross-appropriation"
provides for the possibility of resistance and contestation.[9] Sewell's example is work-relations, and the "other contexts" he cites notably include
statutes and legal arguments (as well as strikes, socialist tracts, and economic treatises).[10] Waldron is concerned with free access to and fair distribution of the products of culture-worlds, whereas Sewell is concerned
with how the autonomy of culture-as-theory explains how agents resist
the contraints of power. Yet both the cultural theorist and the normative
theorist are seeking to address the moral problem of how human agents
gain the capacity to successfully contest potentially burdensome social
constraints. And both see "culture," as well as legal institutions, as a key
to that moral problem.

Ancient and modern history alike provide numerous examples of people enthusiastically supporting the coherence-claims of societal cultures
when they are constituted as states.[11] This poses problems in that nationalist sentiment may serve to restrict free access to cultural diversity while
simultaneously rendering it difficult for any "subnational" societal culture
to maintain its own coherence. Waldron advocates "cosmopolitanism"
as an alternative to nationalist loyalties. Is there any rational and just reason for a human agent to choose the constraints of nationalism over the
freedom of cosmopolitanism? That choice might be informed by the Aristotelian argument that humans are by nature "political animals." On this
view, citizenship, defined as active participation in a political community,
is an end unto itself, a fundamental human good that may be chosen in
preference to other fundamental goods, under conditions in which disagreement about ends is seen as legitimate.[12]

Alternatively, someone might reject Aristotle's natural-ends line of argument and yet still choose to accept the cultural claims of a nation-state

[9] I borrow this term from Spinosa, Flores, and Dreyfus 1997.

[10] Sewell 1999, 48–49.

[11] For purposes of this essay, I think it is fair to consider large poleis (like Athens and
Sparta), and Greek *koina* as in some ways similar to modern nation-states. They are, to be
sure, quite different from modern nation-states (above all in the absence of a strong distinction between citizenry and government), but that fact should not blind us to the continuities: Both are political-cultural entities that make explicit demands upon their members
as citizens, in terms of risks and costs, and offer explicit benefits including access to economic, political, and cultural opportunities.

[12] The notion that group membership is a fundamental good in itself is the starting premise of both communitarian political theory (e.g., Sandel 1984, 1998), and policies that seek
to protect indigenous cultures from the encroachments of the nation-state (such as those advocated by Kymlicka). The liberalism advocated by Isaiah Berlin assumes disagreement
over fundamental goods. Liberal perfectionists, such as Joseph Raz (1986), seek to show
that choiceworthy fundamental goods are compatible.

because she believes that citizenship (or even lesser forms of national membership) may be an efficient instrumental means to other desired ends, for example, a fairer distribution of social goods such as wealth, education, or health care. Sewell notes that systems of meaning are not coextensive with national boundaries, but he also urges students of cultural studies to "pay at least as much attention to [states as] sites of concentrated cultural practice as to the dispersed sites of resistance that currently predominate in the [cultural studies] literature."[13] Situating the implicit normative claims of cultural theorists for the value of contestation and resistance within the realm of state politics, between the cosmopolitan's freedom to choose among diverse cultural options and the citizen seeking a fairer distribution of social goods, may help to clarify what is at stake in the developing enterprise of cultural studies.

As we gain a fuller understanding of the spectrum of cultural communities that existed within Hellas it becomes easier to see why attempts to define that extensive culture-zone as a societal culture, capable of providing its adherents with a comprehensive identity or set of values, must fail. These attempts range from Isocrates' complex vision of Panhellenism to politically charged modern appeals to "Greek wisdom"—and each becomes less compelling as our analysis becomes more fine-grained. As soon as we ask questions of any specificity, whether they are standard cultural questions about practice (What do you eat? How do you fight? How do you bury your dead?) or familiar political and ethical questions about justice and obligation (How should you treat others? What do you owe and to whom? Who has the authority to judge behavior?), we realize that no given human agent is adequately described simply as "Greek"—much less, for example, as "Western," or "Islamic." That is *not* to say that umbrella descriptions of extensive culture-zones are analytically meaningless. But it *is* to say that coarse-grained description can offer only very limited purchase when we seek to define the origins or function of the value-identity complex embraced by any given human agent or group of agents. This limitation of analytic purchase demonstrates the patent absurdity of the robust cultural *absolutism* that has sometimes led academic intellectuals (among others) to make grandiose claims about the systematic superiority of Hellas (or the West, or Islam).

Of course the existence of genuinely diverse societal cultures within the wider Greek culture-zone is not particularly surprising as soon as we gain even a passing acquaintance with the diverse histories of different Greek regions: Syracuse is quite obviously not Olbia, but neither are Arcadians Achaeans. Sharper awareness of that multiplicity of Greek historical

---

[13] Sewell 1999, 56.

identities helps us to see that the boasts of self-proclaimed Panhellenists like Isocrates or Thucydides' Pericles, who claimed to speak for "all Hellas," typically masked much more particularistic and politically partisan definitions of Greek culture. Isocrates' apparently expansive Hellas is a zone available for habitation only by members of a well-to-do and highly educated cosmopolitan elite, an elite whose members possessed the material resources and well-educated discrimination that allowed them to appreciate a multiplicity of cultural delights. Moreover, Isocrates' Hellas easily slips discursively into an imagined ancestral Athens, now writ large. We can begin to see in Isocrates' Panhellenism something closely akin to Pericles' frankly imperialistic vision of "Athens as School of Hellas," only now reinscribed on an ostensibly postimperial, cosmopolitan map of the Greek world.[14]

The diverse reality of the Greek culture-zone certainly breaks the bounds of Pericles' and Isocrates' partial and ultimately Athenocentric visions. But does it also break the bounds of the mutual implication of culture and politics that is the assumed framework for their Panhellenic sentiments? Sewell implicitly raises this mutual implication of culture and politics as a normative problem by noting that the constraining quality of semiotic systems must be a product of the way semiotic structures are "interlocked in practice" with other structures—including politics.[15] Must culture, then, be implicated in politics? I think that the answer is yes, whether we define politics broadly as the organized play of power, or somewhat more narrowly, as the enterprise of seeking answers to questions like, How is justice administered, and within what borders? When writing about a particular "culture within Greek culture," the dissident intellectual culture that flourished within democratic Athens,[16] I advanced a strong view about the relationship between politics and culture—that politics is central to any proper understanding of Greek cultural history. While rejecting the extreme position that culture can be *collapsed into* politics (or vice versa—and thus accepting Sewell's claim for the conceptual autonomy of culture-as-theory), I continue to regard that strong view as correct.

Accepting the view that doing serious cultural history means thinking seriously about politics has obvious methodological implications. It means, for example, that if Thucydides' Pericles seeks (as some readers have supposed he does) in the Funeral Oration to create a sphere of "the political" that is fully disengaged from either "the private" or "the cultural," he is doomed to failure. This "separate spheres" conception proved

[14] Isocrates' Panhellenism: Ober 1998, esp. 254–55.
[15] Sewell 1999, 50–51.
[16] In Ober 1998.

unsustainable in the face of the messy and pragmatic conditions of lived experience—as Thucydides' own historical narrative makes eminently clear.[17] But by the same token, the strong view on politics and culture also means that, as they turn to the next phase of investigating the fascinating particularities of diverse microcommunities and their specific practices, practitioners of cultural studies should be paying attention to the question of how those microcommunities and specific practices are implicated in politics—in practical and normative concerns about institutions and ideology, values and interests, justice and legitimacy, which is to say, in the matters that have traditionally been addressed by political theorists.

My attachment to politics as such is not predicated upon some primordial conception of "the primacy of the political," or on a conception of Greeks as animals that are for some mysterious reason "even more political" than other humans. Nor is it entirely based on the traditional (and correct, as far as it goes) explanation for the prominence of politics in Greek culture—because of the relatively small scale of Greek states, and thus the great number of bounded cultural communities (*poleis* and *koina*) within the Greek culture-sphere, state autonomy was both highly cherished and very difficult to preserve.[18] Rather, I would tend to focus my explanation for the persistence of politics in Greek culture on the related issue that is explicitly addressed by the authors of the essays in *The Cultures within Greek Culture*—on the fact that there were many vibrant cultures (and thus a variety of competing and compelling cultural identities) within Greek culture.[19] Perhaps ironically, the more squarely we face up to that multicultural Greek reality, the more clearly we can see why "the political" could never be forgotten by the ancient Greeks. Politics was a vehicle by which the thin coherence of the polis was maintained, and by which the constraints associated with coherence were contested.

The issue of "the politics of cultures within culture" need not necessarily be posed with primary reference to the state. That is to say, we could today focus on the political consequences of the existence of diverse cultures within either Protestant or Sunni culture, or within France or Saudi Arabia. As early modern European and contemporary world history shows (clearly and often tragically), the question of politics and culture transcends the

---

[17] See, further, Ober 1996, 161–87 (chapter 11: "The Polis as a Society: Aristotle, John Rawls, and the Athenian Social Contract"); Ober 2001.

[18] The fourth-century B.C. Greek writer, Aeneas Tacticus, *On the Defense of Fortified Places*, gives a vivid sense of the interconnectedness between internal politics (the search for unity) and the inevitability of internal division and conflict (the persistent fear of treason), under conditions of systematic external threats.

[19] It is related because it is possible to speak of, for example, "Athenian culture." But it is nonidentical because cultural distinctions obviously do not map directly onto political distinctions between states.

physical bounds of the nation-state. That said, however, looking at the state as a site of strong cultural claims remains important because (inter alia) the mass of ordinary people cannot easily escape their physical situation within a state. In classical antiquity, as in modernity (outside highly mobile societies like that of the United States), many people have of necessity lived out their lives quite close to where they happened to be born. Some nonelite people do indeed move far from their original homeland, but too often it is under duress: compelled by the harsh exigencies of power (war, economic change) to go not where they choose, but where they may have a better hope of survival. Both the fact of staying at home, and the fact of mandatory migration have obvious bearing on the history of the perpetuation and diversification (as well as the evolution and hybridization) of cultures.

Of course it is not the case that everyone stays home by necessity or moves abroad only under duress. Modern cosmopolitans (market-capitalists, academics, members of international aid organizations), like some of their ancient Greek counterparts (traders, sophists, philosophers), move about the world quite freely. Some may even consider themselves to be "citizens" of a culture-sphere so expansive that it potentially encompasses the globe and all of its diverse cultures. Waldron, attacking communitarian versions of Aristotle's claim that membership in a territorially defined constitutive community is a fundamental human good, on the grounds that "thick" communitarian conceptions of politics and culture problematically compromise fundamental human freedoms, notes that a cosmopolitan need not necessarily be a world traveler; the key thing is that

> he refuses to think of himself as *defined* by his location or his ancestry or his citizenship or his language. Though he may live in San Francisco and be of Irish ancestry, he does not take his identity to be compromised when he learns Spanish, eats Chinese, wears clothes made in Korea, listens to arias by Verdi sung by a Maori princess on Japanese equipment, follows Ukrainian politics, and practices Buddhist meditation techniques. He is a creature of modernity, conscious of living in a mixed-up world and having a mixed-up self.[20]

Waldron's rejection of the thick cultural coherence associated with communitarianism (and by both communitarians and their critics with "the Greeks"), and his vivid description of the diverse pleasures associated with what we might call "cosmopolitanism as a cultural practice," allows

---

[20] Waldron 1992, 754. Waldron later (1992, 761) adds to this list the propensity of cosmopolitans to collect the artworks of indigenous peoples: "Their apartments are likely to be decorated with Inuit artifacts or Maori carvings." Needless to say, such things are not within the means of the poor.

us to return to the normative question raised above: Should we regard free access to an expansive and various global culture-sphere as an ideal? If so, does that cosmopolitan ideal direct us toward a normative preference for transcending the political—at least insofar as politics implies the existence of bounded political communities with constraining cultural tendencies? Should we regard state-based politics as the undesirable and dispensable remainder of a localist parochialism that has become outmoded by the diverse opportunities opened by modern cosmopolitan cultural practice? Is politics as it is practiced in bounded communities, with its constraint-producing tendency to interlock in practice with semiotic structures, a systematic threat to cultural diversity as a fundamental good?

Any answer to this normative concern is likely to depend on another question that recent work in classical cultural studies implicitly poses: Just who do we think "we" are? We (readers of this book) may decide that not only our enjoyment of cultural variety, but also the best protection of our autonomy as individuals, entails defining "ourselves" as those who take a cosmopolitan rather than a "bounded political" view of the world. But arguably this imaginative step requires that "we" also imagine ourselves as enjoying the level of wealth, leisure, and education necessary to place ourselves easily within Waldron's (or even, mutatis mutandis, Isocrates') cosmopolitan vision. If we hope to move from the realm of thought to that of practice (if this is the world as we know it, rather than an ideal world in which everyone is well off), we will be faced with the fact that we cannot actually become practicing cosmopolitans without detaching ourselves in various ways from the less-advantaged "rooted-identity masses"—that is, those lacking the necessary attributes and attitudes to live as cosmopolitans. In short, cosmopolitan practice, of the sort Waldron describes, remains (outside of the world of ideal theory) class-specific. Many, perhaps most, of the people of the world still lack the wealth necessary to acquire Japanese audio equipment, the leisure and education necessary to enjoy opera, understand the politics of distant places, or even to learn new languages. For them, Waldron's vision of the cosmopolitan present must remain either an aspiration or a threat to a valuable cultural identity. Or, perhaps, both at once.

To the extent to which "we" do define multicultural cosmopolitanism as our goal, and to the extent to which we succeed in achieving our desire to inhabit an open and free cosmopolitan sphere, incidentally filled with diverse multicultural pleasures, we may forget politics—at least for a while. But, in the absence of a comprehensive and reliable "apolitical world system" capable of conscientiously and consistently guaranteeing universal conditions of distributive justice, the freedom and pleasures that "we cosmopolitans" enjoy are not attained or sustained outside of the play of power. And the play of power currently leaves most people within their bounded communities or forces them into the wider world as refugees. And so, whoever we think we are, we will, sooner or later, more or less tragically, be brought back to politics.

If this is (for modern cosmopolitan intellectuals) an all-too-familiar and depressing modern story, so, a fortiori, was it familiar to Greeks. The interesting thing for students of Greek politics and cultures is that Greeks (I am thinking here especially, but not uniquely, of Athens) did not nec- essarily find politics depressing. Greek writers remained highly attuned to both politics and culture (as something akin to Sewell's definition of culture-as-theory), and to their mutual implication. It is certainly the case that specific writers in particular moods were quite capable of consigning "politics" to a grim realm of base necessity ("the cave" of Plato's *Repub- lic*), or to a glorious realm fit for the sort of heroic endeavors that only seem possible once cultural diversity and the private sphere have been transcended (Pericles' Funeral Oration, again). But Greek, and especially democratic, political practices (e.g., Cleisthenes' institutional reforms in postrevolutionary Athens; see chapter 2) embraced as exciting and mean- ingful the serious business of constantly building and deconstructing (through iterated public and private practices) political solidarity from within a variety of cultural communities. Far from the very thick sort of cultural coherence typically associated by political theorists with "the Greeks," Athens provides an example of a societal culture manifesting the sort of "thin coherence" advocated (as a analytic approach) by Sewell. Rather than explaining political excitement and meaning-creation entirely in the language of constraint and hegemony, I would point to the ways in which politics and the state may be instruments whereby non-elites (or at least some non-elites; see chapter 5) gain enhanced access to cultural re- sources that enable them to resist some forms of social power, as well as the opportunity for enhanced welfare.

While "umbrella" culture-zones cross state boundaries, diverse cultures persist within the bounds of a given state—inside of the political entity that lays claim to the authority to control passage across borders, to con- fer citizenship, to define the terms under which justice will be adminis- tered. Greek states (like modern nation-states) sought to monopolize the legitimate use of force, that is, to define the distinction between force and violence. But they also sought to establish standard rules governing the public (and some aspects of the private) behavior of all those who inhab- ited the state territory—especially in terms of their relations with other territorial residents. This sort of political work was not a simple matter in the face of persistent cultural diversity. As Kymlicka points out, the au- thority of "national" political-legal rules and the authority of the cultural rules binding members of societal cultures within the state territory can come into open conflict.[21] Mutatis mutandis, clashes between the state and substate communities are familiar enough to us from Greek literature, perhaps most famously in tragedy. Is the state necessarily acting wrongly when it seeks to constrain a particular form of cultural expression? It does not take a hypersophisticated reading of, for example, Sophocles' *Antigone* or Euripides' *Bacchae* to see why that simple formulation might be open to challenge.

The overarching authority-claims of states have traditionally been facilitated by the creation of a national identity based on (inter alia) standardized narratives (e.g., the racial myths celebrated by the Athenian institution of the Funeral Oration); a standardized civic education (e.g., the Spartan *agōgē*); and the promulgation of rules, rituals, privileges, and disabilities that differentiate citizens from noncitizens, insiders from outsiders—in brief, by the state's claim to be isomorphic with the societal culture. States are defined physically by their borders, which may be both politically and culturally demarcated; for example the "witnesses" to the sacred oath taken by young Athenian warriors-in-training (ephebes) included the "boundary-markers of the territory" (*horoi tēs chōras*; see chapter 9).[22] Differential rules applying to citizens and noncitizens, insiders and outsiders, may determine who can enter the state territory and for how long (cf. the Spartan practice of periodic expulsion of foreigners [*xenēlasia*]) and under what terms (cf. the Athenian head-tax on metics [resident foreigners]). Moreover, differential rules will typically determine who, having entered, can successfully claim access to what immunities and what privileges in respect to political participation (ordinarily limited to native males) and cultural participation (cf. the Eleusinian mysteries, in which any Greek-speaking individual, man or woman, free or slave, might be initiated).

The success of such access claims will typically rest on the petitioner's degree of cultural integration. Once again, the *opportunity* to integrate is seldom equally available to all and the *process* of integration (or assimilation) is never without costs for those seeking membership in the community. Modern national approaches to the integration of outsiders into the body of citizens (i.e., those with the highest level of immunity and participation rights) have ranged from denying citizenship to most immigrants, while freely offering citizenship to notional "cultural or racial insiders" who happen to live outside of the national territory by accidents of history (e.g., Israel, Germany); to frankly coercive assertions of cultural hegemony (e.g., in "English language only" laws in some U.S. states); to the now highly contested American ideology of the melting pot

---

[21] Kymlicka 1995.
[22] See below, chapters 6 and 9.

(the myth that we have all assimilated to a cultural mélange that changes over time as the mix evolves).[23]

Cosmopolitan political theorists, embracing a universalistic conception of human rights, have sought to challenge the legitimacy claims of nation-states by pointing out that differential treatment (including, in strong versions of cosmopolitanism, differential access of citizens and noncitizens to the state territory) is hard to justify on the basis of the arbitrary contingencies of birth or cultural affinity.[24] For those who reject the Aristotelian notion that the bounded political community represents an intrinsic human good (and thus that the political community is worthy of protection as such), moderate versions of this argument can gain considerable purchase within ideal theory.[25] But, as Yael Tamir has argued, in the real world non-elites have rational instrumental reasons for actively supporting the persistence of the nation-state. While fully acknowledging the historical complicity of the nation-state in the exploitation of lower classes, and the problematic pressure the state often brings to bear on minority cultures, Tamir suggests that non-elites have also substantially benefited from membership in a nation-state.[26]

Athenian history shows that citizenship can indeed serve to integrate the interests of elites and non-elites, by ensuring that some risks and some opportunities are shared across class lines.[27] A "shared risk pool" (expressed in welfare benefits) limits the potentially catastrophic costs of risk taking and thus allows the non-elite individual to take advantage of inherently risk-laden opportunities. So, for example, in Athens the relatively poor citizen could afford to participate in the high-risk, high-opportunity business of war because he knew that if he were killed, the state would guarantee his son's upbringing.[28] Among the benefits the state may offer is access to education (whether technical or civic; see chapter 6), which once again allows the individual to engage in a wider range of activities (including cultural choice and political participation) than would otherwise be available to him. And this in turn promotes social, cultural, and physical mobility for individuals and for disadvantaged groups. Paradoxically, it may only be via the maintenance of a certain degree of rooted national-cultural identity that the non-elite can

[23] Strauss 1994.

[24] I am indebted to Michael Blake, for his discussion, in an unpublished paper, of this issue. See now Blake 2003

[25] I am indebted here to Don Moon, for his discussion of "moderate cosmopolitanism."

[26] Yael Tamir, "Global War, Class Struggles," Moffett Lecture, Princeton University, December 13, 2001.

[27] Ober 1989.

[28] In the polis, war was an opportunity (as well as a risk), not only because of hope for plunder, but because it built networks of solidarity among citizens of different statuses.

actually hope to share in the benefits of openness, change, and cultural mobility.

Tamir's argument was developed as an answer to cosmopolitan political theorists like Waldron, who focus explicitly on the social constraints imposed by communities that base membership on cultural identity. But similar arguments can also serve as a challenge to the consistently proresistance and anticoherence normative stance taken by many cultural theorists.[29] Under certain conditions some people may reasonably *prefer* that the constraints of the bounded national culture *not* be contested, because successful contestation makes it that much easier for elites to exit the shared national risk-pool in favor of the pleasant world of diverse cosmopolitan pleasures. Waldron and modern cosmopolitan theorists are deeply concerned with social justice and far from advocating this sort of abandonment. But the justice concerns of political theorists do not represent the standard elite response to the successful contestation of interlocked political-cultural constraints. The highly cosmopolitan Isocrates was perhaps more typical—and notably parsimonious in his material contributions to the Athenian community.[30] The exit of each member of the elite in turn means a smaller pool of shared resources and thus reduced access to welfare benefits for those who remain behind. Of course, in ideal cosmopolitan theory there would be no nations from which to exit, and each individual would contribute fairly to a global pool which would in turn be fairly redistributed. But non-elite people make their choices in the world as they find it, not the world of ideal theory.

The interlocking of politics with national culture is a particularly fraught question today, in the context of an increasingly globalized economy and a broad acceptance of the legitimacy of fundamental human rights. If nation-states offer their relatively disadvantaged populations certain opportunities, the "nation-state-centered global regime" also limits the opportunities open to people desiring to move freely between nations. Those inconvenienced will include both well-off cosmopolitans and the desperate victims of mandatory migration. Can the nation-state justify closing its borders to some or all outsiders? Can it justify offering differential access to rights and

<hr/>

[29] Discussed by Sewell 1999, esp. 52–55.

[30] Isocrates' parsimony is obvious from the introduction to his *Antidosis*. Of course this is only anecdotal; other Athenians with cosmopolitan tendencies may have been generous liturgists. Waldron's (1992: 776) ideal cosmpolitans are "people whose primary allegiance is to some international agency—who are genuinely and effectively citizens of the world." Such people are surely admirable; but the non-elite individual may fear (and he may be right to) that for every such a one, there are a dozen "tough-minded" international bureaucrats and global capitalists whose decisions may have catastrophic consequences for him. He furthermore knows that he has absolutely no purchase on their decisions because they are in no sense politically accountable to him.

privileges to those who reside within its borders, based on the fortuitous fact of being born a citizen? There is no very tidy practical answer to these questions. But some attention to history, to the risks historically shared and cultural costs historically assumed by insiders, surely needs to be taken into account. If denying territorial access to some noncitizens is an affront to freedom of movement, it is also unfair suddenly to dilute the expected welfare benefits of those insiders who have already paid substantial costs (whether through taxes or having accepted cultural assimilation in exchange for participation rights) and have undertaken substantial risks (e.g., military service).[31]

When the differential-access issue is framed in these historical and quasi-contractarian terms, we may find that there are ways to justify admitting or not admitting a given stranger who requests permission to dwell within our national territory. We may concede that the claim of the indigent refugee to the basic means of subsistence trumps our own "contractual" expectations as paid-up insiders, because her basic human rights cannot be exercised in the absence of a subsistence minimum. But the claim of the well-to-do cosmopolitan (who has no intention of assuming risks or paying costs) may not trump our insiders' contractual expectation to a share of goods for which we have, in a meaningful sense, already paid. These issues are relevant when thinking about the ways in which culture-based communities—and especially state-communities—were created, maintained, challenged, and subverted within the Greek world. Again, we need not delve far into Greek literature to discover a profound concern with the problems of cultural assimilation and justice that are raised when suppliants request admission to a state's territory, whether they are exiles, wandering cosmopolitans, or entire displaced populations.[32]

If one accepts Tamir's contention that the nation-state does (at least under democratic conditions) bring substantial benefits to local nonelites, it becomes easier to see why official acknowledgement of deep and abiding intranational diversity (e.g., through the special legal protection of subnational societal cultures, as advocated by Kymlicka) may potentially impose its own substantial burdens. If the games of "preserving subnational societal cultures versus maximizing resources for welfare" and "cultural contestation versus maintaining thin cultural coherence"

---

[31] The war-orphan example (above) shows how assumptions based on risk-benefit calculus cross generational lines: the father assumed risks on the assumption that his son would gain benefits. The same sort of thinking might go into an Athenian slave's determination to do what is necessary (in terms of extra work, acceptance of cultural assimilation) to buy his freedom, and thus make it possible for his children to live as free persons. The point is that the implied "contract" between cost-paying—risk-taking persons and the benefit-and-opportunity-granting state must be understood as extending forwards in time, beyond the current generation.

[32] See, recently, Forsdyke 2000.

are based on a zero-sum calculus, then those "less-advantaged" persons within the nation, who depend upon national unity to preserve their access to desired goods and opportunities, may quite rationally and reasonably resist diversity claims—at least diversity claims of the sort that seem to pose threats to national unity. And this may in turn help us to understand why the play of power at a microcultural level includes the activity of willful human agents in the formation and maintenance (as well as resistance and contestation) of cultural constraints.

What, then, of the *least* advantaged? In Athens, this was the slave population, subject to systematic oppression, although also covered (at least in principle) by certain legal immunities (see chapter 5). Ian Morris has drawn attention to the inability of archaeologists to discover archaeological traces of a distinctive slave culture in the Athenian industrial village of Thorikos. As an explanation for the archaeological invisiblity of a distinctive slave culture, Morris suggests that "Athenian male citizen culture as a whole was unusually hegemonic, filling every corner of the conceptual landscape, allowing no space for alternatives."[33] If we assume for the moment that Morris is correct in this claim, it is worthwhile asking how Athenian cultural hegemony functioned in terms of human choice. Is it possible that benefits associated with membership in the cultural community of Athens (even the small benefits and marginal membership available to slaves) served as positive incentives to acquiesce in accepting and sustaining Athenian national culture?[34] Rather than regarding the slave residents of Thorikos only as passive victims of hegemony, perhaps we should imagine even these most harshly disadvantaged Athenian residents as willful agents, capable of making rational (if fundamentally unsatisfactory) choices about cultural assimilation, capable of appropriating and cross-appropriating symbols (in ways that would be archaeologically invisible), even in the face of the systematic and brutal exploitation of their labor.[35] As the least advantaged residents of Athenian territory became more culturally Athenian (and so less materially distinguishable from poorer Athenian citizens), they were (at least marginally) more likely to be beneficiaries of legal immunities as well as gaining greater access to the resources of Athens' diverse semiotic systems and the diverse contexts in which they were deployed.[36]

[33] Morris 1998, 196–97.

[34] See below, chapter 5; Edward Cohen (2000) makes the case rather more strongly than I believe is warranted by the evidence.

[35] Cf. Sewell 1999, 48–49, on the possible options for cultural resistance open to "an impoverished worker" who must accept work from the only manufacturer in her district—a condition not far removed from slave labor.

[36] Or at least so critics of Athenian democracy, like Pseudo-Xenophon (1.10–12), supposed. Cf. Ober 1998, 18–19; see also chapter 5.

Obviously none of this is meant to justify the morally indefensible Athenian institution of slavery, but rather to make it possible to think about how agency may be exercised by even the most oppressed of people, and in ways that may affirm as well as contest cultural coherence. If we think of ideology as enacted through interpellation, through the social process of being "hailed into being," under conditions in which authoritative speech is implicated in relationships of power, we might better understand why (in Althusser's famous example) someone responds to the policeman's "Hey you!" Her response may not be entirely involuntary. She may answer (in part) because she has the capacity to recognize her own social situation and opportunities: Even though she recognizes that it is not without a cost to her, she can see that overall it may be in her interest to sustain the cultural rules under which her opportunities (if never infinite) are enhanced and her future (if always circumscribed) may be relatively more open.[37]

Of course, the politics-culture game need not always be understood as zero-sum; and not all diversity claims need be regarded as threats. Although the polis-dweller's cultural choices may be limited relative to the choices open to a cosmopolitan elite, this certainly does not mean that he gained a unitary identity from just one societal culture. The contemporary "cosmopolitan versus communitarian" debate (in which Waldron's article intervenes) may obscure the fact, revealed in the essays in *The Cultures within Greek Culture*, that even the most "home-bound" polis-dweller (like his modern counterparts) participated in a spectrum of cultures.[38] Indeed, Athenian "national culture," with its frank discursive and institutional recognition that every Athenian (whether citizen male, woman, metic, or slave) belonged to a wide variety of cultural groups (cultic, regional, kinship-fictive kinship, occupational), can be read as an acknowledgment that relatively unmanaged diversity (and its associated freedoms, of association and expression) was vital to the flourishing of the democratic state. Internal cultural variety, and the capacity of individuals to construct complex selves out of those diverse cultural resources, could and did bring substantial benefits to the political community (see chapter 2).[39] But those benefits were only reaped once some assimilation-costs had been paid, which meant that some level of national unity (in Athens, expressed inter alia in the political language of *homonoia* ["like-mindedness"]) had been accepted. Athenian cultural hegemony may sometimes *seem* to be

[37] On Althusser and agency, see further, Butler 1997.

[38] Waldron 1992, 777, associates communitarians' depictions of Athens qua "small-scale community" with "the aboriginal hunting band . . . or the misty dawn in a Germanic village." As noted above, this misconception of Athens as a thick, intimate and face-to-face society is a persistent error in contemporary political theory.

[39] This is a central argument of my book in progress on the organization of knowledge in democratic Athens; see also chapter 2.

all-embracing precisely because (as K. H. Allen 2003a demonstrates) Athens was *actually* so culturally diverse.

The balance between cultural diversity and national unity within a political community is invariably a delicate one, and the balance can easily be lost. Under the pressure of real or perceived threats (e.g., enemy attack, economic change) the dangers associated with intrastate diversity may come to be perceived as too high. And this can, in the wrong circumstances, lead to reactionary attacks on the very idea of cultural diversity (e.g., ultranationalist movements in the United States and Europe), or to violent devolution of a nation into cultural-ethnic fragments (e.g., the former Yugoslavia). In Greek terms, as Arlene Saxonhouse and Peter Euben have argued, an abiding "fear of diversity" was driven by a sense that an intolerably high level of diversity will inevitably lead to open civil conflict, to *stasis*.[40] But (as Saxonhouse and Euben also point out) this conviction is not the *inevitable* default position of all Greek political thought. Moreover, the sense that it is indeed possible for the diversity-unity equation to fall out of balance may at times have been driven by rational welfare concerns and attention to real social costs. The fear of excessive diversity is not invariably driven by an atavistic horror of "otherness." As soon as we recognize that capacity to contest coherence and gain access to diversity are not the *only* good things that people might reasonably seek, that thin (yet resilient) cultural coherence may be valued because it allows people to go on together (whether or not that is regarded as a good in itself), we also recognize why politics must remain central to thinking about culture.[41]

Stasis was a terror that perpetually stalked the Greek political landscape (see chapter 8). Nicole Loraux has argued, with special reference to Athens, that *stasis* was an ontological condition of the ancient Greek state. She points out that some of Athens' multiple microcultures—defined especially along the lines of class and gender—existed in a steady condition of conflict.[42] Loraux's point is undeniable in one sense, but it is essential to keep in mind the distinction between endemic low-level conflict, and the hot conflict that was ordinarily called *stasis* by the Greeks. Aristotle (like other Greek writers) argued that *stasis* was most readily provoked by the perception of injustice—the conviction that the benefits of communal life were not being distributed on an equitable basis.[43] Given the diverse range of cultural communities within any given political community, and

---

[40] Saxonhouse 1992; Euben 1990.

[41] The question of whether cultural-community rootedness is a good in itself is the point at issue in the debate between liberal and communitarian theorists. My point here is that we need not take a position on the matter of community as a final good in order to see why it might be a cherished possession.

[42] Terror of *stasis*: Ober 2000; Loraux 1997 (trans. 2002).

[43] See, on this general point, Balot 2001.

the multiplicity of possible ways a community might define the conditions of equity (if justice is "to each according to his x," then what is x?), the potential for *stasis* within the state remained high.

Politics, seen from this perspective, is the attempt to manage, through imposing a standard system for the administration of justice, the dangers associated with diversity. Politics sought to keep disputes, which invariably arose in the culturally diverse state, from escalating into full blown *stasis*. That, I think, is the central point of much ancient Greek political theory and practice. But to use an umbrella term like "Greek theory and practice" is akin to speaking of "Greek culture"; a more fine-grained analysis reveals that Greek political theories and practices were (like the cultures within Greek culture) very diverse. Quasi-aristocratic regimes (real: Sparta; and imagined: Aristotle's "polis of our prayers" of *Politics*, book 7) found it necessary to deny the presence of meaningful diversity within the ruling body and sought to control the effects of persistent diversity within the state territory by the distribution of people with different social attributes into naturalized status and function groups (Aristotle's "natural slaves") or rigid castes (Spartan helots).

A democratic regime (such as Athens) was quite different. Even while emphasing the value of *homonoia*, it allowed for the existence of considerable diversity within the citizen body, based on individual choice and microcultural identity. And it left the boundary between citizens and noncitizens much hazier (at least in certain respects) than aristocratic regimes could tolerate.[44] In lieu of fixed castes, democracies developed standard (even hegemonic) institutional and ideological means whereby diverse persons and groups found common ground for resolving disputes, and whereby an internally diverse body of citizens could make binding decisions about state policy. This is a practical example of Sewell's "interlocking" of semiotic and political structures. What was produced was no doubt constraint. But this constraint was not based on thick coherence; it preserved the possibility of contestation, while offering at least some benefit for most (if not all) residents. The borders were clearly defined, but remained relatively open to immigrants. Democratic Athens continued to distinguish citizens from noncitizens, men from women, free from slave— but certain immunities were extended to all residents of the national territory, and there was at least some possibility for assimilated outsiders to join the body of the citizens (see chapter 5). The cultural resources for public contestation (e.g., theater and dissident political theory) were quite rich.

Sometimes "politics as diversity-management" failed, and in the wake of failure *stasis* erupted. Is it possible to make a normative judgment about

---

[44] See chapter 5; the lack of boundary distinctions is especially clear in terms of work, since citizens and noncitizens engaged in many identical forms of labor.

when the resort to *stasis* should be regarded as a reasonable response to the injustices that inevitably arose within multicultural communities? We cannot ignore the day-to-day suffering that injustice in respect to distribution inflicted upon the disadvantaged of even the most democratic of Greek states. Yet the damage caused by *stasis* might well be worse. Overt *stasis* resulted in conditions of extreme material deprivation: widespread death, exile, destruction of property, and theft. *Stasis* meant hunger, loss of shelter, and constant fear of arbitrary physical violence. Violent civil conflict (an extreme form of contestation) is surely justifiable when an existing regime institutionalizes conditions of extreme deprivation and reasonable when there is a possibility that engaging in *stasis* will replace a systematically violent regime with a regime that allows the disadvantaged enhanced opportunity to ameliorate their condition.[45] This calculus explains the periodic helot uprisings against the Spartan regime.[46] And it explains the well-documented democratic Athenian resistance to the "Thirty Tyrants" in the *stasis* of 404–403 B.C.

The Athenian *stasis* and its aftermath revealed very clearly the different conceptions that certain Athenian microcommunities held regarding justice. A generous reading of the intentions of the temporarily dominant oligarchs ("the Thirty") suggests that they attempted to create a unified political community by ridding Athens of various categories of persons they regarded as undesirable (sycophants, demagogues, wealthy metics), and by establishing a caste system that would exclude all but the well-to-do and properly educated from exercising participation rights.[47] The resistance to the Thirty was led by those who had been Athenian citizens under the former, democratic regime. But the resistance movement was joined by a large number of Athenian metics and slaves.

The metics and slaves who fought the Thirty had been systematically disadvantaged under the old democratic regime. Yet they chose to undertake very substantial risks, fighting alongside the citizens, in order to help restore democracy. In the aftermath of the successful prodemocracy *stasis*, full citizenship was proposed for noncitizens who had fought for the democracy. But in the end, most of them were apparently granted a more limited set of new privileges and special immunities. Those privileges and immunities were guaranteed by a public decree. The stele on which the decree was inscribed lists the name and *occupation* of each recipient. Whereas a citizen would be officially identified by his deme membership—that is, by

---

[45] I do not claim that these are the *only* conditions in which civil conflict is justified.

[46] Cartledge 2001, 127–52 (chapter 10: "Rebels and *Sambos* in Classical Greece: A Comparative View").

[47] Generous reading of intentions of the Thirty (i.e., that they actually had a plan beyond plunder): Osborne 2003; Krentz 1982. My own reading of the motivations of the Thirty is rather less generous: see chapter 8.

his membership in a particular local microcommunity defined by geography and kinship—the noncitizen was identified by his membership in a microcommunity defined by his work.[48] There is no way to tell whether or not the metics and slaves who fought for Athens' democracy during the stasis of 404–403 believed that they had been fairly compensated for the risks they assumed. But they did in fact take those risks. And presumably they chose to do so because they believed (perhaps rightly) that the restoration of the democratic state offered them (and their descendents) opportunities and benefits that they would not have enjoyed otherwise.

After the democracy had been restored, the Athenians performed various community-wide rituals and developed new legal and ideological means to encourage official forgetfulness about the stark divisions that had been revealed in the course of the civil conflict.[49] The hegemonic cultural instruments of the state once again sought, with considerable success, to reassert a level of political unity adequate simultaneously to disguise cultural variety and to allow for its perpetuation, to preserve cultural coherence and provide space for cultural resistance.[50] This is exemplary not only of the cultural work that democratic politics can do, but of the work it *should* do—because it pushes, if only in fits and starts, towards a better and more just social order.

[48] *IG* II² 10 = RO 4, with helpful commentary and bibliography.

[49] Wolpert 2002.

[50] Cf. Sewell 1999, 54, on cultural consensus as a difficult achievement, necessarily hiding conflicts; 57, on the task of cultural analysts as explaining coherence as well as resistance.

CHAPTER FIVE

Quasi Rights: Participatory Citizenship and Negative Liberties

This essay had its origins in 1997, when Phillip Mitsis invited me to participate in a New York University workshop on political rights and duties.* In preparation for the workshop, he suggested I read an essay by Fareed Zakaria (Zakaria 1997: see now Zakaria 2003), arguing that the goal of promoting liberal constitutionalism in American foreign policy could (and indeed should) be uncoupled from the goal of promoting democracy. Zakaria's policy recommendation was based on the claim that democracy may emerge from the values and institutions associated with liberal constitutionalism, but that the reverse is historically unknown. Citing cases from the nineteenth and twentieth centuries, Zakaria argued that democracy as such does not promote individual liberty; it does not lead to legal arrangements concerned with guarding the rights of the individual. Zakaria's position on "illiberal democracy" has deep roots in nineteenth- and twentieth-century liberal thought—it owes debts to Benjamin Constant's celebrated distinction between the individual-centered rights of the moderns versus the political rights of the ancients, and to Isaiah Berlin's elaboration of Constant's position. It also has profound implications for how great powers interested in furthering the spread of human rights should go about doing so. It suggests that such powers might do well to support the establishment and maintenance of dictatorships and oligarchies, so long as they appeared likely to become appropriately benevolent in respect to their support of liberal values and the rule of law. On the other hand, if Zakaria is right, there is no reason for great powers to waste national energy and treasure seeking to promote democracies abroad.

The history of classical Athens offers a challenge to Zakaria's empirical claim that democracy does not promote rights (or at least "quasi rights"). Boundaries and boundary crossing are key elements of the "democracy-ergo-rights" story offered here. It might appear that democracy, as a citizenship-centered regime, would be prone to limit rights to citizens. But the history of Athens suggests that, in practice, immunities transgress the border between citizens and local noncitizens. Moreover,

* This essay was first published in *Social Philosophy and Policy* 17 (2000): 27–61. Reprinted with permission of Cambridge University Press.

the transgression is in some cases enshrined in Athenian law. Analyzing the emergence of quasi rights in Athens therefore offers a way to explore how and why a citizen body might choose to extend important legal protections beyond the ranks of the citizenship—and thus potentially open the way for a universalization of privileges once reserved for members of a closed community. A conference on democracy organized by the Social Philosophy and Policy Center of Bowling Green University in 1998 provided the ideal forum in which to develop and test my ideas on this topic.

• • •

THE RELATIONSHIP BETWEEN PARTICIPATORY democracy (the rule of and by a socially diverse citizenry) and liberal consitutionalism (a regime predicated on the protection of individual liberties and the rule of law) is a famously troubled one. The purpose of this essay is to suggest that, at least under certain historical conditions, participatory democracy will indeed support the establishment of liberal constitutionalism. That is to say, the development of institutions, behavioral habits, and social values centered on the active participation of free and equal citizens in democratic politics can lead to the extension of legally enforced immunities from coercion to citizens and noncitizens alike. Such immunities, here called "quasi rights," are at least preconditions for the personal autonomy and liberty in respect to choice making that are enshrined as the "rights of the moderns." This essay, which centers on one ancient society, does not seek to develop a formal model proving that democracy will necessarily promote liberal constitutionalism.[1] By explaining, however, why a premodern democractic citizenry of free, adult, native males—who sought to defend their own interests and who were unaffected by Enlightenment or post-Enlightenment ideals of inherent human worth—chose to extend certain formal protections to slaves, women, and children, it may point towards the development of a model for deriving liberalism from democratic participation. Development of such a model could have considerable bearing on current policy debates.

---

[1] Weingast 1997 develops the game-theoretic basis for a rational-choice model along these lines. Although my argument here focuses on social practices and values rather than on rational choice, it is compatible with Weingast's model (see chapter 8). I received very helpful comments on earlier versions of this paper delivered at New York University, the University of California at Santa Cruz, Stanford University, and Princeton's University's Center for Human Values. Special thanks to Barry Strauss and Phillip Mitsis, for discussions that led to the writing of this paper, and to Emily Mackil for editiorial assistance and substantive comments.

DEMOCRACY VERSUS LIBERALISM?

The notion that democracy has any meaningful relationship to liberalism is often denied. Fareed Zakaria, for example, argues for a sharp distinction between democracy and constitutional liberalism. For Zakaria, democratic citizenship has no intrinsic value and democracy should be valued only if it were shown to be an efficient instrument for obtaining the desirable end of constitutional liberalism—for protecting what are sometimes known as the "rights of the moderns." Other political means for obtaining this same desired end would, for Zakaria, be equally acceptable and, indeed, preferable if those means proved more efficient. Although he is unable to point to a contemporary example of liberal constitutional autocracy, Zakaria sees no principled reason to prefer democracy to a hypothetical autocratic alternative. Zakaria therefore suggests that American foreign policymakers should reorient their priorities—away from encouraging the growth of democracy abroad in favor of fostering the growth of liberal constitutionalism—even if that means supporting autocracy.[2]

If we suppose, with Zakaria, that democracy is nothing more than an instrument for gaining the higher end of protecting the rights of individuals and minority groups, there seems no innate reason to prefer being a "democratic citizen" to being a "rights-holding subject" of a benevolent nondemocratic sovereign. And so the only reason to prefer democracy to autocracy is the presumption that democracy is more likely than autocracy to foster the growth of liberal ideals and constitutional governmental structures. But Zakaria claims that this is not the case. His quick survey of modern European history and contemporary developments in the third world leads to a simple conclusion: "Constitutional liberalism has led to democracy but democracy does not seem to bring constitutional liberalism."[3] Leaving aside various other problems with Zakaria's argument (e.g., his tendency to conflate "constitutionalism" *simpliciter* with the special form of "*liberal* constitutionalism"), this essay attempts to use the example of classical Athens to rethink the relationship between (first) the core

---

[2] Zakaria 1997. For a good discussion of the traditional conflict between the liberal "rights of the moderns" (religious liberty, liberty of conscience, thought and expression, rights of person and property) and the democratic "rights of the ancients" (freedom of political speech and participation-rights), and an argument that these can be conjoined within a conception of deliberative democracy based on reasonable plurality, see Cohen 1996.

[3] Zakaria 1997, 28. Zakaria's examples of constitutional liberalism leading to democracy include nineteenth-century Britain, Hong Kong, and contemporary "semidemocratic" East Asian regimes. His examples of democracy failing to bring about constitutional liberalism include sub-Saharan Africa, Haiti, Central Asia, and "the Islamic world": ibid., 26–29.

values that constitute the primary commitments of contemporary liberalism, (next) the constitutional "rule of law," and (finally) participatory democracy—with its focus on the duties and privileges of the citizen.

Zakaria's primary focus is foreign policy, but the claim that democracy has nothing to do with the desired end of achieving constitutional liberalism has much wider policy implications. If this is correct, then there is (for example) no reason for liberals to worry about "democratic citizenship" per se or "the education of citizens." Rather the proper concern would seem to be with the liberal education of a few elite leaders capable of guaranteeing that a constitutional apparatus is properly established and maintained. Assuming that constitutional liberalism is the only desired end and that democracy is a dispensable instrument will therefore lead to a preference for an educational system with some of the same general goals (if not any of the specific features) of the educational system designed to produce Guardians in Plato's *Republic*. But if democracy does foster liberal values and the rule of law, then a very different sort of civic education would seem to be in order (see chapter 6).

Dragging ancient Greece into the debate over democracy and constitutional liberalism is not idiosyncratic. Zakaria acknowledges that the modern emphasis on individual liberty "draws on a philosophical strain, beginning with the Greeks."[4] But his position on the relative importance, and ultimate separability, of democracy and liberalism builds on Isaiah Berlin's celebrated elaboration of Benjamin Constant's distinction between "positive liberty" (i.e., participatory political community building, or political share holding, which Constant specifically identified with Greco-Roman antiquity) and "negative liberty" (i.e., the distinctively modern individual freedom from interference by others in the processes of personal choice making). For Berlin, the core "classical republican" idea—that participatory politics undertaken by "citizens" was a precondition to the secure maintenance of individual rights—was incoherent since he supposed that negative liberties could just as well be ensured by a sovereign for his subjects. Zakaria's argument builds on Berlin's claims that negative liberty "is not incompatible with some kinds of autocracy, or at any rate with the absence of self-government" and that it is a mistake to suppose that there is any "necessary connexion between individual liberty and democratic rule."[5]

While it is obviously impossible to prove the existence of a *"necessary connexion"* between democracy and liberal values by reference to a single historical case study (or indeed by multiple historical cases), I will argue

---

[4] Ibid., 26.

[5] Constant 1988, 307–28; Berlin 1969. On Berlin's conception of negative liberty and his debt to Constant, see Gray 1996, 5–37, esp. 20. Berlin quotes: Berlin 1969, 14, 56, cited by Skinner 1998, 115.

that in ancient Athens something resembling modern liberal values did in fact emerge, for the first time in recorded human history, quite directly from the development and experience of the first recorded large-scale experiment with democratic political processes. And thus, whether or not one supposes that participatory democracy is a good in itself (for the record, I do), there is some reason to suppose that a democracy may indeed foster the values, institutions, and behavioral practices conducive to the development and maintenance of constitutional liberalism. This is still a long way from a straightforward causal argument: I am not claiming that democracy is a necessary and sufficient condition for either constitutionalism or liberalism. But I do think that a case can be made that the habits associated with the practice of democracy have a lot better chance of leading in those desirable directions than do the habits associated with autocracy.

I will argue, then, that the answer to the question, Is the practice of democracy conducive to the development of negative liberties? is at least a qualified yes. The answer is qualified first because classical Athenian democracy never evolved into a fully liberal regime—never extended participation rights to all those residents who would be regarded as appropriate rights-holders under any modern regime claiming the title "liberal" or "democratic." And it is further qualified because the rights which were guaranteed by the Athenian regime never had the ontological status of "inherent or universal human rights." In Athens individual rights were acknowledged as performative and contingent rather than being regarded as natural or innate. I have dubbed them "quasi rights" because the Athenians never supposed—as modern rights theorists sometimes do—that rights had a universal or metaphysical existence, that they were either God-given or naturally occurring. Rather, for the Athenians, rights were to be enjoyed by those who demonstrably deserved them, and—this is the key point—only for so long as other rights-holders were willing to acknowledge them and willing voluntarily to act consistently and collectively in their defense. The Athenians, were in this sense, "rights pragmatists."

The Athenians developed a detailed, and emphatically procedural, code of law. But they recognized that, absent appropriate political behavior, the law code was meaningless—mere written words without substance or authority. In this they were highly realistic. Laws, even in the most mature of liberal and constitutional regimes, remain in force only for as long as the behavior of the powerful generally conforms to them. Law codes will survive the challenge of serious misbehavior by the strong only when society is willing to respond with superior strength in defense of the law. Modern constitutional regimes depend, of course, on government agents to enforce the law. And so, when these agents misbehave, the only viable response is a multiplication of government agencies charged with investigating and prosecuting other agents of the government. That process can continue, as recent U.S. history suggests, ad nauseam, if not ad infinitum. The result is a growth of political cynicism on the part of the populus. Government, politics, and the rule of law itself come to be seen as a sideshow—occasionally entertaining but generally annoying and largely irrelevant. By contrast, the Athenian citizens depended directly and immediately upon one another to enforce laws and to reify, in action, the values on which laws were predicated. For the Athenians, democracy meant that the collective strength of the individually weak "many" was available for deployment against the capacity for coercion possessed by powerful individuals and syndicates. Although they were indeed concerned to prevent the misuse of governmental authority Athenians never forgot that threats to human dignity are just as likely to emanate from private individuals capable of monopolizing social power.

My second main argument concerns democratic ideology and the legal consequences of political sociology: The democratic Athenians included within the privileged category of "free and equal citizens" many persons normatively regarded by traditional Greek "social mentality" as incapable of being citizens on the grounds of their putative dependence and moral inferiority (i.e., day-laborers, small-scale traders, and craftsmen possessing little or no real property). I will suggest that this inclusiveness led to the development of what I am calling "quasi rights." Moreover, it soon opened the way (in legal practice as well as in political theory) for the extension of legal immunities in the form of negative liberties to other Athenians regarded as dependent and inferior: children, women, slaves, and resident foreigners. I will *not* argue that this "liberalizing" tendency to extend immunities beyond the boundary of the citizen body was the conscious or stated intention of the Athenian democratic regime or anyone associated with it. Rather it was an unintended effect of ideological complexity. But the fact that the Athenian citizenry did not *intend* to foster extracitizen liberalism only strengthens the argument that (at least under the conditions pertaining in classical Athens) the practice of participatory democracy itself can foster liberal practices and values and can, moreover, extend those practices and values into new and unexpected social contexts.

DEMOCRACY IN THE ATHENIAN STYLE

The primary body of Athenian rights-holders and rights defenders was the citizen body: the demos. This large (ca. 30,000 persons) and socioeconomically diverse group was defined by age, gender, and (ordinarily) by birth: typically the Athenian citizen (*politēs*) was a male over eighteen years of age, legitimately born of an Athenian father and Athenian mother, whose neighbors had formally (by voting in local assembly) accepted him as such, and whose name had been inscribed in his ancestral township or neighborhood (deme) citizen-list.[6] The citizen body was thus homogeneous in terms of gender and ethnicity (or imaginary ethnicity: some citizens were naturalized foreigners). But it remained highly stratified in terms of wealth and income. Economic distinctions had been specifically linked to constitutional participation-rights in the early sixth-century B.C. (predemocratic) governmental system established by the reformer-lawgiver, Solon. Each of the four Solonian census classes enjoyed specific participation-rights, based on a sliding scale of annual income measured in terms of agricultural produce. These census classes were never abolished, but by the fourth century B.C., if not before, they were ignored in political practice ([Aristotle] *Athēnaiōn Politeia* 7.4). Rich and poor Athenian citizens were political and legal equals: each citizen was an equal voter (*isopsēphos*), enjoyed an equal right to public speech (*isēgoria*), and an equal standing before the law (*isonomia*).[7]

By classical Greek (and pre-twentieth-century Western) standards, the most remarkable feature of Athenian citizenship is an absence: despite the range of wealth classes within the citizen body, there was no property qualification for the active exercise of citizenship; the landless Athenian day-laborer was in meaningful institutional terms the political and legal equal of the largest landowner. For Aristotle (and other ancient theorists) it was precisely the absence of property qualifications for citizenship that distinguished democracy from oligarchy.[8] By instituting democracy, the Athenians had agreed, in effect, to extend the frontier of citizenship (and its associated protections) wide enough to enclose the entire native adult male (hereafter NAM) population—to extend the border of political belonging remarkably far (by contemporary Greek standards), but (in principle) no further.

Despite having defined the citizenship as a body of politically equal share-holders, Athenian citizens remained intensely aware that wealth-inequality translated inevitably into inequalities in social power. And they were well aware of the manifold humiliating and painful ways in which the misuse of the superior power of those who were rich, well connected, well educated, and consequently strong could play out in the lives and on the bodies of the poor, isolated, relatively ill-educated, and

[6] See Whitehead 1986, 67.
[7] For a general discussion of Athenian democratic equality, see Raaflaub 1996, 139–74.
[8] Aristotle, *Politics* 1291b3–34.

weak. Among the primary ethical goals of the Athenian demos was to limit the practical effects of social-power inequality by political and legal means. The story of the development and manifestation of quasi rights in democratic Athens can be told in terms of the concurrent development of a strong civic identity among the members of the demos, the elaboration of a popular and political ideology to explain that identity, the creation of governmental and legal institutions to defend that ideology, and the evolution of self-conscious habits of employing democratic ideological and institutional powers (including judicial authority). In Athenian popular ideology and elite political theory alike, these concurrent developments were achieved and maintained by the day-to-day actions of numerous "poor" Athenian citizens (*penētes*: i.e., those who had to work for a living—in actuality an economically diverse group that included middling landowners and day-laborers). The "poor" employed their collective political and legal power to counter the social power of a much smaller body of leisure-class (*plousioi*) elite citizens (again, an internally diverse group, ranging from the marginally leisured to the extremely wealthy).[9]

It was by institutionalizing what Robert Dahl has called "the Strong Principle of Equality" (the assumption that all persons within the relevant group are competent to participate in decision making and that no one individual or junta can or should be counted upon to make better decisions about the best interests of the group or its individual members than they could make for themselves) that the Athenians instantiated and maintained a direct and participatory form of democratic self-governance. Democracy worked in practice because the Athenians assured, through public speech, daily behavior, and legal procedure, that structures of patronage (and other forms of socioeconomic domination with overtly political effects) were strictly limited in practice. The quasi rights enjoyed by Athenian citizens were predicated upon the conviction that each citizen and the citizen body as a whole would and should be committed to the defense—notably, although not exclusively, through the enactment and vigorous implementation of a code of laws and legal procedures—of each citizen's freedom of speech, association, and action (*eleutheria*), political and legal equality (*isotēs*), and personal security from degradation or assault (*sotēria*). Within the boundaries of the citizenship, the citizens themselves would police one another's behavior on a day-to-day basis. When necessary they would employ social and legal sanctions to ensure

[9] The story of how the demos came to be defined in terms of "nonleisured" Athenians (or, conversely, all NAMs) rather than of the elite is important and interesting, but not my main focus here: cf. Ober 1996, esp. chapter 6; Hanson 1996; Strauss 1996; exchange between Raaflaub and Ober in Morris and Raaflaub 1998, 67–85.

conformity to a standard of behavior that limited the material and psychic effects of socioeconomic inequality.[10]

This sort of policing may seem to be exactly the sort of social control opposed by the sort of liberalism advocated by J. S. Mill in *On Liberty*. But Mill, and his fellow British liberals, were (I think rightly) impressed with the defense of the relative openness of Athenian society praised by Thucydides' Pericles in the Funeral Oration (2.37.2): "Our public life is conducted in a free way, and in our private intercourse we are not suspicious of one another, nor angry with our neighbor if he does what he likes; we do not put on sour looks at him which, though harmless, are not pleasant."[11] Pericles' point is that in comparison to the obsessive concern with all aspects of public and private behavior manifested by aristocratic-oligarchic Sparta, the Athenians took little notice of one another's private lives and affairs. Pericles' comments point to a distinction that will be important to my argument: the contrast between the concerns of the democratic polis and those manifested by the normative (idealized standard) aristocratic polis. One serious problem with some recent political theoretical discussions of ancient Greece is a tendency to reify "the polis" as a single analytic category by conflating Athens, Sparta, Plato's Kallipolis, and the "polis of our prayers" of Aristotle's *Politics*.

If it was remarkably extensive by contemporary Greek standards, the Athenian definition of the citizen as a NAM is, of course, highly exclusivist by twenty-first-century standards: children, and, much more problematically, women and non-native residents (including numerous slaves) were excluded from the ranks of the demos.[12] The Athenian political-legal order has, therefore, been regarded by some scholars as predicated on an ideology grounded in a stark distinction between "citizens" and "others." Moreover, it has been argued that the exclusion of "others" from the participation-rights associated with political standing was not an unfortunate blindspot of an otherwise admirable system, but a foundational premise of the system itself. On this reasoning, the Athenians were only able to maintain the standards of non-exploitative behavior within the "citizenship boundary" by emphasizing the distinction between the microcosmic, internal civic realm of "polis as state (or citizen-estate)" and the macrocosmic, external realm of "polis as whole society."[13] Because, it

[10] Strong principle of equality: Dahl 1989. Policing: Hunter 1994; D. Cohen 1991.

[11] Trans. B. Jowett, with revisions of Hornblower 1991, loc. cit. On Mill and Athens, see chapter 2.

[12] Athenian demographics regarding citizens and their families: Hansen 1986. The number of foreign residents and slaves was large, but cannot be accurately estimated. In any event, citizens cannot have been more than about one-fifth of the total population at any time during the democracy.

[13] On the distinction: Ober 1996, chap. 11, with literature cited.

is argued, the Athenian citizen body was officially defined in the naturalizing terms of gender and ethnicity, its ideological underpinnings were not only exclusivist but essentialist, and Athenian political essentialism is best understood as forthright misogyny and racism.[14] Viewed in this harsh light, Athenian democracy would seem to be not only contingently, but irremediably illiberal, a graphic illustration of Zakaria's argument that democracy in and of itself has nothing to do with the values espoused by liberal constitutionalism.

IDEOLOGY AND SUBVERSION

Although I am very aware of the illiberality of Athenian democracy—when it is viewed at any particular moment in its history, and when it is contrasted to contemporary liberal ideals—I suggest that focusing exclusively on the binary opposition between "citizen" and "other" elides too much of the ideological complexity central to Athenian politics and society.[15] "Ideology" is defined here not as "false consciousness" but as including the logic of common practices as well as commonly held ideas and normative values.[16] Ideology has no metaphysical existence outside of ongoing lived experience. Like a river, ideologies must be continuously replenished from multiple sources; while rivers and ideologies may appear to exist in a steady state, no river and no ideology can stand still. And yet very unlike the waters of a natural river, the raw material of ideology is willful human activity: thought, speech, and action. Ideology is necessarily pragmatic and performative, in the sense of being a living set of beliefs, norms, protocols, and responses. Ideology is not, therefore, just a fixed and given part of people's mental furniture, but it is publicly performed through thinking, saying, doing, and writing by self-conscious, choice-making human agents. Although a dominant ideology may close off some avenues of choice (and seek to close off others), no ideology (and a fortiori no democratic ideology) has the totalizing capacity to reduce human interactions to a predetermined set of rote behaviors.[17]

Moreover, although every ideology, by definition, is held by more than one person, not even the most dominant ideology will be perfectly standardized or can function as a seamless whole within a group of persons manifesting any meaningful degree of social diversity. A highly robust

[14] Bipolarity of Athenians and others: Cartledge 1993. Link to democracy: Roberts 1996. Racism and misogyny: Morris 2000.

[15] See Ober 1996, chapter 11.

[16] The distinctions between what people say and what they do, and what people say in official circumstances and what they say among intimates, is relevant here, but hard to specify.

[17] See, for example, Ober 1996, chapter 5, on the inevitability of criticism.

ideology will be eagerly embraced and more or less accurately performed by a lot of people, frequently, and in many and various contexts, but never by all of the people, all of the time, and everywhere: the performance of culture is not limited to "authorized personnel." Performances by different-minded or inappropriate persons, or under peculiar circumstances, may result in challenges to the dominant ideology, and as a consequence culture changes. The dissonance between official performances and "alternative" performances will necessarily affect attitudes and force questioning of established norms, and so may lead (sooner or later) to substantive revisions of the ideological context itself and of those social identities that depend upon it.[18]

Furthermore, ideology not only informs history, it exists within history. Political ideology, as one part of social context, is responsive to other contextual shifts (e.g., demographic change); the social and political order inevitably changes over time in reaction to events (broadly construed).[19] In response to internal (alternative performance) and external (eventual) factors, every given ideology will evolve and may occasionally be rapidly and radically transformed through the diachronic processes affecting social and cultural reproduction: Even with the best (or worst) will in the world, no human group (or dominant subgroup) can maintain a genuinely stable ideology or political culture indefinitely. Yet it is not necessary to suppose that all aspects of an ideology will change at the same rate: some elements may prove to be much more durable than others.

In some recent discussions of ancient Greek social attitudes a useful contrast is drawn between long-term and relatively stable "mentality" and the shorter-term, more variable and responsive "ideology."[20] Following recent work by Ian Morris and Leslie Kurke, I would suggest that by the sixth century B.C., a fairly cohesive and deeply engrained "mentality" had developed among an important subset of the NAM population of the Greek city-states. This mentality emphasized values characteristic of what is sometimes called the hoplite or "middling" class—that is, those NAMs who owned enough land (or equivalent wealth) to feed their families, may have owned one or more slaves, and fought in the ranks of the heavy infantry. The middling sensibility privileged a common, public,

[18] Butler 1997 offers one account of the relationship between performance and culture; my thanks to Susan Lape for clarifying for me how Butler's work can be applied to Athens. My own understanding of how dominant ideologies are challenged by alternative performances is sketched in Ober 1996, 148–54.

[19] See Morris 2000.

[20] Morris 2000, chapter 4. In my own work, I have tended to use the term ideology to cover both aspects of thought and practice, and it is important to keep in mind that there is no practical way to segregate "mentality" from "ideology" in the thought of any given person at any given time.

inward-looking, and political center (*to meson, to koinon*) over the individualized, sometimes foreign-oriented, and diverse private realm (*to idion*). It privileged the values of the relatively large (perhaps 40 percent of the NAM population) "moderate and middling" ranks of society (*hoi metrioi, hoi mesoi*: generally associated with the heavy-infantry hoplites rather than the elite cavalry). It tended to reject the values of the small (perhaps 5–10 percent of NAMs) leisure-class, luxurious, and cosmopolitan elite. And by the same token, it excluded from consideration all NAMs with inadequate property, those incapable of arming themselves as hoplites.

The middling mentality emphasized moderation, self-control, self-sufficiency, self-sacrifice in the common interest, and the high intrinsic value of citizenship itself. By the same token it rejected any celebration of luxurious living, ostentatious public displays of wealth, or fascination with extra-polis (and especially extra-Greek) relations. The middling mentality honored freedom (qua lack of dependency) and equality (among the ranks of the *mesoi*). It placed the hard-working (on his own land), hard-fighting (in common with his fellow infantryman), male warrior-landowner at the center of the social and political universe, and counterpoised that central figure with the marginal categories of women, foreigners, and the unfree, generally. The unfree included chattel slaves (or, in the case of Sparta serf-helots) but also those NAMs who lacked the material resources necessary for inclusion among the ranks of the *mesoi*.[21] By about 500 B.C. many Greek poleis were dominated by a republican political order defined by the middling mentality—in these regimes, which Aristotle would variously define as aristocracies, "polities," or as moderate forms of oligarchy, propertyless men were denied citizenship, but property qualifications were low enough that it was the *mesoi* who ruled.[22]

HISTORICAL DEVELOPMENT OF ATHENIAN DEMOCRACY

The historical development of Athenian democratic citizenship is a large topic, fruitfully and recently re-examined by Brook Manville.[23] In Athens,

[21] Chattel slaves, either Greek prisoners of war or (more often) non-Greeks imported specifically to serve as slaves, could be bought and sold as ordinary property. Helots and other unfree "serfs" were tied to the land; they could not be bought or sold but otherwise lacked liberties and immunities.

[22] Morris 1996, 19–48; Kurke 1992; and (believing it to be a reality rather than an ideology) Hanson 1996.

[23] Manville 1990.

the victory of the middling mentality was signaled by the constitutional reforms of Solon (594 B.C.) and paradoxically confirmed during the relatively benevolent (and generally antiaristocratic) reign of the tyrant Pisistratus (546–528 B.C.). The major step from the republican conception of the "rule of those in the middle rank" to a more radical form of democracy which enfranchised even propertyless laborers was taken in 508–507 B.C., in the aftermath of a popular uprising against a Spartan-sponsored attempt to install a narrow oligarchy as the government of Athens. This Athenian Revolution, and the constitutional order that emerged from it, set the stamp on Athenian civic identity and laid the groundwork for the developed democratic order of the fifth and fourth centuries B.C.[24] From this time on, it would be the demos, qua the body of NAMs, who ran Athens according to their own conceptions of the best interests of the demos and the polis. This meant that democratic Athenian political ideology was in an important sense, and from the beginning of the democracy itself, in conflict with the less capacious "middling mentality."

Within the middling mentality, the core values of freedom and equality were linked to sufficient property holding. And thus the marginal penumbra of "unfree-dependent, unequal-inferior, politically useless noncitizens" included all those NAMs (perhaps 50 percent of the total) who were regarded as inadequate in terms of wealth. By extending the border of political inclusiveness so as to include even genuinely destitute NAMs as actively participatory citizens, the Athenians counterpoised their political practice and an emerging democratic political ideology to the norms fostered by the well-established (although never uncontested) middling mentality. Just as archaic Greek culture had been defined by a fierce contest between an ideology favorable to luxuriousness (*habrosunē*) and the eventually and generally victorious middling (*metrios*) mentality,[25] much of the drama of Athenian culture may be sketched in terms of the tension between the middling mentality (especially as it was reformulated in the work of critical intellectuals) and an increasingly self-confident and coherent popular democratic ideology. In democratic Athens, the core *metrios* values of freedom and equality among citizens were maintained, but redefined by being stripped of any strong association with property holding. And with that radical redefinition came the possibility that in practice and over time, the values of freedom, equality, and security of the person might prove robust enough to survive their application in even more unexpected contexts and to persons outside the ranks of the NAMs.

In the democratic Athenian case, given the forthrightly pragmatic orientation of democratic government and the prominence of political life in

---

[24] Ober 1996, chapter 4.

[25] For the struggle between *habrosunē* and *metrios* mentality, see Morris 1996 and Kurke 1992; Kurke 1999.

the organization of society as a whole,[26] we may expect political ideology to be especially responsive to public performance and misperformance. And so, as I have argued in detail elsewhere, it was. In the citizen assembly and People's courts and in the public square—but also on the streets, in the fields, and workshops, and in mercantile and service establishments— citizens gathered, conversed, persuaded or failed to persuade, and chose courses of action accordingly. They behaved towards one another conventionally or innovatively, were noticed or ignored, and were rewarded and punished accordingly. They took note of all of this activity, forming opinions, thereby confirming or challenging their presuppositions, and resolving or changing their minds. And in so doing, they reproduced political culture and reconstituted social structures by their variously accurate and subversive performances of popular ideology.

Considerable traces survive of some public Athenian discussions—most especially the preserved (as inscribed stone stelai) records of Assembly decisions and (in the literary record) speeches of prosecution and defense written by or for litigants in the People's courts. Because these epigraphic and forensic corpora can be analyzed, in the aggregate, for their ideological content, it is possible to speak with some confidence about the content of Athenian political ideology.[27] But it is important to keep in mind that these inscriptions and speeches, as records of the most overtly political and most highly public of Athenian discussions, are at once descriptive and normative: They employ not only the speaker's suppositions about the actual experienced reality of Athenian social life and the attitudes of the demos, but they also refer to social relations and attitudes that the speaker supposes (and supposes his audience to believe) *should* pertain in the democratic city.

Our records thereby point to the matrix of convictions about actuality and normativity that constituted Athenian democratic ideology—or at least the part of that ideology suited to public assertion. Because our surviving records tend to concern relations between citizens, and because the judges (assemblymen and jurors) of the speech contests recorded in our surviving documents were Athenian citizens, sitting in a specifically "citizenly" politico-juridical capacity, these records are a particularly good indication of the ideological "party line" of the Athenian demos qua exclusive corporation of political share-holders. It is probably safe to say that these documents quite accurately define a good part of the ideological spectrum but fail to reproduce the entire spectrum: they portray

---

[26] Lévêque and Vidal-Naquet 1964 (trans. 1996); Meier 1990; Vernant 1982. My argument does not embrace reductive claims about the "primacy of politics" in Greek culture (Rahe 1992), but likewise rejects the attempt to read Athens as primarily family- and cult-centered.

[27] Inscriptions: Whitehead 1993. Speeches: Ober 1989.

Athenian political ideology as more unitary, coherent, and stable, and less liable to subversion by outside (i.e., noncitizen) pressures, than we may suppose it was in the experience of Athenian social life "in the round." The fraction of Athenian ideology to which we have relatively easy access is highly relevant to the question of the relationship between democracy and liberal values: I will suggest that maintaining this public ideology in intracitizenry contexts was essential if the Athenian "citizen many" were to retain the functional capacity to restrain, by political and legal means, the social power of the wealthy few. And that capacity was essential to the survival of both democracy and the liberalizing tendency exemplified in the expansion of quasi rights.

We are considerably less well informed about how citizens talked with one another in less obviously public fora. And, outside of the works of Athenian dramatists, pamphleteers, and philosophers, we have only scant traces of day-to-day interactions between citizens and noncitizens, or among noncitizens. In order to assess the extension of quasi rights within the wider Athenian society, I have looked at two sorts of evidence, and have attempted to read them against each other. First, there is the relatively official record of public forensic speeches, which include descriptions of legal and quotidian practices and make normative claims. Second, I have looked at the ways in which philosophical and dramatic texts critically expose the extension of protections within both Athenian society and utopian (or dystopian) imaginary societies. My claim will be that certain quasi rights were applied to noncitizens more often and in more diverse contexts than could be predicted by an interpretive model that emphasizes binary opposition between citizens and others as the primary principle of Athenian sociopolitical organization. The extension of negative liberties is due to a variety of factors and these probably cannot be isolated. They must, however, include conscious attempts at subversion on the part of noncitizens. There is, furthermore, the citizens' recognition (whether fully conscious or not) of contradictions between the three spheres discussed above: the relatively exclusivist claims of the traditional *metrios* mentality, the more capacious democratic political ideology, and the complex lived experience of social life. Both subversive activity and the capacity to recognize contradictions should, I suppose, have something to do with the historical development and subsequent complexity of Athenian ideology. They should also help us to understand that ideology's insistence on juxtaposing political (and legal) authority to nonpolitical (especially economic) forms of social power.[28]

[28] The contrast, among republics, is with societies like that of ancient Rome, in which religious, social, economic, and political power were concentrated in the hands of an aristocratic oligarchy.

I would not claim that it is possible, by employing the approach sketched above, to give a historically satisfactory account of Athenian social life in the round. But that is not my goal here: I hope only to show that there is reason to assume considerable discontinuity between what we might call the demos' "official intention"—the distribution of positive and negative rights exclusively *within* the closed context of the society of Athenian citizens (the "politico-polis"), and the functional distribution of negative liberties within the more open and fluid society comprising the entire population of the residents of the territory of Attica (the "geo-polis"). The general point I hope to make is that Athens was, at least in this respect, from the beginning of the democratic era, considerably more liberal than certain of its own premises allowed. The trend towards liberality was particularly noteworthy in the fourth century B.C.— the age of Plato and Aristotle. As noted above, Athens never evolved into a society that could fairly be described as "essentially liberal" in modern terms. The liberalizing trend was perhaps slowed, or even reversed, in the aftermath of the Athenian loss of formal independence to the autocratic Macedonians after 322 B.C.[29] How liberal Athens might have become had its independence been maintained remains entirely conjectural.

PSEUDO-XENOPHON AND ARISTOTLE: CITIZENSHIP AND ITS DISCONTENTS

The fascinating late fifth-century polemical pamphlet by an anonymous malcontent sometimes called "The Old Oligarch" (Pseudo-Xenophon, *Athēnaiōn Politeia*) seeks to teach its reader that Athenian democracy is the efficient and rationally self-interested rule of the "bad" (because poor and uneducated) many (*hoi polloi, to plēthos,* or *ho dēmos*) over the "good" (wealthy and cultured) few. The pamphlet seems initially to encourage hopes for an antidemocratic coup d'état, but it ends on a decidedly discouraging note: The last paragraph of the text begins in medias res, "But someone might interject that no one has been unjustly disenfranchised at Athens" (3.12). The implied context here is the potential for oligarchic opponents of the democracy for fomenting a civil war. In the classical Greek polis, the ordinary stake in a civil conflict was enfranchisement— membership in the citizenship qua political community of the polis. The end result of successful revolutionary action would be a change in the

[29] On democracy in postclassical Athens, see Habicht 1997. On the ways in which postclassical Athenian political culture may have resorted to essentializing ideological tactics, see Lape 2004.

composition of the citizen body.[30] And thus, the probable supporters of a revolutionary movement were those who were currently disenfranchised—and especially those who regarded their disenfranchisement as unjust. Pseudo-Xenophon replies to his hypothetical interlocutor that although a few men had in fact been unjustly expelled from the community of citizens by the Athenians for official malfeasance of one sort or another, the number was very small indeed, "but to attack the democracy at Athens not a few (*oligoi*) are required." Successful revolution apparently requires "many" (*polloi*) who, because they believe themselves to be unjustly disenfranchised, will support a change in regime. At this point in the essay, Pseudo-Xenophon's tendency to use "demos" as a synonym for "the unleisured many" (*hoi polloi*) rather than "the citizenry" tout court plays out. With the demos-*polloi* securely in control, it is impossible to suppose that "many" will be disenfranchised and so revolution is shown to be impossible on the original sociological premises of the argument. Pseudo-Xenophon concludes his tract and his practical lesson: at Athens, where it was the members of the demos who held the magistracies, how would anyone suppose that the many (*hoi polloi*) would ever be disenfranchised? And so "in view of these considerations, one must not think that there is any danger at Athens from the disenfranchised" (3.13).

Pseudo-Xenophon's somewhat cryptic argument is elucidated by a text written just a century later: Aristotle's *Politics*. Like the Old Oligarch, Aristotle was deeply concerned with the relationship between citizenship and civil unrest. Among Aristotle's goals in the *Politics* is the elucidation of the sources of civil conflict and the discovery of ways in which civil war might be prevented via pre-emptive and meliorative constitutional adjustments. Aristotle is at one with Pseudo-Xenophon in seeing the goal of civil war as the enfranchisement of those who regarded themselves as worthy of the status of citizen (or disenfranchisement of those thought to be unworthy of citizenship). And the prime cause of civil unrest was, consequently, the discontent of those who were unjustly (as they supposed) disenfranchised. Although Aristotle has many suggestions for minor constitutional tinkering that might serve to reduce tensions, it is clear from his account that he thinks the most straightforward way to solve the problem of citizenship and political unrest would be for the citizen body of the polis to be coextensive with the body of those who both desired and deserved the status of citizen. If there were no body of noncitizens

---

[30] On this passage of Pseudo-Xenophon, cf. Gomme 1962, 61–62, 67–68. The association of revolutionary change in the *politeia* with a change in the dominant element in the citizen body (*politeuma*) is a key issue for Aristotle in the *Politics*.

within the polis who wanted to be citizens, there would be no reason for a civil war aimed at revising the criteria for citizenship.

It is this concern with citizenship and its discontents that unites the "practical" discussion of the middle books (according to the traditional arrangement) of the *Politics* with books 1 and 7. Book 7, the account of the "polis of our prayers," presents a hypothetical polis in which the felicitous situation sketched in the previous paragraph obtains in practice—the body of "potential citizens" is coextensive with the body of "actual citizens" and thus the polis not only manifests a high degree of happiness, but also is optimally stable. With the right sort of attention to the processes of social reproduction (especially formal education, sketched in the fragmentary book 8), the "polis of our prayers" should not be subject to the subversive misperformances that led other (real) poleis into a seemingly never-ending series of constitutional-sociological changes (*metabolai*: cf. [Aristotle] *Athēnaiōn Politeia* 41.2 for an account of the twelve major Athenian *metabolai*). But in order to arrive at this happy end, Aristotle must necessarily decide what the appropriate criteria for citizenship actually should be. This work is undertaken in book 1, where Aristotle sketches the hypothetical origin of the fully developed polis from first principles.

In briefest summary, Aristotle suggests that the polis is the natural context for human flourishing, indeed the only context in which humans can hope consistently to achieve their highest ends. The polis is imagined as growing up organically from the conjunction of men and women into families (*oikoi*) for purposes of biological reproduction, then families into villages and clans for the purpose of security, and then villages and clans into the polis for the purpose of achieving justice and autarky.[31] Given the polis' evolution via the conglomeration of families, which are (in Aristotle's view) properly composed of husband, wife, children, and slaves, the society of the ideal-standard polis itself was made up of native adult men, native women, their children, and their slaves. The activities of each of these categories of persons was necessary for the existence and maintenance of a proper polis, but not all of these persons will be considered to "have a share" (*metechein*) in the polis. Indeed, as in Athenian ideology, only NAMs were regarded by Aristotle as potential citizen–share-holders. Aristotle explained the exclusion from share holding of non-NAM residents by reference to their innate psychologies: due to specific defects in their deliberative capacity (*to bouleutikon*), women, slaves, and children simply could not function as citizens. Male children were only temporarily impaired; they were expected to have developed appropriate deliberative

---

[31] For a fuller account, see Ober 1996, chapter 11.

capacity upon achieving adulthood. Women and slaves, however, although manifesting somewhat different psychologies, were permanently and irremediably impaired. Aristotle gives his reader no reason to suppose that a woman or a (natural) slave would ever (justly) desire any of the attributes or protections of citizenship, at least as long as she or he were treated justly by her or his husband-master (*kurios*).

There is a serious practical problem with this naturalizing scenario, one that would be clear enough to any classical Greek, and Aristotle faces it quite squarely (if chillingly): Some Greek-owned slaves were Greek citizens of other poleis, men who had been captured in war and sold into slavery. These persons remained "psychological citizens." As such they were necessarily unhappy in their status as slaves and thus a likely source of ideological-constitutional subversion. Aristotle's solution is a sketchy doctrine of "natural slavery" which posits the existence of persons who are "slaves by nature." He tentatively identifies most barbarians, and especially those of Asia, as likely natural slaves. The best polis will abjure enslaving those who are not slaves by nature, but may actively seek out opportunities to acquire natural slaves by imperialistic warfare.[32]

With the development of the doctrine of natural slavery, Aristotle's "natural polis" is complete. At first glance it appears to be a democracy on something like the Athenian model: all NAMs seem, on the psychological premises of the argument, to suit the criteria for "share-holding citizens." Yet in the last chapter of book 1 (1.13) Aristotle introduces a further complexity that mandates a good deal of further discussion of citizenship: those persons (including many NAMs) who worked for others, and received directions from them, were in some important sense assimilated to slaves. Such persons are summed up under the related categories of *banausoi* (craftsmen) and *thētes* (laborers). These quasi slaves did not enjoy the leisure that we are now reminded (the point was made in the *Nicomachean Ethics*) is necessary to the development of political virtue. Moreover, it seems that the labors of *banausoi* and *thētes* could, in and of themselves, be regarded as having corrupted any genuine and innate political capacity. It was precisely in their approach to the political standing of "sub-*metrios* NAMs" that Athenian democrats differed from those who advocated more restricted criteria for the active exercise of citizenship. And thus, by equating *banausoi* and *thētes* with slaves in his treatment of normative citizenship, Aristotle diverges from democratic definitions of citizenship, and leans toward the thinking of earlier and more overtly oligarchic political theorists, like Pseudo-Xenophon.

[32] For Aristotle's doctrine of natural slavery, see Aristotle, *Politics* 1252a24–1256b40, and the discussion of Garnsey 1996 with literature cited.

Elsewhere in the *Politics*, however, Aristotle treats democracy as the best of the "commonly existing" regimes (the alternatives being oligarchy and tyranny). Aristotle's recognition of the (contingent, if not absolute) justice of democratic practice on the grounds of what might be called "natural citizenship" (for Aristotle, lack of innate psychological impairment), and his simultaneous methodological acknowledgment of the endoxic force of settled sociological judgments of his elite interlocutors who regarded many NAMs as quasi slaves, is the source of considerable tension in the argument of the *Politics*. The seriousness with which Aristotle treats certain of the claims underpinning democratic government (e.g., the "summation argument" in support of the potential validity of collective decision making) is among the most interesting and (for a modern democrat at least) most attractive features of his text. But for our current purposes, the important point is that Aristotle's philosophical-psychological-naturalizing premises take the place of Athenian popular ideology in the project of explaining the basis of share holding and social justice in the polis.

Like Aristotle, the Athenian demos was very concerned with the issue of justice. But unlike Aristotle's "polis of our prayers," in which all potential citizens were both actual citizens *and* leisure-class and where all productive labor was to be the province of natural slaves, the Athenian democracy had to reconcile the concerns of a socially and economically diverse citizen body with the concerns and interests of other residents of the "geo-polis" without reference to a well-developed naturalized teleology. Unlike Aristotelian political theory, Athenian civic ideology had no well-articulated psychological premises with which to explain why citizenship (and its attendant privileges and protections) should be restricted to NAMs and denied to women and slaves—or for that matter, to resident foreigners (metics: a large category of persons, to which Aristotle himself belonged, but one of very limited analytic importance within the argument of the *Politics*). Although the Athenians did attempt (with varying degrees of success) to naturalize political distinctions based on gender, there is reason to suppose Athenian NAMs regarded slaves and metics as psychologically similar, or even identical to themselves.

Pseudo-Xenophon makes special note of the startlingly uppity behavior (*akolasia*) of Athenian slaves and metics, and he relates this phenomenon to the culture encouraged by democracy and to its material bases: He points out that in Athens "you" are not permitted (*oute . . . exestin*) to hit slaves and foreigners at will, nor will a slave stand aside for you. Pseudo-Xenophon's own explanation for this disturbing (to his implied reader) state of affairs is that the lower-class individuals constituting the Athenian demos were not recognizable as citizens: they were no better dressed or any more handsome than individual slaves and metics. Hence, if an elite gentleman were allowed free license to strike slaves at will, he might well strike an Athenian citizen, mistaking him for a slave (1.10). And so, he claims, it was in order to ensure their own physical security that the demos forbade the casual beating of slaves. Moreover, he suggests that the Athenians' willingness to grant equality in regard to speech (*isēgoria*) to metics and slaves, and to allow slaves to become rich, as well as their tendency to manumit slaves were all quite rational (*eikotōs*: 1.11–12). He claims that the explanatory key is the material importance to the lower-class Athenians of Athenian naval power—like Aristotle (*Politics* 1327a40–b16) Pseudo-Xenophon relates naval might directly to the social conditions that fostered democracy (1.2; 1.11–12). The navy required the availability of considerable free capital (*chrēmata*) and a variety of specialized trades (*technai*). He argues that metics provided the necessary skills while money was acquired by taking a portion of the earnings of slaves. If, as was the case at Sparta, your slave feared me, he might simply give up making money so as not to be at risk on account of his possession of wealth. Pseudo-Xenophon implies that this would not be a problem for the Spartans, whose land-based military organization did not demand the accumulation of capital; whereas for the Athenians the drying-up of the capital resources now gained by extracting the surplus value generated by the willing labor of profit-motivated slaves (who were presumably saving up to buy their manumission) would impair the operations of the navy.

For Pseudo-Xenophon the underlying premise is self-interest. The Athenian demos protected slaves and metics from physical mistreatment first because they feared being mistaken for slaves or metics. Athenians next protected property rights of slaves and metics because they believed they could profit from the willing labor of slaves and metics who would work productively only if they were secure in their possession of property and some part of the fruits of their labor.[33] The Old Oligarch's highly tendentious explanation for Athenian liberality in respect to slaves and resident foreigners is reiterated by Plato and other ancient critics of democracy. Their point is that when compared with more restrictive citizen regimes (like Sparta), democracy was perversely (yet rationally) unwilling to patrol the boundaries between citizens and noncitizens. The Athenians allowed noncitizens access to protections that should (in aristocratic thought) "properly" be restricted to citizens alone. This perversity

---

[33] The Greek text is partially corrupt here; see Bechtle 1996, who discusses the difficulties and offers a sensible solution. The point, for Pseudo-Xenophon, is that because the Athenians enter into legally binding financial agreements with their slaves, under the terms of which the slaves are eventually able to manumit themselves, the free Athenians are not able to do whatever they wish in respect to slaves and are therefore "slaves to slaves."

was explained by democracy's critics in terms of political sociology: the presence of poor ("ill-dressed, ugly") laborers and craftsmen within the Athenian citizen body. It was, they claimed, because the ordinary citizens (*hoi polloi*) themselves were "slave-like" when compared to the "good and beautiful" (*kaloi k'agathoi*) elite that they extended certain protections to slaves.

While rejecting the Old Oligarch's premises about natural inferiority of the poor, I would suggest that he is right to link the extension of privileges to the sociological diversity of the Athenian demos. Once the "natural" association between participation-rights and high social standing had been breached, there was a strong tendency for certain negative liberties to be extended beyond the citizen body itself.

DEMOSTHENES 21: QUASI RIGHTS AND THE LAW ON *HUBRIS*

It is hard to say how closely Pseudo-Xenophon's (undoubtedly polemical) claims about Athenian treatment of metics and slaves reflects the lived experience of most real persons in classical Athens. But his statement about Athenian unwillingness to tolerate overt public violence to non-NAMs is supported by an important Athenian legal statute: the law (*nomos*) dealing with acts of *hubris*. As N.R.E. Fisher has exhaustively demonstrated, *hubris* refers to the propensity for and the act of deliberately seeking to disrespect or dishonor another person through outrageous speech (gross verbal insult) or action (physical violence).[34] Aristotle (*Rhetoric* 2.2.1378b23–31) usefully associates the tendency to commit *hubris* with the possession of wealth (especially new wealth) and other elite attributes. But our best single source for the Athenian law on *hubris* is the politician-orator Demosthenes' prosecution speech, *Against Meidias*, composed in 346 B.C. The speech is especially relevant to my current purposes, because, in the course of exposing the extent and illegitimate application of his opponent Meidias' wealth-power via acts of *hubris*, Demosthenes explores in detail the existence and function of the quasi rights of personal (as well as communal) liberty, equality, and security within the citizen body.[35]

Demosthenes argues that, in the face of potentially destabilizing economic inequalities among the citizens, the maintenance of liberty (qua the right to do what one wishes and especially to speak out in public), equality (of opportunity and political voice), and individual personal security (living without fear of being constrained by the actions of stronger

---

[34] Fisher 1992.

[35] I offer a detailed analysis of this speech in Ober 1996, chapter 7.

persons within one's own society) are functionally essential components of democratic Athenian culture. For him, the maintenance of these quasi rights was among the primary purposes of democracy: Without them, the powerful would rule the state in their own interests and democracy would cease to exist. The possibility of "benevolent" oligarchs, who would recognize the justice of granting negative liberties to the weaker many, is as foreign to Demosthenes' thought as "enlightened" democrats, who accept the moral superiority of aristocrats, are to the thought of Pseudo-Xenophon.

Demosthenes' prosecution speech offers a particularly eloquent defense of the notion that the maintenance of quasi-right protections is predicated *not* on any natural or divine dispensation, or on the contractual delegation of powers to an abstract sovereign, but upon political participation—the willed activity of the concerned individual citizen and of the collective citizenry in the defense of the outraged individual. Demosthenes (21.223–225) explicitly reminds his audience of jurors that Athenian laws have no independent existence or agency; it is only the willingness of the citizens actively to work the machinery of the law (as voluntary public prosecutors and jurors) that gives the law substance and force. The modern reader is forcefully reminded that there was no meaningful distinction in Athens between "citizenry" and "government." In Athens it was the aberrant powerful individual or syndicate, rather than "the government," that threatened the freedom, equal standing, and fundamental dignity of the ordinary (non-elite) citizens. Demosthenes' speech is a testament to the assumed determination and capacity of the demos to restrain the hubristic individual. At the same time it offers ample evidence for the very considerable scope of action and opportunity of the wealthy elite, and the relative security of their property rights.

In the midst of his demonstration that Meidias (by punching Demosthenes in the theater of Dionysos, while the latter was serving as chorus-producer for his tribe) was guilty of the worst sort of *hubris*, Demosthenes pauses to quote the (typically highly procedural) Athenian law forbidding acts of *hubris*:

> If anyone treats with *hubris* any person, either child or woman or man, free or slave, or does anything unlawful (*paranomon*) against any of these, let anyone who so wishes, of those Athenians who are entitled (*exestin*), submit a *graphē* (written complaint) to the *thesmothetai* (legal magistrates). Let the *thesmothetai* bring the case to the *Hēliaia* (People's court) within thirty days of the submission of the *graphē*, if no public business prevents it, or otherwise as soon as possible. Whoever the *Hēliaia* finds guilty, let it immediately assess

whatever penalty it thinks right for him to suffer or pay. Of those who submit *graphai* according to the law, if anyone does not proceed, or when proceeding does not get one-fifth of the votes, let him pay one thousand drachmas to the public treasury. If he (the accused) is assessed to pay money for his *hubris*, let him be imprisoned, if the *hubris* is against a free person, until he pays it. (Dem. 21.47, trans. MacDowell, adapted)[36]

Having cited the law in full, Demosthenes then points to its remarkable scope: "You hear the generous consideration (*philanthrōpia*) of the law, men of Athens: it does not even allow acts of *hubris* against slaves. Well by the very gods!" Demosthenes then proposes a sort of thought-experiment: What if someone were to transport a copy of this law to "the barbarians from whom slaves are imported to Greece," and were to praise the Athenians by pointing out that despite the many wrongs they have suffered at the hands of barbarians (a reference imprimis to the Persian wars of 490–78 B.C.) and their consequent natural enmity, "nevertheless [the Athenians] don't think it right to treat insolently even the slaves whom they acquire by paying a price for them, but have publicly made this law to prevent it, and have before now imposed the death penalty on many who transgressed it." Demosthenes suggests that in these circumstances, the grateful barbarians would immediately appoint "all of you" to the honorific position of *proxenoi*, "local consuls," who look after the interests of persons from some specific foreign locale (Dem. 21.48–50). Demosthenes' explication of the *hubris* law is constructed in the form of an a fortiori argument, to show how spectacularly wrongful was Meidias' behavior in punching a fellow citizen who was performing a public liturgy. And Demosthenes himself, with his "by the very gods!" seems a bit startled by the results of his own explication of the law's scope and by its failure to distinguish between citizens and noncitizens as protected persons (cf. Aeschines 1.17).

A few other aspects of the law on *hubris* (which cannot, unfortunately, be dated or securely assigned to a specific lawmaker) merit our attention here. First, its provisions are remarkably broad: Not only does it proscribe *hubris* against all categories of residents of Athenian territory, it prohibits the commission of any action that was *paranomon*—which can be translated either as "unlawful" or "against what is customarily regarded as proper"—against the same extensive list of persons. Since neither *hubris* nor *paranomon* is specifically defined by the law, it was up to the voluntary prosecutor to convince his audience of jurors that a given action was, when viewed in context and judged by prevailing community standards, "hubristic" or "legally-customarily improper." We can now see why

---

[36] MacDowell 1990, loc. cit.

Pseudo-Xenophon would have regarded it as prudent for a visitor to Athens, evidently used to freely asserting his superiority at home, to refrain from engaging in behavior towards anyone that might be regarded by Athenians as demeaning or otherwise offensive.

The *hubris* law points to an important distinction between positive (participation-) rights and negative liberties. Although citizens have no special standing among those protected by the law, it is only "Athenians who are entitled" (i.e., citizens not suffering from full or partial disenfranchisement [*atimia*]) who are empowered to initiate a prosecution under the anti-*hubris* law. As in the case of other Athenian criminal actions, if a voluntary prosecutor were to initiate a legal action, but failed to pursue it in court, he himself would suffer *atimia*. Moreover, if the prosecutor failed to convince one-fifth of the jurors of the justice of his claims (the votes of jurors—generally 500 for this category of delict—were counted after the carefully timed speeches of prosecutor and defendant were complete), then he must pay a stiff fine (roughly three years' wages for a skilled craftsman). Clearly, the Athenians were concerned to prevent frivolous prosecutions and they backed up their concern by putting the voluntary prosecutor, as well as the defendant, at risk. The exercise of positive rights can entail serious consequences, but it is the exercise of positive rights by "the enfranchised" which defends the negative liberties of the entire resident population.

Finally, the law draws a distinction between the potential punishment of a person convicted of *hubris* against free persons as opposed to *hubris* against slaves: the man convicted of the latter will not face prison, even if he is unable to pay an assessed fine. It is worth noting however, that a monetary fine was only one of the possible penalties that might be suggested by a successful prosecutor and accepted by the jury. Demosthenes appears to claim (the syntax allows some vagueness) that "many" persons had in fact been executed for committing *hubris* against slaves. Demosthenes may, of course, be engaging in hyperbole. We do not know how often (if ever) Athenian citizens actually were prosecuted for *hubris* against non-NAMs, or, if they were prosecuted, what the rate of conviction or the seriousness of the assessed punishment might have been. It seems, on the face of it, unlikely that a man would be prosecuted for *hubris* against members of his own *oikos*, whether slave or free. But then it also might seem, on the face of it, unlikely that the Athenian citizens would pass or keep on the books a law that is so little concerned with citizens as a specially protected category. The law on *hubris* confirms Pseudo-Xenophon's claim that metics and slaves could not be struck with impunity at Athens, but it shows that the scope of protection was (in the letter of the law, anyway) even broader: children and women were granted identical protections.

METICS AND SLAVES

Before turning to gender roles, we should pause to consider briefly other evidence for the formal or informal application of negative liberties to metics and slaves. Although ownership of real property ordinarily remained a monopoly of Athenian citizens, the Athenians sometimes granted metics the right to own real estate (*enktēsis*); others were granted remission of the head-tax ordinarily paid by resident foreigners (*isoteleia*). A detailed study by E. Cohen amply demonstrates that Pseudo-Xenophon was right that metics and even slaves could and did accumulate considerable private fortunes and that their property rights were as secure as any Athenian citizen's.[37] Cohen also argues that in certain sorts of civil lawsuits (*dikai*) concerning property, metics and even slaves could represent themselves rather than depending on legal representation by an Athenian citizen, and by the same token they could initiate prosecutions, even against citizens.[38] Metics and slaves enjoyed as much religious freedom as anyone in Athens; they were treated as functional equals in the context of certain important Athenian cults and rituals, notably the state-sponsored and state-protected Eleusinian Mysteries.[39]

But given that citizenship, with its specific participation-rights, remained centrally important, what of naturalization? An Athenian law dating to the mid-fifth century predicated citizenship on birthright, mandating double native descent—an Athenian father and Athenian mother—for those persons accepted as citizens by the demes. This restriction was ideologically buttressed by resort to the myth that Athenians were autochthonous—originally born of the earth of Attica. Public speakers could claim that with autochthony came a common inborn patriotism.[40] Yet naturalization was in fact possible, for individuals and even for groups of persons, by special decree of the citizen Assembly. Some metics, and even former slaves, were in fact enfranchised in this way. In the best-known case (because the family's complex legal affairs are well documented in the corpus of Demosthenes' forensic speeches), the family of the extremely wealthy former-slave and bank-owner Pasion became prominent members of Athenian society.

[37] *Enktēsis* and *isoteleia*: Whitehead 1977. Wealthy metics and slaves: Cohen 2000.

[38] Cohen 1973 and 2000.

[39] On the question of religious freedom and the law against impiety: Parker 1996, 207–11, 214–15. On metics and slaves in Athenian religious life: Cohen 2000.

[40] Periclean citizenship law: Boegehold 1994, with literature cited. Autochthony ergo patriotism: Ober 1989, 261–66. Cohen 2000 discusses the evidence for naturalization in detail. He also argues that the citizenship law potentially allows any individual to be legally accepted as a citizen as long as he was born of two long-term noncitizen residents of Attica, but I do not believe that the evidence he cites supports the sharp legal distinction between the terms *astos* and *politēs* upon which his argument depends.

Pasion's son, Apollodorus, went on to became a well-known Athenian politician and public speaker. In several preserved forensic speeches, Apollodorus speaks openly of his ancestry (see chapter 1). Although he allows that he and his relatives owed a special debt to the Athenians for the gift of citizenship, he claims that this indebtedness is a source of his own intense patriotism and his dedication to the good of his adopted polis.[41]

Metics (regularly) and slaves (more often than is generally acknowledged) served in the Athenian armed forces.[42] Their faithful service led, on several occasions, to formal proposals in the citizen Assembly for mass manumission of slaves and mass enfranchisement of metics (see chapter 4). Although in each case the Athenians eventually balked (sometimes after the decree had been successfully challenged in the People's courts), there was clearly, from time to time at least, considerable sympathy (and potential, if not fully realized, ideological space) for the inclusion within the Athenian citizen body of many persons who were obviously not "autochthonous." Indeed, even the standard story of Athenians as a pure "earthborn" race was counterbalanced by the equally well-known and celebrated story of Athenian receptiveness to foreign immigrants in mythological times.

In practice, it is certain that many "nonethnic" Athenians slipped into the ranks of "the Athenians" without being approved by special decree of the Assembly. This was perhaps especially common in periods of revolutionary political change (Aeschines 1.77; Demosthenes 57.26 [*diapsēphismos*]). But it also occurred on the more casual and endemic level of the deme registration procedure: the deme assemblies voted to accept as citizens any number of men who fell short of the double-descent requirement. The periodic calls for "cleansing of the deme lists" (e.g., in the 340s B.C.) are evidence for Athenian concern for maintaining the fiction of the citizen body as a closed corporation, but also point to the fact that it was indeed a fiction, and that many persons undoubtedly were registered as "Athenians" because their neighbors had, for whatever reason, chosen to ignore actual ethnicity in regarding them as worthy of that distinction.[43]

CONTROLLING WOMEN (AND CHILDREN)

Pseudo-Xenophon limits his criticism of Athenian laxness in the matter of treatment of non-NAMs to metics and slaves. But in the *Republic* Plato

---

[41] The procedure for enfranchisement and its relative rarity: M. Osborne 1981. Family of Pasion and Apollodorus: Ober 1989, 212–14; Trevett 1992.

[42] Metic service in Athenian armed forces: Whitehead 1977, 82–86. Slaves in military service: Hunt 1998.

[43] Cohen 2000 discusses the evidence in detail.

(562b–63d) seems to pick up where the Old Oligarch had left off, noting that the freedom and equality characteristic of democratic regimes lead not only to metics becoming equal to citizens, but the young equal to the aged and women equal to men. Plato's Socrates had advocated a sort of cross-gender role equality within the closed and carefully educated ranks of Calipolis' Guardian class (on the analogy of the similarity of the nature of male and female dogs, to which the Guardians are frequently compared). But Plato clearly regards the putative equalization of gender relations within the real world of the democratic polis to be among its most grievous faults. Plato's claim here (like Pseudo-Xenophon's, above) is part of a critical project and cannot be taken as a simple description of Athenian reality. But, in light of the specific inclusion of women in the Athenian law against *hubris* and the frequent assertion by modern scholars that women in democratic Athens were actually much less free and less equal to men than they were in aristocratic societies (e.g., among archaic poleis and in classical Sparta),[44] it is worth asking whether there might be some real-world basis to Plato's complaint that democracy encouraged the extension of privileges across gender lines—just as it did across the lines of metic versus citizen and slave versus free.

In the context of a discussion in the *Politics* about what sorts of institutional arrangements are suited to each regime-type, Aristotle makes a suggestion that has considerable bearing on the general topic of women's standing in democratic and nondemocratic poleis:

> The controller of children (*paidonomos*) and the controller of women (*gunaikonomos*), and any other office that has authority of this sort of superintendence (*epimeleia*) is aristocratic, and certainly not democratic. For how is it possible to prevent the wives of poor men (*aporoi*) from going out [of the house]? Nor is it oligarchic, for the wives of oligarchs live luxuriously. (1300a4–8)

Later, Aristotle notes that

> peculiar to those poleis which enjoy greater leisure and are more prosperous, and which in addition take thought for orderliness (*eukosmia*), are the offices of guardian of women, guardian of the laws, guardian of children, and gymnasiarch, and, in addition to these, the superintendence of gymnastic games and the Dionysian festival contests, and any other spectacles that there may be. Of these sorts of offices, some are clearly not democratic, such

---

[44] For the claim that women in aristocratic Sparta were excessively free, see Aristotle, *Politics* 1269b12–1270b6. Greek democracy as oppressive to women: Katz 1999.

as that of guardianship of women (*gunaikonomia*) or guardianship of children (*paidonomia*), since poor men (*aporoi*) necessarily use their wives and children as subsidiary workers (*akolouthoi*) due to their lack of slaves. (1322b37–23a6)

The two comments directly link the sorts of behavior that could reasonably be enforced by agents of the government with the sociologically determined propensities of the sort of citizens definitive of various regime-types: That which was suitable for leisured aristocrats was simply impracticable in a democracy, dominated as it was by people constrained to work for their living.

The office of the *paidonomos* is otherwise unattested, but *gunaikonomoi* did exist in some poleis—including postdemocratic Athens.[45] Aristotle's explanations for women's behavior under different regimes (and his silence on the matter of children's behavior) suggests that he was more interested in *gunaikonomoi* than *paidonomoi*. He supposed that, were a *gunaikonomos* appointed, the wives of citizens would be prevented (or officially discouraged) from "going out" and from living luxuriously. In the case of oligarchy, in which citizenship was defined specifically by reference to wealth, Aristotle assumes that oligarchs' wives lived luxurious lives with the tacit approval (or even open encouragement) of their husbands. Display and enjoyment of wealth is assumed to be central to the oligarchic identity and, that being the case, there was no reason for an oligarchic regime to seek the appointment of an official whose duty would be to restrain luxurious behavior.

The case of democracy is more complex and Aristotle's commentary is fuller: Aristotle assumes it is simply impossible (even if it were in principle regarded as desirable) to prevent the wives of working men from leaving their homes. His reasoning in the first passage is clarified by the second: the "poor" *oikos* lacked slaves, and so it depended on the productive labor of all of its members (including women). Some part of this labor was typically carried out, we must suppose, in extrahousehold contexts. Once again, as with Pseudo-Xenophon on the lenient treatment of slaves, the association between what sort of behavior is allowed and the socioeconomic basis of democracy is to the fore: for Aristotle, it is specifically because in a democracy the citizenry included slaveless "poor men," who were constrained to act (and to allow other members of their household to act) in certain ways due to their lack of material resources, that the aristocratic office of "controller of women" is particularly unsuited to a democracy.

---

[45] *Gunaikonomoi* at Athens and elsewhere: Garland 1981. See D. Cohen 1991 on the scholarly myth of seclusion of women at Athens.

There is nothing wrong with Aristotle's reasoning in these passages: he allows us to suppose that Greek men (including democrats) would, on the whole, prefer that their women stayed at home and out of sight.[46] A regime which restricted citizenship to those men financially able to keep women at home, and one concerned with ensuring good order via supervision—that is, an aristocracy—would be likely to appoint a magistrate with the duty of assuring that this norm was enforced in practice. As we have seen, in Aristotle's view oligarchs lacked the motivation to prevent private luxuriousness among women. But under a democracy, regardless of the normative preference of the NAMs, there was, practically speaking, no way for the regime to survive unless women went out of the home to work. If the women of the poor could not work, the poor would starve and thus material necessity trumped whatever normative preference for the seclusion of citizen women might have pertained among the Athenian NAMs. And thus we might begin to develop a context for taking seriously Plato's comment about the tendency of democracy to promote relatively greater practical equality of women and (citizen) men without invoking a self-conscious liberalism among the NAM population.

It is impossible to determine whether or not Athenian women valued as a substantive liberty, the lack of legal restrictions on their freedom of movement and association. Yet if we regard the creation of a formal government officer "in charge of controlling women" as a move specifically designed to place limits on women's life-choices, then we might want to question the scholarly habit of correlating Greek democracy with oppression of women, aristocracy with intergender liberality. We are, however, still a long way from making an argument for a *positive* correlation between democracy and (relatively) liberal gender-role relations or attitudes. If we accept that it was quite common for Athenian citizens' wives and daughters to work outside of the home, and that this material necessity was recognized (at least in negative terms) in Athenian institutional arrangements, do we have any warrant to go further? Do we have reason to suppose that the lived and performed Athenian experience of gender roles was otherwise more liberal than the "official" normative line? Or that Athenian ideology responded over time to the fact that women's labor was essential to the survival of democratic culture?

The best source of evidence for the last question, at least, is Athenian drama: At Athens tragedy and comedy were officially sponsored by the

[46] Cf. Thucydides 2.45.2: "If I may speak also about the women who will now be widows, I shall define it all in a brief admonition. For great is the glory for you not to be worse than your existing nature, and not to be talked about for good or evil among men" (Trans. J. S. Rusten, rev. by Hornblower 1991 loc.cit.).

democratic state and famously depict strong, willful, even overtly "political" women. When watching Aristophanes' *Ecclesiazusae* (ca. 393 B.C.), Athenian citizens were confronted with a comic scenario in which women are made citizens by decree of the Assembly and subsequently undertake a radical reorganization of the polis along social lines that were hyperegalitarian (among the free population).[47] I suppose that comedy (I am deliberately leaving tragedy to one side) had an institutionalized critical function. The Athenians intended for comic poets to present on stage culturally subversive material, to make visible the ideological contradictions and evasions by which the Athenians ordinarily lived their personal and (especially) their political lives. And I suppose that the democracy challenged itself in this way because of an implicit recognition of the dangers inherent in ideological ossification, and a recognition of the essential role that sharp and profound internal criticism plays in the continued flourishing of a democratic political order.[48] In the terms employed above, we might suggest that drama very literally "alternatively performed" aspects of Athenian ideology and thereby stimulated the democratic imagination and opened the way for other (imitative, reactive, creative) alternative performances outside the Theater of Dionysus. A reconsideration of the Athenian law on *hubris* may help us to think about the relationship between drama, Athenian democratic ideology, and the wider Greek context.

I would suggest that the *hubris* law might be read as a (nonintentional) democratic counterpart and rejoinder to aristocratic laws establishing "controllers of women" and perhaps similar, less well attested, offices for control of other categories of noncitizens.[49] We may suppose that both democratic Athens and the normative aristocratic polis passed their laws intending imprimis to protect the standing of the citizen body. In both cases, there was a deep concern with behavior, especially in public (although perhaps also in private) that might be contrary to, and thus threatening to the established rules (i.e., *paranomon*), thereby manifesting the potential to destroy the regime that was maintained by adherence to those rules. The general Greek assumption that law code and regime are intertwined, fragile, and so incapable in practice of surviving serious

[47] See further Ober 1998, 122–55.

[48] The argument is made in detail in Ober 1996, chapter 10.

[49] Although Aristotle's concept of aristocracy is defined, philosophically, as the rule of those possessing political virtue, the fact that some nondemocratic poleis did indeed have "controllers of women" allows us to use the term aristocracy rather more broadly than Aristotle ordinarily did. Some scholars have supposed (although it is not provable) that the *hubris* law was enacted by Solon, to whom also are attributed laws restricting the behavior of Athenian women at funerals (Plutarch, *Solon* 21.5). But the point here conerns laws enforced under the democratic regime.

breaches is familiar from Aristotle's *Politics* and interestingly reconfigured by Plato's *Crito*—a text that has caused liberal readers considerable anguish.[50] In this conviction, then, Athenian democrats seem similar to the aristocratic upholders of the *metrios* ideal (although compare chapter 10, below).

The contrast between Athens and the normative aristocratic regime arises in where the threat to "laws and regime" was perceived to *originate*, how it was *manifested*, and how it was *answered*. The aristocratic ideology that eventuated in *gunaikonomia* legislation saw a prime need for behavioral control to be exerted upon those noncitizens most intimately connected to citizens: children and (especially) "citizens' women." If we take Aristotle's *Politics* as our source, the threat was thought to be manifested by the inappropriate public appearance of those who should remain invisible, and by the enjoyment of luxury by those who should not live in a luxurious manner. Although presumably children were also potentially sources of dangerous behavioral deviance, in Aristotle's account it is wives and daughters of citizens who are the primary objects of concern: Evidently the women of aristocrats manifested some tendency to "go out in public"—that is, to imitate the very public-oriented lives of their husbands, brothers, and fathers. And/or they tended to want to live overluxuriously in private—that is, to conform to the behavioral norms typical of the archaic *habrosune* ideology, an ideology which had conflicted with the *metrios* ideal normatively embraced by classical aristocrats (at least those of the Aristotelian sort). Because manifestations of these tendencies were affronts to the *metrios* ideal, the preservation of "good order" required scrutiny of women and official suppression of their subversive practices. The potential threat was answered by the creation of a formal government office: a bureaucracy (in effect) that was assigned formal responsibility for rooting out women's misbehavior and chastising any breeches uncovered. The rest of the citizen-aristocrats were, by implication, left to pursue other matters, public and private.

By contrast, the Athenian democratic ideology construed the threat to public order, the prime suspect of "paranomic" activity, as the hubristic individual—he who was strong enough and arrogant enough to seek to establish pre-eminence via the humiliation of others within the polis. By combining the language of the *hubris* law itself and Demosthenes' normative language in explicating that law,[51] we may say that Athenians saw women, children, slaves, and (presumably) foreigners, along with the

[50] Plato's *Crito*: Kraut 1984. Cf. chapter 7, below.

[51] This would be problematic procedure if the primary concern was the intention of the original lawmaker, but since that is unknowable and undatable, per n. 49, above, I am concerned here with the way the law was used and understood in fourth-century practice.

weaker of the citizens (i.e., those commanding few resources) as the potential objects of illegitimate activity, rather than the willful originators of threats to the public order. The powerful hubristic individual was imagined as seeking to establish hierarchical relations within the polis on his own terms by demonstrating his capacity to humiliate, by outrageously insulting weaker persons by speech or deed (especially sexual violation), and by seeking to do so with impunity. And if he (or the class of powerful persons he represented) were successful in establishing a secure "personal" social hierarchy within the polis, a social space free from the legal authority of the democratic state, it would clearly mean the end of the effective rule of the demos; this is why a successfully perpetrated, unchastised act of *hubris* could be characterized as signifying "the overthrow of the democracy."[52]

Equally distinctive is the Athenian notion of how to respond to the threat of *hubris*—not by the establishment of a formal office, a hypothetical "controller of hubristic persons," but rather by the willful intervention of "whoever among the enfranchised Athenians so wishes." The voluntary prosecutor (NAM in good standing) took it upon himself to initiate a legal action before a large body of citizens and at considerable legal (as well, we must assume, in some cases, less formal but very real) risk to himself.[53] The maintenance of good order in Athens was consequently dependent upon the presence of individuals willing to serve as voluntary prosecutors—whether out of a concern for the public good, desire for personal revenge, self-aggrandizement via public display, or (most likely) some combination of these. Unlike the normative aristocratic polis, which assigned the responsibility for investigation and chastisement to an appointed individual and (potentially and in principle) left the rest of the citizens out of it, in democratic Athens the entire citizen body was (potentially and in principle) involved in the maintenance of public order through the prosecution of the deviant individual.[54]

How should we read the Athenian legal conflation of women, slaves, and weaker citizens as potential victims, rather than originators, of subversive behavior? In light of the strong women depicted in Attic drama, it seems illegitimate to read the *hubris* law as proof that Athenians saw women as

[52] Phrase *kataluein ton dēmon* (or similar expressions) and its association with *hubris*: Aristophanes, *Ecclesiazusae* 453; Thucydides 3.81.4 (*stasis* on Corcyra). See chapter 10, below.

[53] Demosthenes' description of the various bad things done to him in private life by Meidias and his cronies illustrates the potential harms that could arise from challenging the powerful, even in Athens.

[54] The Athenians annually appointed many magistrates (by election or, more often, by lot) to undertake various aspects of public business: Hansen 1991, 225–45. But the work of magistrates was subject to the authority of popular assemblies and law courts, and did not include moral policing.

fundamentally "apolitical" or incapable of agency. The women of Aristophanes' *Ecclesiazusae*, for example, seem to manifest all the characteristics of Aristotle's "natural citizens." Their stated motivation in seeking to seize control of the government is the communal project of "saving the polis." Led by the attractively portrayed character Praxagora, the citizen women of the play seek to reconcile various aspects of *metrios* mentality and democratic ideology. Their program of collectivization would end in freeing all Athenian NAMs from the necessity of labor and in equalizing opportunity for the enjoyment of such pleasures (especially food and sex) as the society had to offer.

Notably, Praxagora is not portrayed as an elite woman: she is the wife of Blepyros, a citizen who owns but a single cloak and depends in part upon his Assembly pay for the sustenance of his family (cf. Aristotle, *Politics* 1300a1–4). Praxagora "goes out in public" when necessary, without prior approval of her husband, and not only to engage in economically productive work. She excuses a nocturnal absence by claiming that she was called out to aid a friend undergoing childbirth (*Ecclesiazusae* 526–34). Her excuse points to an Athenian world of female friendship, association, and mutual aid—a world that would presumably be restricted in an aristocratic regime characterized by presence of a *gunaikonomos*. Praxagora had no slave attendant and so ventured out all alone—she explains that she donned Blepyros' male clothing in order to appear more formidable to potential cloak-thieves. We are reminded of Aristotle's comment that among the poor, women (and children) perform the sorts of tasks (in this case, defense of property) that the wealthy delegated to slaves. The point, once again, is the problematic (from the perspective of the *metrios* mentality) inclusion of poor men among the active-citizen body, which leaves open the possibility of the (situationally contingent and partial) assimilation of the women (and other non-NAMs) to citizens.

It is not easy (maybe not possible or even desirable) to sustain a claim that any given drama guides its audience to a simply positive or negative evaluation of that possibility. But it seems highly likely that drama was at once informed by the complexity of democratic ideology, and contributed in some measure to how Athenians thought about the evolving matrix of social and political values with which and by which they lived their lives.

Conclusions: Ancient Politics and Modern Theory

I have suggested that in classical Athens the practice of participatory democracy led to the development of a regime that was at once constitutional and fostered something like modern liberal values. Democracy promoted the development of both positive participation-rights and negative liberties. Whereas participation-rights were limited to NAMs, certain negative liberties were (at least in legal principle) extended to all residents of Athenian territory. If we regard the NAM body as a collective sovereign, the Athenian case might (ironically) be taken as proof of Berlin's contention that subjects of an autocrat may enjoy negative liberties. But the sociologically diverse Athenian demos is very different from Berlin's imagined unitary sovereign, and I have argued that it is the *ideological* complexities associated with the *social* diversity of the citizenry that is the key to understanding the development of what I have been calling "quasi rights." The Athenian constitutional order developed from and was sustained by a complex and contradictory ideology. The contradictions of the ideology were exposed by both "external" critics like Plato and by institutionalized critics, notably the comic poets. The experience of regularly being confronted with contradictions between social norms and the implications of politial practices was an important aspect of the education of the democratic citizen. It encouraged habits of public deliberation, cut against the binary opposition between "citizens and others," and so promoted a distribution of relations of justice that was considerably wider than the majoritarian logic of participatory democracy might otherwise have demanded.

The more general question of what Greek democracy might mean for contemporary politics and political thought has been asked, overtly and implicitly, in much recent work by both political theorists and classicists.[55] I conclude by reiterating three reasons that the study of the Athenian experience of democracy seems to me useful to modern political theorists.

First, the Athenian example highlights the potential interpretive leverage gained by assessing a variety of text genres (here: historiography, comedy, forensic oratory, and partisan pamphlets, as well as political philosophy), and by juxtaposing practices, law, ideological assumptions, normative statements, and formal philosophical claims. The modern academic tendency (which is, happily, far from universal) of subdividing the study of politics such that political theorists and philosophers deal with "ideas" while the analysis of past political practices and ideologies is delegated to historians, leaves too much out of any given picture. The establishment of sharp dichotomies between "rational discourse" of intellectuals and the ideological assumptions common to ordinary people tends to obscure how indebted intellectual thought may be to ordinary political discourse and ideological presuppositions. Athenian political texts discourage this sort of dichotomous thinking, in part because they were written in a "predisciplinary" era.

---

[55] Euben 1997; Ober and Hedrick 1996 sums up a good deal of recent work, and the bibliography of that volume points to more.

Second is the overt Greek concern with the practical and ideological effects of social-power inequality, especially that produced by wealth inequality. The Greeks approached the issue of wealth-power from a perspective very different from that generally assumed by modern writers, who find it difficult to approach issues of wealth and class outside of the interpretive framework defined (in schematic terms) by Adam Smith (and his advocates and critics), on the one hand, and Karl Marx (with his advocates and critics), on the other. Whereas it would be very foolish to suppose that the ancient approach to "social life and politics" is inherently superior to modern discussions, it is, I think, potentially valuable in offering a precapitalist, pre-Marxist viewpoint.

Third, and for me the most important, is the unambiguous classical Athenian focus on the pragmatic and performed status of political privileges and legal immunities. Lacking any clear distinction between citizenship and government, or any metaphysical basis for the assertion of rights claims, the Athenians saw that establishing and maintaining individual dignity and democratic public authority must be predicated on the actions of society's members. If rights were not consistently and accurately reperformed by most of the people most of the time, they would simply cease to exist. This understanding might offer some purchase on the failure of traditional forms of liberal universalism to come fully to grips with assertions of "group rights" (see chapter 4) predicated on the establishment and maintenance of a specific group identity.[56] Moreover, the Athenian democrats' willingness to trust "voluntarism" and general reluctance to delegate important authority to specific governmental agents may offer an alternative to the modern tendency to associate the maintenance of rights directly with the strength of the formal institutions established by a powerful (if potentially threatening) central government.

Of course no polis—not even democratic Athens at its best and understood in the best possible light—is an appropriate model for the establishment of a modern state regime. My point is not that we should take Athens as a paradigm, but that the history of the democratic polis is "good to think with." It offers us, as moderns, a perspective on the possible spectrum of relationships between democratic politics, political sociology, and moral values that is at once strikingly familiar and radically alien. As such Athens may present a therapeutic challenge, not only to those who would deny any connection between participatory democracy and the extension of negative liberties, but to a complacent "end-of-history" tone that sometimes seems to affect even the best work by contemporary liberal thinkers.

[56] See, for example, C. Taylor et al. 1994.

CHAPTER SIX

The Athenian Debate over Civic Education

Going on together implies a process of sociocultural reproduction over time; it demands that some shared values be passed on from generation to generation, that citizens be taught how to take on a particular civic identity. This sort of social reproduction and identity-formation is a primary function of education and a fortiori of civic education. The issue of civic identity is especially to the fore in political regimes that depend on the willing and active participation of a politically engaged and competent citizenry. And thus, civic education is a common concern for republican theorists, including (in very different ways) Rousseau and J. S. Mill. If one supposes, as I do, that among the sources of democratic persistence is a capacity to stay in touch with a revolutionary sensibility, one that retains the sense that the regime is amendable to substantial institutional change, without losing its value-centered identity, then civic education becomes a particularly difficult matter: An education that focuses on the primacy of obedience, sameness, and continuity—whether it resembles the one for which the Spartans are famous, or the one that was advocated by Plato in the Republic—*is simply inappropriate for democratic citizens if they are to be taught that revolution is among their most important legacies.*

A participatory democracy, on the Athenian model, will have to find ways to develop each citizen's "democratic soul"—that is, to teach the moral psychology, ethical judgment, and conception of justice and law that is appropriate to the democratic citizen. And it must do so without resolving the productive tension between coherence and diversity. Democratic citizens must somehow learn to "think alike while thinking differently." Here I propose that Athenian civic education, unlike the educational regimes advocated by Plato and other Greek political theorists, centered on practice: It was by doing politics, by "working the machine" of local and polis-wide governance, and by reflecting on the practice of his fellows citizens that an Athenian was educated in the core values of the democratic community. And it was by participation in political practice that he came to grasp the meaning of historical legacies and to reproduce the revolutionary capacity of his community over time. The distinctive practice-centered Athenian approach to civic education is one important way in which the Athenian polis diverged from the "standard polis" imagined by many political theorists, ancient and modern.

This chapter, which originally appeared in a collection of articles on education in Greek and Roman antiquity, returns to two speeches, by Pericles (as reported by Thucydides) and Demosthenes (Against Meidias), *that also figure in other chapters, in order to see how these by-now-familiar texts participate in a debate between the democratic political system and its critics.* This essay benefited from conversations and a working relationship with Brook Manville (see Manville 1997 on "both/and" thinking in Pericles' funeral oration). Recent and important work on civic education includes Allen 2004, Balot 2004, Lape 2004, and Poulakos and Depew 2004.*

• • •

CIVIC EDUCATION AIMS AT TEACHING the citizen how he ought to behave and how he ought to expect others to behave towards him—in contemporary parlance what his "rights" and his "duties" amount to in principle and in practice. My argument runs as follows.

I want to claim first that strongly democratic regimes (like Athens) are confronted with a civic education dilemma in that democratic citizens must learn both to "think alike" and to "think differently." On the one hand, they must be taught to agree to carry out their civic lives according to a set of more or less clearly articulated general principles even while recognizing that consistently adhering to these principles may require a high level of personal sacrifice. On the other, democratic citizens must also retain the capacity to challenge accepted conventions—or at least to listen attentively to those who do so. The dichotomy between conformity to established norms and respect for genuinely original thinking renders it difficult to imagine the design of a formal curriculum of democratic civic education. How is it possible systematically to teach individuals to be good democratic citizens in both senses: to be consensual and dissident at once and in turn?

My second point is that the democratic Athenian polis regarded education in democratic values as extremely important to social and political flourishing, and especially as a counterweight to the "standard" reciprocal and competitive values that characterized Greek aristocratic culture. But the Athenians did not establish a formal set of institutions designed to teach citizens about their rights and duties until the reform of the *ephēbeia* in the later fourth century B.C. Rather, as Yun Lee Too suggests (Too 2001a), the Athenians expected that governmental and legal institutions, along with the public discourse characteristic of the democratic polity, would offer an adequate instruction in civic values.

* This essay was first published in Yun Lee Too, ed., *Education in Greek and Roman Antiquity.* (Leiden: E. J. Brill, 2001), 273–305. Reprinted with permission of E. J. Brill.

Next, I hope to show that intellectual critics of the democracy (my primary example will be Plato) shared with the democrats a conviction that "standard (aristocratic) Greek values" were misconceived and that education of citizens was necessary if superior alternative values were to be promoted. But, as Andrea Nightingale suggests (Nightingale 2001), Athenian intellectual critics of democracy regarded the relatively informal democratic Athenian approach to civic education as fundamentally inadequate. Athenian critics of democracy devised theoretical models of formal educational institutions designed to teach each resident of the polis to act in ways that were appropriate to his or her station—that station to be determined by his or her moral capacities. Curricular models designed to reflect and reinforce a moral hierarchy were (implicitly or explicitly) offered as alternatives to the egalitarian Athenian approach, which sought to teach the same values to each citizen, without regard to his particular moral capacity. Critical approaches to education were concerned with producing consistently ethical behavior that would support a unitary conception of "the good." From this moral perspective, the very existence of citizens who might think both "alike" and "differently" was an affront. It was taken by critical writers as symptomatic of democracy's incoherent commitment to making unequals into equals and to doing so under the banner of freedom-as-license.

Finally, I hope to bring the arguments developed by Too and Nightingale into a dialectical relationship by arguing that there was a real debate between the democracy and its critics over the question of civic education, and that this debate was ultimately a productive one: it led to improvements in the classical Athenian democratic polity, and it can help us to think more seriously about the problem of civic education in our own, decidedly postclassical, societies.

Value-Consensus versus Free Speech

Athenian democracy was intimately associated with "public voice"—with the capacity and the willingness of citizens to speak up about public concerns and to do so in public. The practice of democracy assumed that citizens had a capacity to reason together, in public (as well as in private), via frank speech, and that the results of those deliberations would (in general and over time) conduce to the common good. Deliberating meant listening as well as speaking; accepting good arguments as well as making them.[1] As Aristotle suggests (*Politics* 1281a40–b10, 1286a24–31, in the so-called summation argument), democratic judgments may be superior

---

[1] Deliberative practice: Gutmann and Thompson 1996. Frank speech (as a translation for *parrhēsia*): Monoson 2000.

to those made in oligarchies or tyrannies because judgments made in democratic assemblies aggregate the perceptions of many diverse people. The understanding of a collectivity can be superior to that of each of its parts because of the tendency of open democratic deliberations to draw upon the insight of many individuals, each with his own distinctive point of view. Thus it was not only the *principle* of freedom of speech (as a defense of negative freedoms) but also the constant and positive *exercise* of free speech (in deliberations about the common good) by persons with diverse ideas that was essential for the flourishing of the democracy (see chapter 2).[2] If all those within the citizen body think and were to say just the same thing about the same issues, then public deliberation would be of no substantial benefit in that there would be no testing for better arguments and no meaningful aggregation of multiple viewpoints. In this case the view of the collective whole is no better than the view of any individual, and so practicing democracy becomes a waste of time.

Yet if multiplicity of viewpoints is a precondition for the effective practice of democratic deliberation, it is equally true that Athens could not operate without some agreed-upon postulates and common ground rules. A democratic society centered on deliberative decision making is dependent on shared assumptions, since there can be no independent way for citizens to judge the relative worth of arguments that arise from radically different postulates. And so it is not surprising to find that Athenian democracy did indeed assume that citizens would ordinarily share certain premises: in addition to a commitment to freedom of speech, key Athenian assumptions included the equality of citizens' potential political worth, and the importance of preserving the personal security of each individual against outrageous treatment by powerful individuals or syndicates (see chapter 5). Any argument made in an Athenian deliberative assembly that included among its premises the fundamental inequality of individuals or the irrelevance of protecting weaker citizens against outrage was unlikely to gain support.

If some consensus about basic values was essential to democratic deliberation, too much consensus would preclude innovative responses to changes in the external (foreign policy) or internal (social, cultural, political) environment. Athens confronted the omnipresent danger that its governing assumptions would become too elaborate, too entrenched, too fully "naturalized"; this would inevitably limit the society's capacity for making best use of genuinely original thinking and thus would constrict its capacity to respond creatively to emerging opportunities and challenges. The tension between the need to foster heterogeneous viewpoints

---

[2] Summation argument: Keyt, "Aristotle's Theory of Distributive Justice," 238–78, in Miller and Keyt 1991; cf. Ober 1998, 319–26.

and homogeneous premises, and the impossibility of ever definitively fixing the "right" place to draw the line between diversity and sameness, sets up a dilemma that lay at the heart of Athenian civic education. The disinclination to resolve that dilemma animated Athenian democratic culture.[3] Democracy could not flourish at Athens (or, I think, elsewhere) without social critics—any more than vocal critics could flourish in a society lacking democracy's core commitment to free speech. But how might future citizens be taught to respond appropriately (speaking and listening at appropriate times in public fora, voting as assemblymen for better rather than worse policies, judging well as jurors or executing policy as lotteried magistrates in ways that were more rather than less just) within the ambiguous conceptual terrain laid out by that necessarily unresolved dilemma?

A vibrant democracy depends on the efforts, not only of citizen advocates dedicated to promoting its continued existence, but also of citizen dissidents who advocate its revision or even its replacement.[4] Yet establishing and maintaining a dialogue between the consensus that guided the democracy at any given point in time and its critics is no simple thing. To the extent that critics reject the currently operative value-assumptions that govern democratic discourse, they will not gain a hearing in deliberative assemblies. And so the dialogue between the democracy and its critics could not be carried on according to ordinary principles of democratic public debate. Indeed, it is at first glance difficult to see how such a dialogue could have taken place at all: the most important critical voices often belonged to those with no expressed interest in improving the existing regime, and the democracy never acknowledged, in any explicit or officially sanctioned way, that its critics were anything but pests. Returning to civic education: teaching tolerance for pests might be possible, but that was not enough. How could an educational system teach someone when it made sense to be attentive to pests and when it was best to ignore them?

I would like to suggest, first, that there actually *was* a dialogue between Athenian democracy and its critics, in that each side did address a common set of concerns and did attend to the arguments (explicit and implicit) made by the other side; and, next, that the dialogue, especially as it was carried out in the fourth century B.C., did in fact remain, on the whole, a fruitful one, in that critical speech remained free and the democracy was bettered thereby. One key part of that dialogue centered on the

[3] Conflict between difference and sameness as core features of Athenian political thought: Euben 1990.

[4] Cf. Walzer 1988, for the distinction between valuable "internal" and dangerous "external" modern critics of democracy. I do not think that this distinction holds for the Athenian experience, at least in the fourth century B.C.

education of citizens. The issue of education was particularly salient for Athenian democracy and its critics in that it necessarily asks what premises should be common to the members of a political community, whose responsibility it should be to teach those common premises, and in what institutional framework they should be taught. On the whole, those who claimed to speak for the Athenian democracy contended that an adequate civic education emerged from democratic processes, from "working the machine" of democratic government. The critics of democracy, for their part, contended that process alone was inadequate, that without a special system of education, devised and run by experts, the diversity of viewpoints among citizens would inevitably lead to catastrophic civil conflict.

Socrates versus Meletus

I begin my story about the Athenian debate over civic education in the middle, at the trial of Socrates in 399 B.C.—a pregnant moment at which the dialogue between democracy and its critics might seem to have broken down, and in a way that must be particularly disturbing to anyone concerned with free speech and the status of the dissident citizen in a democratic polity. In a well-known passage from Plato's *Apology* (24c–25c), Socrates seeks to demonstrate by cross-examination that his accuser, Meletus, has given no serious thought to the question of the education of the youth of Athens. Prompted by Socrates, Meletus readily asserts that it is "most important" that "the youth be the best possible." Socrates then demands that Meletus declare precisely *who* improves the youth. Repeatedly nudged along by his interrogator, Meletus replies with the following list of "improvers": the state laws (*nomoi*); the body of potential jurors (i.e., 6,000 registered *dikastai*); those who voluntarily attend law courts (presumably referring to "bystanders" [*periestēkotes*]); the 500 members of the Council (*bouleutai*); and the Assemblymen (*ekklēsiastai*: potentially all citizens in good standing). And so, in short, "all of the Athenians"—except Socrates. Socrates then proceeds to show why this is a silly sort of answer, claiming, on the analogy of horse training, that the capacity to improve any given creature is limited to "one person" or to "a few." By contrast, when "the many" associate with creatures in an attempt to improve them, they invariably end up by corrupting them. And so, "although it would be a great happiness for the youth if one person alone corrupted them, while the others benefit them, in fact, Meletus, you have sufficiently displayed that you never yet gave any thought to the youth."

It is obviously impossible to say just how a real Athenian jury might have responded to this interchange between Meletus and Plato's

Socrates.[5] But I suppose that most jurors would have readily agreed with Meletus' assertion that the improvement of the youth was indeed a matter of utmost importance, and with his attempt to identify the institutional bodies that benefited the youth of Athens. Conversely I think that Athenian jurors would have been put off by Socrates' equine analogy, which sought to show that the efforts of "the many" to educate the youth must necessarily lead instead to their corruption, and that only "the one" or "the few" were possible candidates for true educators.

Reduced to its basics, Meletus's list of "improvers" comes down to a claim that "it is first the laws and public institutions of the polis, and then those who participate in their use, who educate and thereby improve the youth of Athens." Such claims would not have rung odd in the ears of an experienced Athenian juror. Other litigants in preserved Athenian courtroom orations make similar and explicit claims about the important educational role played by decision-making bodies in the democratic state. Aeschines (3.246) argued to an Athenian jury in 330 B.C. that the wrestling grounds (*palaistrai*), formal educational institutions (*didaskaleia*), and poetry (*mousikē*) do not, in and of themselves, adequately educate (*paideuei*) the youth of the polis. More important, claimed Aeschines, was the educational function of the decisions of democratic assemblies (*ta dēmosia kērugmata*). And in the same year the orator Lycurgus (1.10) opined that the jurors he was addressing knew perfectly well (*eu iste*) that their votes to condemn the defendant would not only serve the momentary purpose of punishing a wrongdoer, but would be an incentive to the youth (*neoteroi*) to pursue the path of civic virtue. He asserted that there were two primary elements involved in the education of the young (*ta paideuonta tous neous*)—the punishment of wrongdoers and the rewards granted to honorable men (*andres agathoi*). The youth, beholding these two alternatives (i.e., the stick of punishment and the carrot of reward), would turn away from wrongdoing out of fear, and be attracted to right behavior out of a desire for good reputation (*doxa*). Examples could be multiplied, but the basic point is clear enough: Meletus' opinion on the subject of the role of Athenian democratic institutions in the moral education of the Athenian citizenry was not idiosyncratic nor should it be regarded as a "straw-man" fabrication on the part of the author of the *Apology*.[6] Rather it was a reflection of a core ideological conviction, openly celebrated by public speakers and presumably cherished by ordinary Athenians, regarding

[5] The actual historicity of the exchange is not important to the argument I am developing; the point is that Plato's Socrates elicits answers which an ordinary, nonphilosophical Athenian might be expected to give.

[6] Ober 1989, 160–63, for other examples.

the values of the democratic state and the educational mission of democratic institutions.

The sort of education that Plato's Socrates, Meletus, and the Athenian litigants whose courtroom discourse is preserved in the oratorical corpus had in mind was not instruction in arts and letters per se. Rather, they all referred to the general area I have been calling "civic education": public morality, civic virtue, and normative ethics. What did Meletus and his (fellow nonphilosophical) Athenians suppose that democratic civic education amounted to? What political and ethical values were taught by the jurors and other educators cited by Meletus? And can we be any more precise about the institutional loci of Athenian civic education?

RIGHTS AND DUTIES

I would like to claim that there was in fact a quite clear Athenian ethical code and that it was indeed taught in Athens' legal and governmental institutions, by Athenian jurors, councilors, assemblymen, and so on. The code that emerged from Athenian political and legal practices embraced a strong sense of consequentialist duties—that is, a responsibility to sacrifice individual interests, when called upon, to promote the greater good of the whole. The Athenian conception of the citizen's duty to participate with his fellows in furthering the public good was implicit in (inter alia):

- Mandatory military service and (for the well-to-do) mandatory payment of taxes and liturgies
- A Solonian law enabling a voluntary prosecutor to bring legal charges against a malefactor on behalf of an injured third party
- Incentives to public service: The state made it possible for every citizen to participate in all major deliberative assemblies, and in various magistracies, through pay for service on juries, and (by the end of the fifth century) in the citizen Assembly. Ordinary citizens, even those without a polis-wide reputation, were encouraged to serve as magistrates through the mechanism of filling most state magistracies by lot.
- Disincentives to the avoidance of public service: The most obvious of these was the ruddle-dipped rope that was used to clear the Agora during meetings of the Assembly—citizens marked with the red dye of the rope (i.e., those who continued to hang about the Agora rather than attending the assembly) were subject to fines.
- Promotion of self-sacrifice and euergetism through public commemorations (notably honorific inscriptions and the rituals associated with state funerals for the war dead)

- Social sanctions upon selfish behavior. These are most obviously manifest in the discourse of the lawcourts, where opponents were typically castigated for a failure to perform an expected level of public duties.[7]

The Athenian ethical focus on duty and public responsibility was counterbalanced by a strong commitment to deontological immunities—that is, to a general right of noninterference that was manifest in (inter alia):

- The (possibly Solonian) law forbidding *hubris*: It was forbidden to "outrage" anyone—man or woman, free or slave, adult or child. This law reflects a concern with ensuring the integrity of the body and the personal dignity of each Athenian
- The oath taken by the Athenian magistrate upon taking up his office, promising that he would not use his public authority to arbitrarily redistribute private property
- The basic law restricting the passage of laws against individuals (i.e., all laws must ordinarily be generally applicable to all Athenians); the key exception was publicly enacted honors for individuals
- The core Athenian commitment, reiterated time and again by public speakers, to maintaining the freedom, political and legal equality, and security of the individual citizen[8]

Finally, Athenian duties and rights were sustained by a highly robust conception of personal accountability. Among the institutions ensuring accountability were:

- The Solonian law allowing the indictment before the people of a magistrate on grounds of misuse of power
- Formal procedures for the preliminary scrutiny (*dokimasia*) and final financial accounting (*euthuna*) for magistrates
- The procedures of *graphē paranomōn* and *graphē nomōn mē epitēdeiōn theinai*, whereby the proposer of a decree in the Assembly or a law to the *nomothetai* could be indicted for having proposed a measure inimicable to the established values of the Athenians
- the risk assumed by the prosecutor in public legal actions (e.g., the disabilities suffered if he were to gain less than one-fifth of the votes cast)[9]

Athenian public culture (both institutions and discourse) "taught" each Athenian the extent of his duties and rights, and how they were to be kept

[7] Fuller discussion of these relatively well-known features of Athenian public life can be found in Ober 1989; Hansen 1991.

[8] For a fuller discussion of Athenian rights (or "quasirights"), see chapter 5, above.

[9] In addition to the works cited in note 7, above, see Todd 1993; Hansen 1975; Roberts 1982.

in balance. That ethical code never became rigid or dogmatic because the public practices through which young Athenians learned democratic ethics tended to evolve over time, in part as a result of a fruitful engagement with critical voices. One reason that the engagement *was* ultimately productive is that there *was* some common ground between democratic Athenians and critical philosophers, at least in a negative sense: they shared a refusal to accept, in any unmediated way, the values that are ordinarily thought of (by modern classicists and political theorists) as constituting "standard" Greek ethics.

STANDARD GREEK ETHICS VERSUS DEMOCRATIC-CRITICAL ETHICS

The standard ethical code exemplified by much of the preserved canon of Greek literary culture may be roughly summed up as reciprocal and agonistic, focusing on conjoined values of "tit-for-tat reciprocity" and "zero-sum competition." Thus, the standard ethical code enjoined a Greek first to seek to help his friends (those who had done him good) and then to harm (or at least avoid helping) his enemies (those who had done him wrong). Greek standards of reciprocity demanded that help and hurt received from others be paid back in a measure that was at least equal, and preferably greater than, the help or hurt received. Next, the standard code enjoined the Greek to seek to gain preeminence over his rivals in an ongoing round of agonistic contests. In these manifold contests, which ranged from drinking games at symposia, to interfamily feuds, to warfare between states the gain by the victor was more or less directly proportionate to the loss on the part of the loser(s). It is obviously impossible to say whether or not most classical Greeks, across all social categories, would subscribe to this standard ethical code. But it is, I believe, certainly true that this code, or something very much like it, characterized a variety of interpersonal relations and educational institutions favored by an influential and vocal segment of elite Greek society. It is perhaps not too much to say that insofar as Greek literary culture was didactic in purpose, it focused on teaching the aristocrat (and especially the young aristocrat) to value reciprocal and competitive ideals. Moreover, the reciprocity-competition matrix defined a substantial part of relations between Greek states. In the generally anarchic Greek international environment, the "standard code" remained largely unchallenged.[10]

---

[10] Standard Greek ethics: Dover 1974; Blundell 1989; D. Cohen 1995; Allen 2000b, 59–65. Anarchic Greek international scene: Lebow and Strauss (1991). It is worth noting that the "standard code" was potentially contradictory, in that "helping a friend" might come into conflict with seeking personal victory.

It has, however, been rightly noted that the standard reciprocal, agonistic code of ethics was counterbalanced, at least in certain spheres of Greek life, by a set of ethical norms which might be called "cooperative values." These focused on the virtuousness of seeking a common good (common to the polis, the demos, or some relatively substantial subset of polis or demos) through moderation of appetite, restraint on self-aggrandizement, and the willing contribution of one's personal fortune, one's time, and even one's own life. These cooperative values are especially associated with the public realm, with the intra-polis and explicitly political "world of the citizen." And they seem to be especially to the fore in the public discourse of the democratic polis. As Meletus' response to Socrates suggests, practices related to the public space of citizenship were seen as having a meliorative role in educating each member of society, and especially subadult "potential citizen" males in cooperative values. That civic education took cognizance of the standard code of reciprocal and agonistic ethics, but sought to regulate and delimit its operative sphere.[11]

Within the Greek world, cooperative values were certainly not unique to democracies. The concern with educating the youth in cooperative values through public institutions may well be a general feature of the Greek polis: the Spartan *agōgē* (upbringing) can be seen as one, remarkable and extreme, manifestation of this general concern in a nondemocratic context. The *agōgē* was a formal institution, aimed at teaching Spartan youths aged seven to twenty how to live and fight as warrior-citizens. The Spartan youths were reared apart from the rest of society, and the *agōgē* was marked off from (although congruent with) the rest of Sparta's public institutions. The goal of this education was to teach each Spartan to conform precisely to the military ethos that defined Spartan society—to serve as a fully cooperative soldier, taking and giving commands as befit his station, and never shrinking back or advancing beyond his assigned place in the ranks. The presumption was that having graduated from the rigorous civic and physical training of the *agōgē*, the young Spartan was now fit to take up his public role as a hoplite in the phalanx and as a citizen in the Spartan assembly. The *agōgē* taught the young Spartan to collectivize the values implicit in the standard code: the friends he would seek to help and the enemies he would harm were the friends and enemies of the Spartan state. Enemies were internal as well as external: they included, especially, the subject helot population whose labor provided the warrior class with the leisure to concentrate

---

[11] The polis's focus on the importance of cooperative behavior in the service of the collectivity may be traced back to the "*metrios* values" that emerged in the archaic period; for a survey, see Morris 1996. Cooperative values in Athens: Herman 1993, 1994, 1995.

primarily upon military training. The individual warrior might seek to gain a reputation for excellence, but that reputation was gained not by standing out from the crowd, but by being an exemplary "Similar" (*homoios*).[12]

In Athens, as the Socrates-Meletus exchange suggests, the education of the citizen in cooperative values was quite different; there was no *agōgē* or other formal system of state-supported civic education (at least until the reform of the *ephēbeia* in the mid 330s, about which see below). In Athens public institutions ostensibly designed to achieve other ends (justice, public policy) carried an additional burden of educating the young Athenians in civic values. Plato's Meletus and actual Athenian litigants claimed that ordinary public institutions were in fact well suited to educating the youth, at least so long as those citizens who manned the institutions were fully cognizant of their role as educators, took their duties seriously, and kept a watchful eye upon the lessons being taught by the decisions they made. Plato's Socrates and actual philosophers scoffed at the notion that this sort of informal approach could perform the arduous task of ethical training.

A major burden of Athenian civic education was offering an attractive alternative to the problematic values exemplified by the standard ethical code. The influence of those traditional values could never be obliterated, nor would it have been socially desirable to do so. The standard code remained operative within aristocratic Athenian society and was manifest in various aspects of elite private education and behavior.[13] Close regulation of public behavior potentially informed by the reciprocal and agonistic code was imperative to the survival of Athenian democratic government. It would not do for an Athenian who regarded himself as superior to his fellows by dint of, for example, his great wealth to seek to assert his superiority over those of his fellow citizens whom he regarded as his inferiors and class enemies. For the democracy to flourish, the claims of equality among citizens must ordinarily prevail. Overt manifestations of the standard code must normally be restricted to private life, and could be regarded as problematic even within the private sphere.[14] Yet suppression is only one part of the story. Athenian public life depended on the persistence of rightly manifested reciprocal and competitive values—for example, on competitions between speakers in the Assembly to devise and present to their fellows the best policy. The incorporation of reciprocal and agonistic values into an

---

[12] Spartan *agōgē*: Cartledge 1987; Kennell 1995. Spartan "similarity" versus Athenian "equality": Cartledge 1996.

[13] See, for example, Kurke 1999.

[14] For surveys of the mechanisms of Athenian social control, see Hunter 1994; D. Cohen 1991.

overarching framework of cooperative values and their revaluation by the political community was essential to the long-term workability of the Athenian political order.[15]

As I have argued elsewhere (see chapter 5), Athenian democratic culture was predicated on the three closely interrelated political values of equality, freedom, and security. And respect for these values was, consequently, the foundation of the ethical system "taught" by Athens' informal approach to civic education. For the Athenians, equality meant legal and political equality, equal access to justice, equal votes, and an equal option to exercise public speech. Legal and political equality did not entail equal access to material goods, but legal and political equality were sustained by a limited redistribution of material goods (via pay for public service, welfare benefits to the handicapped and orphans, distribution of food at public festivals, and so forth). Freedom meant the independence of the polis from foreign domination, the positive liberty of the citizen to participate in various aspects of governance and public life, and the negative liberty of the individual to do more or less as he wished in his private life. Security meant that the weaker citizen (especially a poor man, one lacking formal education or powerful friends) was in principle immune from being subjected to coercion, to unanswerable physical assault or verbal humiliation by his stronger neighbor, whereas all citizens (and especially wealthy citizens) were protected from certain forms of the arbitrary exercise of magisterial and majority power, especially with regard to private property.[16]

The relationship between the "value triad" and democracy was itself reciprocal: Maintenance of democratic institutions (with their implicitly educational role) and the general hegemony of democratic ideology assured the continued freedom, equality, and security of each individual citizen and of the citizenry as a collectivity. Conversely, it was the consistent tendency of each citizen and the citizenry as a collectivity to act as free, equal, and secure entities that assured the maintenance of the democracy.[17] The issue before us is to understand how these core Athenian political values were supported, explicitly and implicitly, by a code of civic ethics visible in the public language and institutional practices sanctioned and fostered by the democratic polity.

I would suggest that Meletus' response to Socrates did more than proclaim a cultural ideal; it was quite an accurate portrayal of lived social reality. Athenian public practices (notably those listed above) did in fact educate (and indeed improve) the citizens by promoting a code of normative

---

[15] This is the burden of Ober 1989. See also Whitehead 1983, 1993; D. Cohen 1995.

[16] Equality, freedom, security: Ober 1996 and chapter 5; and see also the essays by K. Raaflaub, E. M. Wood, and M. H. Hansen in Ober and Hedrick 1996.

[17] Ober 2000.

ethics that was sufficiently clear and coherent to allow for sociocultural reproduction of patterns of behavior consistent with the freedom, equality, and security of the individual and the community. It was the reliability of this process of sociocultural reproduction via informal civic education that ensured the practical stability of the democracy over time, that allowed democracy to recover from the oligarchic interludes of the late fifth century, and that sustained the democracy through the crises of the Peloponnesian War era and the tumultuous fourth century.[18]

DEMOCRACY'S CRITICS ON CIVIC EDUCATION

Like the demos of Athens, classical political philosophers confronted the problems of what principles might serve to regulate standard reciprocal and agonistic ethics and how to transform those traditional aristocratic values into patterns of conviction and behavior aligned with richer conceptions of justice and the common good.[19] But the philosophical response to this challenge was very different from that of the Athenian democracy. Socrates' criticism of Meletus in Plato's *Apology* sets the stage. In Socrates' argument, because Athens *lacked* a formal system of public education to inculcate excellent values, that is to say a system designed and implemented by competent experts, it followed that no Athenian (except Socrates himself) took any care at all for the improvement of the youth. Or, if "the many" did seek to "train" the youth, they would necessarily end up corrupting them. And thus (given Athenian intransigence to learning the sort of lessons offered by Socrates) the Athenians remained dismally ill-educated.

The putative failure of the democratic state to offer a substantive education in values is an important contextual aspect of various detailed proposals for systems of civic education developed by philosophically minded Athenian writers in the course of the fourth century: for example, by Xenophon (*Memorabilia, Cyropaedia*), Plato (*Republic, Laws*), Isocrates (*Areopagiticus*), and Aristotle (*Politics*). In each case, the philosopher (I am using the term broadly) was concerned with establishing (in theory) a formal educational system that would ensure that experts were responsible for inculcating the youth with the "right" ethical and political values. And in each case that substantive education in values was intended to yield consistently good social outcomes by ensuring that potential citizens

[18] Concept of social reproduction: Gutmann 1999.

[19] Nehamas, "What did Socrates Teach?" in Nehamas 1999, offers an insightful assessment of the first steps in the history of the philosophical confrontation with what I have been calling "standard ethics" (as codified in the teaching of the so-called sophists).

embraced a unitary notion of "the good" and possessed the intellectual capacities and special skills adequate to achieving that unitary good. By contrast, the democratic polis never offered its citizens a unitary conception of the good. Just as the democratic polis refused to assign the task of civic education to a separate educational institution or to educational "experts," it avoided the attempt to instruct citizens about the final ends of human life.

The Athenians were not inclined to create a formal educational system along the lines envisaged either by the Spartans or by the philosophers, not only because they recognized the useful dichotomy between "thinking alike" and "thinking differently" and the educational effectiveness of their own public practices in instructing citizens in that dichotomy, but also because doing so would have had distinctly antidemocratic implications in terms of limiting the freedom of each citizen to identify and pursue somewhat different conceptions of his (individual) good. This is not to say that Athens was self-consciously liberal in a way that would have pleased a strong modern liberal dedicated to the priority of individual choice making in the hierarchy of values (e.g., Isaiah Berlin). But it is to say that despite hegemonic tendencies implicit in democratic political discourse, Athens was (at least potentially) much more open and flexible in allowing for the individual pursuit of happiness than was a Spartan-style education in virtue or the theoretical, philosophical projects that are often identified as the only meaningful examples of Greek civic education.[20]

The philosophical critics of democracy were convinced that political regimes lacking a unitary, well defined, and carefully articulated conception of the good, along with a formal, institutional curriculum for teaching the youth to pursue that unitary good, faced catastrophic problems with social cohesion. The specter of civil war (*stasis*) loomed over fourth-century philosophical projects concerned with civic education: the fear was that citizens who had not been convinced as youths to support a unitary, state-sanctioned conception of the good would too readily fall into violent conflict with their fellows, as competing conceptions of the good were actively promoted and as friends to be helped and enemies to be hurt were variously defined.[21] Diversity among conceptions of the good was regarded as especially problematic in the absence of any final and definitive means to arbitrate amongst diverse goals. That final and definitive means might, in the view of the philosophers, be provided even in

---

[20] At this point my argument seeks to bring Too's (2001b) conception of Athenian "education by law" and Nightingale's (2001) analysis of the complex political-contemplative goals of Platonic and Aristotelian education into a productive relationship through the mediating practices and ideology of Athenian democracy.

[21] Cf. Ober 2000.

subutopian regimes by a detailed and substantive code of law: it is no accident that discussions of civic education and state law are closely intertwined in classical political philosophy (as Too 2001a and Nightingale 2001 have shown in their discussions of Plato's *Crito, Republic, Laws,* and Aristotle's *Politics,* books 7–8).

The Athenian solution to the relationship between law, education, and the "diversity-of-goods problem" was quite different from the solutions proposed by classical philosophers. As Too (2001a) notes, Athenian public speakers frequently and vociferously expressed their respect for the law code; it is hardly surprising that Meletus' first response to Socrates' demand for the names of "improvers of the youth" is simply "the laws." This sort of response presumably came quite naturally to an Athenian: It is mirrored in various forensic speech appeals to "the authoritative laws."[22] And in Plato's *Crito* Socrates imagines the "laws of Athens" themselves as dissuading him from any thought of escaping prison (see chapter 7). They do so in part by reminding Socrates of the reciprocal obligation he owed to the laws on the grounds of the education (*paideia*) they, the laws, had provided for him.[23] But Socrates of the *Apology* does not regard "the laws" as an adequate description of the educators of the youth. He demands that Meletus tell him *who* improved the citizens: "I am not asking this, best of men, but rather what human being is it who knows first of all this very thing, the laws?" (24e).

Socrates' refusal to accept Meletus' first answer ("the laws") is, of course, imperative to the development of his argument dismantling the case against himself as a solitary corrupter of youth. But it also points to the fact that "the laws of Athens," in and of themselves, were indeed inadequate either to educate the youth of Athens in civic values or to decide between disputes about diverse goods. This inadequacy is a product of the origins and nature of the Athenian law code. Unlike many other ancient legal systems, which assumed a suprahuman authorship for fundamental law, and then developed from that foundation a detailed body of substantive law, the Athenians knew that their law was the product of fallible human activity. Their law code was relatively simple and highly procedural. In the absence of an unassailable foundation and a detailed code of substantive law, it was legal and governmental processes—the "working of the machine" of law and government—that (contingently) settled disputes about the good and educated future citizens. The Athenians expected that citizens would be educated, not just by the spirit or the wording of the law, but by engaging in (and observing others engaging in)

---

[22] Authoritative laws: Hansen 1991, 173–74.

[23] Socrates' obligation to Athenian laws in the *Crito*: see Kraut 1984, Ober 1998, 179–83; and chapter 7, below. Cf. Nightingale 2001, 151–54, for the special form of reciprocity in Plato's *Republic*.

political and legal processes: by serving as jurors, magistrates, assembly-men, and so on. The Athenians assumed, I believe rightly, that a clear code of ethics arose not only from a public discourse centered on freedom, equality, and security, but also from the logic inherent in fair and consistent public practices. And they supposed that "practices in use" could be effective educators.

If the argument I have developed above is along the right lines, we should expect a distinction to be drawn (at least implicitly) by the classical philosophers between a "proper" system of education, with a formal curriculum and a particular institutional locus within society, and an informal Athenian education by everyday discourse and practice. In a memorable passage in the *Republic*, Plato directly addresses the potential of democratic institutions and discursive practices to miseducate young people, even those with a "naturally" philosophical character. Although Plato's Socrates does not state explicitly that he is referring to Athens in this passage, it is clearly Athens that lies behind his description. Socrates warns his interlocutor, Adeimantus, against supposing, as do the many, that it is certain private educators (*sophistai idiōtikoi*) who corrupt the youth (492a). Socrates is referring here, of course, to the so-called sophists, who offered to teach young Athenians (and especially the aristocrats who could pay their fees) a particularly strong and naturalized version of what I have been calling "standard ethics," along with the practical techniques (especially rhetoric) for securing victory over their rivals. Rather, says Socrates, it is "the many," those who accuse the private teachers, who are themselves the "great sophists" who educate most completely and mold the young and the old, men and women, making them just as they want them to be (492a–b). Adeimantus, who imagines education to be a formal affair with a particular social locus, wonders when it is that this education by the many takes place. Socrates emphasizes the omnipresence of democratic education, replying that it is

> when many gathered together sit down in assemblies, courts, theaters, army camps, or any other common meeting of the multitude (*plēthos*), and, with a great deal of uproar (*thorubos*), excessively blame some of the things said or done and just as excessively praise others, shouting and clapping; and, besides, the rocks and the very place that surrounds them echo and redouble the uproar of blame and praise. Now in such circumstances, as the saying goes, what do you suppose is the state of the young man's heart? Or what kind of private education will hold out for him and not be swept away by such blame and praise and go, borne by the flood, wherever it's headed so that he'll say the same things are noble and shameful as they do, practice what they practice, and be such as they are? (*Republic* 492b–c)

Socrates goes on to explain that the education of the young carried on in public assemblies is reinforced by legal norms and practices, since he who is not persuaded by the clamor of public meetings to conform to a demotic code of behavior is disciplined though disenfranchisement, fines, and death. Such education is, in Plato's view, totalizing and hegemonic: No mere sophist or private arguments (*idiōtikoi logoi*) can hope to prevail (*kratēsein*) against these forces. And so no human *ēthos*, however educated, can, or has, or shall prevail against this sort of *paideia* (492d–e).

In light of the argument that I have been developing here, someone might suppose that Socrates of the *Republic* is *contrasting* democratic co-operative values with the version of standard ethics taught by the sophists. But this is hardly the case: for Socrates of the *Republic*, democratic values and the techniques taught by the sophists are cut from the same cloth. He claims that democratic education-by-practice is so effective that the so-called sophists themselves, who are generally thought to be the rivals of the many, in fact teach nothing but the opinions (*dogmata*) of the many— the very things that the many proclaim (*doxazousin*) when they are gathered together in assembly.

Socrates' lesson equating democratic values and sophistic technique is reinforced by a vivid metaphor: The sophists call what they teach wisdom (*sophia*). But it is nothing more than the "wisdom" that is learned and might be transmitted by the keeper of a great and ferocious beast. The keeper is quickly trained to cater to the beast's needs, its informal bellowing, and its response to different sorts of speech. In the end he will learn to provide the beast with whatever it wants. Having been well trained, the keeper, although self-evidently the beast's servant, then claims to have mastered (and to be able to teach others) the secrets of beast-management (493a–b). Moreover, Socrates concludes, the basic point can be generalized: the painter, poet, and politician—like the sophist—merely learns to accommodate himself to the angers and pleasures of "the many and various foregathered folk"; they make the many their masters, and of necessity produce what the many praise (493c–d).

This is, of course, a hostile description of democratic civic education, meant first to conflate democratic values with sophistic rhetorical techniques and then to draw a sharp contrast between the casual but all-pervasive democratic practice and the carefully thought-through educational regime that trains the Guardians and leads to the production of philosophers in Callipolis. I certainly do not think that Plato is correct to make an easy association of sophism with democratic values. But stripped of its rhetorical trappings, Plato's description of the implicit *processes* of education in the democratic city is not so far off the mark. Nor is it very far from what most ordinary Athenians thought should and did take place in the public space of the polis. Plato asserts, in essence, that the normative claims implicit in Athenian political and legal institutions (including accepted-sanctioned forms of public discourse) constitute and teach the ethical system which arises from and reproduces over time the prevailing political and social structure. Thus, once again, it is the "working of the machine" that is said to educate the citizens in ethical values and that education-through-practice is regarded as effective in reproducing citizens obedient to a distinctive ethical code. Put in more positive evaluative terms, we may say that the practice of democracy is a form of civic education, and it is the success of Athenian civic education that sustained the democratic system over time, provided its resilience, and drove out (or incorporated) competing ethical systems.[24]

DEMOCRATIC RESPONSES TO THE CRITICAL CHALLENGE

Plato's critical account of democratic education focuses our attention on a key aspect of Athenian civic education: ethical claims arise not only from substantive (content) values—for example, the values explicitly asserted in the oath of the ephebes—or in judgments of juries on particular cases, but also from accepted forms of public discourse, and finally, pervasively and importantly, from what we may call "process values" or the "implicit ethics of procedure." Among the educative processes of the democracy, as Plato quite rightly suggests, are the rules and customary practices governing deliberative and judicial assemblies: the Council of 500, the Ecclesia, and the People's courts. But he also suggests (and again rightly) that the education of democratic citizens took place in military venues: in the army camps. And, we might add, on the triremes.[25] And in the formal gatherings of Athenians at religious festivals. And during informal meetings in the civic space of the Agora.[26] Plato seems to me tendentiously wrong to claim that the values taught in each of these venues arise from nothing more than the unexamined and ill-informed opinions of "the mob." In his account, democratic civic education becomes ideological in the worst sense of the term: seeking to enforce conformity with a crude form of "standard" ethics, the lowest common denominator of popular prejudices. I would maintain, quite to the contrary, that Athenian institutions taught a complex lesson that integrated cooperative with reciprocal-agonistic values, and moreover that those educating institutions themselves changed in response to social criticism. If we approach each of the various

---

[24] For modern analogies, see Macedo 1998, 2000.

[25] Educational values of hoplite and trireme service: Hanson 1996; Strauss 1996.

[26] Religious festivals: see essays by Arnaoutoglou and Millett in Cartledge, Millett, and van Reden 1998.

Athenian "civic-educational" venues historically, it is possible to trace institutional changes that may reasonably be linked to the capacity of the democratic order to respond (at whatever remove, and in terms that remained fundamentally egalitarian) to concerns raised by democracy's critics.

Particularly striking examples (each of which has been analyzed in detail in recent scholarship) of democratic reforms enacted from the late fifth through the mid-fourth centuries B.C. include:

- The establishment, beginning in the late fifth century, of a formal law code (answering the charge that democratic law was internally inconsistent)
- Formalized processes in the late fifth, and continuing into the fourth, century, for distinguishing processes of lawmaking from the everyday establishment of state policymaking through decrees of the Assembly (responding to the claim that democratic lawmaking in the Assembly was arbitrary and driven by momentary passions)
- Mid-fourth-century reforms in the method of military recruitment (an attempt to address issues of fairness in respect to consequentialist duties potentially demanding self-sacrifice)
- Establishment (beginning in the 350s B.C.) of financial magistracies which gave more scope for expert management of state funds (a move to allow expertise to have a more substantial role in the processes of governance)
- The elaboration (in the mid-330s B.C.) of the formal training of eighteen- and nineteen-year-old citizen soldiers in the *ephēbeia* (discussed in more detail below: an explicitly "educational" reform answering the charge that democratic education lacked substance)[27]

In no case is it possible to claim that there was a *direct* relationship between dissident criticism and democratic reform. But I think that there is a close enough match between "critical challenges" and "democratic reforms" to justify the assumption that (at a remove) the democracy acknowledged that valid concerns had been raised by its critics. Moreover it responded, in measured and responsible ways (if not in ways that the critics would regard as satisfactory), to those concerns.

[27] Detailed list of changes: Rhodes 1979–80; update in Rhodes, "Judicial Procedures in Fourth-Century Athens," 303–19, in Eder 1995. I differ from Rhodes's conclusion that these innovations represented some sort of falling off from the fullest flower of radical democracy; it seems to me that they are each fully consistent with and furthered core democratic principles, especially the democratic commitment to constant innovation. Allen 2000b, 44–45, argues, on the basis of democratic limitations on the punishment powers of civil and military magistrates, that "[i]t was in the fourth century that Athens was truly a radical democracy."

So far I have made four main points about the Athenian debate over civic education:

1. Ordinary citizens of democratic Athens and Athenian intellectuals critical of democracy agreed in rejecting some aspects of the "standard" reciprocal-agonistic ethical code but had quite different views about the values that should be established in its place, and how and by whom those alternative values should be taught
2. Because of democratic dependence on diversity of viewpoints for effective deliberations, an engagement with critical discussions of (for example) civic education was essential to the capacity of the democracy to adapt to changing circumstances
3. The engagement between democracy and its critics contributed to significant institutional innovations
4. Institutional innovations, even those not obviously to do with education, were directly relevant to the question of Athenian civic education because Athenian civic education operated through public practices

In sum, the dialogue that took place between democracy and its critics meant that the Athenians organized their public practices somewhat differently (and somewhat better) and the ethical lessons learned by the Athenian youth via public practices therefore changed for the better over time. The question remains: where and how did the salutary engagement between the democratic many and the critics of democracy take place, given that critics did not deliberate in public assemblies?

In the passage cited above from the *Republic*, Plato associates the educational public processes of the democratic polis with theatrical and oratorical discourse. I do not think that he was wrong to do so. The central tenets of the civic ethics taught to each Athenian by the procedural rules of Athenian public institutions were (more or less clearly) formulated and contested in the texts of plays presented in the Athenian theater and in preserved Athenian orations. But Plato *is* wrong, I think, when he claims that the discourse of the theater and the civic assemblies was no more than a distillation of the lowest common denominator of demotic sensibilities, nothing but the articulation of the "great beast's bellowings." Instead, I would suggest that dramatic and oratorical discourse were primary sites at which contrasting voices advocating the values currently pertaining among the democratic majority and those promoted by its critics were brought together and articulated in an idiom that made the dialogue between them usefully accessible to the citizenry.

Plays and major speeches were written by playwrights and orators who necessarily bridged the gap between critical and democratic discourse: Aristophanes was famously featured by Plato (in the *Symposium*) as a participant in a "critical-intellectual" conversation and yet he obviously had to remain closely in touch with democratic sensibilities if he hoped to win prizes at the dramatic contests. The same familiarity with both contexts—"aristocratic, critical, and intellectual," on the one hand, and "demotic, democratic, and ordinary," on the other—can be assumed for Athens' highly-educated, elite public orators.[28] My point, then, is that Athenian playwrights and orators were familiar with, and indeed may have participated in, discussions within what I have elsewhere character- ized as Athens' "critical community."[29] And that familiarity sometimes led them to incorporate critical notions into plays and speeches presented to the Athenian public.

If this line of thought is correct, then at least some passages in Athen- ian plays and public speeches will have been informed by critical argu- ments: plays and speeches served as public "carriers" for critical ideas developed by dissident thinkers. As noted above, the original authors of those critical ideas may not have had any conscious intention of improv- ing democracy.[30] Yet I would suggest that whatever their original inten- tions, the force of critical ideas was transformed by the shift in context. When critical thinking was carried beyond "private" discussions among intellectual elites into the deliberative public arena, it became a resource for the betterment of the democracy. When ordinary Athenians attended plays and listened to public speakers, they were indirectly exposed to the thinking of critical intellectuals, but that thinking was reconfigured to suit democratic purposes. In the process of reconfiguration, critical thought became a valuable "heterogeneous" resource, one that helped to coun- terbalance the potentially deadening tendency of democratic ideology to seek a homogeneous consensus.

The civic focus and critical content of much Athenian drama is by now fairly well known and has been discussed in a wide array of specialty studies.[31] But the idea that public rhetoric could manifest a critical (as well as a democratic) function has received less attention.[32] I will there- fore conclude this discussion of the debate between the democracy and its critics over civic education by looking at a few passages from two famous speeches delivered before (or at least composed as if for delivery before) Athenian audiences: Thucydides' account of Pericles' Funeral Oration (dramatic date 431–430 B.C.) and Demosthenes' speech 21, *Against Mei- dias* (346 B.C.). In each case, the speaker replies cogently and dialectically

[28] Backgrounds of Athenian political orators: Ober 1989, 112–18.

[29] Critical community: Ober 1998.

[30] Intentions of critics: ibid.

[31] Theater as a critical resource: see Cartledge 1990; Euben 1986; Winkler and Zeitlin 1990; Goldhill and Osborne 1999; Monoson 2000; Allen 2000b; further references in Ober 1998, 50n72.

[32] But see Farrar 1988 on Pericles; Yunis 1996 on Demosthenes.

to searching criticisms, including (at least implicitly) criticism of the democratic reliance on teaching civic values through participative political processes.

The Funeral Oration, given by Thucydides to Pericles in book 2 of his *History*, is today the best known ancient account of Athenian democracy. The speech alludes directly to the relationship between free speech, effective deliberation, and the capacity to aggregate the judgment of a large body of citizens (2.40.2). It presents as clear a snapshot of democratic Athenian ethics as one could ask for: at once consequentialist and deontological, concerned with personal responsibility and with refuting alternative ethical conceptions. Pericles presents his celebration of Athens and its democratic culture in the context of the war against the Spartans; he explicitly juxtaposes Athenian values, learned through voluntary participation in the life of the city with the Spartan alternative, based on a mandatory, standardized system of education. Sparta is the overt critical foil, but rebutting the arguments of such Athenians as might prefer to see Athens embrace Spartan values informs the speech's polemics. Pericles is careful to draw a clear distinction between Athenians, who live their public lives freely and in the open, to the dour and secretive Spartans, whose military efficiency was bought with the coin of endless and laborious practice (2.39.1). Pericles celebrates the Athenian capacity to embrace both thoughtful public deliberation and decisive action, noting that among all other people, deliberation and decisiveness were regarded as antithetical (2.40.3). Pericles' Athenians are committed to equality of public opportunity, which is said to lie at the core of the democratic approach to governance (2.37.1). They are free in public life and they feel no need to keep track of their neighbors' private affairs (2.37.2).

But for all of the distinctiveness he attributes to Athens, Pericles also appropriates what democracy's critics might claim as specifically Spartan virtues, notably the central Spartan value of obedience to the law. Pericles' speech is framed by introductory and concluding appeals to the absolute responsibility of the citizen to obey the law (2.35.1, 3; 2.46.1). Pericles specifically denies that Athenian liberality leads to lawlessness. Quite to the contrary, obedience to written law, magistrates, and unwritten customs is what ultimately provides for the Athenian determination to defend the injured. That is to say, a "Sparta-like" dedication to lawfulness underwrites the quintessential Athenian commitment to the defense of individual immunities (2.37.3; cf. chapter 5). Throughout the speech, Pericles emphasizes that individual self-sacrifice is at once a duty and, for Athenians, a voluntary choice; willingly embracing one's duty to sacrifice is what leads to glory, for the individual and for the polis as a community (e.g., 2.43.1). Finally, the "standard" agonistic and reciprocal code is at once appropriated (2.41.1–3; 2.42.4) and refuted as an adequate stimulus to truly appropriate behavior (2.40.4–5; 2.45.1).

Eighty-five years, much political history, much critical writing, and a number of institutional reforms separate the dramatic date of Pericles' Funeral Oration from that of Demosthenes' speech *Against Meidias*: the democracy had been twice overthrown and twice restored; Plato and Xenophon had flourished, written much, and died; Isocrates was near the end of his career but still very active; and Aristotle was at the height of his powers. The Athenian legal system had been put on a more systematic basis. Like Thucydides' Pericles, Demosthenes emphasizes the essential bastions of democratic culture: the fundamental importance of the freedom, formal equality, and security from outrage of each citizen.[33] But Demosthenes is more explicit than Pericles about the ways in which working the machine of democratic public practices, especially the legal system, maintained those essential qualities.

Demosthenes claims that the primary threat to democratic freedom, equality, and security originates with the agonistic desire of the powerful individual to demonstrate his superiority to all others and in every sphere of life: not only in private relations, but in public. Demosthenes' Meidias bears a striking resemblance to Plato's character Callicles of the *Gorgias*: like Callicles, Meidias is impatient with restraints on his capacity to assert his superiority, restraints that were imposed upon him by the rules and ethical standards established by the democratic many. Plato's Callicles detects something unnatural in this situation. He believes that he has seen through the artificial, deceptive culture established through the assertion of collective power by a mass of those who were individually weak. He is consequently optimistically and arrogantly confident of his own ability to return to what he supposes is a proper "law of nature."[34] Demosthenes wastes no time in trying to establish a counterclaim for the naturalness of the rule of the many. Instead he implicitly accepts the "Calliclean" assumption that the democracy was sustained only by the collective determination of numerous, individually feeble, citizens to maintain a set of conventions that would restrain the natural tendencies of powerful individuals to seek to dominate others. At the center of the formal system of contraints was the Athenian code of law, notably the law forbidding outrage (*hubris*).[35] But one of Demosthenes' major points is that the law in and of itself is insufficient to restrain the behavior of those who rejected the values of freedom, equality, and individual security. Rather, it

[33] Freedom, equality, and security in Demosthenes 21: Ober 1996, chapter 7.
[34] Plato's Callicles: Ober 1998, 197–213.
[35] Athenian law against *hubris*: chapter 5, above.

is the law-abiding behavior of the citizens, and their willingness to "work the machinery" of the law, as voluntary prosecutors and as jurors, that keeps the likes of Meidias and Callicles from successfully flaunting the values espoused by democratic ethics.

In the *Crito*, Plato's Socrates had discussed the relationship between education, law, and appropriate individual behavior, positing (50a–b) that for him to escape from prison after having been convicted would constitute an injury to the polis because the polis could not survive if the laws were without force (see chapter 7). Socrates' position grounds the maintenance of legal authority on an individual's private decision to behave ethically. The basis of the Socratic ethical-legal order is a just contract between the laws and the individual citizen. According to the terms of that contract, Socrates had agreed to abide by the procedural forms of Athenian law and to obey the judgments rendered by the polis (in the form of the decisions of jurors who abide by the procedural rules), even though those judgments might be substantively incorrect and so do him harm. His voluntary obedience was given in exchange for having received from the laws specific goods: his birth (because of the laws regarding marriage), his nurture (*trophē*), and his education (*paideia*). But in the course of the dialogue Socrates had opened the door to an alternative conception of legal authority, noting that "a good deal might be said, especially by a *rhētōr*, on behalf of that law (*nomos*), now to be broken [by the proposed escape], which requires judgments judicially rendered to be authoritative" (50b; see further chapter 7).

Demosthenes, a *rhētōr* in fact, walked through that open doorway in *Against Meidias*, by providing a detailed brief for why the laws must remain authoritative if the dignity of ordinary citizens is to be protected from attacks by powerful, wealthy, clever men. His speech returns time and again to the educational aspect of legal decisions. Demosthenes assumes that the powerful will always desire to demonstrate their superiority in agonistic fashion by harming and shaming the weak. He does not suppose that they would be restrained by any internal concern for abstract justice: the dangerous and powerful are assumed to be proponents of what I have been calling "standard ethics" and they do not regard their ordinary fellow citizens as "friends." Nor are the laws themselves, mere inscribed letters, capable of guaranteeing compliance with democratic ethics. Rather, the appropriate insurance of legal authority and the democratic values promoted by the law is the collective judgment of the citizenry when they are gathered as jurors. Vigorous public punishment of outrageous behavior will serve to teach the many the source of their own power and will intimidate powerful individuals, forcing them into compliance with the will of the many. It is thus the mass of citizens "working the machine," acting as jurors on the initiative of a voluntary prosecutor, that is the collective agent that preserves the authority of law and educates the citizenry in democratic values.[36]

In both speeches briefly considered here, I would suggest that we can hear a debate being carried on in at least three discursive registers: an assertion of a specifically democratic set of ethical assumptions, a critical challenge that seems to threaten those assumptions, and a thoughtful response to that challenge. In each case the response takes the critical challenge seriously and seeks to answer it. Those Athenians who listened to such speeches, and responded to them in their turn, became active participants in the debate. And that, I suppose, is how and where a productive dialogue between democracy and its critics took place. Because of the established structures of democratic society, that dialogue was incorporated into the informal processes of civic education—as well as eventually contributing to the creation of formal educational institutions.

We must resist the tendency to imagine that we can know the workings of the dialogue I have sketched above in great detail. I would certainly *not* want to claim that Thucydides meant the readers of Pericles' Funeral Oration to recall some particular Laconophile tract, nor, a fortiori, that Demosthenes had a copy of Plato's dialogues in hand when he composed his speech against Meidias. Aligning particular passages in critical texts with corresponding arguments in public orations is a way to illustrate the debate in broad strokes; it cannot prove that there was a direct intertextual relationship among the works we happen to have preserved, or that any given critic was in contact with any given orator. But it is precisely the lack of specificity of the debate over civic education that rendered the ideas developed in critical circles capable of being reconfigured in ways that were accessible and palatable to democratic audiences.

ENVOI: CIVIC EDUCATION AFTER THE LOSS OF ATHENIAN INDEPENDENCE

My story has focused on the fifth and early-to-mid-fourth centuries— the "classical" period during which (except for two brief intervals in 411–410 and 404) Athens was both a democracy and a fully independent state. The loss of full independence after the battle of Chaeronea

---

[36] Demosthenes 21: MacDowell 1990. Greek edition with commentary: Erbse, "Midiana," in Erbse 1979; Harris 1989; Wilson 1991.

in 338 B.C. was certainly a blow to the seamless Athenian conception of liberty, one that had correlated national freedom in the realm of foreign policy with the political agency of the demos and the individual freedom of the citizen. But the end of national independence did not terminate the Athenian commitment to teaching democratic civic values. The cultural and institutional history of Athens in the last decades of the fourth century B.C. anticipates some aspects of Hellenistic approaches to education and should warn us to avoid the oversimplistic distinction between a "civic" classical era and an "individualistic" Hellenistic period.

The first Athenian steps towards squaring a commitment to democratic culture with the realities of Macedonian power were taken in the mid-330s B.C. with the program of civic renewal associated with the Athenian orator and financial magistrate, Lycurgus.[37] That program included the reform of the *ephēbeia* in 335–334 B.C., an institutional innovation that represented democratic Athens's first major concession to the idea that it might be desirable to teach the youth of the city about their civic obligations in a structured and state-sponsored setting. Before the 330s, the Athenians had employed as border-guards young citizens, who were probably called ephebes (*ephēboi*), but whether they were given any formal training by the state is unknown.[38] But beginning in 335–334, the *ephēbeia* came to include a strong educational component. Upon turning eighteen, Athenian citizen males were now inducted into a two-year program that conjoined military training and moral education. The supervisors of ephebes were called *sōphronistai*. As such, they presumably were expected to ensure that their charges learned the value of *sōphrosunē* (moderation, self-possession), a cardinal virtue according to democratic conceptions of citizenship and critical Athenian political philosophers alike.[39] Ephebes who learned their lessons and behaved well were honored in public inscriptions praising their orderliness (*kosmiōtēs*) and discipline (*eutaxia*).[40] It would be very nice to be able to specify the educational practices that lie behind the epigraphic encomia. Unfortunately, although Pseudo-Aristotle describes the weapons training offered the ephebes, he records nothing of the actual content of the civic and moral education they received qua ephebes (*Ath. Pol.* 42).

[37] S. C. Humphreys, "Lycurgus of Butadae," in Eadie and Ober 1985, offers an overview of Lycurgus's program.

[38] Ephebes as border-guards before 335 B.C.: Ober 1985, 90–95.

[39] On *sōphrosunē* and democratic citizenship, see Allen 2000b; as a philosophical concept: North 1966.

[40] Inscriptions collected by Reinmuth 1971; for a typical example, see RO 89. Detailed overview of the institution: Pélékidis 1962. Lycurgan reforms and the Athenian *ephēbeia*: Marcellus 1994, 123–69.

Critical-philosophical ideas surely had something to do, at least indirectly, with the new educational emphasis of the *ephēbeia,* initiated with the reform of 335–334.[41] Should we go further, to say that the reformed institution is evidence for the capitulation of democratic ideology to a philosophical educational agenda? Had the Athenians, in effect, admitted that Socrates had been right to scorn Meletus' opinion on the sources of civic education in the democratic polis? Surely not.

The reformed *ephēbeia* was markedly democratic in its institutional structure. The key officials, the *sōphronistai,* were selected in a two-step process: First, three men over age forty were chosen from each of the ten Athenian tribes; the electors were the fathers of the year's ephebic class. Next, ten of these men were elected as tribal *sōphronistai* by the demos. The selection procedure recalls well-established democratic procedures for electing generals.[42] Making the education of ephebes a responsibility of elected magistrates demonstrates Athenian concern for educating the youth, but it surely would have been regarded by the Socrates of the *Apology* as a far cry from the desirable goal of restricting the training of the youth to "one" or "a few" genuine experts. Whatever the ephebes learned about civic values was taught to them under the direct supervision of officials chosen by and ultimately accountable to the demos. And it was official subsets of the demos (tribes, council, demes) that decided whether the deportment of each year-class of ephebes was worthy of public, epigraphic commemoration. The new educational focus of the *ephēbeia* augmented, without replacing, the Athenian conviction that public institutions should bear the primary burden of civic education. It is notable that the two clearest surviving rhetorical expressions of that conviction (by Lycurgus and Aeschines, cited above) both come within a few years *after* the reform of the *ephēbeia.*

Rather than seeing the institutional change as an admission that democracy was incapable of reproducing itself over time, the *ephēbeia* reform of 335–334 points to the future of Athenian democracy, a future in which democratic ideals would be carried forward by cultural media which might have surprised both Meletus and Socrates. After 322 B.C. many of the public institutions that had served to educate previous generations of citizens were overthrown or drastically altered by oligarchic governments. And yet Athenian democratic culture remained vital through these oligarchic interludes, as demonstrated by the Athenians' determination to restore democracy whenever they regained some measure of political autonomy. The processes and the media by which Hellenistic Athenians remembered and learned to cherish democratic values have

---

[41] This is argued in detail in Marcellus 1994, 85–169.
[42] Procedures for electing generals: Hansen 1991, 233–38.

only recently begun to receive serious scholarly attention. The story of how a philodemocratic code of behavior survived the eclipse of democratic governmental institutions would be a desirable sequel to this chapter in the history of classical Athenian civic education.[43]

[43] For Athenian political history after 322 B.C., see Habicht 1997. On the continued vitality of democratic ideology after 322 B.C. and New Comedy as one key medium for the transmission of an evolving conception of democratic citizenship, see Lape 2004. Rhodes and Lewis 1997 collects decrees that demonstrate the flourishing of democratic institutional and discursive forms, especially in Athens, after 322 B.C..

CHAPTER SEVEN

Living Freely as a Slave of the Law:
Why Socrates Lives in Athens

> Since you were born, nurtured, and educated [through the laws], can you assert that you do not belong to us [viz. the laws], both as our son and slave, you yourself as well as your ancestors?
>
> —Plato, Crito 50e

This essay was written for a Festschrift in honor of Mogens H. Hansen, whose scholarship on the history of Athenian democracy and its modern relevance has set new standards for the field.* The central argument of my essay had been briefly sketched in a footnote to Ober 1998. I suggest that it is possible to resolve an apparent inconsistency in Socrates' position on legal obedience, as it is laid out by Plato in the Apology *and* Crito, *by reference to the procedural focus of Athenian law.*

When invited to contribute to the Hansen Festschrift, I thought immediately of Hansen's fine essay on "the trial of Socrates from the Athenian point of view" (Hansen 1995). My essay inverts Hansen's 1995 piece, by approaching "Athenian law from the Socratic point of view." So I took the occasion of the invitation to expand the germ of an idea and to continue my long and fruitful dialogue with Hansen, a dialogue that had already figured prominently in The Athenian Revolution *(Ober 1996, notably chapter 8). My essay employs (and not only as homage) what I take as a signature Hansenesque interpretive move: seeking to solve a familiar and seemingly intractable problem in classical scholarship by reference to a text-based understanding of how Athenian institutions worked in theory and practice. By so doing, I attempt to leverage a technical problem in Plato scholarship in order to address the big issue of the individual and the community that Hansen had raised in reference to Socrates and Athens.*

Reconstructing the view of Plato's Socrates of his own legal and moral responsibilities in the face of Athenian law, rather than the view of the generalized individual in the face of a generalized "rule of law," offers a solution

* This essay was first published in P. Flensted-Jensen, T. H. Nielsen, and L. Rubinstein, eds., *Polis and Politics: Studies in Greek History* (Copenhagen: Museum Tusculanum Press, 2000), 541–52. Reprinted with permission of Museum Tusculanum Press.

to the particular scholarly crux with which the essay is concerned: Plato's Socrates does not contradict himself by stating in the Apology that he would disobey a legal order to cease and desist from philosophizing, while holding in the Crito that he had no choice other than to "persuade or obey" the laws according to which he was born, raised, and educated. It also bears on the remarkable decisions that the historical Socrates made in 399 B.C.—first to defend himself at this trial (rather than maintain a dignified silence), and then to accept capital punishment after being unjustly convicted on charges of impiety (rather than accept the offer of an easy prison escape).

I argue that certain solutions that Socrates developed in order to square his moral commitments with his behavior day by day were particular to Socrates (as an Athenian citizen who lived from 469 to 399 B.C.) and to democratic Athens (as a particular polis, that developed a particular sort of legal regime). As such, Socrates' answer may not offer a solution for just any would-be Socratic in the face of any given regime of law. Socrates sought general answers to moral problems, for example, When is it permissible to do morally relevant harm? But this essay is meant to show that Socrates also teaches us that individuals must decide how any general answer relates to the rules governing their local communities; and he thereby shows us why sensitivity to local context is not to be equated with moral relativism.

Socrates' position on legal obedience, as reconstructed here, is directly relevant to the issues that motivate this collection as a whole: he is concerned with identity-formation (birth, upbringing, education), with persistence (can a legal regime survive in the face of an unwillingness of citizens to obey?), and with the possibility of absolute justice. Socrates willingly accepted a lapse of substantive justice on the part of fallible human agents, and thus his own death, in favor of maintaining the integrity of procedurally just rules under which legal judgment is to take place. By doing so he preserved both the integrity of his longstanding critical position, and acted to preserve and to educate the community whose open culture had rendered his critical project possible. Important recent scholarship bearing on the concerns of this essay includes Weiss 1998 (on the Crito) and Carey 1998 (on substantive law in Athenian law courts).

• • •

AMONG MOGENS HANSEN'S MANY Athenian interests, one individual and one political value stand out: the individual is Socrates and the value is freedom, especially in its negative sense of freedom to pursue one's personal goals. Here I will seek to illuminate, with a philosophical torch assembled largely from Hansen's historical investigations of Athenian legal procedure, a few small corners of a big question about Socrates and freedom: does the acceptance by Socrates (i.e., the literary figure depicted in Plato's *Apology* and *Crito*: hereafter simply Socrates)[1] of communal obligations he owed as a citizen unduly compromise his freedom as an individual? Linked to this normative question is a historical question about Socrates' identity: How Athenian, in terms of embracing values implicit in Athenian legal and political practices, was Socrates? I will suggest that both Socrates' Athenian-ness and his idiosyncrasy bear on the problem of his ethical obligations to the state. I make three main points:

1. Although Socrates regarded other polities as substantively better, Athens was the right polis for Socrates because (inter alia) the procedural emphasis of Athenian law rendered a commitment to obeying the laws fully compatible with the freedom of Socrates as an individual to choose and pursue his distinctive life goals. And so Athens never confronted Socrates with a hard choice between his freedom of conscience and his duty as a citizen.
2. A hypothetical law against philosophizing would not confront Socrates with a hard choice, because he would regard such a law as formally invalid.
3. When he disobeyed the order of the Thirty to arrest Leon of Salamis, Socrates was not breaking the law because the order lacked authority under the law code that Socrates regarded as being in force at the time.

Socrates is often, and not unreasonably, lumped in with other fifth-century B.C. intellectuals who chose to reside in Athens. Aristophanes in the *Clouds* caricatured Socrates as a model mad scientist-sophist and, a half-century after the trial, Aeschines (1.173) referred in a legal oration to "Socrates the sophist." But Socrates was quite different from most fifth-century sophists and scientists; not only was he an Athenian citizen, he was deeply concerned with the obligations of citizenship. Sophists tended to move about; their choice of residence in Athens was certainly not a matter of ethical responsibility. Socrates, by contrast, was unwilling to live (*Apol.* 37c–e) or even to travel outside of the city of Athens. In the *Crito*, his steadfast preference for a specific locality is offered (in the speech of the Laws [*Nomoi*]: 52b; cf. *Phaedrus* 230c) as proof that he fully accepted

---

[1] I do not suppose that Plato's Socrates in any given dialogue is identical to the historical Socrates, but I do suppose that Socrates as he is depicted in the *Apology* and the *Crito* represents Plato's initial understanding of the ethical quandaries confronting the historical Socrates and Plato's understanding of why the historical Socrates acted as he did when faced by Meletus' indictment, at the trial, and in the few days prior to his execution. See, further, Ober 1998, 159–60. Kateb 1998 argues for distinctly different depictions of Socrates in the *Apology* and the *Crito*.

the contract between himself and the Athenian laws—that is, he willingly offered his obedience to the law in exchange for his birth, upbringing, and education. The *Nomoi* point out that since Athenians enjoyed freedom of movement, if Socrates had ever become disenchanted with the laws, he could have left Attica at will. His continued presence thus marked his continued acceptance of the social contract (51d–e). In sum: Socrates had incurred contractual obligations to the state because he was born and raised as a citizen of Athens, and he signaled his acceptance of those obligations, day by day, through his willing continued residence in the polis of his birth.

Much of the modern scholarship on the *Crito*, notably Richard Kraut's important *Socrates and the State* (1984), is concerned with the problem of whether or not Socrates' position on obedience is authoritarian. Kraut attempts to absolve Socrates of authoritarianism by arguing that the "obey-or-persuade" doctrine enunciated by the *Nomoi* implies that Socrates can seek to persuade his community that the law is wrong either before or after knowingly breaking the law. Moreover, the *Nomoi* may regard him as acting justly, even if he breaks the established laws of Athens, so long as his actions are consistently moral and he defends them in valid moral terms. But this argument is hard to square with the actual text of the dialogue: The *Nomoi* tell Socrates, "you must do whatever the polis and *patris* (fatherland) commands, or else persuade it of what is just" (51b; cf. 49e–50a, 51e–52a).[2] The options are obey or persuade. This would seem, on the face of it, to mean "obey [existing law] or [successfully] persuade [the law to change (via legislation) or those who enforce it to change their interpretation of it]," not "obey or [seek to] persuade [on the basis of sound moral arguments, although you may break the law if your arguments fail to persuade]." The persuade options countenanced by the *Nomoi* certainly must include legislative changes in statutory law (through ordinary processes of *nomothesia*) and convincing jurors to accept a particular interpretation of the law. But the either-or wording does not allow for defending law breaking (in past or future) on the basis of a sound moral argument that nonetheless fails to persuade the legal authorities. Among the maddening aspects of Socrates in the *Crito* is his refusal to acknowledge that he faced a hard choice between obedience to (potentially) unjust law and freedom to follow a conscience that identified injustice with wrongdoing.

Some recent commentators on the *Crito* have suggested that making legal authority the primary interpretive problem is an error, arguing that Socrates' refusal to escape from prison is adequately governed, in philosophical terms, by his preliminary acceptance of two premises: First, that one must not do harm under any circumstance (49a–c: this is said to have

---

[2] Kraut 1984, 82–90.

been established in a prior discussion). Next, that legal disobedience constitutes one sort of "doing harm."[3] The long speech of the *Nomoi*, on this reading, is irrelevant to Socrates' choice; it is best understood as a rhetorical sop to Crito, who is unable to accept the consequences of the "do-no-harm" doctrine without such palliatives. But this interpretation makes for a very lopsided dialogue (much more rhetoric than philosophy) and it requires Socrates' concluding comment, to the effect that the argument of the *Nomoi* is so persuasive that he is unable to hear any other, to be an example of simple irony—of saying the opposite of what is in fact the case. Without some strong warrant for such an assumption, this seems a desperate measure.[4]

The *Nomoi* of the *Crito*, those that Socrates feels obligated to obey and those he imagines as dissuading him from leaving prison, are not universal principles of jurisprudence, not the just laws of a state in the abstract, but rather "the laws (*hoi nomoi*) and the community (*to koinon*) of the polis" (50a)—that is, the laws and the accepted norms of social life in democratic Athens.[5] The home state that Socrates never voluntarily leaves is Athens; the laws he agrees to obey by his day-to-day residence are the laws of Athens. And so, before we reject the prima facie exclusionary force of the either-or condition, or resort to assumptions about where and how Socrates is being ironic, it seems worthwhile to investigate how much personal freedom that obedience to established Athenian law allowed Socrates. I will argue that, given the highly procedural focus of Athenian law, Athenian practices of lawmaking, and prevailing Athenian assumptions about the relationship of law to the governing body, Socrates was not constrained by the laws of Athens in ways that would have unacceptably limited his personal freedom to choose and pursue those activities (specifically philosophizing) essential to his personal happiness (*Apol.* 38a) and moral well-being. In Athens, Socrates was both free and obedient, and he lived what he regarded as a consistently dutiful life in respect to law and morality without suffering a crisis of conscience.

Under a system of state law in which substantive law took precedence over procedure, and in which judicial magistrates could make substantive

---

[3] Miller 1996; White 1996.

[4] On Socratic irony, see now Vasiliou 1999, 2002.

[5] Kraut 1984, 81–82, claims that the *Nomoi* of the *Crito* blend together real Athenian laws and an idealized jurisprudence. This seems to me not to be the case: the *Nomoi* explain the logic behind the laws of Athens in what may be fairly described as jurisprudential language, but the logic is a specifically Athenian legal logic, one that arises from the law code. I think therefore it is misleading to say (Kraut 1984, 82) that "someone who violates the city's orders [i.e., an actual Athenian law] is not necessarily departing from the philosophy of the Laws [the *Nomoi* of the *Crito*]," although as I will suggest below, Socrates can disobey an order that he regards as invalid due to its failure to conform to established Athenian judicial procedures.

law by establishing new legal precedents, Socrates might well have been confronted with a hard choice between doing philosophy and obeying the law.[6] And so he would either have to accept a severe constraint upon his freedom, or leave the city, or break the social contract sketched by the *Nomoi* of *Crito* by willingly breaking the law. In Athens Socrates was not confronted with this hard choice. This does not mean that Socrates thought of Athens as an ideal state, or that he regarded democracy as intrinsically good, or that he thought his fellow Athenians were unlikely to do wrong and cause harm. He certainly regarded his own conviction by an Athenian jury on a charge of impiety as substantively unjust and perhaps he guessed that he could have avoided that fate in a "better" city. But Socrates regarded harm to himself as less important than the opportunity to live a consistently ethical life. That opportunity was provided him by the procedural focus of Athenian law.

Procedural law is concerned with establishing fair rules for legal practices, rather than with carefully defining legal terms in an attempt to achieve consistently good outcomes. Under a legal regime in which impiety was strictly defined, Socrates would confront a problem if and when his dialectical investigations demonstrated that a prevailing legal definition was flawed. If, for example, established substantive law defined a specific and detailed set of beliefs as constituting piety and mandated that citizens hold such beliefs, and if Socrates determined philosophically that those beliefs were foolish, Socrates would have to choose between his conscience and the law. But Athenian law avoided such difficulties because it avoided detailed definitions of abstract terms like "piety."[7] In accepting the authority of Athenian law, Socrates accepted the established procedures by which he would be judged if he were accused of a delict, but he was not constrained to accept a detailed, substantive definition of that delict. Athenian law forbade (inter alia) impiety, *hubris*, slander, and assault. By living in Attica and thereby accepting the law, Socrates acknowledged that these things were morally reprehensible and worthy of punishment. So, for example, because Athenian law forbade impiety (*asebeia*) Socrates accepted that *asebeia* (properly so understood) was a crime, and that a citizen formally accused of *asebeia* would be tried according to a specific set of procedures. But when indicted on a charge of *asebeia*, Socrates was not constrained to accept the detailed definition of *asebeia* offered by the prosecution. Nor was he constrained to accept that his behavior (even if accurately described by the prosecutor) would have constituted *asebeia*. Rather, Athenian law invited each juror to

[6] On substantive law and precedent making as lawmaking, see Scalia 1997.
[7] Proceduralist emphasis of Athenian law: Todd 1993.

weigh the competing assessments of prosecutor and defendant regarding what sorts of behavior carried out under what conditions constituted impiety.

Socrates, of course, claimed not to know anything certain about moral truths, including (as shown by the *Euthyphro*) piety. And so he may not have known what impiety was in any absolute sense. But he was sure that truth must be logically consistent with itself. And so he could be sure that *asebeia* could not be what Meletus supposed, because Meletus contradicted himself under cross-examination (*Apol.* 27a). Thus, whether or not Socrates was a pious man in an absolute sense, he was not (by his own lights) guilty of *asebeia* as defined by his legal opponents. Socrates evidently expected that the jurors could in fact be persuaded by this sort of logical demonstration, in that he claims that he was not seriously endangered by his "new accusers," despite their rhetorical skill (*Apol.* 17b, 18b; cf. chapter 6). The "old accusers"—the slanders that had long circulated in the city against him—were something else again and almost impossible to refute in the span of a legal defense. But the point is that the legal process by which Socrates was tried was procedurally fair. Socrates willingly accepts the authority of a legal system that gives the defendant a chance to establish, by logical demonstration if he chose, that the prosecutor's definition of what constitutes a delict is faulty. In this sense, at least, Athenian legal procedure potentially maps quite closely to the procedure of Socratic dialectic. Neither process assumes that it is possible to arrive at a final truth, but both processes assume that better definitions of contested evaluative terms can be arrived at and agreed upon, and worse definitions rejected.

The procedural emphasis of Athenian law thus goes a long way towards explaining Socrates' willing obedience to it. A more substantive law code (perhaps that of Sparta, Crete, Thebes, or Megara: *Crito* 52e, 53b) might indeed foster a "better" political regime. But such a law code was not subject (as were Socrates' working definitions of moral terms) to constant elenchtic examination, and so it would also be more likely to employ (at some point) a seriously flawed definition. Thus the "better" regime was more likely to confront Socrates with a hard choice between loyalty to philosophy and to the duties of citizenship, a choice he did not face in Athens. Athens may have been less "good" by Socrates' lights than Crete or Sparta, but Athens offered Socrates the unique capacity to be simultaneously an obedient citizen and a free individual. This is at least one reason why, given a daily choice of his place of residence, Socrates consistently chose Athens.

Let us consider two potential complications to this general account of why Socrates was content with Athenian law. First there is the possibility that a jury might seek to punish Socrates by forbidding him to philosophize or that the Athenians might pass a law forbidding philosophizing.[8] The problem arises obliquely from Socrates' statement (*Apol.* 29c–30b; cf. 37e–38a) that he would not obey the jurors if they freed him on the condition that he abandon pursuit of his philosophical conversations. Brickhouse and Smith attempt to square Socrates' statement in the *Crito* that he must always obey the law with his refusal in the *Apology* to obey a hypothetical gag order, by pointing out that an *asebeia* trial was an *agōn timētos*, meaning that if the defendant were found guilty, the jury decided between competing penalties offered by the litigants. Athenian trial procedure made no provision for jury-mandated penalties. Since Socrates knew the prosecutors planned to call for his execution, he was in no danger of being slapped with a gag order.[9]

But Kraut points out that a law forbidding philosophizing *could* be passed by the Athenians at any time. If they did so, Socrates would seem to face a quandary. According to Kraut, "Socrates . . . has no alternative: faced with a law against philosophy, he could not give it up, and he would not leave the city; he is unavoidably committed to disobeying a valid law."[10] But I think that Socrates could refuse to accept the validity of such a law on the following argument:

1) Socrates believed that Apollo's response to Chaerephon's query as to whether any man was wiser than Socrates amounted to a divine order to Socrates to philosophize. Now, this is admittedly a peculiar interpretation of what Mogens Hansen has shown is a highly ambiguous referential oracular statement.[11] Delphic statements are notoriously problematic as perfomative speech acts (e.g., as warnings or orders; see chapter 9); it was unlikely that many of the jurors felt that by saying "no one" is wiser than Socrates the god had in fact unambiguously ordered Socrates to ceaselessly expose the ignorance and folly of his fellows. It not surprising that Socrates must interrupt his description of the oracle with a request that the jurors not shout him down (*Apol.* 21a). But the jurors' doubts would gravely concern Socrates only if he cared more about avoiding harm to himself than maintaining his own ethical consistency. Socrates seems very sure of his ground here, and his interpretation of the oracle as a divine order clearly constituted an important part of why he regarded his own philosophizing as self-evidently pious.

[8] See Kraut 1984, 13–17, 83. The following argument is expanded from Ober 1998, 172n32, 182n51.
[9] Brickhouse and Smith 1989, 137–53.
[10] Kraut 1984, 15–17, quote: 16.
[11] Hansen 1995, 34.

2) The established Athenian law code, the law that Socrates felt constrained to obey, explicitly forbade impiety. Although the law did not define impiety, it was reasonable for Socrates to suppose, as he clearly did (*Apol.* 33c, 37e), that under any coherent definition, willfully disobeying a god's order would be impious. Therefore, if Socrates were to avoid impiety, as he must if he were to fulfill his agreement with the *Nomoi*, he must also philosophize.

3) The (hypothetical) law forbidding philosophizing therefore mandated impiety (at least in the case of Socrates). By mandating a course of action explicitly forbidden by an existing law, the hypothetical law contradicted an established Athenian law. It is, of course, Socrates' peculiar definition of what constituted a god's order that introduces the contradiction, but since Athenian law was silent on the substantive content of impiety, Socrates was free to hold this opinion.

4) The Athenian law code, and Athenian lawmaking procedure, as revised and re-established in the legal reforms of 410–399 B.C., did not tolerate contradictory laws. According to Athenian legal principles, the passage of a new law required the repeal of any established law contradicted by the new law; if a conflict between laws were detected, the older law prevailed unless and until it was repealed.[12] Socrates, then, could regard the law against philosophizing as invalid as long as the law against impiety remained on the books.[13] Most Athenians might not recognize that the antiphilosophizing law was invalid on procedural grounds, but, as shown by his actions as *prytanis* in 406 (see below), Socrates distinguished between obedience to majority will and obedience to the established law.

5) Since only valid laws must be obeyed, Socrates need not obey the antiphilosophizing law, on the grounds of its procedural irregularity, until and unless the law against impiety were repealed (by majority vote of a board of *nomothetai*).

As the trial of Socrates itself demonstrates, the Athenians cared deeply about piety; repeal of the law against impiety is so farfetched as to be uninteresting as a hypothetical. But what about the possibility that the Athenians might pass some other law that would require Socrates to do wrong

[12] Hansen 1991, 169, 175, notes that the lawmaking procedure takes the form of a trial against existing laws.

[13] A prosecutor who indicted Socrates under the hypothetical antiphilosophizing law, anticipating this defense, might assert that the antiphilosophizing law was valid until and unless it was condemned under the procedure for indicting unsuitable laws (see below). But Socrates could respond that, since it is impossible to be both pious and impious simultaneously, both laws could not simultaneously command his obedience. The invalidity of the newer law was thus demonstrated by the fact that it mandated illegal behavior.

according to his own lights? The force of the argument of the *Nomoi* in the *Crito*, to the effect that Socrates must "obey the law or persuade it" is clarified by considering fourth-century Athenian lawmaking (*nomothesia*) procedure. Mogens Hansen has illuminated how that procedure worked in practice, and conveniently lists the main steps in his indispensable *Athenian Democracy*. Hansen's step no. four (1991, 168–69) is especially relevant: "A proposal to change the existing laws must be published before the Monument to the Eponymous Heroes in the Agora, to enable any citizen who wishes to have a say in the matter." Thus, before a problematic new law became authoritative, Socrates had ample opportunity to "persuade": to argue, in public and privately, against the passage of any proposed law that would make the polis an unacceptable home for him by requiring him to choose between doing wrong and disobeying the law. If such a law were ultimately passed, Socrates might, under Athenian law, continue to seek to "persuade" the law to change by indicting its proposer under the procedure for prosecution on the charge of establishing unsuitable laws (see Hansen 1991, 175). Failing that, he was free to leave the polis: as the *Nomoi* point out, his continued presence in Attica was voluntary.

Socrates would not have a similar opportunity to "persuade" in respect to the law under a legal system in which substantive law could be created when a judicial magistrate's ruling established a new binding precedent. Nor would the option of persuasion be available to (for example) those who lived in Sparta under the laws of Lycurgus. Although Socrates himself, with his aversion to making public speeches (*Apol.* 31c), might not choose to avail himself of the chance to persuade in respect to the law, the possibility of melioration via deliberation was surely attractive in principle to the practitioner of dialectic—once again, while Sparta might, at any given point *be* better as a society, it had little possibility of *becoming* better, through deliberative processes, than it currently was. Socrates (in the *Apology* and the *Crito*) remains at least guardedly optimistic about the possibility of moral improvement of each and every Athenian via the persuasion of rational discourse.[14] And thus the claim of the *Nomoi* that persuasion was a complementary alternative to obedience was both realistic and in tune with Socratic aspirations.

The *Nomoi* that address Socrates were currently in force at the time of his imprisonment in 399 B.C. These same *Nomoi* claim to have promoted his birth and upbringing and so they are also the laws that pertained at the time of Socrates' birth in 469 B.C. and during his youth in the mid-fifth century B.C. The *Nomoi* are, therefore, the ancestral laws of the democratic Athenian state. Aristotle, in the *Politics* (1281a, 1282b) points out

---

[14] Ober 1998, 184–85.

that a fundamental change in the laws implies a change in regime, and vice versa. Assuming that, in Socrates' view, the laws of 469 B.C. were fundamentally the same as those of 399 B.C., there remains the question of whether Socrates was or would be bound by Athenian legal regimes other than the ancestral regime promulgated by the democracy. Specifically, did orders issued under the regime of the Thirty Tyrants justly command Socrates' obedience? Socrates notoriously remained in Athens during the reign of the Thirty, rather than joining the democrats either at Phyle or Piraeus. Does the argument of the *Crito* imply that Socrates-in-Athens should obey any existing Athenian government? Or (like Theramenes as described by the Aristotelian *Ath. Pol.* 28.5) any government with a claim to constitutionality? The issue comes to the fore in Socrates' description of his refusal to obey an order he received from the Thirty to arrest Leon of Salamis and bring him to the city for execution (*Apol.* 32c–d). Although the text does not allow a definitive answer to the question of the extent of Socrates' duty to a constitutional nondemocratic legal regime, his behavior in 404 B.C. suggests that he did not accept that the ancestral (fifth-century, democratic) Athenian law code had been nullified by the government of the Thirty. If we suppose that Socrates regarded the Athenian laws in force before the coup remained in force during it, then Socrates' refusal to arrest Leon of Salamis is fully consistent with a stance of steadfast obedience to the (ancestral) laws.

The government of the Thirty was not a full-fledged new constitutional regime in that, as Krentz has shown, there cannot have been a full new law code passed by the Thirty.[15] Nor would an Athenian necessarily conclude that the existing Athenian law code had been formally repealed when the Thirty erased laws inscribed on the Royal Stoa and took down other written laws; erasing a copy of a law does not constitute its nullification.[16] A possible model for thinking about the status of Athenian law under the Thirty is provided by the Eukrates *nomos* passed in 337–336 B.C. (see chapters 1 and 10). This Athenian law threatens with disenfranchisement (*atimia*) and property confiscation any member of the Areopagus Council who fulfills his official function while "the *dēmos* or the *dēmokratia* is overthrown."[17] The implicit premise of this law is that democratic Athenian law is the law of Athens, irrespective of who is actually in charge at any given point in time. The democratic law is imagined as pertaining during a period in which the "*dēmokratia* and the *dēmos*" had been replaced by a tyranny. The tyranny is seen as a lapse in the effective power of the demos to govern, but not in the legal authority of the established law over all Athenians, and especially over Athenian

[15] Krentz 1982, 60–62. Socrates calls the government an *archē* (*Apol.* 32d4).
[16] Boegehold 1996, 205–7.
[17] Meritt 1952, 355–59 = *SEG* 12.87. See, further, chapter 10, below.

magistrates. Socrates might well have reasoned likewise. He certainly refused to equate the power of the demos to effect its will with the authority of Athenian law, as demonstrated by his resistance to the popular will of the Assembly when he served as *prytanis* during the indictment of the Arginusae generals in 406 B.C. That resistance was predicated explicitly on the grounds of procedural irregularity (*paranomos: Apol.* 32b4). Moreover, his resistance to the demos when serving as *prytanis* is equated by Socrates with his resistance to the order to arrest Leon (*Apol.* 32c). In both cases, it seems, those in power demanded one thing, but Socrates rejected that demand as inconsistent with the established law. Finally, the *Nomoi* that address Socrates in the *Crito* speak as if their authority (and Socrates' obedience to it) had been uninterrupted during the course of Socrates' life.[18]

So I would suggest that in 404 and 399 B.C. Socrates, like his fellow Athenians some sixty years later, assumed that the ancestral law code (the one under which he had been born and had grown up) remained in place throughout a tyrannical interregnum. And, unlike Socrates' peculiar interpretation of the force of Apollo's oracle, this assumption may have been quite consistent with the thinking of the ordinary Athenians on the jury—and as such it required no special explanation.

As Socrates reports the Leon incident, he was ordered by Athenian magistrates (the Thirty) to seize another Athenian. Mogens Hansen has shown that under normal circumstances, Athenian law held that magistrates, giving orders within their sphere of competence, must legally be obeyed.[19] In this case it may initially have appeared to Socrates that the magistrates in question could legitimately command his obedience, since when ordered (*metapempsamenoi me . . .* 32c5) to come to the Tholos, Socrates did so. But the order given him upon his arrival was a peculiar one: to seize and transport another citizen from Salamis (*agagein ek Salaminos . . .* 32c6) to the city, with the clear understanding that Socrates would be bringing him to Athens for execution. Instead of going to Salamis, Socrates went home, thus refusing to obey the order.

Did the magistrates mandating the arrest of Leon issue a legally binding order to Socrates? I would suggest that Socrates reasoned that the transport order had no validity under the pertaining (ancestral) system of law—that is, either giving such an order lay outside the magistrates'

---

[18] The *Nomoi* do not, therefore, consider the revisions and recodifications of 410–399 B.C. as an interruption in their continuous authority, even though new laws were added and some laws in effect before 403–402 B.C. were not included in the revised law code (Hansen 1991, 162–64). In this sense, then, the *Nomoi* must be regarded as representing the underlying jurisprudential logic of Athenian law, as well as the laws themselves.

[19] Hansen 1991, 229.

sphere of authority or the "magistrates" were not genuine magistrates, having been appointed extraconstitutionally.[20] Either way, someone who considered the ancestral law still to be in place need not suppose that the Thirty had the legal authority to order him to *agagein* an Athenian. Now, it is indeed the case that under certain circumstances, an Athenian magistrate or an ordinary citizen might seize a citizen. Mogens Hansen notes the frequency of use of *apagōgē* procedure by the Thirty. According to this procedure an Athenian might be legally executed if he had been identified as a malefactor (*kakourgos*) and was apprehended by a magistrate (or a citizen volunteer) in a criminal act (*ep' autophoro*).[21] But there seems to be no existing provision in ancestral Athenian law that would authorize a magistrate to issue a binding order to an Athenian citizen to travel elsewhere in Attica in order to seize another Athenian and transport him to the city for execution. And so, when Socrates ignored the magistrate's invalid order, he put himself at risk (as he points out: *Apol.* 32d), but he did not compromise his stance in regard to the duty owed by a citizen to the established law.

I have tried to show that in democratic Athens Socrates was, by his own lights, free to pursue his life goals and still able to live the dutiful life of a law-abiding citizen. In his conviction that Athens, uniquely, offered its citizens a conjunction of freedom and the fulfillment of the citizen's life, Socrates is very Athenian: in tune with parts of the idealistic vision offered in the Funeral Oration of Thucydides' Pericles (see chapter 6) and sharing core assumptions with his ordinary fellow-citizens about why it is better to live in Athens than elsewhere.

But of course Socrates was neither a politician nor an ordinary Athenian. Some of the assumptions that allowed Socrates to square his own cherished freedom to pursue philosophy with the strictest obedience to the law—notably the pious duty he supposed had been assigned to him by Apollo's oracle—were peculiar to himself. Socrates of the *Apology* and *Crito* does not, therefore, offer a full-featured general description of how anyone else, living under any other legal regime, might square personal freedom with obedience to the law. But neither does he claim to do so. Socrates leaves each would-be Socratic to figure out the details of his own ethical life, which is presumably why the *Crito* was not Plato's last word on political obligation and the law. The deep personal idiosyncrasy

[20] I would like to think that the magistrates' lack of authority was established after they had been engaged by Socrates in an elenchtic conversation on the subject of legal authority; but imagining that interchange in detail would require Mogens Hansen's skill in inventing Socratic dialogue; see, for an example, Hansen 1995, 22–24. Meanwhile, see Xenophon *Memorabilia* 1.2.29–38.

[21] Hansen 1976, 31n4, 36ff.

that lurks within a distinctively Athenian persona, all the while coinciding with a commitment to universal values and reason, helps to explain why Socrates remains such an engaging, elusive, and occasionally maddening figure. And I conclude by noting that those characteristics are not completely alien to the man to whom this essay is offered.

CHAPTER EIGHT

Social Science History, Cultural History, and the Amnesty of 403 B.C.

This essay began as a response to a panel of papers, organized by William Tieman and James Quillin, that was presented at a meeting of the American Philological Association in 2001.* The panel was meant to test the explanatory power of two families of historical method. "Social science history" refers here to approaches to historical explanation that derive from rational choice decision theory. Developed primarily by modern economists, rational choice theory takes humans as "rational agents" who always and everywhere make choices aimed at the maximization of their own utility (which may include, for example, seeking greater access to wealth, power, and reproductive opportunity) by strategically taking into account the actions of others. On the other hand, "cultural history" refers here to a family of historical approaches related to some parts of contemporary anthropological theory. Cultural history views humans as products of and participants in discrete cultures, engaged in the employment of cultural resources to negotiate diverse identities and create meanings. Those meanings vary considerably from culture to culture (see chapters 4 and 9). The two methodological approaches were tested against a single historical problem: the unexpected decision by Athenian democrats to declare an Amnesty in the aftermath of the oligarchy of the Thirty.

It is only fair to say that my own intellectual commitments fell more on the side of the cultural historians; I had tended to regard rational choice theory (despite its merits in other sorts of disciplinary explanation) as operating at a level of abstraction that is too high to offer a satisfactory explanation for many of the kinds of phenomena that historians are concerned with explaining. Rational choice theory has great explanatory power when it is employed within clearly bounded domains: for example, it explains a great deal about the operation of markets in modern economies. But those markets operate in environments that are bound by legal regulations. The theory assumes that sustainable communities will achieve an equilibrium among rational agents, but the great range of equilibria possible in the "Game of Life" make it hard to assess how

---

* This essay was first published in the *Transactions of the American Philological Association* 132 (2002): 127–37. Reprinted with the permission of the American Philological Association.

much it explains about historical phenomena. That said, the value of so-
cial science lies precisely in its drive for general explanations (like rational
choice) that will organize complex sets of data. This can be a salutary
corrective to the tendency of cultural historians to drift into a mode of
explanation that is so intensely "local" as to obviate any sort of cross-
cultural relevance—and that thereby renders history useless for political
theorizing. The goal of this essay is to elaborate an interpretive position
(originally sketched out in Ober 1996, chapter 2) that allows for both
cultural specificity and general human political nature to play roles in
historical explanation.

The test case, the Athenian Amnesty of 403 B.C., is a key moment in
terms of the Athenians' willed commitment to go on together. Without
the Amnesty, those Athenians who had suffered under the Thirty, and
who were driven by the memory of past crimes, would have had re-
course to a full range of institutional resources when seeking their re-
venge. Being denied the chance for "justice as meting out fair deserts"
demanded of them a substantial sacrifice. But without their sacrifice,
the capacity of the community as a whole to go on would be fatally
weakened, as was that of so many other Greek communities in the fifth
and fourth centuries B.C. The distinctive political culture of democratic
Athens is thus implicated in the Athenians' ability to get past civil con-
flict, and go on together into a new era, one that would be marked
(inter alia) by Plato's and Aristotle's deep philosophical investigations
into the relationship between moral psychology and political organiz-
ation. Although this essay begins with a debate among historians,
moral philosophy (in the form of Stuart Hampshire on justice as con-
flict) comes in at the end as a sort of arbitrator of that intradisciplinary
debate.

• • •

IF WE ARE TO BELIEVE THUCYDIDES, XENOPHON, PLATO, Aeneas the Tac-
tician, and Aristotle (among other Greek historical and philosophical
sources), *stasis*—violent conflict among citizens within the civic space of
the polis—had emerged as one of the biggest stories of Greek history and
political philosophy by the latter part of the fifth century B.C. And *stasis*
continued to dominate Greek thinking about "what threatens the polis
most" throughout much of the fourth century, B.C. as well. Why communities fall into a state of *stasis*, and how that problematic tendency might
be controlled, are clearly motivating questions (perhaps *the* motivating
questions) for Greek historians beginning with Thucydides, and for the
first generation of systematic Greek political philosophers. *Stasis* was

little short of an obsession among Greek writers (including dramatists) in the late classical period.[1]

As every reader of Thucydides' harrowing narrative of the civil conflict on Corcyra (3.70–85) learns, *stasis* could be devastating in its material and moral effects. Thucydides suggests that *stasis*, once begun, developed a terrible momentum of its own: killing and atrocity led to retribution-killing and counteratrocity in a widening downward gyre. Physical violence was compounded by referential instability within evaluative language: bodies, property, and the meaning of the everyday terminology of politics and morality—all were at risk. At the bottom of the downward spiral of *stasis* lay the material destruction of the polis as a public and privately held physical space, the disintegration of the citizenship as a community of persons, and the semiotic collapse of a common discourse that had once united citizens with diverse interests and backgrounds. For the Greeks of the late classical period, the experience of devolutionary *stasis* was as bad as it gets—the mutilation of a community by civil conflict was arguably more devastating (at least in historical retrospect and philosophical prospect) than that inflicted by plague, natural disaster, or enemy invasion. *Stasis* eliminated the possibility of public grandeur, individual nobility, ordinary dignity, even baseline human decency. The social and psychological trauma inflicted by *stasis* seemed peculiarly resistant to therapeutic redress.

It is not at all peculiar, therefore, that historians of late classical Greece have been consistently interested in studying the best documented *stasis* of the era—the short reign of the Thirty at Athens and its aftermath. The Athenian story is all the more compelling for its apparent atypicality, for its "arrested development." Instead of vindictively turning upon their foes and thus completing a Corcyra-like downward spiral into chaos, the victorious Athenian democrats abruptly halted the cycle of retribution, by declaring and enforcing an amnesty. This decision (although no doubt influenced by prudential concerns about the Spartan response to an antioligarchic purge) earns the frank praise of the author of the Aristotelian *Athēnaiōn Politeia*.

> On this occasion [the implementation of the Amnesty of 403 B.C., after the fall of the Thirty], they [the Athenian democrats] seem to have reacted to their previous misfortunes, both privately and communally (*kai idiai kai koinēi*) in a manner more noble and public-spirited than all other people (*kallista dē kai politikōtata tōn hapantōn*). Not only did they wipe out all prosecutions for

[1] *Stasis* in Greek political philosophy and drama: Ober 2000. Loraux 1997 (trans. 2002) discusses the ways in which *stasis* was internalized as a negative concept to cover a wide range of conflicts, including those arising from gender. Of course, *stasis* was a deep concern of many archaic poetic texts as well, notably those of Solon and the Theognid corpus.

past acts (*aitias exēleipsan*), but they paid back out of common funds the
money that the Thirty had borrowed from Sparta (40.3)

If the *Ath. Pol.* is to be believed (and, whoever its author, we may suppose
that he had access to a very considerable body of "constitutional history"
now lost to us) the Athenians acted somewhat differently ("in a manner
more noble and public spirited") than "all other people" when faced with
the *stasis* situation. Even if overstated, this claim offers historians of classical Greece an intriguing puzzle—how to explain the Athenians' startling
and distinctive (if not positively anomalous) behavior in 403 B.C.?

For those who accept that there is a puzzle here (i.e., that the democratic Athenian action in establishing and maintaining the Amnesty was
unusual and was not predetermined, by the certainty of massive Spartan
punishment or some other exogenous factor), then at least two, rather
different approaches to explaining the democrats' distinctive choice making are possible: In the first, "type-A," approach, the historian begins by
supposing that the historical situation faced by the Athenians was distinctive, and that the Athenians reacted pretty much the way that other
Greeks (or even, other non-Greek communities) would have if faced with
the same distinctive circumstances. In a second, "type-B," approach, the
historian supposes that the *stasis* situation faced by the Athenians was
fairly typical, but that democratic Athenian political culture was quite
unlike the political culture of most other Greek communities. In this second case, the historian's answer depends on showing that the Athenians
reacted to a "standard" *stasis* situation in a distinct way because of their
distinctive political culture.

Of course, explanations of types A and B are not mutually exclusive and
in the real world of historical explanation, we would probably not expect
anyone to propose a purely "type-A" or "type-B" explanation. But it is, I
think, reasonable to suppose that we could arrange historians' attempts at
an explanation of the events of 403 B.C. (at least the attempts of those historians who accept *Ath. Pol.*'s claim for the distinctiveness of the Athenian
course of events in the period after the fall of the Thirty) along a spectrum
defined by the "ideal types" of A: distinctive circumstances-standard responses or B: standard circumstances-distinctive response. The different
assumptions made by "type A" as opposed to "type B" approaches to understanding the events of 404–403 B.C. may clarify the debate carried out
in a recent collection of articles concerning the aftermath of the Athenian
stasis. The debate is over the relative worth of "social science history"
which favors "type-A" and "cultural history" which leans on "type-B"
explanations.

James Quillin has usefully defined social science history as the "use
of reductionist analyses and case studies in order to create generalizable

models of human behavior"; and cultural history as the attempt to "analyze in all their specificity the cultural expressions and discourse of a particular locality and moment."[2] Social science history asserts that, if we can filter out local variables, we will be left with a coherent sequence of events, motivated by a systematic causal mechanism. The goal is to be able to explain precisely *why* something happened. The record of the past is treated as a fertile source of "real-world" case studies. The historian sifts case studies in order to find cross-cultural regularities in causes and effects with the aim of generating (through standard forms of hypothesis building and testing) one or more generalizable models for human behavior. Once the model is in place (i.e., once it has been tested against an adequate number of well-documented case studies), it can be used to explain other examples (including examples that are less well documented) of relevant "historical behavior." Doing social science history is thus a circular process, but the circularity is not vicious: the process moves from reasoning on the basis of historical cases, to the construction of hypothetical models, to testing the model against other cases, to revision (if necessary) of the model. The proof of the worth of the model ultimately lies in its analytic power, in its capacity to connect a single cause (or set of causes) with historically diverse effects, to show that the same cause yields similar effects cross-culturally and transhistorically.

Cultural historians (among others) object that the models generated by social science history are believed (at least by their inventors) to have greater explanatory power than can readily be accepted by those who honor all of the recalcitrant particulars of specific historical situations. Let me illustrate the problem with an example from a field outside of social history per se: Robert Wright's *The Moral Animal*, an account of recent developments in the field of evolutionary psychology.[3] In Wright's lively prose, various events in the private life of Charles Darwin become a case study to demonstrate the analytic power of some of the central claims made by evolutionary psychologists. This is certainly a witty and provocative idea, since evolutionary psychology applies Darwinian principles (along with rational choice decision theory, which is also favored by many social science historians) to explain diverse aspects of human behavior. But if Wright's strict *pars pro toto* argument holds, presumably any other human life would be just as exemplary, and so each human life, in the end, tells only one story—the story of how making rational choices that maximize an individual's own reproductive chances, along with maximizing the survival chances and subsequent reproductive chances of an individual's offspring and kin, provide the motor driving every individual

---

[2] In the oral version of one of the papers to which this chapter was originally written as a response. See Quillin 2002.

[3] Wright 1994. The term "evolutionary psychology" has largely replaced "sociobiology."

human (and every animal) existence. That is to say, Darwin, just like anyone else, instinctively micromanaged his life (although obviously not
completely consciously); his choices were determined by the imperative
to improve the likelihood of the reproduction over time of his own gene-
tic material. In this vision of human motivation, apparent differences in
human lives (e.g., Darwin v. Plato), and in the organization of human
societies (e.g., nineteenth-century England v. fourth-century B.C. Athens),
are due to environmental differences alone: we humans (as individual -
genetic-utility maximizers) are faced with a wide range of contextual circumstances, so our societies look rather different. Yet underneath, all societies and all individuals are necessarily (because biologically) committed
to the same mechanism of choice.

To many historians this will, I suppose, sound at least unlikely, and
perhaps pernicious. The notion that each human life should (at the right
level of reductive abstraction) tell exactly the same story about motives,
because each individual human is motivated by the same causal drive to
reproduce, seems to fly in the face of a huge body of empirical evidence
pointing to a wide diversity among human lives and cultures. And so historians might conclude that models built on this combination of genetics
and rational choice theory are either silly or malicious. Or, more charita-
bly, they may allow that the level of reductive abstraction necessary to get
each life and each society to tell the same story is so high as to be ultimately without historical explanatory power. At a more advanced level
of intellectual generosity, the historian may simply say that Wright's version of evolutionary psychology lacks the power to explain the phenomena that professionally interests him or her.

Now, in choosing Wright on evolutionary psychology as a paradig-
matic case to exemplify what many cultural historians (inter alios) may
find wrong with social science history, I have intentionally taken an example of reductionist "scientism"—one outside of the realm of history as
such and one which I suppose would be vigorously championed by none
of the authors involved in the current historians' debate over social science
and culture. The question of how much weight one can put on analytic
models derived directly or indirectly from social science becomes murkier
in genuine historical practice: How, for example, should we explain the
underlying causes of revolutionary movements? In a hotly debated case
study (still well outside of the ambit of classical Greek history), historians
of early modern England argue about the origins of the "English Revolution" of the mid-seventeenth century. Are the events of the 1640s best
explained by reference to underlying economic and/or technological
changes—that is, causes that could be extrapolated to other historical cases
of revolutionary action? Or—as is argued by the so-called Revisionists—
should historians be focusing on very specific and local responses to very

specific and local events?[4] This debate is a long way from evolutionary psychology, but the basic concern is the same: explanatory models derived from social science are regarded by some historians as implausible, in that they do not manifest an adequate "fit" to the observable empirical data; or they are regarded as irrelevant, in that they do not gain any substantial "purchase" on the phenomena that the historian feels professionally committed to understanding.

And so we come to cultural history itself, which focuses directly upon cultural difference, specificity, contingency, and the capacity of local societies to construct their own local meanings. Cultural history tends to be concerned with functional explanation: how members of a society, or subgroups within a community, negotiated a set of meanings that allowed them to continue to live in an existing community. And thus cultural historians seek to understand the logic of relationships embedded in a society's discourse (as preserved in texts) and implied by its practices. Cultural historians tend to be particularly sensitive to the role played by ambiguous or even apparently contradictory representations of lived experience. They read ambiguities and contradictions as evidence for strategic negotiations between individuals and between diverse social groups—for example, between elites and non-elites, men and women, insiders and outsiders. The structure of society is seen as a dynamic, but fairly stable context for these ongoing negotiations, which, on the political plane, will determine who wields what sort of power under what circumstances and on the basis of what sort of legitimacy claims. Although cross-cultural comparisons are certainly possible within cultural history—indeed such comparisons are quite common—the goal is typically to elucidate what is *distinctive* about each society, rather than to find the "unitary underlying cause" that produced similar historical effects.

There are various explanatory problems that arise from the cultural historian's focus on the specific and the local, on context and negotiation. One set of problems is familiar from critiques of positivism. While sharing the historical positivist's love of the particular, cultural historians today tend to distinguish themselves from practioners of traditional positivist historiography—that is, from the attempt to establish secure facts about the past "for their own sake," to describe "what Alcibiades did and suffered."[5] Among the perceived problems with the positivist approach to classical Greek history is that, after the monumental work of the nineteenth-century historians of classical Greece (e.g., Grote and Busolt), Greek historians suffered a drought of significant and securely established new facts. The spate

[4] See, for example, the discussion of the controversy in Zaret 2000.
[5] For a defense of the positivist approach, arguing that it need not fall victim to a simplistic view that it is possible to establish a completely "objective" account of the past, see Rhodes 1984.

of important inscriptions discovered in the course of the excavations of the Athenian Agora allowed positivists to enjoy a second spring in the mid-twentieth century. But in recent decades the slowed pace of excavation and publication has reduced the supply to a trickle. This left most positivist historians with two main options: either revisit a well known controversy and attempt to resolve it by establishing a new important fact (e.g., the existence of a "Peace of Callias" in the mid-fifth century), or extend the range of what are considered significant facts.

The first approach has resulted in the publication of many books and articles but it has not, I think, actually resolved many controversies (the Peace of Callias is exemplary). The second approach, the extention of the range of relevant facts, has had the salutary effect of widening the chronological and geographic range of Greek history, stimulating excellent new work on Hellenistic and "epichoric" history. But among historians who study the great central and southern Greek states (especially Athens and Sparta) in the fifth and fourth centuries B.C., the "extension of the fact" has sometimes led to a focus on details so fine that it threatens to reduce their readership to the disappearing point. M. I. Finley fulminated against this second approach, damning the "democracy of facts"—the tendency to suppose that everything that can conceivably be known about the past should be known, and that everything known is of equal value.[6]

A related problem associated with the relative paucity of major new facts for "mainstream" classical Greek history, and the high value attached to important new evidence about (say) classical Athens, is the tendency of some historians to restrict access to evidence. Those who "own" publication rights to important unpublished inscriptions, for example, sometimes delay publication for extended periods, meanwhile allowing private access to the new material to a limited circle of students and colleagues. There are reasonable enough explanations for this pattern of professional behavior, but it does lead to the suspicion that priviledged access is sometimes given or withheld for extraneous reasons, thereby raising concerns about fairness, and perhaps arousing (unwarranted) disdain for practioners of the positivist approach in general.

Of course there are some recent and laudable successes of positivist history to which Greek historians can proudly point. I think of Mogens Hansen's splendid series of articles from the 1980s with titles beginning with "How many?, "How often?" and so forth. Hansen's work established, to most scholars' satisfaction, a number of new and important facts

---

[6] Finley 1985. I write as one who spent years laboring happily to produce new, if minute, facts (e.g., precise measurements of windows) about classical Greek fortifications. There is no doubt that such work can be fun; the question is whether the facts it produces will be regarded as useful by one's professional colleagues.

about how the Athenian Assembly functioned. His conclusions left historians of Athenian democracy dancing with glee, because we felt that we had learned something new after finishing each article. The experience of sheer delight in the establishment of important new facts is an experience shared (I believe) by most historians. This may be because there is, after all, a bit of the positivist in all of us, but it is also (and importantly) because we recognize that established facts are what allow us to test our models and theories; if my approach easily accounts for a new fact, I expect that to count when my fellow historians evaluate my work. But, for classical Greek historians, encounters with really important new facts remain rare and cultural history offers one way to extend the scope and broaden the significance of what we might hope to accomplish. Those Greek historians still fascinated by the "mainstream" poleis in the classical period, who are unimpressed with the explanatory claims of social science history, who despair of ever solving old riddles, who are uninterested by the study of minutiae and who may be disenchanted by limited access to new material, have consequently sought to develop a fresh approach to local and specific history, one that focuses more on the social and cultural meaning of discourse and practice than on the establishment of new institutional or chronological facts.

But there remains a problem, the social science historian contends, in that cultural history fails to offer an adequate explanation for change. The question of *why* new things happened, *why* historical actors make the (sometimes very unexpected) choices they do, can get lost in the pleasures of thickly describing *how* people negotiate identities and existences within and against pre-existing protocols. In extreme cases, the cultural historian's assumption that negotiation within established protocols is what really matters approaches the ontological claim that cultural rules are "always and already" in place. At this point, the historical enterprise itself seems to be in doubt: if social rules, substantial enough to ensure that action is coextensive with negotiations within the frame they define, are "always and already" pre-existing, then the space left for meaningful social change shrinks to zero. Ontologically based and historically based explanations for social and cultural phenomena are not necessarily incompatible. But I think they occupy interpretive spheres that remain distinct enough that cultural historians must acknowledge that at some point (one might dispute just where) an argument ceases to be historical in that it has lost the capacity to address even the possibility of change.

The cultural historian must also be ready to make some hierarchical choices among the universe of significant meanings. Presumably anyone impressed by Finley's attack on the "democracy of facts" should be equally critical of an approach based (explicitly or tacitly) on a "democracy of meanings." The attachment of the cultural historian to the local and specific makes it easier to fall into the "democracy-of-meanings" trap: after all, if each society (or subcommunity; see chapter 4) is distinct, negotiating meanings in respose to an infinitely variable environment, then there are by the same token an infinite variety of meanings that can be generated and negotiated by participants, and then described by the astute historian. But which of these had any measurable effect on the course of (say) classical Athenian history understood as an integral part of Greek history? How do we rank the meanings that substantially affected people's actions, as opposed to meanings that were so local and specific as to have had no significant part to play in the larger issue that we (those engaged in a given scholarly problem) have agreed we should be trying to explain? The distinctive Athenian response to a *stasis* situation in 403 B.C. provides a case in point.

The Athenian *stasis* of 404–403 and its distinctive outcome seems to be a particularly good testing ground for the competing claims of social science history and cultural history. It may also provide a particularly good paradigm case of why historians should pay attention to both approaches. As I suggested above, understanding *stasis* is a genuinely important historical (and political) issue and was recognized as such by contemporaries. It is not susceptible to charges that, as a phenomenon, it is epiphenomenal, minute, or of narrowly local concern. Understanding the Athenian *stasis* demands that the historian confront the issues of change and discontinuity. The *stasis* of 404–403 represented a radical break in the continuity of Athenian life, and Athenian politics and society in the fourth century were clearly not identical to the politics and society of the pre-*stasis* fifth century. And yet there is also a very real issue of cultural-political continuity: one need not accept the teleological perspective of the Aristotelian *Ath. Pol.*, which sees the restored democracy of the fourth century as the culmination of a political development dating back at least to Solon in the early sixth, to accept that the Athenian political structures and social protocols that emerged in the aftermath of the restoration of 403 manifest an organic connection with those that had pertained before the reign of the Thirty.

So where does all this leave us? Perhaps in a place that is best understood in terms of contemporary moral philosophy. In a recent refutation of Plato's claim that human reason might finally bring an end to all conflict (in the polis and in the soul), Stuart Hampshire argues that there will always be conflict over *substantive* questions associated with justice and fairness (e.g., who deserves what in terms of distribution of goods and punishments). But, he asserts, there is a high degree of cross-cultural agreement about the need for *procedural* justice and fairness based on institutionalized "adversary reasoning" (i.e., dispute-resolution procedures, predicated on "hearing the other side," that decide who gets what in any given situation).[7] Hampshire's line of reasoning should be quite familiar to Greek historians who have followed recent scholarship on the procedural focus of Athenian law (see chapter 7). But Hampshire's conjunction of an acceptance that conflict over questions of morality and substantive justice is inevitable—even between sincere, well-meaning, and rational persons—with an argument that a deep commitment to fair procedure is an attribute common to communities embracing very diverse values, also provides an analogy for the debate between social science history and cultural history. There are substantive differences among social science historians and cultural historians in terms of what they suppose are the most historically relevant phenomena, in their understanding of human motivations, and in their judgment about whether change or continuity is of greater interpretive moment. Yet there is, or so I imagine, a substantial common ground between social science historians and cultural historians: they are not historical positivists (despite a delight in and a respect for facts) and they are committed to avoiding strongly ontological explanations in order to leave space for social and cultural change (whether or not they are primarily interested in explaining change). Moreover, I suppose that both sides in the debate (along with positivist historians) share a basic faith in the procedural means by which Greek historians test one another's arguments.[8]

I discussed the problem of historical models and paradigms (although not in the specific context of social science or cultural history) in a short essay first published in 1989.[9] I argued that the employment of models is necessary and inevitable if history is to make any advance, and that we test one another's model-based explanations by reference to the specifics of the historical situation, by paying attention to what established facts the model does and does not explain. Any model that requires a great deal of analytic machinery, and yet explains rather little about the evidence we care to explain, will not be judged very useful. By contrast, a model that explains a great deal in comparison to the machinery it needs to muster is likely to be judged both elegant and useful. It comes down to a matter of how good the "payoff" is: how much we feel we have learned about the society in question, how much of the recalcitrant mass

---

[7] Hampshire 2000, arguing that "hearing the other side" is the core cross-cultural principle of fairness. He offers "weighing of evidence for and against a hypothesis in a social science" and "the weighing of evidence in a historical . . . investigation" as prime examples of adversary reasoning (19–20).

[8] Hampshire 2000, 45, suggests that those who "share certain professional attitudes and customs, and a common professional morality" constitute the "true communities" of modernity.

[9] Reprinted in Ober 1996, chapter 3.

of evidence gets organized, and how efficiently it is organized. Rethinking this series of methodological claims in terms of Hampshire's substantive conflict–procedural agreement distinction, I would suggest that there is actually quite a high degree of agreement about *evaluative procedure* among historians who continue to disagree sharply on matters of *interpretive substance*. This is why historians who have mastered a common body of facts (e.g., historians of classical Athens), and yet employ very different approaches for explaining those facts, feel that they can fairly evaluate one another's work. It is why a fair-minded positivist can acknowledge that a work of a given social science or cultural historian is "good of kind" (even if not to his taste).[10] And it is why (a fortiori) cultural and social science historians can and should engage in productive dialogue over important questions, including the Amnesty of 403 B.C.

[10] I take this opportunity to express my pleasure in my long dialogue over "how to do Athenian history," with a model "fair-minded positivist," Peter Rhodes. See now Rhodes 2003.

CHAPTER NINE

Greek *Horoi*: Artifactual Texts and the Contingency of Meaning

Horos is a Greek term for "boundary" and "boundary-marker." This chapter moves from the concern with cultural specificity to the closely related issue of the historical contingency of the cultural meanings employed within a given community. With reference to the issue of "thinking alike and thinking differently" raised in chapter 6, it is clear that some level of "thinking alike" about key political concepts is essential for a community to persist over time—and, by the same token, some of those concepts will be very difficult to recover once the community has gone out of existence. Physical boundaries of various sorts, from national borders to private property lines, are necessary for the sustained existence of any complex and place-structured political community. Those boundaries will need to be marked in some way, but cultural traditions about boundary marking vary considerably.

This essay, which originally appeared in a collection of essays on the archaeological interpretation of texts and artifacts, confronts the interpretive complexity introduced by physical boundary-markers (e.g., slabs of stone inscribed with a few letters) as "texts" that are read easily by the members of a local community, but which may remain enigmatic to would-be interpreters who are denied a share in the full panoply of cultural resources bearing on the making and reading of local meanings.* This is a familiar (if sometimes inadequately acknowledged) problem of historical interpretation: the classical historian is constantly reminded of his lack of essential cultural knowledge when seeking to understand cultural artifacts (whether it is a literary text or a stone pillar). The problem of boundaries and locally bounded cultural meanings is not, however, uniquely a matter for historians. The issue of boundaries, how they are defined, what sort of constraints they impose, and how their presence and significance is communicated, is very relevant to the question of citizenship and assimilation (cf. chapter 4) and thus is a central issue for political theory.

Part of the argument of this chapter builds on my understanding of speech act theory, as it was originally conceived by J. L. Austin and developed by subsequent interpreters. Speech is, of course, a universal

---

* This essay was first published in D. Small, ed., *Methods in the Mediterranean: Historical and Archaeological Views of Texts and Archaeology.* Mnemosyne Supplement 135 (Leiden: E. J. Brill, 1995), 91–123. Reprinted with permission of E. J. Brill.

attribute of human communities—it is (as Aristotle recognized in the Pol-itics) the core competency that allows us to share social and technical knowledge with our fellows and thus to be the "especially political" ani-mals that we are. It is quite possible for humans to become adept at com-municating in a variety of once-local languages—it is, for example, the capacity of contemporary classicists to read a language that is no longer "native" to anyone that makes it possible to make sense of Greek texts. Yet as every immigrant learns, baseline linguistic capacity is only part of what is needed to grasp and to participate in the political meanings that animate a given community. If we hope to make ancient Greek politics a resource for ourselves, we need to recognize the bounds of our own under-standing. Moreover, as Austin saw clearly, the conditions for "felicity"— that is, for successful uptake of a performative speech act—are culturally specific. Absent a culturally specific set of felicity conditions, linguisti-cally comprehensible statements will not serve as speech acts, and thus will have no capacity to effect social change. Boundaries help to define the con-texts in which certain statements, by certain persons, will bring about so-cial change and those by others will remain "infelicitous." Defining the conditions for felicitous speech is among the most important political work done by culture.

Recent classical scholarship that bears on this essay's concerns include Ma 2000 (on speech acts and historical interpretation); Stanton 1996, Langdon 1999 (on rupestral horoi of Attica); Cole 1999–2000 and 2004 (on the role of boundaries in Greek religious ritual); and L'Homme-Wéry 1996 and 2000 (on Solon and Athenian conceptions of territorial borders).

• • •

THE GREEK *HOROS* (boundary-marker) is a good starting point for a med-itation on the social meanings that may be deduced by historians and archaeologists from the interrelationships between text and material arti-fact, on the one hand, and between reference, performance, and social context, on the other. In its most obviously recognizable form, the *horos* is a stone stele inscribed with the Greek letters ΟΡΟΣ.[1] It may thus ap-pear to be a rather simple sort of artifact (a block of stone) carrying a

---

[1] Examples (including such variants as ΗΟΡΟΣ [with three- or four-bar sigma], HOPO, OPO, OPOC [lunate sigma], OPOC A' ["*horos* no. 1"]): *IG* I² 902A, *IG* II² 2502–24 (some twenty other examples are noted, but not actually printed, by the editors of *IG*); Traill 1986, 117, #7. See now Langdon 1999 for discussion of letter forms and chronology. As we will see, there are formally simpler (anagraphic) types of *horos*; but these are not so easily recognized as *horoi*. I would like to thank Charles Hedrick, Merle Langdon, Hans Lohmann, Adrienne Mayor, David Small, Greg Stanton, John Traill, and Brent Vine for comments and offprints that helped me to write a piece with which some of them have substantial disagreements.

rather simple sort of text (a word). Neither the artifact's form nor the text itself makes any claim to uniqueness. It can be iterated (copied or cited) by almost anyone in almost any context. At the same time, both the veracity and felicity of any given *horos*'s claim to mark a boundary is a direct function of its specific location. The *horos* informs its reader that a border has been established at a particular point in space, and implicitly commands the reader to act accordingly. This command is an example of a written speech act in the form of a declarative statement: but what, precisely, is that statement?

I Am the *Horos* of the Agora

Two narrow stone stelai, discovered still in situ during the excavations of the west side of the Athenian Agora, make the *horos*' declaration explicit. Each stele is inscribed, in archaic lettering, with the following text: "I [the stele] am the *horos* of the Agora."[2] On one level that sentence is a straightforward truth claim, a statement in the form of a declarative sentence that is either true or false. In order for the statement to be true (i.e., both accurate and coherent), the *horos* of the Agora must remain fixed in its original position and the Agora must exist. If someone were to pull up the Agora *horos* and carry it somewhere else, the statement it proclaims would no longer be accurate, since it would no longer mark a boundary of the Agora.[3] And if no one knew what "the Agora" was, the statement would cease to be coherent. Likewise, iteration is likely to entail a loss of veracity: for example, the statement that marks the beginning of this section of my essay is false (when read as a declaration) in that the page on which it appears is obviously not the boundary of the Agora.

The veracity of the *horos* is thus directly tied both to its physical situation and to the existence of an identifiable referent for the space that it claims to delimit. Yet presumably no one (in ancient Athens or today) would understand as *merely* referential the sentence, "I am the *horos* of the Agora"—that is, as representing nothing beyond a banal statement of fact in the form "*x* is *y*" (similarly, no reader of this essay would be likely to take the section heading as a false referential claim being made by the page itself). In using the first person singular in order to proclaim

---

[2] ΗΟΡΟΣ ΕΙΜΙ ΤΕΣ ΑΓΟΡΑΣ: Agora inscription inv. nos. I 5510 (total height: 1.20 m., white island marble), I 7039 (original height: 0.68 m. above ground level), both dated to ca. 500 B.C. by context pottery and letter forms. A third, similar *horos* (I 5675) was found out of place. See Thompson and Wycherley 1972, 117–19; Camp 1986, 48–52; Daverio Rocchi 1988, 16.

[3] I am excepting here the case in which a legitimate authority moves the *horos* and reestablishes the boundary, for example, in order to extend the space encompassed by the Agora.

itself "the *horos* of the Agora," the stele was doing rather more than just informing a curious bypasser that "this point just happens to be where the Agora begins"; in asserting its presence in the first person, the *horos* takes for itself the role of watcher-over and guardian of the frontier it marked. As permanent watcher and guardian (one that remains present in the absence of its human author) the *horos* issued a command to the reader: "I order you not to cross the frontier unless you are are among those entitled to do so." Thus, in the process of being informed that the Agora begins "right here," the ancient Greek reader of the Agora *horos* was also enjoined to act in a certain way. If, for example, he had committed homicide, he was ordered to proceed no further: according to Athenian law, murderers (and certain other malefactors) were forbidden to enter the Agora.[4] The *horos* is thus an example of what some speech act theorists call the performative-constative: that which is grammatically a statement of fact (a truth claim with a referentially clear subject and object) is also an action: that is to say, the statement does something, it performs a significant and obviously recognizable social function.[5]

The question one usually asks of a performative statement is not whether it is true or false, but whether it is felicitous or infelicitous, that is, whether the intended speech act (in this case, an order) was efficaciously delivered and received—whether the "uptake" was successful (this is, of course, not the same as asking whether or not the order was in fact obeyed).[6] Achieving felicity is a matter of context. It requires that the

[4] The Greek term for "watcher-over" or "guardian" is οὖρος, formally identical to the Ionian form (used by Homer) for *horos* and often used in compounds related to the protection of liminal zones, for example *pulōros* (gate-keeper), *thurōros* (door-keeper), *phrouros* (guard); even if, as is generally supposed, the two terms ὅρος and οὖρος do not share a common root, the concepts (border-frontier, watcher-guard) are intimately related in Greek practice and thought. On "egocentric" (first person) inscriptions and their assertion of presence, see J. Svenbro, "J'écris, donc je m'efface. L'énonciation dans les premières inscriptions grecques," in Svenbro 1988. Laws limiting access to the Agora: Andocides 1.71, 76; Aeschines 3.176; Demosthenes 24.60; cf. MacDowell 1978, 111; Camp 1986, 51.

[5] For a cogent introduction to speech act theory, see Petrey 1990, who points out (42–56, contra E. Benveniste) that a speech act need not take the specific grammatical form of an imperative; cf. Searle 1969, 68. On commands or orders as speech acts: Searle 1969, 64, 66.

[6] The distinction between felicity and obedience is clarified by considering the order-issuing authority's reaction to a failure to obey. That reaction can be quite different if the authority in question believes that uptake occurred (i.e., that the person given the order understood the order and the relevant social rules) or did not occur (i.e., the person ordered failed to grasp the sense of the order). An example of the first (felicitous) case is a licensed motorist ignoring a stop sign. An example of the second (infelicitous) case is a recent arrival to the state of Montana crossing a fence marked with orange paint (indicating "no trespassing"). While it may be that, legally speaking, "ignorance of the law is no excuse," in ordinary social practice the distinction is frequently highly relevant.

parties in question—she who gives the order and he who receives it—be willing to operate according to the same general set of social conventions. Furthermore, the receiver of the order must accept the legitimacy of the authority giving the order.[7] Not every speech act which takes the form of a declarative sentence requires that the statement be true in order to achieve felicity.[8] But in the case of the *horos*, the felicity of the speech act does indeed seem dependent on its veracity, that is, upon its being both properly located and referentially coherent.

The relatively prolix (four-word) Agora *horos* informs its readers of the name of the space it delimits; moreover, because the Athenian Agora was public space, the inscription clearly implies that it was established by public authority (i.e., by the government of the polis of Athens). Thus anyone who knows the rules associated with the Agora will understand how he or she is expected to act and by what body he or she might be expected to be punished for misbehavior. The simpler (one-word) form of *horos*, described in the first paragraph of this chapter, does not name what it delimits or who authorized it; rather it assumes that its readers will be able to supply those names and the associated rules for themselves. For the knowledgeable member of the society that established it, the one-word *horos* says a good deal: "I am the boundary of *x*, established by the legitimate authority *y*, and you are accordingly ordered to act in the prescribed manner *z*." The fundamental interpretive problem presented by the laconic one-word *horos* is how we, not being members of ancient society, are to fill in the values of *x*, *y*, and *z*.

The problem of interpretation is compounded by the fact that the one-word *horos*—as a single artifact bearing a single, unaltered text—could, in the course of its existence, quite easily come to delimit referentially different spaces. And it could thereby come to demand completely different sorts of behavior of its reader. Suppose, for example, that a man marked the border of his privately owned plot of land by erecting a *horos*. After his death, his son dedicates the land to a god. In this case the *horos*, which once marked the border of a private field, now marks the border of a sacred temenos. Alternatively, a one-word *horos* stone

---

[7] Conditions for felicity: Austin 1975, 14–45; Searle 1969, 62–71; Petrey 1990, 12–13.

[8] For example, a gangster boss says in the presence of his henchmen, "X is a dead man." His minions answer, "Right, boss." In actuality X is, at the moment, alive and well; both the boss and his henchmen know this. Yet the boss's statement is obviously not a false description, but a command to murder X. The henchmen do not aquiesce to a false description of reality, but indicate their intention to obey an order. The boss's statement is a felicitous (if reprehensible) speech act because the henchmen grasp the boss's meaning and accept his authority.

might be removed from its original position (e.g., marking private land) and then formally installed in a different position (e.g., to mark an existing sacred temenos). In either case, a text which originally signified and performed the sentence, "I am the *horos* of private land; I order you not to trespass," later signified and performed a different sentence, "I am the *horos* of the sacred temenos; I command you to perform the appropriate ritual." Exactly the same physical object, exactly the same text; and yet the former values x and z were quite easily changed to a and c. The one-word *horos* thus provides a particularly clear example of the impossibility of complete authorial control of textual meaning: the individual who cut the original *horos* had no control over its subsequent meanings in the two hypothetical cases just noted. And thus, even if modern archaeologists can assign particular x, y, and z values with a high degree of probability to a given *horos*, we must not suppose that they have therefore isolated *the* unitary and permanent meaning of the sign.[9]

Below, I will look at several examples of ancient Greek *horoi*, beginning with some ancient literary descriptions of artifacts unattested archaeologically and concluding with several series of *horoi* discovered by field archaeologists, artifacts for which there is no secure literary attestation. I hope to make two main points: First, the *horos* is a marker of socially vital distinctions. Second, grasping the nature of the distinctions in question depends on a knowledge of changing and historically specific social codes. Looking at how several texts treat *horoi*, and examining the *horos* as an "artifactual text"—as a text that is an artifact, and at the same time an artifact that is a text—should help to elucidate some semiotic issues and methodological problems involved with moving back and forth between texts and artifacts, history and archaeology. Along the way I hope to demonstrate that problems addressed by literary theorists and philosophers of language are not simply clever-but-irrelevant word games; rather these problems have direct bearing on the everyday work of historical and archaeological interpretation.

---

[9] *Horoi* marking sacred lands: *IG* I² 858, 860; II² 2596–2612 (e.g., ΟΡΟΣ ΙΕΡΟ, ΟΡΟΣ ΤΕΜΕΝΟΥΣ, with or without name of the relevant deity added). Historical mid-fourth century B.C. examples of erecting *horoi* to mark as sacred land which had formerly been cultivated privately: By officials of the Amphictyonic League in lands claimed by Amphissans (decree apud Demosthenes 18.154: *kai stēlais dialabein tous horous*). By the Athenians in the territory known as Orgas on the Megarian border (*IG* II² 204); cf. Ober 1985, 216n16; Daverio Rocchi 1987. For a stimulating treatment of the diverse "social meanings" of the *horos* as a sign, and the "plasticity" of *horos* as a symbol, see Louis Gernet, "Mortgage *Horoi*," in Gernet 1981, esp. 309.

ATHENA'S STONE: *HOROS* OF THE PLOWLAND

In book 21 (403–5) of the *Iliad*, in the midst of a fight with the god Ares, the goddess Athena picks up a stone which, as Homer informs us, was "lying there on the plain, [it was] dark, rough, and huge; former men had established it as a boundary of the plowland."[10] The brief reference does not, at first glance, give the reader a great deal to go on: The stone's great size (*megan*) points to Athena's superhuman physical strength. And the reference to "former men" (*andres proteroi*) and their artifacts has obvious parallels with other poetic references to the ancient residents of the Troad and their artifactual remains.[11] Athena's stone plays a minor role in the epic, but is a valuable starting point for investigating a *horos* in a literary text as a complex archaeological artifact.

The stone in question was rough (*truchēn*) and so apparently unworked, ergo a natural object, rather than an a priori artifact. Yet it had been "established" (*thesan*) as a *horos* by the act of men. What precisely were the human actions (words or rituals) which constituted the establishment? We cannot say. It is perfectly possible to suppose that the men of old had physically moved the stone from somewhere else to the edge of the plowland. And thus the very act of setting it into place could have constituted its establishment (thus LSJ s.v. τίθημι, A). But it is equally possible to suppose that the plowland itself was laid out only as far as the location of a stone that was already lying (*keimenon*) in place. In this case some pronouncement or ceremony presumably would have been performed (LSJ s.v. τίθημι, B) in order to establish as *horos* a stone that remained in situ. The status of the stone as an artifact seems somewhat less problematic in the first case than in the second. Yet, unless the stone were part of a recognizable series (i.e., either built into a continuous wall or one of a line of similar stones), there would be nothing about this very stone to distinguish it as as a holder of special meaning. To "later men" (let us say, modern field archaeologists surveying the Trojan Plain), Athena's stone would not be recognizably a *horos*, but just another big hunk of rock. Homer's readers, on the other hand, know that the stone Athena picked up was once a *horos*, but only because he informs them of

---

[10] Full quote: "But she [Athena], drawing back, seized a stone in her mighty hand, it was lying there on the plain, dark, rough (*truchēn*), and huge (*megan*); former men (*andres proteroi*) had established it (*thesan*) as a *horos* of the plowland. With this she struck furious Ares on the neck, loosing his knees."

[11] For example, 2.811–815 (the poet mentions a steep mound which men call Batieia, but the gods know it as the *sēma* of Myrine); 23.326–33 (Nestor points out to his son a dead stump flanked by stones which he posits may either be the *sēma* of a long dead man or a race marker established by "former men" (*epi proterōn anthrōpōn*).

this fact; the poet's text imparts meaning to an otherwise unremarkable object. But the text does not enable its readers to move from the stone mentioned in the text to any given material stone visible in the field: the *Iliad* passage may alert the archaeologist surveying the Troad to the possible function of actual "dark, rough, huge" stones, but it does not *eo ipso* allow him or her to establish the function of any given stone.[12]

The Homeric passage underlines the contingency of signification: The "former men" knew the stone was a *horos* because they operated according to an agreed-upon common code of signs and behavior (a language of words and actions) and were participants (even if indirectly) in the act which established the stone as a boundary. Once they were gone, the code was lost (except to knowledgeable poets) and so the once-established meaning slipped from the object. Later historians, attempting to reconstruct the code used by the former men, will not be able to restore the earlier meaning unless they are lucky enough to have available a text that is quite specific about the location and appearance of the object. In this case, Homer's text takes us part of the way, but not quite far enough.

Homer does name the space delimited by the *horos*: he tells us that the stone once marked the boundary of the plowed land. Thus the natural object, once it had been established as an artifact, differentiated the land that was cultivated from that which was not. Why had the former men thought it necessary or desirable to mark this distinction by establishing a *horos*? Once again, the text fails us. The poet does not indicate whether the boundary had a significance that was religious: was the wild land sacred to some deity? Or economic: was the uncultivated land owned by someone other than the owner of the cultivated land, and/or put to some different economic use (e.g., as grazing grounds)? Nor does he identify the authority by which the stone was established as a boundary: The decree of a king? An agreement among family groups living in the area? A divine pronouncement? We cannot even say whether the authority was sacred or secular, public or private. Moreover, lacking any further textual elucidation, we cannot say what the intended practical effect of the existence of the boundary would have been—that is to say, how the behavior of the "former men" would have been altered after the *horos* had been established: Were only certain persons given (or denied) permission to pass the boundary? Was it forbidden to cultivate land beyond it? We do not know. And a fortiori we have no idea what sanctions might have been imposed upon those who chose to ignore the boundary-marker or whose responsibility it was to enforce the sanctions.

---

[12] Unless, of course, the geology of the region were such that the appearance of big, dark, rough stones on the surface could confidently be assigned to human agency.

Homer's text does, however, make one further and very important point about the boundary-stone: if (per above) its meaning as a boundary was not transhistorically fixed, neither was its physical location. The marker could be and was moved (albeit by divine force). Through Athena's action in grabbing it up, the stone was clearly stripped of any remnant of its former meaning as a boundary. After it had been used to bash Ares, the stone was no longer in situ and so could no longer be regarded as marking a boundary (existing or historical) even by those who had been informed by a poet of its (former) status. By employing the stone as a weapon, Athena in effect annulled its claims in regard to the delineation of space and returned the human artifact to the status of natural object. And thus, even the field archaeologist capable of locating the edges of ancient field systems would not recognize the displaced rock as a *horos*.

The fact that Homer felt it was worthwhile to mention that Athena's stone had once been a *horos* points to the significance attached to the establishment of physical boundaries in Greek culture.[13] To the members of the society that had installed it, the *horos* proclaimed that certain territory was "this, not that"—it marked a difference and enacted a distinction where distinction had not previously existed. And thus the establishment of a *horos* was a way of imposing human, cultural, social meanings upon a once-undifferentiated natural environment. The land was brought under human economic control by the work of cultivation and under semiotic control by the closely associated act of instituting markers. These markers had a functional purpose: they indicated different uses to which "this land" could properly be put as opposed to "that land" on the other side of the established boundary. Moreover, the distinctions thus marked had social ramifications: as signs of human control, markers could have the effect of establishing not just what the land could be used for, but *who* had the right to use, perhaps even to tread upon, the demarcated terrain.

If *horoi* were centrally important symbolic and social markers, then it mattered a great deal who had the power to establish or to disestablish them. Possession of the authority to make or unmake distinctions, to attach new and widely accepted significance to objects (e.g., unworked stones), is surely one of the most fundamental measures of human power.[14] This is particularly clear when the decision to create a distinction has obvious economic effects. In complex human societies, determining who can use parcels of arable land, and for what purposes, has immediate and obvious economic implications. So historians and archaeologists certainly do want to know the nexus of human relationships and decisions that

---

[13] Boundaries are, of course, important in other cultures as well; see, for example, in the Old Testament Genesis 31.44–48, Jos. 22.26ff., Is. 19.19–20; and in general Green and Perlman 1985; Ispahani 1989.

[14] See Ober 1989, 338–39.

established *horoi* point to. But Homer's account of Athena's stone and its former status also reminds us that the *horos* itself may be able to tell us next to nothing about those relations and decisions; indeed, we may not even know a *horos* when we stumble over it in the field.

SOLON: *HOROS-ANNULLER AND HOROS*

The contingency of the social meanings proclaimed by *horoi*, and the problems of historical interpretation raised by that contingency, become very clear when we turn from the mythic world of Homer to the historical figure of Solon. In a poetic passage listing his accomplishments, quoted by the Aristotelian *Athēnaiōn Politeia*, Solon speaks of the promises he was able to fulfill by exerting his own power (*kratei*) and by bringing to bear force (*bia*) combined with justice (*dikē*).[15] He asserts that if the extent of his reform program is ever brought into question, the black earth, supreme mother of the Olympians, will be his witness at the tribunal of Time: "For on her behalf I annulled (*aneilon*) the *horoi* which had been established everywhere, so that being formerly enslaved, she is now free."[16] Solon's claim to have acted as disestablisher of *horoi* and liberator of the earth is closely connected in his poem to another liberation: the freeing (*eleutherous ethēka*) of Athenians—the repatriation of those Athenians who had been forced into exile or sold abroad as slaves and the freeing of those who remained in Attica but were forced into a slavish condition and trembled at their master's every whim.[17] Solon pointedly contrasts (through a *men-de* construction) these acts of liberation—which were accomplished by power, force combined with justice—to his writing of laws (*thesmous . . . egrapsa*) that would be applied equally to bad and good alike.[18]

---

[15] [Aristotle], *Athēnaiōn Politeia* 12.4 = Solon F 36 (West—all Solon Fragments are hereafter cited by West number), lines 15–17. I follow the reading of the Berlin papyrus (ὁμοῦ), adopted by Linforth 1919, West, and Chambers (Teubner ed.) rather than that preferred by Kenyon in her Oxford edition (νόμου). For discussion of this important crux, see Ostwald 1969, 3n5; Rhodes 1981, 176; Stanton 1990, 56n5.

[16] Ibid., lines 3–7.

[17] Ibid., lines 8–15: "To Athens, to their divinely-founded homeland, I brought back many persons who had been sold, some unjustly some justly; some of those had fled out of dire necessity, they no longer spoke the Attic tongue after wandering in many places; and others who were subjected here to shameful slavery, fearing the whims of their masters, I made into free men." (trans. P. J. Rhodes, Penguin edition, adapted)

[18] Ibid., lines 15–20: "These things, on the one hand [I accomplished] by my power . . . but on the other hand, I wrote laws for good and bad people alike, providing straight justice for each man" (trans. Rhodes, Penguin edition, adapted). I am following the Berlin papyrus and the reading of Linforth 1919 and West (θεσμοὺς δ') rather than Kenyon and Chambers, who read θεσμοὺς θ'. See Rhodes 1981, 177.

Despite enduring academic uncertainties about Solon's precise constitutional position, the interrelationship of political power, authority over *horoi*, and changes in social relations are explicit in this fragment. Solon freed the earth by annulling *horoi*, just as he freed the Athenians by announcing their liberation. In both cases, previously existing distinctions were declared invalid. Solon's action meant that Athenians would no longer be subdivided into separate status categories of free and slave; to be an Athenian (male) now entailed being a free person, a citizen.[19] And whatever distinctions, marked by *horoi*, that had formerly pertained in respect to use of the "black earth" were now eliminated. But what distinctions *did* the pre-Solonian *horoi* mark? Even without knowing as much as we might like about the conditions of archaic slavery, we may hope to explain in general terms what it might have meant for an individual Athenian to be enslaved or to be freed. It is much more difficult to guess what it meant for "black earth" to be in a condition of slavery or freedom. It is commonly assumed by scholars that the *horoi* annulled by Solon were written records of indebtedness or encumbrance, more or less similar in function, and perhaps in form, to well-attested (archaeologically and in literary sources) inscriptional *horoi* of the fourth century B.C. These were quite detailed records cut into stelai, set up on land that was used as collateral to secure a loan. These fourth-century inscribed records publicly proclaimed the terms under which the property they demarcated was hypothecated. If the Solonian-era *horoi* were official land-encumbrance records of some sort, the annulment of *horoi* would mean the annulment of outstanding debt, or at least of the requirement to pay over some part of the crop annually. So presumably the annulment would be part of (or equivalent to) the *seisachtheia* ("shaking off of burdens") mentioned by *Ath. Pol.* (6.1, 12.4) and Plutarch (*Solon* 15.3–5, 16.3). The presumptive beneficiaries of the annulment of *horoi* would have been the poorer Athenian peasants, the persons Plutarch (*Solon* 13.2) says were called *hektēmoroi*.[20]

This scenario may well be generally correct, but it is complicated by the intractable problem of reconstructing archaic notions of "ownership" and "alienability"; moreover, it goes considerably beyond what Solon himself says he did. As Linforth rightly pointed out, "his [Solon's] statement is cast

[19] Association of the sign of the *horos* with power over persons and property: Gernet 1981, 309. Solon and citizenship: Raaflaub 1985, 62–65; Ober 1989, 60–65; Manville 1990, 124–56.

[20] Fourth-century hypothecation *horoi*: Fine 1951; Finley 1951, 1953; Millett 1991. Solonian *horoi* in relationship to fourth-century B.C. hypothecation *horoi* and the link to the *seisachtheia* and the *hektēmoroi*: F. E. Adcock in *CAH* (1st ed.: 1926) II.33–38; A. Andrewes in *CAH* (2d ed. 1982) III(2).377–82; Linforth 1919, 62–66; Gernet 1981, 303–11; Manville 1990, 126–28. Earler literature on the subject: Finley 1951, 199n23.

in a poetical form, sufficiently clear for his readers, who knew exactly what he was referring to, but somewhat obscure to us."[21] That obscurity is intensified by the fact that no archaic artifact has ever plausibly been identified as a *horos* of the sort Solon claims he annulled; there is no archaeological evidence for hypothecation stelai from Attica earlier than the late fifth century B.C. This apparent gap in the archaeological record could be explained by supposing that the *horoi* in question were made of perishable material.[22] But given the absence of evidence for wooden *horoi*, the absence of Solonian-era *horoi* from the archaeological record might more easily be explained by the assumption that the *horoi* in question were unworked and anagraphic stones, similar in form to the *horos* of the plowland mentioned by Homer. If this is correct, the Solonian *horoi* may actually still exist and some may even be visible in the fields of Attica, although they are unrecognizable as *horoi*. Yet if the *horoi* annulled by Solon were unworked, uninscribed stones, they were evidently markers of distinction rather than detailed records of financial transactions. So what distinction might they have marked before Solon's action?

The context of the "black earth" passage implies that the annulment of *horoi* was linked to the establishment (or restoration) of just relations between a powerful Athenian elite (the men Solon calls *meizous kai bian ameiones*, "greater and more fortunate in life": *Ath. Pol.* 12.5 = Solon F 37.4) and the Athenian masses (whom he calls the *dēmos*: F 36.22, F 37.1). As an alternative to the "record of indebtedness–encumbrance" thesis, we might posit that before Solon's action the *horoi* had marked areas of Attica in which the movements of Athenians of a certain status (e.g., *hektēmoroi*, the enslaved, or non-Eupatrids) were restricted (e.g., areas which they could not leave or enter). This is all, of course, mere speculation. It is offered only to show that assuming the pre-Solonian *horoi* to have been financial records of hypothecation or encumbrance is *also* speculative and that internally coherent alternative hypotheses can be offered. In the end, we may be forced to admit that we do not know what a pre-Solonian *horos* would have looked like or precisely what it signified; as in the case of Athena's stone, the meaning of the marker is contingent upon a vanished (or, in this case, legally abolished) matrix of social relations and rules. We simply do not know enough of the social code of pre-Solonian Athens to reconstruct meanings that were presumably

---

[21] Linforth 1919, 62. Cf. Andrewes in *CAH* (2d ed. 1982) III(2) 377: "His [Solon's] hearers knew in detail what he meant but we have to guess, and the word *horoi* does not by itself settle the issue . . . [But] Solon cannot be saying simply that he abolished many boundaries."

[22] Theory of wooden *horoi* to explain the fact that no Solonian-era *horoi* have ever been found: Stanton 1990, 56. Cf. Adcock in *CAH* (1st ed. 1926) II.33–34: "there is no reason to assume that the [boundary] pillars were of stone indelibly inscribed."

easily accessible to most members of early sixth-century B.C. Athenian society.

Solon uses the word *horos* metaphorically in another fragment, when discussing his relationship with the two parts (*dēmos* and powerful men) of Athenian society. He claims that whereas someone else in his position would not have restrained the common people or rested before his agitation had skimmed the butter from the milk, "I set myself (*katestēn*) between them, like a *horos* in disputed terrain (*en metaichmiōi*)."[23] Here the man who elsewhere boasted of having removed distinction-establishing *horoi*, proudly takes for himself the name and the distinction-enforcing role of the *horos*. Rather than being a devisive instrument for the enslavement of that which should be free, here the (metaphorical) *horos* establishes the vital and legitimate distinction that prevents unfair treatment of one social group by another. One implication of Solon's self-description as a *horos* is that the problem he claims to have solved in the first passage was not the result of distinction ipso facto, but rather of the wrong sort of distinction. We may remember that Solon not only freed enslaved Athenians, but established (or at least revised) precisely defined, wealth-based status categories (*telē*) which officially determined the distribution of political powers and responsibilities for all Athenian citizens.[24]

Moreover, Solon's legislation forbidding the future enslavement of Athenians by their fellows may be regarded as the origin of the formal status of the citizen: an impassable *horos* was (metaphorically) erected between the categories of "free Athenian" and "Athenian slave" (but cf. chapter 5). It is very likely that Solon's permanent ban on the enslavement of Athenians took the form of a written statute—a *thesmos*.[25] If so, it was distinct in Solon's mind and poetic description from the original liberation

---

[23] [Aristotle] *Ath. Pol.* 12.5 = F 37.

[24] Wealth categories: *Ath. Pol.* 7.2–4; Plutarch, *Solon*, 18.1–2. Stinton (1976), bothered by Solon's self-description as *horos*, argues that ὅρος should be emended to οὖρος (watcher/guardian), which seems to me quite unnecessary; cf. n. 4, above, on the closeness of the two terms. Rhodes 1981, 179, after discussing various proposed emendations (and noting that ὅρος and οὖρος may be the same word), concludes "I am not sure that the explanation of this sentence has yet been found." But cf. Manville 1990, 126–27: "The metaphor of the boundary stone was certainly apt. For a general theme in all of Solon's reforms was the creation of boundaries—spatial, legal, and even psychological." Loraux (1984) rightly emphasizes the competitive-military connotations of "being in the middle of things" in this fragment rather than the connotation of political "moderation."

[25] *Ath. Pol.* 6.1 mentions forbidding human collateral for debts, establishing *nomoi*, and the *seisachtheia* as three distinct reforms; at 10.1 forbidding human collateral is included in Solon's *nomoi*, and the cancellation is said to be before his period of *nomothesia*. Plutarch, *Solon* 15.3, lumps these altogether under the rubric of the *politeuma* which Solon wrote. Cf. Linforth 1919, 65–66, who considers forbidding human collateral to be a formal law and separate from the liberation itself.

itself, which had been accomplished (according to the fragment quoted above) by personal power and "force combined with justice." Thus power (*kratos*) and force (*bia*) could justly be employed to disestablish illegitimate distinctions; but the establishment of new distinctions through the production of law is described by the poet-statesman simply as "writing" (*thesmous . . . egrapsa*). The differentiation between the conditions he thought appropriate for performing the two varieties of speech act may cast some light on how Solon viewed (at least in retrospect) the role he had played in the restructuring of Athenian society, and how he understood the nature and extent of the powers he had temporarily wielded.[26] The term Solon uses for "disputed terrain," *metaichmion*, refers literally to the space between the spears of opposing armies. Yet clearly Solon's use of the word is metaphorical: setting a *horos* between two armies would be nonsensical, whereas establishing a boundary in a disputed frontier zone is a reasonable and understandable way of preventing destructive conflict. Solon's metaphorical reference to his own political position as a *horos*, marking a disputed frontier, points to the actual role of physical *horoi* in establishing the exterior territorial borders of a self-contained society (a polis), as well as in establishing valid distinctions operative within a society.[27]

Horoi of the Patris

Sometime in the archaic period, perhaps even before Solon's reforms, the Athenian ephebes, eighteen- and nineteen-year-old Athenian soldiers-in-training (see chapter 6), began to swear a standard oath of allegiance to their fatherland (*patris*).[28] According to the preserved fourth-century B.C. copy of the archaic oath, the ephebe swore to respect sacred rites, to obey the laws and those magistrates who acted rightly, not to dishonor his weapons, not to abandon his place in the line, and to fight alongside his comrades in defense of all national assets, sacred and secular. Moreover, "I shall not hand down a lessened *patris*, but one that is increased in size and

[26] It is tempting to suppose that Solon felt that a tyrant was one who used *kratos* and *bia* (rather than the writing of *thesmoi*) to establish new social distinctions. Such a description would certainly suit sixth-century B.C. tyrants such as Cleisthenes of Sicyon (Hdt. 5.67–68).

[27] The existence of a recognized border between poleis is indicated by the ritual of offering border-crossing sacrifices (*diabatēria*), particularly associated with the Spartan army: Jameson 1991, 198 with n. 2, 202, 220, and references cited. See also n. 33, below.

[28] Tod *GHI*, II.204 (=RO 88 = Harding 1985, no. 109), a fourth-century B.C. inscription from the Attic deme of Acharnai which preserves the oath. Its archaic character (pre-Peisistratid and perhaps pre-Solonian) and discussion of earlier literature: Siewart 1977.

strength, [striving] myself and along with all the others."[29] The oath itself is followed by a long list of witnesses (*histores*): "gods, Agraulos, Hestia, Enuo, Enualios, Ares and Athena Areia, Zeus, Thallo, Auxo, Hegemone, Herakles; *horoi* of the *patris*, wheat, barley, vines, olives, figs."

What did the ephebes and those administering the oath have in mind as a referent for the words *horoi tēs patridos* (boundaries of the fatherland)? The grammar of the second part of the list of witnesses is not absolutely clear. The witness list begins with the term "*theoi*" (gods). The gods in question are then named: a total of eleven divinities, including personifications of "increase, growth, and leadership" (Thallo, Auxo, Hegemone). So far so good. The second part of the list begins with the term "*horoi* of the *patris*" and continues with five major products of arable agriculture. And here lies the crux: is this part of the list paratactic—a series of (six) separate witnessing entities, one of which is "*horoi*"? Or is the phrase *horoi tēs patridos*, like *theoi*, a collective noun whose elements are described by the (five) words that follow? On the second hypothesis, we might suppose that "wheat, barley, vines, olives, figs" is a collective metonym for "the *horoi* of the *patris*." Or (on an even closer parallel with *theoi*) that among a larger set of *horoi tēs patridos*, the particular *horoi* that will witness the oath are (again metonymically) the several products. According to the first (paratactic) hypothesis, the *horoi* are not defined as agricultural products; their physical form remains textually indeterminate. According to the second (metonymic) hypothesis, the *horoi* themselves are actually agricultural products.[30] The metonymic reading certainly makes for better syntactic parallelism (*theoi/horoi*). Moreover, according to Plutarch (*Alcibiades* 15.4), a metonymic reading was adopted as early as the late fifth century B.C. by the politician and general, Alcibiades, who supported his policy goal of boundless imperialism with the argument that the Athenians had sworn to treat as their own *patris* any place in which wheat, barley, vines, olives, and figs were grown. But we need not accept Alcibiades as an unimpeachable authority for the original, archaic reference; his manipulation of the language of the oath falls squarely within the sophistic tradition of twisting accepted meanings to support otherwise dubious postions.[31]

[29] ο⟨ὐ⟩κ ἐλάττω παραδώσω τὴν πατρίδα, πλείω δὲ καὶ ἀρείω κατά τε ἐμαυτὸν καὶ μετὰ ἁπάντων (lines 10–12).

[30] A paratactic reading is assumed by Vidal-Naquet 1986, 122: the ephebe guarantees "to protect the boundary-stones of his country, and with them, the cultivated fields." A metonymic reading seems to be assumed by Siewart 1977, 109. The latter reading might be supported by Thucydides' reference (6.13.1) to the sea as the *horos* between Athens and Sicily.

[31] For Alcibiades' reputed skill as a speaker: Plutarch, *Alcibiades* 10.2–3, 13.1–2; as a sophistic interlocutor: Xenophon, *Memorabilia* 1.2.40–46.

Supposing that wheat, barley, and so forth actually are *horoi* requires that we accept a set of referents for the term *horoi* that is at odds with the referents implied by the Homeric and Solonian passages discussed above. Yet even on a paratactic reading, the syntax of the witness list obviously implies a close relationship between the *horoi* of the fatherland and the various agricultural products. This relationship is hardly unexpected: "Athena's stone" marked the border of the plowland and the *horoi* Solon annulled to free the "black earth" certainly had something to do with the use of arable land. As an alternative to a purely metonymic or purely para-tactic reading, one might be tempted to try a metaphorical compromise: the wheat, barley, vines, olives, and figs refer metaphorically to the actual stone boundary-markers which delimit the fields in which these products were grown. This hypothesis allows the ephebes to imagine as witnesses familiar and concrete entities ("boundary-stones," which, as we have seen above, could assert both their presence and a truth claim by "speaking" in the first person) rather than an abstraction ("borders") reified as a set of agricultural products. Moreover, given its general "watching-over and guarding" function (see above), the *horos* qua boundary-stone would seem to make an eminently suitable witness to an oath. And yet the meta-phorical reading raises its own problems: just as the "*horos* of the Agora" formally delimited the physical space of the Agora, the "boundary-markers of the *patris*" should delimit the physical fatherland, the polis itself. Thus *horoi tēs patridos* can hardly refer to each and every field-boundary in Attica.

In order to try to solve the conundrum, we will have to look outside of the text of the oath itself, and consider some aspects of its context. In Athenian myth and fourth-century B.C. military practice, the ephebes were associated with and responsible for patrolling the frontier zones of Attica.[32] Assuming that this association of ephebes with the frontier ex-tended back to the time of the archaic oath, we might narrow the meta-phoric reading suggested above: the referent implied by *horoi tēs patridos* was, I would suggest, the line of field *horoi* which defined the outermost reaches of Athenian agricultural enterprise. Within this line of *horoi* was the fatherland. The territory outside the line was in some sense wilder-ness: undesignated, undefined, unmarked.

Once again, we are confronted with a complete absence of archaeo-logical evidence that might clarify our literary testimonia. No inscribed Athenian *horos* "of the *patris*" has ever been found.[33] The text of the

---

[32] Ephebes and frontiers: in myth, Vidal-Naquet 1986; in practice, Ober 1985, 90–95. Siewart 1977, 109, claims that the lack of an explicit reference to frontier zones (*eschatiai*) is evidence for the ephebic oath's archaic character.

[33] Markers of national and even ethnic boundaries are mentioned by ancient authors, for example, Plutarch, *Theseus* 25.3 (the stele which Theseus was supposed to have established

oath itself may suggest an explanation for their invisibility. The ephebes taking the oath promise not only to defend their homeland, but also to augment and extend it: "I shall not hand down a lessened *patris*, but one that is increased in size and strength." If the young men swearing the oath took that statement literally (and supposed that the goddesses Auxo and Thallo took an interest in the growth and increase of the *patris* proper, as well as of crops and livestock) then they could not in good conscience allow the *horoi tēs patridos* to remain fixed. It would be their sacred duty to increase the extent of the cultivated land, by pushing back the boundaries of the wilderness.[34] As this process continued and new fields were marked out, the outer line of the *horoi* was necessarily and continually constructed anew. And thus, the precise referent of the phrase *horoi tēs patridos* was inherently unstable—and its semiotic instability was a direct function of the sincerity with which the speech act of the oath was performed.[35] If we imagine the *horoi* in question to be unworked stones designating the borders of agricultural fields, similar to the Homeric example, the exact stones in question would not be the same from generation to generation: an individual *horos* which once designated the boundary of the *patris* would, by the fulfillment of the terms of the oath, become an "internal" *horos*; the distinction it marked would consequently be altered significantly and it would no longer be included in the witnesses for the oath sworn by the next generation of ephebes.

The ephebic oath may be read as a textbook example of a self-deconstructing text: the deathless "witnesses" of the oath, the guarantors, intended as fixed and stable points of reference, are themselves destabilized (their meanings radically altered) by the fulfillment of the conditions imposed upon the oath-takers. The demand for augmentation in the oath

---

at the Isthmus, stating on one side "Here is Ionia, not Peloponnesus," on the other, "Here is Peloponnesus, not Ionia"); Xenophon, *Anabasis* 7.5.13 (Thracian tribes which establish piracy zones with *stēlai* set up as boundary-markers). Lycurgus 1.113, 115, could speak of the bones of the Athenian Phrynichus being dug up and "thrown beyond the borders of Attica"; cf. Dinarchus 1.77. Pausanias mentions frontier-markers of various sorts: 2.38.7; 8.25.1, 34.6, 35.2, 38.7. Some actual examples of inscribed polis border-markers (Aitolia, Laconia-Messenia, Boiotia) have been found, for example *SIG*[3] 933; *SEG* 23.297, 35.406; *IG* V.1 1371–72, VII 2792, IX.I 427, IX.I[2] 1, 116. Cf. comments of Roesch 1965, 61–63; Camp 1991, 195n9; Langdon 1985b 13–14n4; and esp. Sartre 1979, 216–17.

[34] On the "internal colonization" of Attica and the expansion of arable agriculture into marginal land on the frontiers, see Osborne 1985, 6–10; Gallant 1982.

[35] The oath, as a form of promise, is a standard form of speech act: Austin 1975, 157–60 ("commissives"); Searle 1969, 54–62: "as illocutionary acts go, [promising] is fairly formal and well articulated; like a mountainous terrain, it exhibits its geographical features starkly" (54). Note that the instability still pertains even if we accept the metonymic hypothesis and accept the agricultural products as the *horoi* in question.

renders impossible the stability of the witnesses who are supposed to ensure that the demand is fulfilled. The changeless referents of the oath and
the established distinctions they mark cannot survive in the endlessly
changing world which the oath itself enjoins. The inherent instability of the
text and its witnesses may in turn have encouraged new (and sometimes
seemingly perverse) citations and interpretations: Alcibiades is able to cite
the oath as authorizing a reckless and (when viewed in retrospect) destructive plan for overseas imperialism. Even if we regard Alcibiades' sophism
as a special case, however, there is surely no doubt that the ephebes who
swore the oath in the postimperial era of the later fourth century B.C., when
the oath itself was reinscribed, had something quite different in mind than
their archaic and mid-to-late fifth-century predecessors: The wording of
the oath might be *patrios* ("ancestral," that is, a word-perfect citation of
the archaic original), but its cultural meaning was not.[36]

Does the claim that the referent of the term *horoi tēs patridos* was unstable, and that the meaning of the oath itself changed over time, necessarily lead to a "strong" deconstructive conclusion—that is, that this text
is evidence for the inevitable and general collapse (or even impossibility)
of meaning itself? I would say not. At the solemn annual oath-taking ceremony each ephebe performed a speech act (more or less sincerely), and
that act was felicitous in that it was comprehensible and regarded as
binding by both the oath-taker and his community. The fact that a historian can show that the meaning of the oath and the identity of some of its
witnesses must have changed over time need not lead us into the functionally useless assumption that words, meanings, signs, and referents
are somehow unreal for the members of any given human society at any
given point in its history.[37] Each generation of ephebes supposed it knew
what the oath entailed and who (or what) were its witnesses. The ephebes
either kept their promise or failed to do so, and were judged accordingly
by their community. It is the social contingency of meaning, rather than
its ontological indeterminacy, that is historically and politically significant.
Accepting cultural meanings as contingent (as opposed to utterly indeterminate) does not make historical explanation impossible. But it does entail
close attention to details of social context. This consideration underlines
the vital importance of incorporating both "historical" and "archaeological" evidence, both texts and artifacts, when we attempt to describe and to
explain what was going on in past cultures.[38]

---

[36] The fourth-century B.C. copy of the oath is prefaced by the statement "the ancestral oath (*horkos patrios*) of the ephebes, which the ephebes must swear" (line 5). The "postimperial" fourth century B.C.: see below.

[37] What I mean by useless: Ober 1996, chapter 2; cf. chapter 8, above.

[38] For a thoughtful and detailed discussion of this issue, see Morris 1992.

BORDERLANDS: *TA METHORIA*

I suggested above that the land which lay outside the *horoi tēs patridos* could be regarded as "wilderness: undesignated, undefined, unmarked." Yet the land beyond the established frontier was not a trackless wilderness in any simple sense; rather it was a border zone that led eventually to the established frontiers of Megara or the poleis of Boiotia. The borderland between poleis was sometimes referred to as *gē methoria* (Thuc. 2.27.2, 4.56.2) or *ta methoria* (Thuc. 2.18, 5.3.5): literally that which lay "between the *horoi.*"[39] Athenian actions which fulfilled the expansivist goals of the ephebic oath tended to bring land once outside of the borders within the full political control of the state. Because this process was incremental, *ta methoria* remained a rather fuzzy category: yesterday's borderland was today's Attic land. The Athenian garrison town of Oinoe provides a good example. Oinoe was described by Thucydides (2.18.1–2) both as "in Attica" (*tēs Attikēs*) and "in the *methoria* between Attica and Boiotia." The chronological reference point of Thucydides' comment is 431 B.C., the first year of the Peloponnesian War. And yet by that time Oinoe almost certainly enjoyed full deme status and so was a constituent part of the Athenian polis.[40] We cannot say for sure how long before 431 the town of Oinoe was founded or when the land it occupied became part of Attica. The very probable archaeological site of Oinoe (Myoupolis in northwestern Attica) has not been excavated, but a good number of surface sherds have been collected; notably none of these has (so far) been dated earlier than the mid-fifth century. It is a reasonable guess (although, pending excavation, no more than that) that the town was founded by Athenians sometime in the late archaic or early classical period.[41] Whenever the town was incorporated, however, the Thucydides passage shows that in the later fifth century Oinoe could still be described as being located "between the *horoi.*" And thus, the term

[39] Cf. Thuc. 1.103.4: Megara allied with Athens because Corinth was attacking the former in a war "about border land" (*peri gēs horōn*); 1.122.2: the Corinthians remind the Spartans that the coming conflict with Athens will be much different from "disputes about border land" (*peri gēs horōn hai diaphorai*).

[40] Thuc. 2.18.2. Status of Oinoe: Whitehead 1986, 48, 373, 403. Description of the site: Ober 1985, 154–55, 224; Lauter 1992. Note that there are two demes named Oinoe in Attica; I refer here to Hippothontid Oinoe, the western of the two. Herodotus (5.74.2) describes both Oinoe and Hysiai (which was never a deme in the Athenian constitutional sense) as "frontier towns of Attica" (*dēmous tous eschatous tēs Attikēs*).

[41] Date of pottery from the probable deme site: Ober 1987, 211–12; Edmonson 1966, 32. Lohmann 1992, 35, suggests that some demes (including Atene and Piraeus) may not yet have been founded at the time (in 508–507 or 507–506 B.C.) Cleisthenes established the political system based on demes, trittyes, and tribes.

ta methoria could be used (even by a self-consciously precise author like Thucydides) conventionally as well as referentially. It proves to be no easier to define with precision what it meant for a classical writer to say that some place was "between the *horoi*" than it is to fix the meaning of the *horos* itself.

The extension outwards of the borders of Attica and Athenian encroachment on the *methoria* were not processes that could be indefinitely prolonged without provoking Athens' neighbors. The wild, uncultivated *methoria* may seem in one sense a structural inverse of the cultured world of the polis, and thus an ideal liminal space for the conduct of *rîtes de passage* such as the *ephēbeia*.[42] But in the world of inter-polis diplomacy, which depended on establishing distinctions that would be recognized and respected by discrete political entities, it was necessary that the *methoria* be defined in functional terms as carefully as was the land within the borders. As in the case of the *horos*-delimited land we have considered above, the permitted uses of the *methoria*—who had a right to do what in that space, and under what conditions—had to be spelled out. Such was the situation in the region of Panakton, a site in the central Athenian-Boiotian *methoria*.[43] By the time of the Peloponnesian War, the Athenians had built a fortress there; the place was captured by the Boiotians early in the war, and they proceeded to slight the walls before handing it back to the Athenians under the terms of the Peace of Nicias. When the Athenians protested the slighting, the Boiotians produced the following explanation (*prophasis*): "As the result of a dispute, there were ancient oaths in force to the effect that neither side was to possess the place, but they were to graze it in common."[44]

It is worth noting that the terms of the agreement cited by the Boiotians stipulate grazing, rather than arable agriculture as the permitted (common) use of the land in question. But regulation under a formal inter-state agreement is far from the romantic image of the frontier zone as an unrestricted and undefined wild space. On the other hand, the Athenian action in building the fort, which (at least according to the Boiotians) contravened the old agreement, demonstrates how very difficult it might be to maintain agreed-upon interborder land-use standards when more than one society was involved. In this case the expansivist ideals we have seen embedded in the ephebic oath (*horkos ephēbōn*) evidently overrode the "ancient oaths" (*horkoi palaioi*) sworn by the Athenian ambassadors to their Boiotian counterparts; the speech act conventions pertaining within

[42] Thus Vidal-Naquet 1986, 106–28. On mountainous borderlands in Greek myth as areas that are "outside and wild," see Buxton 1992, 7–8.

[43] In *methoria*: Thuc. 5.3.5. The site of Panakton: Ober 1985, 152–54; id. 1987, 209–11; Munn 1990.

[44] Thuc. 5.42.1.

Athenian society proved stronger than those employed between the two states in respect to a border region. The Boiotian attempt to "annul" the inter-polis boundary-marker represented by the Athenian fortress at Panakton proved to be unsuccessful in the long run. The fort was rebuilt by the Athenians in the fourth century B.C. and was indeed used as a base for Athenian ephebes.[45]

The Athenians' tendency to augment their own polis militated against the very concept of *gē methoria* as frontier zone and may, ironically, have given impetus to the eventual establishment of relatively stable linear frontiers. I have argued elsewhere that the period after the Peloponnesian War saw a systematic attempt on the part of the Athenians to rationalize their northern and western land frontiers through the construction of a series of fortresses and watch-and-signal towers. This program represented a significant change from former practice: rather than establishing new fields or garrison towns in order to roll back the borders, the Athenians now focused their attention on the attempt to define a stable border line.[46] Although the ephebes continued to swear that they would augment the size and strength of the fatherland, that promise would no longer be fulfilled by extending Athenian control over the *methoria*. The line of border fortifications implied the existence of a fixed linear frontier, or at least signalled an Athenian desire that stability should pertain. Although even in the fourth century B.C. we have no epigraphic examples of Athenian state-border *horoi*, the forts and towers themselves may be thought of as representing a line of border-markers which defined the limits of the Athenian *patris*.[47]

RUPESTRAL *HOROI* OF ATTICA

What effect might the stabilization of the national frontier have had on the production of social meanings assigned to intra-polis *horoi*? This

[45] This has been conclusively demonstrated by a Stanford University survey and excavation; the field work has not yet been fully published but cf. summary in Munn and Zimmerman Munn 1989 and Munn 1990. See now Munn 1996.

[46] Ober 1985, esp. 208–20. This should not be taken as a hard and fast rule: cf. disputes with Thebes over the border zone of Oropos and with Megara over the sacred Orgas: ibid., 214–17.

[47] Even if we do not accept agricultural products as *horoi*, there is no reason to suppose that a border-marker need always take the form of a stele. Herms and other artifacts were evidently commonly used as border-markers: L. Kahn 1979; Sartre 1979; Daverio Rocchi 1988, 53–59. [Demosthenes] 7.40, for example, claims that the border of the Chersonese peninsula was marked by an altar of Zeus "of the borderland." Lycurgus 1.143 claims that his opponent will beg the jurors to be allowed to live "within the walls of the *patris*" (*en tois teichesi tēs patridos*); given the associations of the term *patris* discussed above, this might be taken to mean "within the territory protected and defined by the fortifications of the fatherland" (rather than, or as well as, "within the walls of the city proper").

question brings us back to a consideration of archaeological evidence proper. In the course of the last decade, a fair number of ancient rupestral (rock-cut) *horoi* have been published from various sites in Attica. Although the inscription sometimes includes an indication (severely abbreviated and thus cryptic) of what sort of territory is being delimited, often just the four letters of the word itself (ΟΡΟΣ or OPOC with lunate sigma) were cut directly into an exposed shelf of bedrock. In several cases, the rupestral *horos* is clearly part of a series which defines a line or even a corner.[48] The single-word rock-cut *horos* is, at first glance, the simplest possible sort of text and simultaneously the result of a very basic process of artifact production: the natural bedrock is turned to human uses through the action of inscribing the four letters. The rupestral *horos* can be viewed as a particularly pure example of text-as-artifact and artifact-as-text: viewed as a text the *horos* is nothing but an artifact (a word in lieu of a stele); viewed as an artifact it is nothing but a text (the bedrock is unaltered except for the inscribed letters).

The physical presence of these simple inscriptions on the bare rock of Attica brings us face to face with the *horos*'s basic function: those who chiseled the letters into the bedrock clearly intended to establish a distinction or set of distinctions. Before the letters were cut, the rock face was a simple, brute fact of nature. With the removal of a few chips of stone, that selfsame fact of nature was redefined in overtly cultural terms. The rupestral inscription is, by definition, in situ; indeed its precise situation and immovability seem intrinsically bound up in its meaning. Unlike Athena's stone, the rupestral *horos* (which exists as an inscribed absence of material, rather than a material presence) cannot be picked up or pushed aside. Unless it is chiseled away or covered up (by human agency or a natural accumulation of debris) it both keeps its place and maintains its claim to establish distinction in this particular place. When several *horoi* form a line, we can say with certainty that the social meaning once imposed upon the ground lying on one side of the line was nonidentical to that imposed upon the ground on the other side: As long as there are humans able to construe the four inscribed signs as a word for "border-marker," the rock-cut *horoi* will continue to proclaim, "Over here, *this*; over there, *that*."

But, to an even greater extent than in the cases of *horoi* attested in literary sources, the rupestral *horos* remains silent in regard to both the nature of the significance it marked and the agency which authorized the establishment of a distinction. In the absence of an explanatory context,

---

[48] Series of *horoi*: List in Traill 1986, 117, and, now, Stanton 1996. For other examples of Attic rupestral *horoi* (individual and series), see note 58, below.

we can say nothing with certainty about an isolated single-word rock-cut *horos* beyond the claim that a distinction was once established at the point of its situation. Nor does the existence of a line of *horoi* get us much further, except insofar as we can now plot the distinction spatially. Chronological context turns out to be very hard to come by: Dating rupestral *horoi* can be a hazardous enterprise, close dating is usually impossible. Exposed bedrock has no stratigraphy; surface sherds (when they happen to be found) cannot be securely associated with the date of the inscription's cutting. We lack a dated typological sequence for rock-cut letter forms; and the relationship between the relatively huge, roughly-cut letters of the rupestral *horos* and the careful work of professional stonecutters on nonrupestral inscriptions remains somewhat tenuous.[49]

Yet there is one notable point about Athenian rupestral *horoi* that has been taken by some scholars as pointing to a context: their occurrence is quite widespread within Attica. Several series of one-word *horoi*, all of which resemble one another in that they employ lunate (rather than three- or four-bar) sigmas, have been found on hills in southern Attica: on Mt. Lykabettos, on Alepovouni in the southwestern foothills of Mt. Hymettos, on Kaminia in southeastern Attica near Vari, on Megalo Baphi near Legrena, and on a ridge east of Mt. Merenda.[50] It is certainly possible to argue (if not to prove) that these various inscription series were cut at about the same time. Assuming that to be the case, one may be willing to take the next (rather large) step and suppose that the

---

[49] Traill (1986, 118) states that "the date of the horoi is problematical, but several have been assigned, on good authority, to the 4th century B.C., and I believe all may be dated to that same period"; the authority in question is not identified. My own suggestion (Ober, 1981, 76) that the four (lunate sigma) Alepovouni *horoi* date to the Roman era on basis of letter forms was accepted by Langdon (1985a, 257–58; strongly reiterated in Langdon 1999) and Whitehead (1986, 29n110), but questioned by Stanton (1984, 301–3) and Traill (1986, 119). For attempts to date other rupestral *horoi*, see, for example, Traill 1982, 168; Langdon 1985a, 257, 260; Langdon 1988b, 50; Langdon 1988a, 77–78.

[50] These are tabulated and discussed in Traill 1986, 116–22. Traill #4 = two on Lykabettos (OPOC with lunate sigma; one now lost): *IG* II² 2521; Traill 1986, 117, 119–20. Traill #6 = two (OPOC with lunate sigma) on the ridge of Kaminia near Vari in southwestern Attica: Lauter 1982; Langdon, 1988b. Traill #5 = two (OPOC with lunate sigma) on a ridge and saddle east of Mt. Merenda: Traill 1986, 117, 120. Traill #2 = five (perhaps more: OPOC with lunate sigma) in line along the ridge of Megalo Baphi near Legrena in south Attica: Lohmann 1983, 99–104; Lohmann 1992, 33. Traill #3 = four (OPOC with lunate sigma) on Alepovouni, a western foothill of Hymettos, defining a line and corner: Ober 1981, 73–77. Traill #1 = six (OP/ΠΜ) on the ridge of Panagia Thiti (139 m) southeast of Hymettos: Traill 1982. A new list of eight series of such *horoi* is offered by Stanton 1996.

inscriptions were cut at the direction of a single authorizing agency. And finally, given their scattered proveniences and the rather large areas they seem to define, one who has swallowed the two previous premises might further speculate that the authority in question was the central government of the polis. And it would then seem reasonable to ask what the Athenian government's purpose might have been in establishing boundaries at various places around Attica. This chain of reasoning brings us back (albeit in a rather roundabout way) to the question posed above, regarding the impact of fixed borders upon the internal subdivision of Attica. If the chain is sound and the inscriptions could be dated to the century after the Peloponnesian War, we might be in a position to make some interesting suggestions about fourth-century Athenian attitudes towards borders generally. But if any one of the chain's links is very weak, we will have to admit that the rupestral *horoi* will not help us solve this historical problem.

A number of scholars have in fact asserted that one or more of several south Attic rupestral *horos* series (including the various lunate-sigma series noted above) were cut in the fourth-century B.C. at the behest of the Athenian state, in order to regularize or reorganize the borders between Attic demes.[51] This is an extremely seductive notion in that it transforms the simple *horos* into highly significant evidence for an important political program. It means that historians can employ spatially fixed archaeological evidence to define the precise borders of demes and hence estimate the size, resources, even populations of individual demes. The deme-marker hypothesis turns these otherwise maddeningly laconic markers into evidence that might be applied to a variety of historical puzzles, from Cleisthenes' original plans (see chapter 2) to (per above) the impact of state-border stabilization on the political organization of the polis. On the whole, it would be very good news for historians of classical Athens if the deme-boundary explanation for the rupestral *horoi* were correct.

Is it correct? In 1981, before most of the *horos*-series from other parts of Attica had been reported, I published a series of four rupestral *horoi* from Alepovouni on the slopes of Mt. Hymettos. I suggested that these Alepovouni *horoi*, which describe a corner (three inscriptions in line with a fourth at a right angle to the third) were best explained as

---

[51] Traill 1982; Lauter 1982; Stanton 1984 and 1996; Whitehead 1986, 29n110 (doubting that the Panagia Thiti and Alepovouni series were deme-markers, but accepting the Megalo Baphi series); Langdon 1988b; Lohmann 1992, 33. Langdon 1999, 494, notes that "a consensus has developed . . . that the boundaries so marked were territorial dividing lines between adjacent demes," while demonstrating that this consensus hypothesis is unlikely in respect to the extended Alepovouni series.

marking the corner of a Roman bee-farm.[52] That explanation was challenged in separate studies by H. Lauter (1982, 315) and G. R. Stanton
(1984, 301–3); the latter argued that the letter forms were less diagnostic
than I had supposed and might be much earlier. Lauter and Stanton advanced the classical deme-marker explanation for the four Alepovouni
horoi and for a *horos* on Kaminia. J. S. Traill (1982) meanwhile suggested that a series of *horoi* (reading OP/ΠM, rather than OPOC) on the
Panagia Thiti ridge south of Hymettos were late fourth-century deme-
markers.[53] Shortly thereafter, H. Lohmann (1983) adopted the classical
deme-marker explanation for the recently discovered Megalo Baphi
series. M. Langdon (1985a) in turn rejected the Lauter-Stanton deme-
boundary hypothesis for the Alepovouni *horoi*, partly on the grounds
that deme-boundaries should follow the natural contours of the ground
and should not therefore make right-angle turns. Langdon, following
an earlier suggestion of G. Culley, proposed associating the Alepovouni
horoi with a Roman-era inscription which mentioned "public highlands"
(*orē dēmosia*) in the Hymettos region and concluded that "the temptation to link this information to the *horoi* on [Alepovouni] is practically
irresistible."[54]

By 1986 Traill (1986, 116) was ready to assert that "the demes were
served by rupestral *horoi*" and felt it no longer necessary even to argue
the case that virtually all of the known rupestral *horoi* of Attica (and several nonrupestral examples) marked deme-boundaries. Langdon (1988b),
who found a second *horos* on Kaminia, was subsequently persuaded
by Traill to adopt the fourth-century B.C. deme-marker explanation for
the two Kaminia *horoi*. Yet accepting the explanation Langdon found
"practically irresistible" for the Alepovouni series *and* his preferred
explanation for the Kaminia inscriptions entails separating the Kaminia
series from the Alepovouni series in date and function, and so the argument from similarity of appearance must be discarded. On the other
hand, Traill's interpretation of the Panagia series, with its different text,
raises the possibility that variant types of *horoi* could have the same
(deme-marker) significance.[55] And thus we are left with the possibility

---

[52] Ober 1981, 73–77. Langdon (1999) subsequently discovered and published no fewer
than fifteen other rupestral *horoi* on the same hill, some with lunate sigma, some with four-
bar sigma, and some with single letters above and below the word *horos*. He regards these as
marking private holdings of some sort, but rejects the idea that the holdings were apiaries.

[53] The series was originally published by Eliot 1962, 63–64.

[54] Langdon 1985a, 259. The inscription is *IG* II² 1035 (line 58); the Alepovouni *horoi*
are associated with the Roman inscription by Culley 1977, 270n27.

[55] Traill (1986, 116) suggests that "[T]he peculiarity of 1 [the OP/ΠM series] may be explained by the fact that this group segregated a special pair of demes which belonged to two
different trittyes"; but the argument is circular, since the "fact" in question is actually

that similar texts may have different meanings, and dissimilar texts identical meanings.

My bee-farm hypothesis was, I admit, simply a speculation, based on the ancient reputation of Hymettos as a honey-producing region, the existing vegetation (especially thyme) in the area around the *horoi* themselves, and what I took to be their date. The deme-marker explanation is predicated in part on the existence of *horos* series in different geographical locations around Attica. Does the multiplicity of superficially similar inscriptions move the latter explanation out of the realm of speculative hypothesis? Regrettably, it does not. First, it is not possible to prove that a single agency was responsible for all of the *horoi*: imitation (e.g., by private individuals or by local officials) would explain the physical evidence just as well as unitary authorship. Next, there is no necessary reason to suppose that all of the lunate-sigma rupestral *horoi* were cut at or even about the same time. If we do not assume unitary state authorship a priori, a standard diffusionary model would lead us to expect that formally similar rupestral *horoi* would appear considerably later at locales distant from the point of invention and first use.[56] Third, the form of even the several series of single-word lunate-sigma inscriptions is far from standardized: the notable differences in size and lettering style seem to preclude the possibility that a single lettering crew was at work.[57]

In sum, any given *horos* series *might* have defined a deme-boundary at some point in its history, but equally possibly, it might not have.

Traill's hypothesis, which is in turn based on the assumption that the inscriptions in question are indeed deme boundary-markers. In support of his proposed reading of ὅρ(ος) π(αραλίας καὶ) μ(εσογαίας) ("horos of the coast and inland") Traill (1982, 168–69) cites a series of three *horos* inscriptions on Mt. Paximadi, apparently marking the border beween between ancient Laconia and Messenia: *IG* V, 1 1371 a–c.

[56] Spatial diffusion and chronological seriation: Deetz and Dethlefsen 1965. Note that the distances involved need not be great. Deetz and Dethlefsen's test case of gravestone motif preference showed considerable artifact seriation among several towns located in eastern Massachusetts in the period 1700–1829; the greatest distance involved was about 35km (straight line: Lexington to Groton). Coincidentally, the Alepovouni *horoi* are about 35km (straight line) from those at Megalo Baphi.

[57] Letter heights and inscription length (in meters: Megalo Baphi series based on my estimates from Lohmann's photographs): Megalo Baphi #2: 0.14–0.20 (h) × 1.01 (l); #5 0.15–0.19 (h) × 0.84 (l); Kaminia #2: 0.08–0.12 (h) × 0.42 (l); Alepovouni #1: 0.26–0.32 (h) × 1.10 (l); #2: 0.12–0.17 (h) × 0.60 (l); Lykabettos #1: 0.065–0.13 (h); E of Merenda: #1, 2: 0.12–0.14 (h). Style: Megalo Baphi: stem of rho seems to extend above loop (although this may be a wear mark) and well below the line. Kaminia: Relatively large loop on rho which begins at loop but extends below the line. Alepovouni: large omicrons, rho with very small loop, stem of rho strictly aligned with other letter bottoms. Lykabettos: very large, loopy rho, stem aligned with letter bottoms; Merenda: Large omicrons, rhos with fairly small loops, stems extend below the line.

There exists, at the moment, no means of falsifying counterhypotheses (e.g., that the inscriptions are the traces of a fad for permanently marking the boundaries of private holdings or sacred precincts that began in the immediate environs of the city and eventually spread to the south and east), and no way of refining the chronology.[58] Nor can the Gordian knot be cut by assuming that all Attic rupestral *horoi*, regardless of form or text, are classical deme-markers; there are simply too many *horoi* that must be left out of any single, comprehensive explanation of their meaning.[59] Since some rupestral *horoi* clearly are not deme-markers, the argument becomes completely subjective: *horoi* are deme-markers when they show up in places where one supposes deme-markers should show up; other explanations (or no explanation) can be adduced when they show up where one does not want deme-markers showing up. The level of subjectivity would be considerably lessened if there were independent textual authority pointing clearly to where we should look for deme-borders, but no such evidence has as yet been brought forward.[60]

The argument for accepting the several series of *horoi* discussed above as classical deme-markers (or as markers of a Roman bee preserve)

[58] The distribution pattern of known rupestral *horoi* (map: Traill 1986, 121), from Aleopvouni to Megalo Baphi, could be accommodated by the simplest sort of diffusion model (assuming the city of Athens as the point of origination). The argument of Lohmann (1992, 33) that since the Megalo Baphi inscriptions extend across the heads of two valleys, they must be deme-markers, is far from definitive, since there is no way to preclude a very large temenos or private holding. Sacred precincts defined by *horoi*: n. 9, above. Traill (1986, 119) rather uncomfortably allows for the temenos hypothesis, but only as subsidiary to the deme-marker hypothesis, in the case of the Alepovouni series: "I will not reject the possibility that a hilltop sanctuary shared by two demes . . . might be included within their [the inscriptions'] compass."

[59] For example, four inscriptions reading HO, near the church of Panagia at Thiti: Eliot, 1962, 56–58; Traill, 1982, 168n22 (both assume the inscriptions mark the peribolos of a sanctuary). An inscription on Alepovouni reading ΟΡΟΣ (four-bar sigma), near, but not in line with the other four: Langdon, 1985a, 257–60. Two others (not in series) on the western slopes of Hymettos: ΟΡΟΣ (*IG* II² 2519), ΖΗΝΩΝΟC ΟΡΟC (*IG* II² 2713). Three on hill 337.4 of Hymettos, reading ΟΡΟΣ ΔΙΑΝΟ(ΜΟΥ) (= boundary of the water conduit): Langdon, 1985a, 260–62. Three on the hill of Lathoureza near Vari, reading ΖΩ/ΟΡΟ/ΒΑ: Langdon 1988c. Langdon 1999 underlines the rapid growth in the number of known rupestral *horoi*, and the impossible burden that the increasing body of such inscriptions places on any unified interpretation of their original meaning.

[60] Langdon (1985b, 7) explores the literary testimonia, and concludes that "our search does not yield much evidence." The most important is *Ath. Pol.* 21.4: "He [sc. Cleisthenes] divided up (*dieneime*) the territory by demes into thirty parts." But this is pretty vague. Cf. Lohmann (1992, 33) who baldly asserts that "since literary sources testify to such deme boundaries in Attica, there should no longer be any doubt as to their existence." But he does not cite the sources he has in mind.

requires reading certain very specific sorts of signification onto ambiguous marks, while denying the possibility (or at least the likelihood) of all other possible significations. In the case of the deme-marker hypothesis, the driving force behind the exclusionary reading is the intense longing of historians and archaeologists to be able to delimit specific demes at specific times in history. Yet in the end, the argument rests precariously on the linked a priori assumptions that if a deme was a distinct geographical entity with secure borders, then its borders should be defined by prominent ridges separating agricultural valleys, and so if *horoi* are found on an appropriate ridge, then they must be polis-established boundary-markers.[61] Lacking secure textual evidence for demes as geographical entities or for the nature of their boundaries, the deme-marker hypothesis remains in the category of speculation. The iterability of the marks in question and the potential for the imposition of new meanings on existing marks still defeats the hope of securely fixing their significance. Although the rupestral *horoi* are fixed in their location, and so cannot be grabbed up by a god looking for a weapon or pulled up by order of a political reformer, in the long run their meanings were no more securely fixed than those of Athena's stone, the pre-Solonian *horoi*, or the *horoi* of the *patris*.

The ancient rupestral *horoi* are still too spare; there is as yet no way to provide them with a context secure enough to control the range of meanings they might once have proclaimed. Historians and archaeologists must not allow either the desirability of the most interesting explanation of archaeological evidence (which is certainly the deme-marker hypothesis) or bare assertions by scholars (however distinguished) to stand for proof of a hypothesis's correctness.[62] This rather depressing negative conclusion points to what seems to me an important (although also negative) archaeological point: a text that is nothing other than an artifact, an artifact that is nothing other than a text, has remarkably little to say. Artifacts and texts

[61] The geographical argument that deme (and trittys) boundaries must exist and are defined by natural features, especially ridges: Eliot 1962, 136–38; Langdon 1985b; Traill 1986, 116–22. But cf. Thompson 1971, Whitehead 1986, 27–30. Hansen (1991, 58) suggests that for ancient Greeks the population of citizens was more important than territory. Deme-officials known as *Horistai* are mentioned in *IG* II² 1177, lines 21–24, but (as Whitehead [1986, 141] notes) we have no idea what their duties might have been.

[62] This does not mean that one should not propose speculative hypotheses; indeed, speculation is a necessary and salutary part of the interpretive process. We must have working hypotheses, so that when further evidence is discovered (and I do not suppose that all of the visible rupestral *horoi* of Attica have yet been found or published) those hypotheses can be strengthened or tossed aside. My point is that we should recognize these hypotheses for what they are. We must not suspend critical judgment in the face of an argument from authority. And we must guard against drifting into accepting a hypothesis as a "foundational fact," or discarding alternative hypotheses, simply because we *want* it to be true.

alike gain meaning through their situation in a broader cultural context—when deprived of their context, they are also deprived of their power to impart meaning. The *horos* was intended by those who inscribed it as a speech act: an imperative to the members of society, ordering them to act in conformity with the distinction proclaimed by the marker. But outside of its cutlural milieu, that speech act is infelicitous. Shorn of context, the text-as-artifact–artifact-as-text can refer to nothing outside of its proclamation of self-presence and difference.

CHAPTER TEN

Tyrant-Killing as Therapeutic Conflict: A Political Debate in Images and Texts

This final essay stands in lieu of a conclusion, in that it brings together many of the interpretive issues raised in the other essays: boundaries, identities, knowledge, and persistence—but also moral authority and historical legacy, civil conflict and civic education, and the debate between critical philosophy and democratic ideology. The central idea here is an apparent paradox: the notion that violent political conflict (stasis) might, under certain circumstances, be regarded as a therapeutic means for "healing" a community—and thus for allowing its members to go on together. Therapeutic conflict is not simply cathartic in the sense one might expect from reading Aristotle's Poetics. *Rather it is a matter of politically appropriate mimesis: a matter of citizens learning how to reperform the right historical event (in this case the act of killing a tyrant), in the right way, at the right moment, and with the right attitude—which is to say, not with hot blood but as a matter of political duty.*

The added interpretive element in this essay (in addition to epigraphic evidence, which also figures in chapter 9) is iconography. Political theorists typically seek to gain access to earlier political cultures—and their conceptions of ethics and politics—almost uniquely through texts. But the ancient Athenians, like many other peoples, constructed and understood the political meanings that enabled them to go on as a community in part through visual media. The visual media of concern to me here include sculpture (publicly and privately commissioned) and painted vases. Classical scholars have made striking advances in recent years in terms of their ability to read, in sophisticated ways, the ethical and political messages that ancient viewers might be expected to pick up when viewing works of art. Diversity and coherence are essential parts of this story: A given work of art might have a strong "standard" message, one that every local reader could be expected to read off in the first instance. But it might also offer members of diverse subcommunities the option of alternative readings, depending, for example, on their social background and political tastes.

Among the politically potent iconographic motifs of classical Athens was that of the heroically nude tyrant-slayers, Harmodios and Aristogeiton. This essay was initially written for a conference, organized by

Kathyrn Morgan and held at the University of California, Los Angeles, on the topic of "popular tyranny."* The conference papers looked at various aspects of the complex relationship between democracy and tyranny in Greek (and especially Athenian) culture. I argue here that the image of the tyrant-slayers was important both in the debate between Athenian democracy and its critics and in the Athenians' collective capacity to get through periods of conflict without becoming psychologically or institutionally stuck in the attempt to achieve absolute justice after a period of violent civil conflict.

The tyrant-slayer image allowed potentially devastating and relatively protracted periods of civil conflict, which had engaged and polarized thousands of Athenians, to be reimagined (and imaginatively reperformed) as brief moments of therapeutic violence. Rather than a long, grinding stasis, the events of the late fifth century B.C. could be imagined as a heroic moment, in which individual hero-citizens dispatched an individual malefactor-tyrant, leaving the community to realign the legacy of its democratic past with its hoped-for democratic future. The act of tyrannicide thus becomes a special kind of legacy-gift, and the esteem of the community is reflected in its reiterated iconographic commemoration of that act. The images of the tyrant-slayers, along with stories told and songs sung in their praises, served to educate future generations of Athenians in the values of the democratic community—as well as reminding them of the personal sacrifices necessary for it to persist over time. Yet, at the same time, looking at the critical response to that powerful set of tyrant-slayer images and narratives allows us to assess ways in which democracy's critics worked to keep alive the possibility of creative misperformance, and thus the essential capacity for thinking (and reading and viewing) differently.

An important newly published tyrannicide inscription from democratic Eretria (Knoepfler 2001, 2002) sets out the legal duties of citizens faced with threats to the democratic order, and makes explicit the binary "democracy versus oligarchy-tyranny" contrast developed in this chapter.

• • •

MY STARTING POINT IS the evolving relationship between Athenian democratic ideology and the arguments developed by politically dissident Athenians—that is, those who were not willing to accept that democracy was the best of all political worlds, or even the best that could reasonably

* This essay was first published in K. Morgan, ed., *Popular Tyranny: Sovereignty and Its Discontents in Ancient Greece* (Austin: University of Texas Press, 2003), 215–50. Reprinted with permission of University of Texas Press.

be hoped for.[1] I have argued elsewhere that democratic ideology, with its quasi-hegemonic tendencies, was challenged in texts produced by members of an informal yet self-consciously critical "community of interpretation."[2] Here, I hope to show that the contest between democratic ideology and a dissident sensibility that sought political alternatives informs some notable moments in the long and intellectually fertile Greek engagement with the concept of tyranny.

As the papers collected by Kathryn Morgan in *Popular Tyranny* (Morgan 2003a) demonstrate, the general issue of "the tyrant, his nature and what to do about him" was conceptually very important *within* Athenian democratic ideology and equally important within what I am calling the "dissident sensibility." But the tyrant issue was also important for debates *between* democrats and their critics from the early fifth through the late fourth centuries B.C. Both democrats and dissidents agreed in general terms on why tyranny is at once morally and politically unacceptable: the tyrant is wicked because he uses illegitimately acquired public power systematically to alienate from "us" that which is most dear to us.[3] Tyranny, by embodying a negative political extreme, the intolerable *politeia* (or non-*politeia*), in turn helps to define what "we" require "our own" *politeia* (present or hoped-for) to secure and ensure for us. It also helped dissident Greek intellectuals to explore the positive political extreme—the ideal or

[1] On Athenian dissidents, cf. Ober 1998. I received helpful responses to earlier versions of this chapter from audiences at UCLA, the University of Toronto, University of Tel Aviv, Johns Hopkins University, and the University of Chicago. Special thanks are due to W.A.P. Childs and Ralf von den Hoff for help with iconographic questions, to Vincent Farenga, for his thoughtful commentary, and to Richard Neer, for sharing an advance draft of the relevant parts of his dissertation (see now Neer 2002) and for his insightful comments on an earlier draft of this chapter.

[2] The argument for "democratic hegemony" is made in Ober 1989, 332–39, and the essays collected in Ober 1996. I suggest in Ober 1998 that democratic ideology is best regarded as "quasi-hegemonic" in light of the extent of opportunities for public and private dissent of various sorts. The term "community of interpretation" is borrowed from Fish 1980.

[3] Because proponents of what I call "democratic ideology" and the "dissident sensibility" agreed that tyrants are wicked does not, of course, imply that all Athenians thought so—the Athenian demos (as depicted in, for example, Aristophanes, Thucydides, book 6, and the Eukrates *nomos* discussed below), and Plato (of *Gorgias* and *Republic*) agreed that there were in fact men in Athens who regarded the tyrant's life as the pinnacle of human happiness, desired tyranny for themselves, and would seek to seize it if given a chance. It is important to avoid supposing that the "democratic-dissident" debate adequately maps the political terrain of classical Athens—it is a debate joined by those who accept that justice includes something like "the common good" and so leaves out self-interested and self-aggrandizing types who sincerely regard their individual and personal advantage as the only good worth pursuing. It is worth noting that Socrates of the *Gorgias* contrasts Callicles' moral beliefs to certain moral convictions (488e–89b: it is preferable to suffer than to do wrong; 491d–e: *enkrateia* is a virtue) held commonly by Socrates and "the many."

best-possible *politeia*, and it helped them to think more deeply about "moderate" political alternatives.[4]

In the context of debate, certain questions arise: Who is the (actual or potential) tyrant? Who are "we"? What should we do about tyrants? The answers to these questions will help to establish some conceptual similarities between democrats and their opponents but also to distinguish democratic ideology from critical challenges. In brief summary: for classical Greek democrats, the tyrant can be defined as *anyone* who would seek to overthrow "we the demos." This demotic definition equates oligarchic revolutionaries with tyrants. An obvious example of conflation is Thucydides' reference to Athenian demotic fears of an "oligarchico-tyrannical conspiracy" (*xunomosia oligarchikē kai turannikē*: 6.60.1). The democratic association of oligarchs with tyrants is, I suppose, one reason that tyranny remained such a lively issue for the Athenians for so long after the threat of "actual" tyranny (of the archaic Greek sort) was past.[5]

Defense of the democracy tended to be equated with resistance to tyrants. That resistance might culminate in tyrannicide, and therefore murderous violence by citizens against fellow citizens. Tyrant-slaying thus becomes, in democratic ideology, a rare example of therapeutic civil conflict. Dissidents, in seeking alternatives to democratic ideology, sought to complicate this simple scenario. They argued that the demos was the real tyrant. They posited a spectrum of regimes as an alternative to the binary "democracy-tyranny" political universe. And they offered alternative narratives about the actions and motives of tyrannicides and about when *stasis* in the polis was and was not therapeutic.

THE DEMOCRATIC IDEOLOGY OF TYRANNY IN ICONOGRAPHY AND TEXT

Among the arresting features of the ideological debate over tyranny is that it can be traced in both textual and iconographic registers. Moreover, the

[4] R. Osborne 2003, rightly emphasizes that after 412 B.C. both oligarchy and "moderate" variants of democracy were granted more serious analytic attention as "third ways" between "radical" democracy and tyranny. But he seems to me to overstate the "sea change" and "transformation" of Athenian political ideology and practice in the era 412–403, and to underestimate the continued salience of tyranny as defining "the worst case" in both the democratic and dissident political imagination in the fourth century. Tyranny continued to hold an undisputed position (e.g., for Plato, in the *Republic*, for whom it is the final point in the degeneration of regimes and Aristotle, in the *Politics*, for whom it is the worst of the "incorrect" regimes) as the undoubted bottom of the political barrel. Consequently, the label "tyrant" retained its bite, even as oligarchy and "moderate" democracy gained (among intellectuals) greater conceptual clarity.

[5] This peculiarity is addressed by essays in Morgan 2003a, written by Raaflaub, Kallet, Seaford, Henderson, and Osborne. Henderson 2003 notes the tendency to equate tyranny and all forms of antidemocratic activity, citing Andocides 1.96–98, as well as the evidence of comedy.

text and iconography of tyrant-killing are mutually implicated and in a variety of ways: texts referring to tyrannicide pay explicit and implicit homage to artistic monuments and the iconography of tyrannicide is often transparently narrative. My discussion of the iconography of "democracy and tyranny" is necessarily selective. I begin with two very familiar monuments (figs. 1, 2, 4) from early and late in the history of the independent Athenian democracy; they are perhaps, for students of Athenian democracy, even overly familiar in that their repeated photographic reiteration may have evacuated for us some of their evocative power.

1. Kritios and Nesiotes tyrannicide statue group, erected in the Athenian Agora in ca. 477 B.C. (figs. 1, 2). The group, which survives in Roman copies, depicts Harmodios and Aristogeiton in the act of assassinating Hipparchus. This monument replaced an earlier tyrannicide group sculpted by Antenor, erected in the Agora in the very late sixth or very early fifth century B.C. and taken as war booty by the Persians in 480–479. The exact date and ideological force (aristocratic? democratic?) of the Antenor group are debatable. By contrast, the Kritios and Nesiotes group seems quite straightforward. Following a general scholarly consensus, elaborated by Burkhard Fehr, Michael Taylor, and others, I take the Kritios and Nesiotes statue group as a self-consciously democratic monument, put up by the Athenians immediately after the Persian Wars to celebrate democratic Athenian unity and boldness in action.[6]

As Vincent Farenga has astutely noted, the expressed ethos of the composition is not one of conflicted values; it suggests no disjunction between inner qualities of being and the external signs of appearing and doing. The monument exists within what Farenga (drawing from Bakhtin) has called a "citizen chronotope."[7] Yet the Kritios and Nesiotes group, with its dramatic and kinetic composition, is also very much an image of "becoming"—the killers, acting as a cooperative team, boldly advancing upon their foe, are caught by the sculptors at the moment just before the death-blow was struck; the viewer is drawn into the action and invited to complete the narrative for himself.[8] As we know from the critical comments of

[6] The Kritios and Nesiotes group: Taylor 1991; Fehr 1984; Brunnsåker 1971; Castriota 1998. Further bibliography: Neer 2002. I leave aside the unanswerable question of the motives of those who erected the original group sculpted by Antenor—whoever they were, whatever the Antenor group's date pre-480, and whatever its precise form. For further discussion and bibliography on the Antenor group, see Raaflaub 2003, who also cites the evidence for the formal honors offered by the state to the tyrannicides and their descendents.

[7] Vincent Farenga, formal comments on an earlier draft of this essay, March 28, 1998.

[8] Fehr 1984, 35–38, on the active unity of purpose and its democratic associations.

Figure 1. Kritios and Nesiotes group. Photo by permission of Museo Nazionale, Naples (Inv. no. 6009–6010).

Figure 2. Kritios and Nesiotes group (restored cast). Photo by permission of Museo dei Gessi dell' Università, Rome.

Thucydides and other writers, the canonical Athenian way of completing the story was with the establishment of the democracy: the kinetic energy of the tyrant-slayers carrying through to the creation of a new identity in which Athenian citizens would not be passive subjects but active participants in the history-making business of public life.[9]

One element missing from the well-known partially-restored Roman copy of the tyrant-slayers monument in Naples (fig. 1) is weaponry. Presumably this is a mere accident of preservation, but the broken swords draw our attention to the weapons employed by the tyrant-killer. The swords are clearly illustrated on a depiction of the moment of the assassination on a red-figure stamnos by the Copenhagen painter, dating to about 470 B.C. (fig. 3).[10] The standard way for a Greek tyrant to "take the point" of his own illegitimacy is literal death by sword (*xiphos*) or dagger (*encheiridion*).[11] The implicit argument of the Athenians' act of re-erecting the statue group, and of the sustained democratic Athenian reverence for the tyrannicides, is that Harmodios and Aristogeiton killed a tyrant and after the death of the tyrant came democracy.

Several of the essays in *Popular Tyranny* noted the tacit popular assumption that "tyrannicide ergo democracy" became a hot topic in Athenian critical-historical literature by the later fifth century B.C. It was explicitly challenged by Thucydides who goes so far (6.53.3) as to claim that, at least by 415 B.C., the Athenian citizenry actually "knew by hearsay" (*epistamenos gar ho dēmos akoēi*) that the tyranny was not overthrown "by themselves and Harmodios" [i.e., in 514] but by the Spartans [i.e., in 510]. But, whatever the complexities of the Athenians' historical memory of how tyranny was ended in Athens, by the later fifth century solidarity with the tyrannicides was clearly regarded, by democrats and their critics, as the essence of traditional democratic patriotism.[12]

The tyrannicide statue group thus came to express the "democratically correct" response of Athenian citizens to threats to the democratic order.

[9] On history making: Spinosa, Flores, and Dreyfus 1997.

[10] The Copenhagen Painter has now been associated with the Syriskos Painter: Neer 2002, 251–52, with n. 143. The four vase paintings probably or certainly depicting the tyrannicide dating from 475–450 and the five from around 400 B.C. were originally studied as a group in Beazley 1948; their connection with democratic and elitist sensibilities is sensitively examined by Neer 2002, 168–81.

[11] Cf. Thuc. 6.58.2: Hippias searches Panathenaic marchers for *encheiridia* after the assassination of Hipparchus, and holds those with daggers guilty since it was the tradition to march in the procession only with shield and spear. Thucydides' account was challenged by [Aristotle] *Ath. Pol.* 18.4, as anachronistic.

[12] Herodotus 5.55–57.1 (noting that Hippias was the tyrant, Hipparchus was his brother, and tyranny lasted for another four years, and that it became harsher after the assassination); Thuc. 1.20.2, 6.53.3–6.60.1); [Arisotle] *Ath. Pol.* 18. For further discussion of these passages, see Raaflaub 2003.

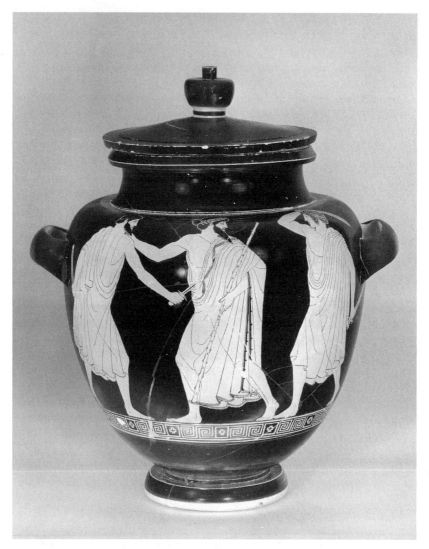

Figure 3. Stamnos by the Copenhagen Painter, showing tyrannicide, ca. 470 B.C. Beazley 1963, 257 no. 5. By permission of Martin von Wagner Museum der Universität Würzburg. Photo: K. Oehrlein

The Athenian quickness to associate subversion with tyranny and the tyrannicide group with active citizen-centered defense of democracy against subversion are illustrated by a comic passage. In Aristophanes', *Lysistrata* (lines 631–34), produced in 411 B.C. the chorus of old Athenian men staunchly declare, "These women won't set up a tyranny over me, for I'll stand on guard, and 'I'll carry my sword in a myrtle bough'; I'll stand to arms in the Agora beside Aristogeiton: Like this! I'll stand beside him." The old men of the chorus, quoting the evidently well-known drinking song (*skolion*), imagine themselves taking up arms in the public space of the Agora, next to the statue group. In taking their stand "beside Aristogeiton" Aristophanes' old men explicitly take on the role of Harmodios. We must imagine the dancers of the chorus, as they sing "Like this!" mimicking the form of the Harmodios statue, assuming for a moment the "Harmodios-stance": right (sword) arm cocked behind the head, preparatory to dealing what B. B. Shefton has called the "Harmodios blow." (fig. 2).[13] To be a defender of democracy against subversion, then, is to "become" Harmodios—and explicitly to become Harmodios as he is depicted in the Kritios and Nesiotes group.

The Copenhagen painter, presumably working within a few years of the erection of the Kritios and Nesiotes monument, is not captive to the statue-group iconography. He depicts (fig. 3) the tyrannicide figures as draped, and thus represents the historical moment rather than, as vase painters around 400 B.C. would (see below) the statue group itself. Moreover, the Copenhagen painter depicts Aristogeiton's position (thrusting home his sword) quite differently from the way he is depicted in the restored statue (draped left arm forward, right [sword] arm behind). Harmodios' position, however, is identical in both vase painting and statue. Harmodios' stance, with raised sword-arm, is also clearly recognizable on two roughly contemporary red-figure vases, one a fragment in Agrigento attributed to the Pan Painter, the other on a badly damaged skyphos from the Villa Giulia.[14]

Although the iconographic sample is small, it appears that the "Harmodios stance" quickly achieved canonical status as the single most stable visual element in Athenian tyrannicide iconography. The Harmodios stance might, therefore, serve as synecdoche for the monument, the event, and its (imagined) narrative continuation. This supposition is strengthened by the Aristophanes passage, which suggests that by the late fifth century B.C. not only the tyrannicides, but the tyrannicide *statue group* itself, and especially the *stance* of the Harmodios figure, were closely associated with the defense of the existing democratic regime against "tyranny." The passage strongly implies that to "stand as Harmodios" was to declare oneself

[13] Harmodios blow: Shefton 1960. Cf. the stage directions added to the translation, in Sommerstein 1990: ad loc. *"striking attitude, right leg thrust forward, right arm raised as if swinging back sword."* I am tempted to add *"with cloak thrown off"* on the strength of Plato, *Republic*, 473e–474a; see below. On the importance of tyrant language and examples from history in this play, see Henderson 2003.

[14] Villa Giulia vase: Beazley 1948: 26 with fig. 1. Agrigento fragment: Beazley 1963, 559.147; Burn and Glynn 1982, 127; Carpenter et al. 1989, 259.

an enemy of tyranny and a defender of the existing democratic regime. And so we might guess that in the context of a debate between democrats and dissidents, the Harmodios stance would become a contested visual icon, just as the story of the act of tyrannicide and its meaning were contested in historical narrative.

If the democrats modeled themselves on the tyrannicides, dissident intellectuals like Thucydides challenged the tyrannicides' motives and character: in Farenga's terms, they sought to complicate the straightforward ethos expressed by the monument by drawing a distinction between the act (assassination) and the inner motives of the actors. That story is well treated in several of the essays in *Popular Tyranny*; there is no need to recapitulate it in detail here.[15] Suffice it to say that in the late fourth century B.C., debates centering on the character of the tyrannicides were still being rehearsed. According to the Aristotelian *Ath. Pol.* (18.5) "democratic writers" (*hoi dēmotikoi*) claimed that Aristogeiton, when captured after the assassination, fooled his captors into destroying their own supporters, whereas "others" (i.e., dissidents) say that he betrayed his comrades.[16]

Some elements of the population were, moreover, suspected by the Athenian democrats of disrespecting the national heroes: As Kurt Raaflaub points out, at some unknown time in the fifth or early fourth century, the democratic state passed legislation forbidding slander of the tyrannicides and prohibiting the use of their names for slaves.[17] Whatever the truth of Thucydides' claim about what the Athenians "actually knew" of their own history, there can be no doubt that from the late fifth century at least, and through the late fourth, the relationship between the assassination of Hipparchus, the overthrow of the tyranny, and the origins of democracy were at the center of the debate between democratic ideology and critical discourse on various levels. The dissident side of the debate is preserved in historical narratives which seek to refute the demotic narrative linking tyrannicide with the origins of democracy. Public iconography shows that the democratic ideology of tyrannicide was asserted at the visual level. And the *Lysistrata* passage suggests that "official" democratic visual icons were recapitulated at the level of gesture (and thus subject to comic attention). We will return below to the question of whether it is possible to detect a critical response to the democratic iconography of tyrannicide.

2. The second well-known image crowns the stele publishing an "anti-tyranny" law, passed on the proposal of Eukrates in 337–336 B.C. The

---

[15] The relevant texts (cited in n. 8, above) are conveniently collected in Stanton 1990.

[16] For further discussion of this passage, see Ober 1998, 359–60.

[17] Raaflaub 2003.

Figure 4. Eukrates *nomos*, documentary relief, 337–336 B.C. Demos crowned by Demokratia. Athenian Agora. Photo by permission of the American School of Classical Studies: Agora Excavations.

document relief depicts personified Demos, seated, being crowned by personified Demokratia, standing (fig. 4). As with the Kritios and Nesiotes statue group, the document relief consists of two figures. But the composition of the relief offers a marked contrast to the drama and suspense of the tyrannicide group. On the relief, Demokratia is "crowning" but Demos is not "doing" much of anything at all. His right arm rests comfortably on his left leg, his left hand would have rested on a staff. He seems completely at peace on his throne, sure of himself, a quietly self-confident Demos, "being" personified. Yet this peaceful image graces an inscription, a *nomos* enacted by the Athenian state in 337–336 B.C., that concerns the possibility of antidemocratic revolution and encourages the violently patriotic act of tyrant-killing. It explicitly exonerates any potential tyrant-killer from prosecution (*hos . . . apokteinōi, hosios estō*: lines

10–11) and threatens with disenfranchisement (*atimia*) and property confiscation any member of the Areopagus Council who fulfills his official function while "the *dēmos* or the *dēmokratia* is overthrown."[18]

The implicit argument made by this monument—its text and its iconography—is striking: What is remarkable is *not* that it implies that to challenge democracy is to embrace tyranny—this was, as Aristophanes' *Wasps* and *Knights* demonstrate, already a familiar enough claim in the late fifth century B.C. (see Henderson 2003). What *is* striking is that it suggests that the overthrow of the "*dēmokratia* and the demos" and the establishment of a tyranny would not terminate the legitimate authority of Demos or the instrumental capacity of the Athenian demos to reward and punish the political behavior of individual Athenians.

In 410–409, in the context of the extended *stasis* of the late fifth century, the Athenians had passed a decree on a motion by Demophantos, mandating the use of a "loyalty oath" to compel a prodemocracy, antityrant response on the part of the citizens, if and when "the demos is overthrown."[19] The Eukrates *nomos* echoes some of the language of the late fifth-century decree. But by the later fourth century, there is no longer any perceived need for an oath to be sworn by each citizen. Now, in the place of the oath-bound individual, democratic governmental authority and the authority of democratically enacted law are imagined as continuous *through* a tyrannical interlude. Under late fourth-century conditions, a coup d'état is indeed imaginable, but the democratic restoration that will follow the collapse of the tyranny (presumably via assassination) is simply taken for granted. Democracy has become an ordinary condition, a "state of being" which may perhaps be in some sense interrupted by tyrannical interludes, but which remains "the once and future" *politeia*—the legitimate form of authority that somehow continues despite any lapse in the actual power of the actual demos. And so, personified Demos (and the political order he represents) will still sit on his metaphorical throne even if "the demos" is (momentarily) overthrown.

We seem to have come a long way from Thucydides' paranoid Athenians of 415 B.C., who feared the establishment of a tyranny because they "knew from hearsay" that it was "not they themselves and Harmodios" who had overthrown the tyrants, but the Spartans. Thucydides' imagined Athenians suppose that, since they cannot expect Spartan benevolence to recur, a tyrannical coup d'état would permanently end the democracy. Five

[18] Meritt 1952, 355–59 = *SEG* 12.87 = RO 79. For a detailed discussion of the relief, its artistic sources, and bibliography, see Lawton 1995, 99–100 (no. 38, with plate 20).

[19] The Demophantos Decree: Andocides 1.96–98, with Raaflaub 2003 and R. Osborne 2003.

years later, and following an oligarchical interlude, the Athenians who voted for the Demophantos decree hoped that the moral authority of a sacred oath might bind each citizen to a democratic code of behavior in the absence of democratic governmental authority, and so allow for the restoration of democracy. After another seventy-five years, and another coup d'état, the Athenians who voted for the Eukrates *nomos* seem much more sure of themselves—even while the dichotomy tyranny-democracy remains at the center of their conception of the political universe.[20]

I will return to "political becoming versus political being" at the end of this chapter; for now the general point is obvious enough—tyranny and democracy were regarded in "official" Athenian ideology as antithetical from the early fifth through late fourth centuries. The antithesis is underlined by the positive democratic valuation of tyrant-slaying. The model tyrant-slayers were Harmodios and Aristogeiton: remembered as heroes in the popular folk tradition, challenged as immoral and selfishly motivated in critical political literature, and so familiarly and so powerfully realized in the statue group in the Agora that "standing like Harmodios" could be employed as synecdoche for prodemocratic resistance to tyranny. By the late fourth century, because individual democrats are assumed to be ready to take up the Harmodios stance and strike the Harmodios blow when the polis was threatened by a tyrant, "old man Demos" can sit comfortably, unarmed, on his throne, accepting his crown from Demokratia.

We may sum up the Athenian demotic agenda (as consolidated by the restoration of 403 B.C.) as follows: tyrants are bad, because the tyrant uses illegitimately acquired power to alienate from citizens that which is "theirs"—especially citizen dignity, that is, the conjoined freedom, equality, and security of the citizen (see chapter 5).[21] Those who seek to replace the democracy with any other form of government are tyrannical. Democracy and tyranny thus define a bipolar political universe; there is no legitimate "third way" between the rule of the demos and the rule of the tyrant as there was, for example, in the Persian Constitutional debate in Herodotus book 3 (on which see Dewald 2003), or in the multi-*politeia* schemata of Plato and Aristotle (on which see R. Osborne 2003). Oligarchs, as nondemocrats, are by democratic ideological definition, tyrants. Killers of tyrants are defenders of democracy and therefore deserve

---

[20] And so, with R. Osborne 2003, I would agree that something very substantial has indeed changed within discourse and practice, but I would contend that those changes must be read in the context of some very substantial ideological continuities.

[21] On freedom, equality, security as the core triad of Athenian democratic values, see Ober 1996, 86–88, and chapter 5, above.

immunity, honors, and celebration. This ideology was reinforced by the events of 411–403 B.C. Obvious examples include the public decree of honors for the killer of Phrynichus, a leader of "The Four Hundred," and the heroizing of the "men of Phyle" for having overthrown the "Thirty Tyrants" (see chapter 8).[22] The Eukrates *nomos* points to the continued salience of the dichotomy through the fourth century.

Why, we may ask, does tyrant-killing remain such a vital notion, given that (with the possible and highly contested exception of Hipparchus) no actual tyrant was ever killed by a patriotic assassin in Athens? As I briefly suggested above, a notable feature of the democratic tyrant-killer ideology is that it offers a rare classical Greek example of *therapeutic* civil conflict (*stasis*) in the polis: a moment in which it is (at least in retrospect) regarded as having been healthy and right for one citizen to run at another with sword drawn and to shed blood in a public place. At Athens, in the difficult years after 403 B.C., the familiar tyrant-killing imagery, which (judging by preserved vases, see below) seems to have enjoyed a floruit around 400 B.C., allowed a highly troublesome period of *stasis*, which lasted for months and exposed divisions within the citizenry (rural/urban, *dēmos/dunatoi*, cavalry/foot-soldiers), to be reimagined by (albeit imperfect) analogy with the democratic interpretation of the events of 514 B.C. and their aftermath. That is, the *stasis* of 404 could be "misremembered" as having been ended by a single moment of legitimate violence. Reenvisioning the *stasis* of the late fifth century via the satisfying image of the demos' heroes confronting and dispatching the aberrant, illegitimate power-holder was among the mechanisms that encouraged forgetfulness regarding the frightening divisions that had emerged among the citizens.[23]

The late fifth-century *stasis* situation was formally ended in Athens at the end of the fifth century not by actual tyrant-slaying, but by the Amnesty decree and its attendant rituals, including an oath and a parade to the

---

[22] Honors for the killer of Phrynichus: Meiggs and Lewis 1988, no. 85. The assassin is not actually described as a "tyrant-killer" but is rewarded for having "done what was necessary." Krentz 1982, 16n2, on the early association of the terminology of "tyranny" with the Thirty. R. Osborne 2003, points to (1) efforts on the part of late fifth- and fourth-century Athenian intellectuals to define a "third way" and (2) suggests that those efforts found expression in constitutional reforms. The first point is certainly true, and the second is, I believe, very likely (see, further, Ober 1998, 369–73, and chapter 6, above). But I do not see that there is any evidence that Athenian "official ideology" ever gave up on the "primacy of tyranny" as democracy's antithesis—or that Athenian intellectuals ever abandoned the "primacy of tyranny" as the worst-case *politeia*. And so, once again, I resist Osborne's argument for a "sea change" comparable to the revolutionary era of the late sixth century.

[23] On the role of forgetting in the Athenian response to *stasis*: Loraux 1997 (trans. 2002), and chapter 3, above. For a detailed discussion of the ideological response to the *stasis*, see Wolpert 2002.

Acropolis.[24] Through those rituals, the *stasis* became a distinct interlude with a beginning and a formalized ending; the ceremony proclaims that before and after the *stasis*, *dēmokratia* was the norm. And this leads organically to the peaceful image of Demos on the Eukrates *nomos* document relief. In the fourth century many democrats and some of their critics (e.g., Isocrates) favored an elaborate pseudo-history which imagined the Pisistratid tyranny as a usurpation, an interruption in a continuous democratic tradition extending from Solon (or even Theseus) onwards. But the tyrant-killer ideology was not forgotten, as shown by the provisions of the Eukrates *nomos* itself. Indeed, the years around 403 B.C. saw a flourishing of public reverence for Harmodios and Aristogeiton. New honors were voted for their descendants.[25] Iconographic citations of the Kritios and Nesiotes statue group on red-figure vases, unknown since the mid-fifth century, suddenly reappear in ca. 400 B.C., most notably in the shield emblem of the Athena Promachos figure on Panathenaic prize amphorae.[26] The appearance of the tyrannicides on the Panathenaic vases is especially significant in that (unlike most vases) Panathenaic amphorae were commissioned by the democratic state.

TYRANNICIDE IDEOLOGY OUTSIDE OF ATHENS

The persuasive power of the democratic Athenian association of tyrant-killers with democrats and tyrants with antidemocrats is elucidated by evidence for tyrant-slayer ideology in democratic poleis outside Athens. Even the briefest glance at the broader Greek geographic and chronological context serves to reinforce Sarah Morris's and Kathryn Morgan's point (Morris 2003, Morgan 2003b) that neither the classical Athenian ideology of tyranny nor the critical intellectual engagement with that ideology existed in an "Athenocentric" cultural vacuum. In the world outside Athens, the Greek experience with full-scale tyranny was not uniquely a phenomenon of the late archaic period. In Syracuse, Pontic Heraclea, and Achaea—to cite just the most obvious examples—tyranny was a serious issue in, respectively, the fifth, fourth, and third centuries. A public inscription (*OGIS* 218) offers detailed information on exactly what tyrant-killing was deemed to be worth in Hellenistic Ilion. Both material goods and special honors were on offer; the extent of these depended

---

[24] Rituals ending the stasis of 404 B.C. Strauss 1985, 69–72. See also chapter 4, above.

[25] See, further, Taylor 1991, 1–5.

[26] Brunnsåker 1971, 104f, no. 6, pl. 23.6. Simon and Hirmer 1976, 157, color plate LI. Further discussion in Neer 2002, 173–77.

on the status (citizen, metic, or slave) of the killer.[27] In the case of a citizen tyrant-slayer, the killer was to receive the following:

> one talent (of silver) immediately upon committing the act
> a bronze statue of himself, to be erected by the demos
> free meals for life in the *prutaneion*
> a front seat at the public contests, along with public proclamation of his
>   name
> a stipend of two drachmas a day, for life. (lines 21–28)

The Iliotes' almost obsessive concern with the danger of tyranny recalls Athenian legislation against tyranny, including the Eukrates *nomos*. A tyrant-killing citizen of Ilion could, however, expect to receive much more than Eukrates' bare assurance of freedom from the risk of prosecution for his act. There are no doubt good contextual reasons (largely irrecoverable given how little we know of the internal history of Hellenistic Ilion) both for the similarity of the concern with tyranny and for the differential reward system. My point here is that the Athenian situation, while distinctive in many ways, was still part of a broader Greek cultural pattern. Athenian citizens, writers, and artists were well aware of the Hellenic world beyond Attica, a world where political relations were sometimes interestingly similar to those pertaining in Athens, even if at other times they were quite different. And by the same token, Athenian history and public iconography might sometimes influence the representation and imagination of tyranny elsewhere in the Greek world.

A public inscription from the polis of Erythrae in Asia Minor, probably roughly contemporary with the Eukrates *nomos* at Athens, brings us back to the question of how politicized debates over tyrant-killing might be carried on at the visual level of public iconography.[28] A decree of "the *boulē* and the *dēmos*" of Erythrae mandates repairs to and honors for a statue of a tyrannicide. Evidently the statue took the form of a standing male figure (*ho andrias*: line 5) holding a sword (*xiphos*). Sometime after the statue was put up (presumably by a prior democratic government),

---

[27] *OGIS* no. 218. My thanks to John Ma for bringing inscriptions from Ilion and Erythrae to my attention.

[28] Dittenberger in *SIG*, 284 with Gauthier 1982. Date: ca. 334 B.C. according to Dittenberger ad loc., on the grounds that Alexander in that year mandated that all the poleis of Asia Minor would be democracies (Arrian, *Anab.* 1.18.1–2, Tod *GHI* II no. 192, lines 3–4). So one might say that oligarchy at Erythrae did not fail, but was overthrown. But we still need an answer for why Alexander reversed Philip's general policy of promoting oligarchy in allied cities. The easiest answer would seem to be that Alexander put in place the government he supposed would be most stable (ergo least troublesome to him) because it was most in tune with what the Greeks of Asia Minor wanted. N.B. the similarity of formulaic language between this inscription (ἀγαθῆι τύχηι δεδόχθαι τῆι βουλῆι καὶ τῶι δήμωι) and the Eukrates *nomos* (ἀγαθῆι τύχηι τοῦ δήμου τοῦ Ἀθηναίων, δεδόχθαι τοῖς νομοθέταις).

Erythrae experienced a period of oligarchy. According to the decree, the Erythraean oligarchs had removed the sword from the tyrannicide statue. Moreover, and most interestingly, the democratic government that erected the inscription attributes a motive to the oligarchs: they removed the sword "thinking that the [statue's] stance (*stasis*) was entirely aimed at them."[29] The ideological force of this political ascription of motive is clarified by our prior consideration of the Kritios and Nesiotes group in Athens and the line from Aristophanes' *Lysistrata*: It seems a fair guess that the Erythraean tyrannicide figure was depicted in the "Harmodios stance" or some Erythraean gestural analogue thereof.[30]

According to the democrats' implicit argument, this "stance" was identified by all Erythraeans, oligarchs and democrats alike, with defense of democracy. The democrats claim that the Erythraean oligarchs had believed that the position taken by the statue, and especially its menacing sword, was "entirely aimed at them"—as opponents of democracy. And so, according to the democratic narrative, by removing the sword the oligarchs had compromised: They left the statue standing, and thereby acknowledged the importance of an established public icon. Yet by removing the sword, supposedly aimed at themselves, the oligarchs accepted a bipolar political taxonomy that associated oligarchs, as antidemocrats, with tyrants. The new democratic government of Erythrae, in a series of pointedly ideological moves that underline the power of public images, decreed the restoration of the sword, ordered that the monument be cleaned up, and mandated that the statue be crowned at appropriate times in the ritual calendar. Moreover, the democrats erected the inscription as a record of their own and their opponents' motives and actions. For any viewer potentially confused by iconographic subtleties, the inscription clarified the political point of the statue's stance, and suggested that the tyrannicide's sword was indeed forever aimed at oligarchs.

The democrats of Erythrae claimed, in effect, that oligarchs and democrats were in full agreement about the association of tyrant-killing with democracy, tyrants with oligarchs. Would the Erythraean oligarchs actually have agreed? Let us assume for the sake of the argument that the oligarchs really did remove the sword from the monument. What might they have meant by doing so? Perhaps, rather than symbolically removing a threat to themselves, the oligarchs were symbolically proclaiming an end to an era of citizen-on-citizen violence, the end of *stasis*. Perhaps they were seeking to make an iconographic statement with a historical point: "tyrant killing was

---

[29] ἐπειδὴ οἱ ἐν τῆι ὀλιγαρχίαι τῆς εἰκόνος τῆς Φιλίτου, τοῦ ἀποκτείναντος τὸν τύραννον, τοῦ ἀνδριάντος ἐξεῖλον τὸ ξίφος, νομίζοντες καθόλου τὴν στάσιν καθ' αὑτῶν εἶναι. Lines 5–6.

[30] On Harmodios and Aristogeiton imagery on coins and statuary outside of Athens, see Fehr 1984, 7–8, with illustrations 2–3.

once a legitimate part of our political life, but it is no longer necessary for any citizen to threaten another with a weapon, because, with the institution of the moderate ('third way') regime of oligarchy, we Erythraeans have put *stasis* behind us. And thus tyranny is no longer a threat." Of course this is just a guess; we have no way of knowing what the Erythraean oligarchs *actually* meant by the act of disarming the tyrannicide statue. My point is that it is possible to suppose that, rather than accepting the democrats' democracy-tyranny antithesis with its associated assertion that tyrannicide was therapeutic *stasis*, the Erythraean oligarchs might have sought to change the discursive playing field.

"Changing the discourse" (in Robin Osborne's terms; Osborne 2003) is, in any event, what dissident Athenian writers sought to do. A self-conscious recognition of the profound symbolic power of the democratic "tyranny ideology," and a consequent recognition of the importance of challenging that ideology, is, I would suggest, among the factors that led fourth-century Athenian dissidents to depict the demos itself as the "true" tyrant, to refine and develop the idea of a spectrum of regimes, and to re-think the place of *stasis* in political life.

REWRITING THE DEMOCRATIC IDEOLOGY OF TYRANNY: PLATO

By the last years of the fifth century B.C., Athenian intellectuals critical of democracy were confronted with an increasingly coherent and pervasive democratic account of tyranny. Moreover, Plato, at least, was convinced that Greek intellectuals, along with oligarchic activists, had explicitly or implicitly internalized the bipolar conception that equated democracy's opponents with tyrants. This is the context of Plato's *Gorgias* and *Republic* (especially books 1 and 2). Socrates' interlocutors (Polus, Callicles, Thrasymachus) argue that the tyrant, the individual who enjoys the greatest capacity to do whatever he wishes, without social restraint and without fear of punishment, lives the happiest possible life. Both Callicles and Thrasymachus posit that democratic sociopolitical conventions were devised by "the many and the weak" to protect themselves against the naturally superior individual who would, if he could, make himself the master of his fellows. For Plato, only philosophers—people like Socrates, Glaucon, and Adeimantus—were capable of resisting the alluring dream of seeking to become a happy tyrant. Plato saw that for as long as anti-democratic elites remained seduced by the superficial attractions of the life of the happy tyrant, the bipolar democratic account of tyranny would stand uncontested, and celebration of resistance to tyranny would remain a stable mainstay of democratic culture. And thus the democrats would retain their monopoly on an antityrannical strand in Greek thought that stretched back through Herodotus, to the lyric poetry of Solon, and perhaps ultimately to Homer's negative depiction of Agamemnon in the *Iliad*.[31]

As several of the essays in *Popular Tyranny* rightly emphasize, Plato was not the first Athenian writer to challenge the political taxonomy that associated opponents of democracy with tyranny. In the fifth century, as Jeffrey Henderson (2003) discusses in detail, Aristophanic comedy explicitly linked the demos with tyranny. In a similar vein, Pseudo-Xenophon (*Ath. Pol.*) implicitly resorted to the imagery of tyranny when he suggested that the demos (qua lower classes) was wicked because it alienates from society's true share-holders that which is theirs, especially their private property. Moreover, he claimed, the demos alienates from share-holders their proper social and political positions and their ideological authority. In the current (democratic) *politeia*, it is the demos that levies taxes, distributes offices (via lottery to the "unworthy"), and sets the ideological agenda (see chapter 5). By this definition, the demos itself, rather than the antidemocrat, could be construed as holding tyrannical authority, and democracy might be re-envisioned as a form of tyranny. According to this line of argument, legitimate (i.e., nontyrannical) government can only arise when the demos has been deposed from its tyrannical position and political authority returned to those few who actually deserve it and are capable of its appropriate exercise.[32]

The force of pre-Platonic attempts to show that "demos=tyrant" was, however, limited in that the "demos-tyrant," unlike a single individual, cannot literally be assassinated: the argument of Pseudo-Xenophon's antidemocratic tract collapsed into aporia at the point of asking the question, what is to be done?[33] And the regime of the Thirty, whatever initial constitutional plans may have been harbored by its "moderates," collapsed into an orgy of violence and greed when faced with the task of actually building a legitimate nondemocratic political order.[34] In the aftermath of 404 B.C., Plato saw clearly that a new (nondemocratic) political order would have to be focused on education rather than assassination—comprehensive political change would have to involve re-education of both the intellectual elite and the mass of ordinary citizens. The elite must

[31] The pro- and antityrannical strands in earlier Greek thought: see Seaford 2003. Cf. Raaflaub 2003 and Kallet 2003, responding to Connor 1977. On Herodotus's very complex depiction of tyranny and tyrants, see Dewald 2003.

[32] On demos as tyrant in Aristophanes, see Henderson 2003. As Raaflaub (2003) points out, "Demos-tyrannos" appears in fifth-century literature explicitly in comedy, implicitly in literature critical of democracy. Kallet 2003 discusses some of the implicit fifth-century and explicit (critical) fourth-century associations of demos with tyrant. Pseudo-Xenophon as a critic of democracy: Ober 1998, 14–23 and chapter 5, above.

[33] Pseudo-Xenophon's aporia: Ober 1998, 23–27, and chapter 5, above.

[34] Possible constitutional-reform plans of the Thirty: Krentz 1982; R. Osborne 2003.

be taught to understand and resist their own enslavement by the tyrant-demos. And the people must be "tamed"—taught to relinquish their tyrannical authority over property, offices, and ideology.

The argument of Plato's *Gorgias* concerns what "we should want for ourselves" and his point is that most people are incapable of wishing for what is actually good for them. Gorgias' two students, Polus and Callicles, actively embrace the "happy-tyrant" ideal. They are students of Gorgias precisely because they suppose that mastery of rhetoric is the royal road to tyrannical bliss. As we have seen, the standard ideology of tyranny emphasized the tyrant's propensity to alienate from others their goods. Polus at one point (*Grg.* 471e ff.) furnishes a variety of "witnesses" to the happiness of tyrants, emphasizing that they can take what they want. But Socrates rejects the argument from witnesses, responding: "You keep trying to refute me rhetorically, as those in lawcourts do," by providing a great number of highly esteemed witnesses. Although Polus could no doubt get almost all Athenians, and foreigners, too, to agree to his position, this will still not budge Socrates from *his* "own possession" (*ousia*: that is, philosophy) or from the truth (471e–472b). The point is that, although the tyrant can certainly use his power to seize the *material* possessions of others, the philosopher remains secure in that no one can deprive him of his "true possession"—even if one were to deprive him of his life. And thus Socrates is able to assert that he cannot be harmed in any meaningful way by a tyrant. This means that the philosopher can commit his life to a new sort of therapeutic *stasis*. As we have seen, the demos imagined tyrant-killing as a uniquely therapeutic form of *stasis*. Plato's Socrates employs some of the vocabulary of *stasis* to describe his own behavior. But Socrates does not seek to kill tyrants, but rather to exterminate, through elenchtic education, his interlocutor's unhealthy desire for tyrannical authority.

Callicles aspires to become a sort of tyrant in Athens through manipulative leadership of the demos. Socrates proceeds to show him that it is the demos that is the real tyrant in Athens, by playing upon the theme of Callicles' role as a "lover of demos." At *Grg.* 491d–492c Callicles predicates the happy-tyrant argument on the natural rightness of maximizing his own pleasure, which in turn means maximizing desire so as to maximize satisfaction of desire. But Socrates shows him that the impulse to maximize desire and pleasure logically results in the lifestyle of the penetration-loving homosexual (*kinaidos*) whose "itches" are, in Callicles' case, "scratched" by the demos (494e).[35] And so, rather than achieving the unrestrained position of the tyrant who can do whatever he pleases,

---

[35] The *kinaidos* as an Athenian social type: Winkler 1990. C. Kahn 1983, 105–7, and Wardy 1996, 81–82, discuss the social, political, and personal ramifications for Callicles of assimilation to the *kinaidos*.

the aspiring political leader ends up as the willing sexual victim of the tyrant-demos. The *kinaidos* metaphor graphically asserts Callicles' inferior relationship relative to the demos. The position Callicles takes up is not that of the bold warrior advancing on his foe, but rather that of a submissive inferior. With Socrates' rude image of Callicles, the would-be tyrant, being penetrated by his demos-lover, sword becomes phallus. The familiar political image of "demos-as-tyrant-killer" is reconfigured in the comic imagery of "demos-as-sexual-aggressor."[36] As long as Callicles remains possessed by the dream of the happy tyrant, he will remain enslaved by the dominant democratic ideology.

The point is reinforced later in the dialogue, this time explicitly in the language of tyranny: Socrates initially posits, and Callicles avidly agrees, that if a man does not wish to suffer injustice he must arm himself with powerful resources. The craft (*technē*) of provisioning oneself with security is to rule over the polis, by being either an actual tyrant or (Callicles' approach) a loyal comrade (*hetairos*) of the tyrannical *politeia* (510a). Yet security, as it turns out, comes at a great cost: the only way to be safe under the rule of a tyrant is to submit to him, agree with everything he says, be ruled by him, and indeed to become as much like him as possible (510b–e)—that is to say, to give up one's individual identity and sense of self. Given that the discussion has been centered on politics in democratic Athens, the "tyrant" in question is once again the Athenian demos, and those who submit to the tyrant-demos by becoming just like it are the public speakers, men like Callicles himself.

The distinction Plato draws between "Socratic politics" and the sort of "tyrannical" leadership in the democratic state sought by Callicles is underlined by Callicles' eventual admission (521a–c) that his own political practice, unlike that of Socrates, does not constitute "going to battle with the Athenians" (*diamachesthai Athēnaiois*) in order to improve them like a medical doctor, but rather it is a form of "menial service" aimed at gaining gratitude (*charis*) and avoiding punishment. Socrates of the *Gorgias* establishes a key distinction between democratic politics as a form of flattery aimed at pleasure, and Socratic politics as a technique of education, by repeatedly employing the language of battles fought within the polis and/or within an individual soul: Socrates' approach to politics is "not via gratification (*katacharizomenon*), but by battling it through (*diamachomenon*)" (513d). The root contrast drawn here is between *charis*-seeking and battle—which we soon recognize as an analogy to the contrast between *charis*-seeking and medical treatment (*therapeia*: e.g., 513e). Paralleling

[36] Image of demos as passive-active lover: Aristophanes, *Knights*, with comments of Nightingale 1995, 187–90, who suggests that in this passage Plato is "harnessing comedy's 'voice of criticism'" (190). Cf. Pericles' injunction in the Funeral Oration to Athenian citizens to "become the lover" (*erastēs*) of the polis, with discussion of Monoson 1994.

the democratic ideology of tyrant-killing as a moment of "therapeutic *stasis*," Socrates of the *Gorgias* correlates therapy and education with "doing battle" with one's fellow citizens and so politics becomes a way of "curing" them. Socrates teaches active resistance to ideological mystification, which is therapeutic for the individual citizen and for the polis. But although Socratic *politikē technē* is imagined via the metaphor of *stasis*, a Socratic "battle within the polis" does not result in the death of either the tyrant-demos, or of the tyrant-demos's orator-servants. Rather, the desired outcome is a new disposition, an elimination of the tyrannical impulse. And so therapeutic *stasis* becomes a metaphor for Socrates' educative mission. We are, in a sense, invited to replace the central democratic image of the tyrant-killer's healing and death-dealing sword with the *Apology*'s image of the gadfly's tonic "sting."

The issue of *stasis* and tyrannicide recurs in the *Republic*. At a pivotal moment in the dialogue, Socrates posits that in order for a truly excellent polis to come into being, either philosophers must be kings or kings and rulers must truly philosophize (473c–e). But this bold vision will not be realized without at least metaphorical violence. Glaucon warns Socrates that his proposal will be attacked by many distinguished people. They will immediately pull off their cloaks, and, stripped naked, grab up whatever weapons lie to hand, rushing forward avidly "as if undertaking noteworthy deeds."[37] So Socrates had better be able to "defend himself by *logos*" (473e–474a). This vivid passage adopts the familiar imagery of the canonical Athenian iconography of tyrannicide: the many distinguished folk will strip, take up arms, and rush forward avidly—imitating the kinetic energy and the heroic nudity of the sword-bearing tyrannicides of the Kritios and Nesiotes statue group. The armed and naked men, anticipated by Glaucon as opponents of a new and quasi-monarchical element in the polis, are counterparts of democratic "tyrant-killers." Their hostile response to Socrates' revolutionary proposal accords with the oath sworn by the Athenians in 410–409 B.C. to oppose the overthrow of democracy by whatever means necessary. Notably, however, it is not just ordinary citizens that Glaucon imagines as rushing at Socrates—although many (*polloi*), they are "not undistinguished" (*ou phauloi*). The would-be assassins who misrecognize Socrates as a would-be tyrant are members of the elite, but they have internalized the democratic account of "the tyrant and what we should do about him." We might say that in opposing Socrates' proposal for philosopher-rulers, they join Aristophanes' chorus of old Athenians, taking up their stand in the Agora next to Aristogeiton, determined that no one will ever set up a tyranny over *them*.

---

[37] οἷον ῥίψαντας τὰ ἱμάτια, γυμνοὺς λαβόντας ὅτι ἑκάστῳ παρέτυχεν ὅπλον, θεῖν διατεταμένους ὡς θαυμάσια ἐργασομένους.

The *Republic* passage underlines, through the familiar topoi of the tyrannicide ideology, the extent of re-education that will be necessary before philosopher-rule could be welcomed—even as an ideal and even among the elite.

Yet later in the dialogue, the optimistic reader is offered reason to hope that Callipolis might be attained: Socrates suggests that, while difficult to achieve, the rule of the philosopher-king was not impossible in practice (*ou gar adunatos . . . oude adunata*: 499c–502c). The gentlemen Glaucon had imagined rushing at Socrates with weapons drawn will be led to admit the logical force of the argument for philosophical rule (501c). Even the masses could come to accept such a regime, if they could just be taught what a real philosopher was really like (499d–500b). The potential depth of popular trust in true philosopher-leaders is suggested at the end of book 7 (540e–541a), where *stasis* imagery once again recurs, although in a very different form. In order for the transition from the old, corrupt regime to a new philosopher-led regime to be accomplished most easily and quickly within an existing polis, the philosopher-rulers will banish all citizens over age ten to outlying agricultural districts; the banished evidently are expected to concur and head off gracefully, leaving their children behind. The situation Plato envisions here recalls a common pattern of Greek civil strife, well known from (for example) Thucydides' depiction of the *stasis* at Corcyra (3.70–82): When a faction takes over the main town of a polis, the opposing faction retreats to strongholds in the countryside. That pattern had recently been played out in Athens, when, in 404 B.C., the Thirty held the city and the democrats held the rural stronghold of Phyle (see chapter 8). Yet in this part of the *Republic* the terrors of *stasis* have been thoroughly domesticated. The demos gives up its urban possessions and progeny without a struggle, evidently seeing that these sacrifices are preconditions to the therapeutic extermination of its own corrupted beliefs and practices. In order to realize Callipolis, the demos is, in effect, alienated from every good that a greedy human tyrant might desire: possessions, homes, children, hope for the future. Yet the division of the city into alienated rural population and privileged city-dwellers is imagined as voluntary. Moreover, the change, once accomplished, is permanent and irrevocable.

In Plato's text, realizing Callipolis requires first that its founders survive a metaphoric act of tyrannicide and then that most of the polis' adult population accepts—once and for all—living conditions ordinarily associated with tyranny and *stasis*. Yet once in place, the society of the *Republic*'s Callipolis, predicated on the strict education of the Guardian class and a set of "noble lies," eliminates all possible sources of conflict within the state and within the souls of its individual members. Callipolis' Guardians could not be alienated from that which was "their own," since ownership (of

family and goods) was either nonexistent or communal. The education of
Guardians ensures that they treat the lower orders strictly in accordance
with justice. The censorship of literature in the ideal city ensures that
Callipolis' residents never learn about the existence of *stasis*. And thus,
Socrates' attempt to exterminate the tyrannical impulse in the souls of his
interlocutors through reasoned argument reaches its end point in Callipolis with the elimination of any possible motive or means for *stasis*. By the
end of the *Republic* Plato has led his reader to a position that is significantly different from that of Socrates as he is presented in the *Apology* and
Gorgias (with his imagery of stings and battle) and, a fortiori, from the citizens of Athens itself, who kept the possibility of "therapeutic *stasis* within
the polis" before themselves through public iconography and patriotic
tyrant-killer tales of the sort objected to by Thucydides.

Plato's conception of politics is obviously very different from that of
Athenian democrats; here I underline two differences particularly salient in
terms of the ideology of tyranny. First, contrary to the attempt of Athenian
democrats to define a bipolar (democratic-tyrannical) political universe,
Plato (like Aristotle and other fourth-century political thinkers) describes
a wide spectrum of political options. In the *Republic*'s hierarchical taxonomy of regimes (Callipolis, timocracy, oligarchy, democracy, tyranny),
Callipolis defines the best possible state, tyranny the worst. But timocracy,
oligarchy, and democracy are distinct (if, after the perfection of Callipolis, unsavory) political alternatives. Second, and equally important, is the
imagination of change. In Plato's scheme, Callipolis, once achieved, remains static, existing in a steady state of excellence. The rules are fixed
and change is regarded as, not only undesirable, but disastrous. As soon
as a mistake is made, as soon as change is introduced, the conditions
of justice are destroyed, Callipolis is irretrievably lost, and the society is
condemned to degenerate through a cycle of ever-worsening political
regimes, ending in the horrors of tyranny (*Republic*, books 8–9).

The democratic vision of political change was, as we have seen, quite different from Plato's, at once more pessimistic about the likelihood and frequency of serious political mishap and more optimistic about the capacity
of existing political values and practices to survive mishaps. Tyrants are
imagined as likely to arise but they are also capable of being resisted and
eventually overcome. For the Athenian, Iliote, and Erythraean *dēmoi* alike,
the figure of the tyrant-killer was thought to be salutary. *Stasis*, at least in
fourth-century Athenian democratic political thought, is simply an inter-
val, an interruption in a continuous democratic narrative. As the Eukrates
law of 337–336 B.C. demonstrates, the moral authority of the demos is
imagined as extending through periods of oligarchic or tyrannical rule;
the demos is regarded as capable of restoring itself in the aftermath of
a healthy moment of tyrant-slaying violence (cf. chapter 3). This robust

democratic optimism may go a way toward explaining the resilience of democracy, in Hellenistic Athens and in the poleis of Asia Minor, in the face of overwhelming Macedonian royal power (see chapter 8).[38]

Re-Envisioning the Democratic Ideology of Tyranny: Dexileos

If the argument I have developed above is along the right lines, we might hope to find iconographic evidence for the debate about the relationship between democracy, *stasis*, tyrants, and tyrant-killers. Linking classical works of art to specific political positions or even to general political sensibilities is fraught with difficulty. But it is not an inherently absurd undertaking. We have no material traces of the tombstone of Critias, the leader of the Thirty at Athens who died fighting the democrats at the decisive battle of Mounichia. But according to a scholion to Aeschines, *Against Timarchus* (DK 88A13), his tombstone featured a relief depicting personified Oligarchia, brandishing a torch and setting fire to Demokratia. The monument also reportedly featured an epigram: "This is the memorial (*mnēma*) of good men (*andres agathoi*) who, for a short while, restrained the *hubris* of the accursed demos."[39] It is tempting to speculate about the artistic sources of this monument's iconography: Might it have drawn on the imagery of personified Justice (*Dikē*) assaulting Injustice (*Adikia*)? An Amazonomachy? A city siege? And it is equally tempting to seek significance in the apparent dissonance between the murderous violence depicted in the relief and the language of restraint employed in the epigram—perhaps a reflection of two phases, quasi-constitutional and openly savage, of Critias's brief career as ruler?[40]

Finally, it is surely significant that on the gravestone of the leader of the gang Athenian democrats called "The Thirty Tyrants," it is Oligarchia and not Tyrannia who is igniting Demokratia. Critias' tombstone, as described by the scholiast, rejects the bipolar democratic reading of democracy's enemies as tyrants. Unfortunately, there is no way to establish that the monument described by the scholiast was ever erected in fact. But the (undatable) story of Critias' memorial, whatever its imagined iconography, points to Athenian tombstones as *possible* iconographic sites of ideological contestation. And it points to the aftermath of the rule of the Thirty as a particularly "hot" ideological era. As we have seen, this same era saw a recrudescence of tyrannicide iconography in Athenian vase painting.

---

[38] Hellenistic democracy: Gauthier 1993; Habicht 1997; Ma 1999.

[39] μνῆμα τόδ' ἐστ' ἀνδρῶν ἀγαθῶν, οἳ τὸν κατάρατον δῆμον Ἀθηναίων ὀλίγον χρόνον ὕβριος ἔσχον.

[40] *Dikē v. Adikia*: Faraone 2002, 331–41; Amazonamachy and city siege: Harrison 1981; two phases of Critias' career: R. Osborne 2003.

Accepting that we should not expect to discover anything nearly so explicit
as an oligarch's tombstone depicting Demokratia in flames, we might, following the scholiast's pointers, find it worthwhile to look for more subtle responses to the democratic ideology of tyranny in the iconography of Attic
tombstones of the decades around 404 B.C.

I have suggested that the memory and imagery of Athens' "tyrant-
slayers" was especially to the fore at the turn of the fifth and fourth centuries. Moreover, on the basis of the passage in Aristophanes' *Lysistrata*,
I posited that that the "Harmodios stance"—warrior moving right to left
(rather than the usual, heroic, left to right), with right sword-arm cocked
behind the head, preparatory to delivering the "Harmodios blow"—came
to serve as a shorthand visual cue to the democratic tyrant-killer ideology.
There is some danger of finding a tyrannicide lurking behind every raised
right arm. But the demonstrable Athenian concern with tyranny and
tyrannicides in the late fifth and fourth centuries renders it more plausi-
ble that visual citations of the "Harmodios stance" during that era were
read by contemporary viewers as something more than politically innocent artistic conventions.

Athenian artists did in fact quote Kritios' and Nesiotes' Harmodios in
designing late fifth- and fourth-century funerary sculpture. A nice example
is the fourth-century funeral relief of Stratocles, son of Procles (Clairmont
1993: 2.217; fig. 5) portraying a hoplite assuming Harmodios' stance while
preparing to strike a fallen foe. As Christoph Clairmont suggests, "the
[Harmodios] motif is well known from the group of tyrant-slayers which is
no doubt reminisced here."[41] In the Stratocles relief, a figure (presumably
Stratocles himself) whose face and dress offer some similarities to Demos
of the Eukrates Relief (mature, bearded, drapery over left shoulder, chest
exposed) takes on the active role of Harmodios. It is perhaps not too
much to guess that an Athenian looking at this monument was invited to
read Stratocles' military service as having served the same role in preserving democratic Athens as Harmodios' assassination of the tyrant—
although how explicit that claim was meant to be, on the part of artist or
commissioner of the tombstone, necessarily remains obscure.

Perhaps the most remarkable visual citation of Harmodios in later
Athenian art is the Albani relief (Clairmont 1993: 2.131; fig. 6)—certainly
funerary in nature, it remains a matter of debate whether it is a public or
a private monument, and it has been variously dated from ca. 430 through
the 390s B.C.[42] Here, a young (unbearded), lightly draped cavalryman has
just dismounted from his horse and prepares to dispatch a fallen, mostly

[41] Stratocles, son of Procles, relief=Clairmont 1993, 2.217. Quote: Clairmont 1993 2,
p. 157.
[42] Albani relief: Clairmont 1993, 2.131, with discussion of date and speculative reconstruction as a public monument of 394–393; Hölscher 1973, 109–10 with n. 529.

Figure 5. Stratocles relief. *CAT* 2.217. Courtesy, Museum of Fine Arts, Boston. Reproduced with permission. ©2000 Museum of Fine Arts, Boston. All Rights Reserved.

Figure 6. Albani relief. *CAT* 2.131. By permission of Villa Albani Torlonia, Rome (Inv. 985).

nude youth with the Harmodios blow.[43] The metamorphosis of Harmodios into an Athenian cavalryman introduces an interesting wrinkle, in light of the strongly aristocratic associations of the Athenian cavalry. The relationship between cavalry and democracy became that much more fraught after 404, due to the active cooperation by the Athenian cavalrymen with the reign of the Thirty.[44] Whatever its exact date, it seems likely that the monument's citation of tyrannicide iconography sought to associate potentially politically suspect elite cavalrymen with defense of democracy.

In an admittedly speculative reconstruction, Clairmont suggests that the Albani relief supported a surviving inscribed frieze listing the Athenian cavalry casualties of 394–393 B.C.—ten horseman and a phylarch lost at the Battles of Corinth and Koroneia (National Museum of Greece inv. 754 = Tod *GHI*: II.104 = RO 7A). Since the inscription was authorized by the Athenian state, Clairmont's reconstruction would make the Albani relief part of a public monument of the mid-390s, honoring the horsemen

---

[43] Cf. Stupperich 1994, 99: "the victor in the Albani relief and the victorious Stratokles . . . who are both shown contrary to the usual direction of the victor as moving from right to left, adopt the stance of Harmodios."

[44] Cavalry and the Thirty: Bugh 1988, 120–53.

who died in defense of the democratic polity. In conformity to the established practices of democratic Athenian public burial, the deceased cavalrymen of the 390s were listed individually on the monument frieze, but the individuality of the fallen warriors was subsumed to the value of community, as emphasized in their common burial and by their common grave monument.

One of the ten dead horsemen listed on the inscribed frieze of 394–393 is Dexileos, son of Lysanias of the deme Thorikos. Dexileos' family evidently decided that the state's communal commemoration was not enough. Shortly after his death and public burial, Dexileos' family erected a large and splendid cenotaph monument in his honor in the Kerameikos cemetery, complete with a sculptural relief and an inscription (fig. 7).[45] The popularity of the tyrant-killer iconography in the 390s is confirmed by an early fourth-century red-figure oinochoe found by excavators in Dexileos' cenotaph precinct (fig. 8).[46] The vase fragment depicts the Kritios and Nesiotes monument itself, with Harmodios to the front in his distinctive stance—although, as Emily Vermeule pointed out in her original publication of the fragment, his sword looks more like a limp rag than a real weapon. Aristogeiton's sword is hidden behind his own right hip. This vase, along with four others of the same early fourth-century date but featuring conventional scenes recalling the Anthesteria "coming-of-age" festival, was apparently deposited by the family of Dexileos in his cenotaph at the time the monument was consecrated.

What, if any, ideological significance ought we to attach to this cluster of artifacts? A possible pointer is offered by Dexileos's peculiar cenotaph inscription (*IG* II² 6217 = Tod *GHI* II.105 = RO 7B), which, surprisingly, lists *both* his birth and death dates—414–413 (archon Teisander) and 394–393 (archon Euboulides). It is the only known Attic funerary inscription to do so. Glenn Bugh, following a conjecture originally made by Colin Edmonson, plausibly argues that the birthdate was added in order to exculpate the horseman Dexileos from the possible charge of pro-oligarchic activities during the reign of the Thirty. The prominent birthdate proclaims that Dexileos was simply too young to have ridden against the democrats at Phyle.[47]

Dexileos' relatives might well have been especially concerned to make some sort of ideological disclaimer because they chose to erect a remarkable, highly visible, and iconographically striking monument to decorate the new cenotaph enclosure. This sort of ostentatious private commemoration had been out of fashion in democratic Athens—and elsewhere in

[45] The Dexileos monument: Morris 1992, 143–44; Ridgway 1997, 3–7, 162; Hölscher 1973, 102–3, 108.

[46] The vase: figure 8 (see Ober and Hedrick 1996, 57 for color photograph). Its excavation context and date: Vermeule 1970. Further discussion and bibliography: Ajootian 1998.

[47] Bugh 1988, 139.

Figure 7. Dexileos relief (394–393 B.C.). By permission of Deutsches Archaeologische Institut, Athens (Inv. P 1130).

Figure 8. Oinochoe fragment depicting tyrannicide monument, ca. 390s B.C. Courtesy, Museum of Fine Arts, Boston. Reproduced with permission. ©2000 Museum of Fine Arts, Boston. All Rights Reserved.

Greece—for a century or more. It might well (and might rightly) be seen as offering a private response, even a covert challenge by a wealthy family, to the democratic practices of commemorating fallen warriors as equals—via funeral oration, common burial, casualty lists, and communal sculptural reliefs.[48] The challenge would be especially stark if we follow Clairmont in imagining the Albani relief as a public monument of 394–393—the iconography of the Albani and Dexileos reliefs is clearly interrelated (whether directly or via a common source). I suggested above that the visual quotation of the Harmodios stance in the Albani relief should be read as asserting that the cavalry defended democracy. The Dexileos inscription, with its implicit claim that "I was too young to be an oligarch, and I died defending democratic Athens at Corinth" might be seen in a similar light, as an attempt to deflect demotic jealousy and ire at ostentatious private self-advertisement by the family of an aristocrat.

[48] Morris 1992, 128–44, discusses the evolving size and splendor of Attic funerary monuments.

This would be an acknowledgment, at the level of the inscribed text, of democratic ideological authority. And the oinochoe dedication, with its portrayal of the tyrannicide monument might be (and has been) read in the same general light, as making a philodemocratic statement of some sort.[49]

But the relief's iconography adds another level of complexity: As Brunilde Ridgway has recently noted, the Dexileos relief is distinctive (although not unparalleled; cf. again, the Albani relief) in depicting the "heroic" horseman (presumably Dexileos himself) who prepares to skewer his fallen foe as draped, and his defeated enemy as nude. Ridgway suggests that this may be an example of a reversal of the ordinary association of nudity—here, rather than heroism, nudity may reflect the helpless position of the defeated warrior.[50] But for our purposes, it is even more remarkable that the nude fallen soldier quite faithfully maintains the familiar sword-arm overhead of the Harmodios stance, even in collapse—although this time the "Harmodios blow" is offered by a dying man as a futile response to the mounted enemy who is spearing him.[51] The nude fallen warrior clutches a shield (rather than a scabbard) in his left hand, but his shield-arm (like Stratocles': fig. 5) is draped with a chlamys and thereby recalls the draped arm of the otherwise nude Aristogeiton figure of the tyrannicide statue group. If the Albani relief (whatever its exact date) presents to its viewer "Harmodios as victorious Athenian cavalryman," thus celebrating the defense of democracy by the Athenian horsemen, then it is tempting to see in the private Dexileos relief a metaphoric overthrow by the aristocratic cavalryman of the democratic tyrannicide-heroes and so, one might suppose, the overthrow of democracy itself.

The Dexileos relief's visual quotation of the tyrannicide group stretches the canonical representation almost to the breaking point. Indeed, if we did not know about the dedication at the cenotaph of an oinochoe depicting the tyrannicide monument, the association of the Dexileos relief with the Kritios and Nesiotes group would be harder to defend. But the oinochoe was deposited at the cenotaph, strong evidence that the people who commissioned the monument were acutely aware of tyrant-killer iconography. Given the fact of the oinochoe dedication, and given the similarity of the iconography of the Dexileos monument to other near-contemporary sculptural citations of the tyrannicide monument, the Dexileos citation may be

---

[49] Vermeule 1970, 105–6, suggests democratic associations of the (private) oinochoe dedication.

[50] Ridgway 1997, 6–7.

[51] Shefton 1960, 174, cites the Dexileos relief as a primary example of the "defensive use" of the "Harmodios blow." The earlier iconographic depictions of the fallen warrior in the defensive "Harmodios stance" cited by Shefton, mostly Amazonomachai, are from vase paintings.

taken as intentional. If intentional, in the atmosphere of the 390s, it could hardly be innocent of political meaning.

Assuming, as I suppose we must, that those who commissioned the Dexileos cenotaph were sensitive to tyrannicide iconography, we may guess that they anticipated that similarly sensitive viewers would respond, one way or another, to it. So how might an early fourth-century Athenian witness read the Dexileos monument, taken as a whole? Might he or she see a visual narrative of an alternative, counterfactual, "aristocratic-utopian" Athenian history—one in which the *stasis* of 404 had resulted, not in democratic restoration following the humiliating rout of the pro-Thirty cavalry in a snowstorm, but rather in the aristocratic cavalry's therapeutic destruction of the democratic aspirations of the "men of Phyle?"

Yet the Dexileos inscription militates against such a straightforward antidemocratic reading. The juxtaposition of the ostentatious private monument, its subtly subversive iconography, and its subtly defensive inscription, with their potentially clashing ideological messages, suggests that reading the Dexileos monument, even for a contemporary Athenian, was no simple matter. Should we then regard the Dexileos monument as so semiotically overdetermined as to be ideologically illegible—to us or to its contemporaries? Perhaps not, if we regard it in light of Isocrates' highly self-conscious "double-pointed speeches" (*logoi amphiboloi*).[52] Kathryn Morgan (2003b) emphasizes the multiplicity of Isocrates' implied audiences. Isocrates' carefully crafted, deliberately ambiguous texts explicitly offered at least two readings depending on the reader's sophistication and political tastes (in the case of the *Panathenaicus*, a pro- or an anti-Spartan reading). Unlike an Isocratean didactic text, the sculptural monument does not teach us how to read by offering a convenient metarhetoric. But with Isocrates' "lesson" in mind, we might view the Dexileos monument as "amphibolic." In common with political texts of the same period, the monument can be read as hovering in the field of tension created by the powerful democratic ideology and a powerful elite impulse to dissent from that ideology. Like an Isocratean *amphibolos logos*, the monument seems to be an artifact specifically designed to be read differently by different subcommunities. Like an Isocratean text (and unlike the Erythrae tyrannicide monument with its clarifying inscription), it resists simple appropriation by any particular political tendency. But that resistance to interpretive appropriation does not render it innocent of political meaning.

The "amphibolic" reading I have suggested for Dexileos's monument is a far cry from the straightforward, oligarchic reading the scholiast offered of Critias' tombstone, and deliberately so. I would suggest that thinking in

---

[52] Isocratean *logoi amphiboloi*: Isocrates 12.240, with Bons 1993.

terms of Isocrates' craftsmanly and self-conscious ambiguity might provide an entrée into a way of viewing some Greek works of art that would take into account the sort of ideological negotiations that scholars have traced in Greek texts.[53] There are other Attic tombstones in which a defeated soldier struggles to respond to his attacker with the "Harmodios blow": for example the very beautiful, although fragmentary, example in Clairmont 1993, 2.130, which is very close iconographically to the Dexileos relief, or the cruder, and perhaps later example in Clairmont 1993, 2.251, or a recently published relief fragment tentatively identified as a public monument of ca. 338 B.C.[54] And a better understanding of these reliefs might help us to read more into other Attic reliefs depicting triumphant draped horsemen and fallen nude infantrymen who do not offer the "Harmodios blow," for example National Museum of Greece inv. 2744, a public monument—again commemorating the fallen of 394—393, or a striking square base found near the Academy depicting three perspectives of the same general battle scene (Clairmont 1993, 2.213).

The tyrant-slayer motif encourages us to explore the close interaction of ideology and dissent, and of text and image. Tracing the complicated and criss-crossing system of cultural references, a task this essay has only begun, requires moving across a variety of media and between various genres: monumental sculpture and vase painting; comic poetry, history and philosophy; inscribed public decrees; public and private funerary and documentary reliefs; and erudite marginalia reporting monuments that may or may not have existed. It leads us to traverse long periods of history, and to move outside of Athens. The point of seeking to trace the web of references across media, genres, time, and space is the chance to glimpse the growing density of associations that elite and ordinary Athenians (and other Greeks, as suggested by extra-Attic epigraphic traces) brought to the problem of "thinking the tyrant." As the political and cultural resonances grew richer, the skilled interlocutor—whether artist or writer or (with Aristophanes' chorus) gesturer—could say more, in different registers and potentially to various subcommunities, with increasingly subtle allusions. Such circumstances demand both imagination and interpretive modesty on the part of the modern reader. At best we will catch only some references, and we should certainly never hope to fix the "full and final" political meaning of any given citation of the visual or literary canons.

The evolving democratic discourse on tyrannicide depended on both stability and change, on both "being" and "becoming": it required the

[53] Neer 2002, attempts a similar task, focusing on Attic vase painting of ca. 530–460 B.C. Texts as negotiating competing social and political ideologies: for example, Ober 1989; Morris 1996; Kurke 1999.

[54] Bibliography on these "Harmodios blow" reliefs: Kaempf-Dimitriadou 1986.

continuity over time of a core ideological association of tyrant-killing with salutary defense of the democratic regime. But (absent serious challenges by genuine tyrants) the democratic discourse on tyranny risked ossification. It gained the capacity to extend its imaginative scope only when faced with substantial dissident responses. These dissident responses might be at the level of text, of iconographic representation, or of political action. Or, sometimes, all three at once. If the oligarchs of Erythrae had never sought to transform the field of play by the act of taking away a tyrannicide's sword, then the restored democrats would have had no chance to make an epigraphic counterclaim to the effect that those who deprived the tyrannicide of his sword had revealed their belief that it was pointed at themselves. Although we should never forget how nasty Greek politics could become in practice, it is in such high-stakes ideological debates that Greek political life reveals its semiotic versatility and intellectual vitality.

Bibliography

Adelman, Jeremy, ed. 1999. *Colonial Legacies: The Problem of Persistence in Latin American History*. New York: Routledge.

Ajootian, A. 1998. "A Day at the Races," 1–13, in *Stephanos: Studies in Honor of Brunilde Sismondo Ridgway*, edited by Kim J. Hartswick and Mary C. Sturgeon. Philadelphia: University Museum, University of Pennsylvania for Bryn Mawr College.

Allen, Danielle S. 2000a. "Changing the Authoritative Voice: Lycurgus' *Against Leocrates*." *Classical Antiquity* 19:5–33.

———. 2000b. *The World of Prometheus: The Politics of Punishing in Democratic Athens*. Princeton, N.J.: Princeton University Press.

———. 2001. "Law's Forcefulness: Hannah Arendt vs. Ralph Ellison on the Battle of Little Rock." *Oklahoma City Law Review* 26:857–95.

———. 2004. *Talking to Strangers: Anxieties of Citizenship since Brown v. Board of Education*. Chicago: University of Chicago Press.

Allen, Katarzyna Hagemajer. 2003a. "Intercultural Exchanges in Fourth-Century Attic Decrees." *Classical Antiquity* 22:199–246.

———. 2003b. "Becoming the 'Other': Attitudes and Practices at Attic Cemetaries," 207–36, in *The Cultures within Greek Cultures: Contact, Conflict, Collaboration*, edited by Carol Dougherty and Leslie Kurke. Cambridge: Cambridge University Press.

Anderson, Greg. 2003. *The Athenian Experiment: Building an Imagined Political Community in Ancient Attica, 508–490 B.C.* Ann Arbor: University of Michigan Press.

Austin, J. L. 1975. *How to Do Things with Words*. Cambridge, Mass.: Harvard University Press.

Balot, Ryan K. 2001. *Greed and Injustice in Classical Athens*. Princeton, N.J.: Princeton University Press.

———. 2004. "The Dark Side of Democratic Courage." *Social Research* 71:73–106.

Barber, Benjamin R. 1984. *Strong Democracy: Participatory Politics for a New Age*. Berkeley: University of California Press.

Beazley, J. D. 1948. "Death of Hipparchus." *Journal of Hellenic Studies* 68:26–28.

———. 1963. *Attic Red-Figure Vase-Painters*. Oxford: Clarendon Press.

Bechtle, Gerald. 1996. "A Note on Pseudo-Xenophon, *The Constitution of the Athenians* 1.11." *Classical Quarterly* 46:564–66.

Berlin, Isaiah. 1969. *Four Essays on Liberty*. London and New York: Oxford University Press.

Bers, Victor. 1985. "Dikastic Thorybos," 1–15, in *Crux: Essays Presented to G.E.M. de Ste. Croix*, edited by Paul Cartledge and F. D. Harvey. Exeter: Imprint Academic.

——, ed. 2003. *Demosthenes, Speeches 50–59*. Austin: University of Texas Press.

Blake, Michael. 2003. "Immigration," in *The Blackwell Companion to Applied Ethics*, edited by Christopher Wellman and R. G. Frey. London: Blackwell.

Blundell, R. 1989. *Helping Friends and Harming Enemies: A Study in Sophocles and Greek Ethics*. Cambridge: Cambridge University Press.

Bobonich, Christopher. 2002. *Plato's Utopia Recast: His Later Ethics And Politics*. Oxford: Clarendon Press.

Boegehold, Alan L. 1994. "Pericles' Citizenship Law of 451/0 B.C.," 57–66, in *Athenian Identity and Civic Ideology*, edited by Alan L. Boegehold and Adele C. Scafuro. Baltimore, Md.: The Johns Hopkins University Press.

——. 1996. "Resistance to Change in the Law at Athens," 203–14, in *Dēmokratia: A Conversation on Democracies, Ancient and Modern*, edited by Josiah Ober and Charles W. Hedrick. Princeton, N.J.: Princeton University Press.

Boegehold, Alan L., and Adele C. Scafuro, eds. 1994. *Athenian Identity and Civic Ideology*. Baltimore, Md.: The Johns Hopkins University Press.

Bons, J.A.E. 1993. "*Amphibolia*: Isocrates and Written Composition." *Mnemosyne* 46:160–71.

Brickhouse, Thomas C., and Nicholas D. Smith. 1989. *Socrates on Trial*. Princeton, N.J.: Princeton University Press.

Brown, Wendy. 1995. *States of Injury: Power and Freedom in Late Modernity*. Princeton, N.J.: Princeton University Press.

Brunnsåker, Sture. 1971. *The Tyrant-slayers of Kritios and Nesiotes*. Stockholm: Svenska Institutet i Athen.

Bugh, Glenn Richard. 1988. *The Horsemen of Athens*. Princeton, N.J.: Princeton University Press.

Burn, Lucilla, and Ruth Glynn. 1982. *Beazley Addenda: Additional References to ABV, ARV* 2 *& Paralipomena*. Oxford: Published for the British Academy by Oxford University Press.

Butler, Judith. 1997. *Excitable Speech: A Politics of the Performative*. New York: Routledge.

Buxton, Richard G. A. 1992. "Imaginary Greek Mountains." *Journal of Hellenic Studies* 112:1–15.

Camp, John McK. 1986. *The Athenian Agora: Excavations in the Heart of Classical Athens*. London: Thames and Hudson.

Camp, John McK. II. 1991. "Notes on the Towers and Borders of Classical Boeotia." *American Journal of Archaeology* 95:193–202.

——. 2000. "Walls and the *Polis*," 41–57, in *Polis and Politics [Festschrift Hansen]*, edited by P. Flensted-Jensen, T. H. Neilsen, L. Rubinstein. Copenhagen: Munksgaard.

——. 2001. *The Archaeology of Athens*. New Haven: Yale University Press.

Carey, Christopher, ed. 1992. *Apollodoros Against Neaira: (Demosthenes) 59*. Warminster, Wiltshire, England: Aris & Phillips.

——. 1998. "The Shape of Athenian Laws." *Classical Quarterly* 48:93–109.

Carpenter, Thomas H., Thomas Mannack, Melanie Mendonça, and Lucilla Burn. 1989. *Beazley Addenda: Additional References to ABV, ARV* 2 *& Paralipomena*. Oxford: Published for the British Academy by Oxford University Press.

Cartledge, Paul. 1987. *Agesilaos and the Crisis of Sparta*. London: Duckworth.

———. 1990. *Aristophanes and His Theatre of the Absurd*. Bristol: Bristol Classical Press.

———. 1993. *The Greeks: A Portrait of Self and Others*. Oxford: Oxford University Press.

———. 1996. "Comparatively Equal," 175–86, in *Dēmokratia: A Conversation on Democracies, Ancient and Modern*, edited by Josiah Ober and Charles W. Hedrick. Princeton, N.J.: Princeton University Press.

———. 2001. *Spartan Reflections*. London: Duckworth.

Cartledge, Paul, Paul Millett, and Sitta von Reden, eds. 1998. *Kosmos: Essays in Order, Conflict, and Community in Classical Athens*. Cambridge: Cambridge University Press.

Castriota, David. 1998. "Democracy and Art in Late Sixth- and Fifth-Century Athens," 197–216, in *Democracy 2500?: Questions and Challenges*, edited by Ian Morris and Kurt A. Raaflaub. Dubuque, Iowa: Kendall/Hunt Pub. Co.

Clairmont, Christoph W. 1993. *Classical Attic Tombstones*. 8 volumes. Kilchberg, Switzerland: Akanthus.

Cohen, David. 1991. *Law, Sexuality, and Society: The Enforcement of Morals in Classical Athens*. Cambridge: Cambridge University Press.

———. 1995. *Law, Violence, and Community in Classical Athens*. Cambridge University Press.

Cohen, Edward E. 1973. *Ancient Athenian Maritime Courts*. Princeton, N.J.: Princeton University Press.

———. 2000. *The Athenian Nation*. Princeton, N.J.: Princeton University Press.

Cohen, Joshua. 1996. "Procedure and Substance in Deliberative Democracy," 94–119, in *Democracy and Difference: Contesting the Boundaries of the Political*, edited by Seyla Benhabib. Princeton, N.J.: Princeton University Press.

Cole, Susan G. 1999–2000. "Landscapes of Artemis." *Classical World* 93:471–81.

———. 2004. *Landscapes, Gender, and Ritual Space: The Ancient Greek Experience*. Berkeley: University of California Press.

Connor, W. Robert. 1977. "Tyrannis Polis," 95–109, in *Ancient and Modern: Essays in Honor of Gerald F. Else*, edited by J. H. D'Arms and J. W. Eadie. Ann Arbor: University of Michigan Press.

———. 1984. *Thucydides*. Princeton, N.J.: Princeton University Press.

Constant, Benjamin. 1988. *Political Writings*. Cambridge: Cambridge University Press.

Culley, G. R. 1977. "The Restoration of Sanctuaries in Attica. II." *Hesperia* 46:282–98.

Dahl, Robert Alan. 1989. *Democracy and Its Critics*. New Haven, Conn.: Yale University Press.

Daverio Rocchi, Giovanna. 1987. "La *hiera orgas* e la frontiera attico-megarese," 97–109, in *Studi di Antichità in Memoria di Clementina Gatti*. Milan: Cisalpino-Goliardica.

———. 1988. *Frontiera e confini nella Grecia antica*. Roma: "L'Erma" di Bretschneider.

Deetz, J., and E. Dethlefsen. 1965. "The Doppler Effect and Archaeology: A Consideration of Spatial Aspects of Seriation." *Southwestern Journal of Archaeology* 21:196–206.

Devins, Neal, and Louis Fisher. 1998. "Judicial Exclusivity and Political Instability." *Virginia Law Review* 84:83–106.

Dewald, Carolyn. 2003. "Form and Content: The Question of Tyranny in Herodotus," 25–58, in *Popular Tyranny: Sovereignty and Its Discontents in Ancient Greece*, edited by Kathryn Morgan. Austin: University of Texas Press.

Dougherty, Carol, and Leslie Kurke, eds. 2003. *The Cultures within Greek Culture: Contact, Conflict, Collaboration*. Cambridge: Cambridge University Press.

Dover, Kenneth James. 1974. *Greek Popular Morality in the Time of Plato and Aristotle*. Oxford: Blackwell.

Dryzek, John S. 2000. *Deliberative Democracy and Beyond: Liberals, Critics, Contestations*. Oxford: Oxford University Press.

Dworkin, R. M. 2002. *A Badly Flawed Election: Debating Bush v. Gore, the Supreme Court, and American Democracy*. New York: New Press.

Eadie, John William, and Josiah Ober, eds. 1985. *The Craft of the Ancient Historian: Essays in Honor of Chester G. Starr*. Lanham, Md.: University Press of America.

Eder, Walter, ed. 1995. *Die athenische Demokratie im 4. Jahrhundert v. Chr.: Vollendung oder Verfall einer Verfassungsform? Akten eines Symposiums 3–7. August 1992, Bellagio*. Stuttgart: F. Steiner.

Edmonson, Colin. 1966. "The Topography of Northwest Attica." Ph.D. Diss. Berkeley, Ca.: University of California.

Eisgruber, Christopher L. 1994. "Political Unity and the Powers of Government." *UCLA Law Review* 41:1297–1336.

———. 1995. "The Fourteenth Amendment's Constitution." *Southern California Law Review* 69:47–103.

———. 2001. *Constitutional Self-Government*. Cambridge, Mass.: Harvard University Press.

Eliot, C. William J. 1962. *Coastal Demes of Attika. A Study of the Policy of Kleisthenes*. Toronto: University of Toronto Press.

Erbse, Hartmut. 1979. *Ausgewählte Schriften zur klassischen Philologie*. Berlin: de Gruyter.

Euben, J. Peter, ed. 1986. *Greek Tragedy and Political Theory*. Berkeley: University of California Press.

———. 1990. *The Tragedy of Political Theory: The Road Not Taken*. Princeton, N.J.: Princeton University Press.

———. 1997. *Corrupting Youth: Political Education, Democratic Culture, and Political Theory*. Princeton, N.J.: Princeton University Press.

———. 2000. "Arendt's Hellenism," 161–64, in *The Cambridge Companion to Hannah Arendt*, edited by Dana Richard Villa. Cambridge: Cambridge University Press.

Faraone, Christopher A. 2002. "The Ethnic Origins of a Roman-Era *Philtrokatadesmos* (PMG IV [296–434])," 319–343, in *Magic and Ritual in the Ancient World*, edited by P. Mirecki and M. Meyer. Leiden: E. J. Brill.

Farrar, Cynthia. 1988. *The Origins of Democratic Thinking: The Invention of Politics in Classical Athens*. Cambridge: Cambridge University Press.

Fehr, Burkhard. 1984. *Die Tyrannentöter, oder, Kann man der Demokratie ein Denkmal setzen?* Frankfurt am Main: Fischer Taschenbuch.

Fine, John V. A. 1951. *Horoi. Studies in Mortgage, Real Security and Land Tenure in Ancient Athens*. Baltimore: American School of Classical Studies at Athens.

Finley, M. I. 1951. *Studies in Land and Credit in Ancient Athens, 500–200 B.C.: The Horos-Inscriptions*. New Brunswick, N.J.: Rutgers University Press.

———. 1953. "Land, Debt, and the Man of Property in Classical Athens." *Political Science Quarterly* 68:249–68.

———. 1985. *Democracy Ancient and Modern*. London: Hogarth.

Fish, Stanley Eugene. 1980. *Is There a Text in This Class? The Authority of Interpretive Communities*. Cambridge, Mass.: Harvard University Press.

Fisher, N.R.E. 1992. *Hybris: A Study in the Values of Honour and Shame in Ancient Greece*. Warminster, Switzerland: Aris & Phillips.

Forsdyke, Sara. 2000. "Exile, Ostracism and the Athenian Democracy." *Classical Antiquity* 19:232–63.

Foster, Stuart J. 1998. "Politics, Parallels and Perennial Curriculum Questions: The Battle over School History in England and the United States." *Curriculum Journal* 9:153–64.

Friedman, Barry. 2002. "The Birth of an American Obsession: The History of the Countermajoritarian Difficulty, Part Five." *Yale Law Journal* 112:153–259.

Gallant, Thomas W. 1982. "Agricultural System, Land Tenure, and the Reforms of Solon." *Annual of the British School at Athens* 77:111–24.

———. 1991. *Risk and Survival in Ancient Greece: Reconstructing the Rural Domestic Economy*. Stanford, Calif.: Stanford University Press.

Garland, B. J. 1981. "*Gynaikonomoi*: An Investigation of Greek Censors of Women." Ph.D. Diss. Baltimore, Md.: Johns Hopkins University.

Garnsey, Peter. 1996. *Ideas of Slavery from Aristotle to Augustine*. Cambridge: Cambridge University Press.

Gauthier, Philippe. 1982. "Notes sur trois décrets honorant des citoyens bienfaiteurs." *Revue de philologie, de littérature et d'histoire anciennes* 56:215–31.

———. 1985. *Les cités grecques et leurs bienfaiteurs*. Paris: Ecole française d'Athènes. Diffusion de Boccard.

———. 1993. "Les cités hellénistiques," 211–31, in *The Ancient Greek City-State*, edited by Mogens Herman Hansen. Copenhagen: Munksgaard.

Gehrke, Hans-Joachim. 1985. *Stasis: Untersuchungen zu den inneren Kriegen in den griechischen Staaten des 5. und 4. Jahrhunderts v. Chr.* Munich: Beck.

Gellner, Ernest. 1983. *Nations and Nationalism*. Ithaca, N.Y.: Cornell University Press.

Gernet, Louis. 1981. *The Anthropology of Ancient Greece*. Baltimore, Md.: Johns Hopkins University Press.

Gillman, Howard. 2001. *The Votes That Counted: How the Court Decided the 2000 Presidential Election*. Chicago: University of Chicago Press.

Goldhill, Simon, and Robin Osborne, eds. 1999. *Performance Culture and Athenian Democracy*. Cambridge: Cambridge University Press.

Gomme, A. W. 1962. *More Essays in Greek History and Literature*. Edited by David A. Campbell. Oxford: Blackwell.

Gray, John. 1996. *Isaiah Berlin*. Princeton, N.J.: Princeton University Press.

Green, Stanton W., and Stephen M. Perlman, eds. 1985. *The Archaeology of Frontiers and Boundaries*. Orlando, Fla.: Academic Press.

Gutmann, Amy. 1999. *Democratic Education*. Princeton, N.J.: Princeton University Press.

———. 2003. *Identity in Democracy*. Princeton, N.J.: Princeton University Press.

Gutmann, Amy, and Dennis F. Thompson. 1996. *Democracy and Disagreement*. Cambridge, Mass.: Belknap Press of Harvard University Press.

Habicht, Christian. 1997. *Athens from Alexander to Antony*. Cambridge, Mass.: Harvard University Press.

Hamilton, Charles D., and Peter Krentz, eds. 1997. *Polis and Polemos: Essays on Politics, War, & History in Ancient Greece, in Honor of Donald Kagan*. Claremont, Calif.: Regina Books.

Hampshire, Stuart. 2000. *Justice Is Conflict*. Princeton, N.J.: Princeton University Press.

Hansen, Mogens Herman. 1975. *Eisangelia: The Sovereignty of the People's Court in Athens in the Fourth Century B.C. and the Impeachment of Generals and Politicians*. Odense: Odense University Press.

———. 1976. *Apagoge, Endeixis and Ephegesis against Kakourgoi, Atimoi and Pheugontes: A Study in the Athenian Administration of Justice in the Fourth Century B. C*. Odense: Odense University Press.

———. 1986. *Demography and Democracy: The Number of Athenian Citizens in the Fourth Century B.C*. Herning, Denmark: Systime.

———. 1991. *The Athenian Democracy in the Age of Demosthenes: Structure, Principles, and Ideology*. Oxford: Blackwell.

———. 1995. *The Trial of Sokrates—From the Athenian Point of View*. Copenhagen: Munksgaard.

Hansen, Mogens Herman, H. L. Bjertrup, T. H. Nielsen, L. Rubinstein, and T. Vestergaard. 1990. "The Demography of the Attic Demes: The evidence of the Sepulchral Inscriptions." *Analecta Romana* 19:24–44.

Hanson, Victor D. 1996. "Hoplites into Democrats: The Changing Ideology of Athenian Infantry," 289–312, in *Dēmokratia: A Conversation on Democracies, Ancient and Modern*, edited by Josiah Ober and Charles W. Hedrick. Princeton, N.J.: Princeton University Press.

———. 1999. "No Glory that Was Greece: The Persians Win at Salamis, 480 B.C.," 15–35, in *What If? The World's Foremost Military Historians Imagine What Might Have Been*, edited by Robert Cowley. New York: G. P. Putnam.

Harding, Phillip, ed. 1985. *From the End of the Peloponnesian War to the Battle of Ipsus*. Cambridge: Cambridge University Press.

Harris, E. M. 1989. "Demosthenes' Speech Against Meidias." *Harvard Studies in Classical Philology* 92:117–36.

Harrison, E. B. 1981. "Motifs of the City-Siege on the Shield of Athena Parthenos," *American Journal of Archaeology* 85:245–363.

Hart, H. L. 1958. "Positivism and the Separation of Law and Morals." *Harvard Law Review* 71:593–606.

Henderson, Jeffrey. 2003. "Demos, Demagogue, Tyrant in Attic Old Comedy," 155–180, in *Popular Tyranny: Sovereignty and Its Discontents in Ancient Greece*, edited by Kathryn Morgan. Austin: University of Texas Press.

Herman, Gabriel. 1993. "Tribal and Civic Codes of Behaviour in Lysias I." *Classical Quarterly* 43:406–19.

———. 1994. "How Violent Was Athenian society?" 99–117, in *Ritual, Finance, Politics: Athenian Democratic Accounts Presented to David Lewis*, edited by Robin Osborne and Simon Hornblower. Oxford: Clarendon Press.

———. 1995. "Honour, Revenge and the State in Fourth-Century Athens," 43–60, in *Die athenische Demokratie im 4. Jahrhundert v. Chr.: Vollendung oder Verfall einer Verfassungsform*, edited by Walter Eder and Christoph Auffarth. Stuttgart: F. Steiner.

Hesk, Jonathon. 2000. *Deception and Democracy in Classical Athens*. Cambridge: Cambridge University Press.

Hignett, Charles. 1952. *A History of the Athenian Constitution to the End of the Fifth Century B. C.* Oxford: Clarendon Press.

Hitz, Zena. 2004. "Plato and the Failings of Democracy." Ph.D. Diss. Princeton, N.J.: Princeton University.

Holmes, Stephen T. 1979. "Aristippus in and out of Athens." *American Political Science Review* 73:113–28.

Hölscher, Tonio. 1973. *Griechische Historienbilder des 5. und 4. Jahrhunderts v. Chr.* Watzburg: K. Triltsch.

Hornblower, Simon. 1991–96. *A Commentary on Thucydides*. 2 vols. Oxford: Clarendon Press.

Humphrey, Caroline. 1992. "The Moral Authority of the Past in Post-Socialist Mongolia." *Religion, State and Society* 20:375–89.

Hunt, Peter. 1998. *Slaves, Warfare, and Ideology in the Greek Historians*. Cambridge: Cambridge University Press.

Hunter, Virginia J. 1994. *Policing Athens: Social Control in the Attic Lawsuits, 420–320 B.C.* Princeton, N.J.: Princeton University Press.

Ispahani, Mahnaz Z. 1989. *Roads and Rivals: The Political Uses of Access in the Borderlands of Asia*. Ithaca, N.Y.: Cornell University Press.

Jameson, Michael H. 1991. "Sacrifice before Battle," 197–227, in *Hoplites: The Classical Greek Battle Experience*, edited by Victor Davis Hanson. New York: Routledge.

Kaempf-Dimitriadou, S. 1986. "Ein attisches Staatsgrabmal des 4. Jhs. v. Chr." *Antike Kunst* 29:23–36.

Kagan, Donald. 2003. *The Peloponnesian War*. New York: Viking.

Kahn, Charles. 1983. "Drama and Dialectic in Plato's *Gorgias*." *Oxford Studies in Ancient Philosophy* 1:75–121.

Kahn, L. 1979. "Hermès, la frontière et l'identité ambiguë." *Ktèma* 4:201–11.

Kallet, Lisa. 2003. "*Dēmos Tyrannos*: Wealth, Power, and Economic Patronage," 117–54, in *Popular Tyranny: Sovereignty and Its Discontents in Ancient Greece*, edited by Kathryn Morgan. Austin: University of Texas Press.

Kapparis, K. A., ed. 1999. *Against Neaira: [Demosthenes] 59*. Berlin: de Gruyter.

Kateb, George. 1998. "Socratic Integrity," 77–112, in *Integrity and Conscience*, edited by Ian Shapiro and Robert Merrihew Adams. New York: New York University Press.

Katz, Marilyn. 1999. "Women and Democracy in Ancient Greece," 41–68, in *Contextualizing Classics [Festschrift for John Peradotto]*, edited by M. Falkner, Nancy Felson, and David Konstan. Lanham, Md.: Rowman and Littlefield.

Katzenbach, Jon R., and Douglas K. Smith. 1993. *The Wisdom of Teams: Creating the High-Performance Organization*. Boston, Mass.: Harvard Business School Press.

Kennell, Nigel M. 1995. *The Gymnasium of Virtue: Education & Culture in Ancient Sparta*. Chapel Hill: University of North Carolina Press.

Knoepfler, Denis. 2001. "Loi d'Eretrie contre la tyrannie et l'oligarchie, I." *Bulletin de Correspondence Hellénique* 125:195–238.

———. 2002. "Loi d'Eretrie contre la tyrannie et l'oligarchie, II." *Bulletin de Correspondence Hellénique* 126:149–204.

Kraut, Richard. 1984. *Socrates and the State*. Princeton, N.J.: Princeton University Press.

Krentz, Peter. 1982. *The Thirty at Athens*. Ithaca, N.Y.: Cornell University Press.

Kroll, John H. 1972. *Athenian Bronze Allotment Plates*. Cambridge, Mass.: Harvard University Press.

Kurke, Leslie. 1992. "The Politics of *Habrosynē*." *Classical Antiquity* 11:91–120.

———. 1999. *Coins, Bodies, Games, and Gold: The Politics of Meaning in Archaic Greece*. Princeton, N.J.: Princeton University Press.

Kymlicka, Will. 1995. *Multicultural Citizenship: A Liberal Theory of Minority Rights*. Oxford: Clarendon Press.

L'Homme-Wéry, Louise-Marie. 1996. *La perspective éleusinienne dans la politique de Solon*. Genève: Droz.

———. 2000. "La notion de patrie dans la pensée politique du Solon." *Antiquité Classique* 69:21–41.

Lane, M. S. 2001. *Plato's Progeny: How Plato and Socrates Still Captivate the Modern Mind*. London: Duckworth.

Langdon, Merle K. 1985a. "Hymettiana. I." *Hesperia* 54:257–70.

———. 1985b. "The Territorial Basis of the Attic Demes." *Symbolae Osloenses* 60:5–15.

———. 1988a. "Hymettiana. II." *American Journal of Archaeology* 1988:75–83.

———. 1988b. "The Topography of Coastal Erechtheis." *Chiron* 18:43–54.

———. 1988c. "The ZW/BA Horoi at Vari in Attica." *Greek, Roman, and Byzantine Studies* 29:75–81.

———. 1999. "Hymettiana III: The Boundary Markers of Alepovouni." *Hesperia* 68:481–508.

Lanni, Adriaan M. 2004. "Arguing from "Precedent": Modern Perspectives on Athenian Practice," 159–72, in *The Law and the Courts in Ancient Greece*, edited by Edward M. Harris and L. Rubinstein. London: Duckworth.

Lape, Susan. 2004. *Reproducing Athens: Menander's Comedy, Democratic Culture, and the Hellenistic City*. Princeton, N.J.: Princeton University Press.

Lauter, H. 1982. "Zwei Horos-Inschriften bei Vari. Zu Grenzziehung und Demenlokalisierung in Südost-Attika." *Archäologischer Anzeiger*:299–315.

———. 1992. "Some Remarks on Fortified Settlements in the Attic Countryside," 77–91, in *Fortificationes Antiquae*, edited by Symphorien van de Maele and John M. Fossey. Amsterdam: J. C. Gieben.

Lawton, Carol L. 1995. *Attic Document Reliefs: Art and Politics in Ancient Athens*. Oxford: Clarendon Press.

Lebow, Richard Ned, and Barry S. Strauss, eds. 1991. *Hegemonic Rivalry: From Thucydides to the Nuclear Age.* Boulder: Westview Press.

Lévêque, Pierre, and Pierre Vidal-Naquet. 1964. *Clisthène L'Athénien: essai sur la représentation de l'espace et du temps dans la pensée politique grecque de la fin du VIe siècle à la mort de Platon.* Paris: Les Belles lettres.

———. 1996. *Cleisthenes the Athenian: An Essay on the Representation of Space and Time in Greek Political Thought from the End of the Sixth Century to the Death of Plato,* translated by David Ames Curtis. Atlantic Highlands, N.J.: Humanities Press.

Linforth, Ivan Mortimer. 1919. *Solon the Athenian.* Berkeley: University of California Press.

Loening, Thomas Clark. 1987. *The Reconciliation Agreement of 403/402 B.C. in Athens: Its Content and Application.* Stuttgart: F. Steiner Verlag.

Lohmann, Hans. 1983. "Atene, eine attische Landgemeinde klassischer Zeit." *Hellenika: Jahrbuch für die Freunde Griechenlands*: 99–104.

———. 1992. "Agriculture and Country Life in Classical Attica," 29–60, in *Agriculture in Ancient Greece: Proceedings of the Seventh International Symposium at the Swedish Institute at Athens,* edited by Berit Wells. Stockholm: Paul Åströms Förlag.

Loraux, Nicole. 1984. "Solon au milieu de la lice," 199–214, in *Aux origines de l'hellénisme: La Crète et la Grèce: Hommage à Henri van Effenterre.* Paris: Publications de la Sorbonne.

———. 1986. *The Invention of Athens: The Funeral Oration in the Classical City.* Cambridge, Mass.: Harvard University Press.

———. 1997. *La cité divisée: L'oubli dans la mémoire d'Athènes.* Paris: Payot.

———. 2002. *The Divided City: On Memory and Forgetting in Ancient Athens,* translated by Corinne Pache. New York: Zone Books.

Ma, John. 1999. *Antiochos III and the Cities of Western Asia Minor.* Oxford: Oxford University Press.

———. 2000. "Seleukids and Speech-Act Theory: Performative Utterances, Legitimacy and Negotiations in the World of the Maccabees." *Scripta Classica Israelica* 19:71–112.

MacDowell, Douglas M. 1975. "Law-making at Athens in the Fourth Century B.C." *Journal of Hellenic Studies* 95:62–74.

———. 1978. *The Law in Classical Athens.* Ithaca, N.Y.: Cornell University Press.

———. 1990. *Demosthenes, Against Meidias: Oration 21.* Oxford: Clarendon Press.

Macedo, Stephen. 1998. "Transformative Constitutionalism and the Case of Religion: Defending the Moderate Hegemony of Liberalism." *Political Theory* 26:56–80.

———. 2000. *Diversity and Distrust: Civic Education in a Multicultural Democracy.* Cambridge, Mass.: Harvard University Press.

———. 2001. *The Princeton Principles on Universal Jurisdiction.* Princeton, N.J.: Program in Law and Public Affairs, Princeton University.

Mackil, Emily. 2004. "Wandering Cities: Alternatives to Catastrophe in the Greek Polis." *American Journal of Archaeology* 108:493–516.

Manville, Philip Brook. 1990. *The Origins of Citizenship in Ancient Athens.* Princeton, N.J.: Princeton University Press.

———. 1997. "Pericles and the 'both/and' Vision for Democratic Athens," 73–84, in *Polis and Polemos: Essays on Politics, War, & History in Ancient Greece, in Honor of Donald Kagan*, edited by Charles D. Hamilton and Peter Krentz. Claremont, Calif.: Regina Books.

Manville, Philip Brook and Josiah Ober. 2003. *A Company of Citizens: What the World's First Democracy Teaches Leaders about Creating Great Organizations.* Boston: Harvard Business School Press.

Marcellus, Henri de. 1994. "The Origins and Nature of the Attic Ephebeia to 200 B.C." D.Phil. Diss. Oxford: Oxford University.

Meier, Christian. 1990. *The Greek Discovery of Politics.* Cambridge, Mass.: Harvard University Press.

Meiggs, Russell, and David M. Lewis, eds. 1988. *A Selection of Greek Historical Inscriptions to the End of the Fifth Century B.C.* Oxford: Clarendon Press.

Meritt, B. D. 1952. "Athenian Inscriptions." *Hesperia* 21:340–80.

Mill, John Stuart. 1846. "Grote's History of Greece [I]." *Edinburgh Review* 84: 343–77. *Collected Works* 11 (1978), pp. 273–305.

Miller, Fred D., and David Keyt, eds. 1991. *Aristotle's Politics: A Critical Reader.* Oxford: Blackwell.

Miller, Margaret. 1996. "The Arguments I Seem to Hear. Argument and Irony in the *Crito*." *Phronesis* 41:121–37.

Millett, Paul C. 1991. *Lending and Borrowing in Ancient Athens.* Cambridge: Cambridge University Press.

———. 1998. "Encounters in the Agora," 203–28, in *Kosmos: Essays in Order, Conflict and Community in Classical Athens*, edited by Paul Cartledge, Paul C. Millet, and Sitta von Reden. Cambridge: Cambridge University Press.

Moles, John. 1999. "*Anathema kai Ktema*: The Inscriptional Inheritance of Ancient Historiography." *Histos*: 1–53.

Monoson, Susan Sara. 1994. "Citizen as *Erastes*: Erotic Imagery and the Idea of Reciprocity in the Periclean Funeral Oration." *Political Theory* 22:253–76.

———. 2000. *Plato's Democratic Entanglements: Athenian Politics and the Practice of Philosophy.* Princeton, N.J.: Princeton University Press.

Morgan, Kathryn A., ed. 2003a. *Popular Tyranny: Sovereignty and Its Discontents in Ancient Greece.* Austin: University of Texas Press.

———. 2003b. "The Tyranny of the Audience in Plato and Isocrates," 181–214, in *Popular Tyranny: Sovereignty and Its Discontents in Ancient Greece*, edited by Kathryn Morgan. Austin: University of Texas Press.

Morris, Ian. 1992. *Death-Ritual and Social Structure in Classical Antiquity.* Cambridge: Cambridge University Press.

———. 1996. "The Strong Principle of Equality and the Archaic Origins of Greek Democracy," 19–49, in *Dēmokratia: A Conversation on Democracies, Ancient and Modern*, edited by Josiah Ober and Charles W. Hedrick. Princeton, N.J.: Princeton University Press.

———. 1998. "Remaining Invisible: The Archaeology of the Excluded in Classical Athens," 193–220, in *Women and Slaves in Greco-Roman Culture*, edited by Sheila Murnaghan and Sandra R. Joshel. New York: Routledge.

———. 2000. *Archaeology as Cultural History: Words and Things in Iron Age Greece*. Malden, Mass.: Blackwell.

Morris, Ian, and Kurt A. Raaflaub, eds. 1998. *Democracy 2500? Questions and Challenges*. Dubuque, Iowa: Kendall/Hunt Pub. Co.

Morris, Sarah. 2003. "Imaginary Kings: Alternatives to Monarchy in Early Greece," 1–24, in *Popular Tyranny: Sovereignty and Its Discontents in Ancient Greece*, edited by Kathryn Morgan. Austin: University of Texas Press.

Mosley, D. J. 1973. "Crossing Greek Frontiers in Arms." *Revue internationale des droits de l'antiquité* 3.20:161–69.

Munn, Mark Henderson. 1990. "On the Frontiers of Attica and Boiotia: The Results of the Stanford Skourta Plain Project," 32–42, in *Essays in the Topography, History and Culture of Boiotia*, edited by Albert Schachter. Montreal: McGill University Department of Classics.

———. 1996. "The First Excavations at Panakton on the Attic-Boiotian Frontier." *Boeotia Antiqua* 6:47–58.

———. 2000. *The School of History: Athens in the Age of Socrates*. Berkeley: University of California Press.

Munn, Mark Henderson, and M. L. Zimmerman Munn. 1989. "The Skourta Plain Project: The 1987 and 1988 Seasons of Survey on the Attic-Boiotian Frontier." *American Journal of Archaeology* 93:274–75.

Neer, Richard T. 2002. *Style and Politics in Athenian Vase-Painting: The Craft of Democracy, ca. 530–460 B.C.E.* Cambridge: Cambridge University Press.

Nehamas, Alexander. 1999. *Virtues of Authenticity: Essays on Plato and Socrates*. Princeton, N.J.: Princeton University Press.

Neils, Jenifer. 1992, ed. *Goddess and Polis: The Panathenaic Festival in Ancient Athens*. Princeton, N.J: Princeton University Press.

Nightingale, Andrea Wilson. 1995. *Genres in Dialogue: Plato and the Construct of Philosophy*. Cambridge: Cambridge University Press.

———. 2001. "Liberal Education in Plato's *Republic* and Aristotle's *Politics*," 133–74, in *Education in Greek and Roman Antiquity*, edited by Yun Lee Too. Leiden: E. J. Brill.

North, Helen. 1966. *Sophrosyne: Self-Knowledge and Self-Restraint in Greek Literature*. Ithaca, N.Y.: Cornell University Press.

Ober, Josiah. 1981. "Rock-Cut Inscriptions from Mt. Hymettos." *Hesperia* 50:68–77.

———. 1985. *Fortress Attica: Defense of the Athenian Land Frontier, 404–322 B.C.* Leiden: E. J. Brill.

———. 1987. "Pottery and Miscellaneous Artifacts from Fortified Sites in Northern and Western Attica." *Hesperia* 56:197–227.

———. 1989. *Mass and Elite in Democratic Athens: Rhetoric, Ideology, and the Power of the People*. Princeton, N.J.: Princeton University Press.

———. 1996. *The Athenian Revolution: Essays on Ancient Greek Democracy and Political Theory*. Princeton, N.J.: Princeton University Press.

————. 1998. *Political Dissent in Democratic Athens: Intellectual Critics of Popular Rule*. Princeton, N.J.: Princeton University Press.

————. 2000. "Political Conflicts, Political Debates, and Political Thought," 111–38, in *The Shorter Oxford History of Europe I: Classical Greece*, edited by Robin Osborne. Oxford: Oxford University Press.

————. 2001. "Thucydides Theoretikos/Thucydides Histor: Realist Theory and the Challenge of History," 273–306, in *Democracy and War: A Comparative Study of the Korean War and the Peloponnesian War*, edited by D. R. McCann, B. S. Strauss. Armonk, N.Y.: M. E. Sharpe.

Ober, Josiah, and Charles W. Hedrick, eds. 1993. *The Birth of Democracy: An Exhibition Celebrating the 2500th Anniversary of Democracy*. Princeton, N.J.: American School of Classical Studies in Athens.

————, eds. 1996. *Dēmokratia: A Conversation on Democracies, Ancient and Modern*. Princeton, N.J.: Princeton University Press.

Osborne, Michael J. 1981. *Naturalization in Athens*. Brussels: Paleis der Academiën.

Osborne, Robin. 1985. *Demos, The Discovery of Classical Attika*. Cambridge: Cambridge University Press.

————. 2003. "Changing the Discourse," 251–72, in *Popular Tyranny: Sovereignty and Its Discontents in Ancient Greece*, edited by Kathryn Morgan. Austin: University of Texas Press.

Ostwald, Martin. 1955. "The Athenian Legislation against Tyranny and Subversion." *Transactions of the American Philological Association* 86:103–28.

————. 1969. *Nomos and the Beginnings of the Athenian Democracy*. Oxford: Clarendon Press.

————. 1986. *From Popular Sovereignty to the Sovereignty of Law: Law, Society, and Politics in Fifth-Century Athens*. Berkeley: University of California Press.

Parker, Robert. 1996. *Athenian Religion: A History*. Oxford: Clarendon Press.

Pélékidis, Chrysis. 1962. *Histoire de l'éphébie attique des origines à 31 avant Jésus-Christ*. Paris: Editions de Boccard.

Petrey, Sandy. 1990. *Speech Acts and Literary Theory*. New York: Routledge.

Pettit, Philip. 1997. *Republicanism: A Theory of Freedom and Government*. Oxford: Clarendon Press.

Phillips, Derek L. 1993. *Looking Backward: A Critical Appraisal of Communitarian Thought*. Princeton, N.J.: Princeton University Press.

Popper, Karl Raimund. 1963. *The Open Society and Its Enemies*. Princeton, N.J.: Princeton University Press.

Posner, Eric A. 2000. *Law and Social Norms*. Cambridge, Mass.: Harvard University Press.

Posner, Richard A. 2001. *Breaking the Deadlock: The 2000 Election, the Constitution, and the Courts*. Princeton, N.J.: Princeton University Press.

Poulakos, Takis, and David Depew, eds. 2004. *Isocrates and Civic Education*. Austin: University of Texas Press.

Quillin, James. 2002. "Achieving Amnesty: The Role of Events, Institutions, and Ideas." *Transactions of the American Philological Association* 132:71–107.

Raaflaub, Kurt A. 1985. *Die Entdeckung der Freiheit: Zur historischen Semantik und Gesellschaftsgeschichte eines politischen Grundbegriffes der Griechen.* Munich: Beck.

———. Raaflaub, Kurt. 1996. "Equalities and Inequalities in Athenian Democracy," 139–74, in *Dēmokratia: A Conversation on Democracies, Ancient and Modern*, edited by Josiah Ober and Charles W. Hedrick. Princeton, N.J.: Princeton University.

———. 2003. "Stick and Glue: The Function of Tyranny in Fifth-Century Athenian Democracy," 59–94, in *Popular Tyranny: Sovereignty and Its Discontents in Ancient Greece*, edited by Kathryn Morgan. Austin: University of Texas Press.

Rahe, Paul Anthony. 1992. *Republics Ancient and Modern: Classical Republicanism and the American Revolution.* Chapel Hill: University of North Carolina Press.

Randall, R. H. 1953. "The Erechtheum Workmen." *American Journal of Archaeology* 57:199–210.

Rawlings, Hunter R. 1981. *The Structure of Thucydides' History.* Princeton, N.J.: Princeton University Press.

Raz, Joseph. 1986. *The Morality of Freedom.* Oxford: Oxford University Press.

Reinmuth, O. W., ed. 1971. *The Ephebic Inscriptions of the Fourth Century B.C.* Leiden: Brill.

Rhodes, Peter J. 1979–80. "Athenian Democracy after 403 B.C." *Classical Journal* 75:305–23.

———. 1981. *A Commentary on the Aristotelian Athenaion Politeia.* Oxford: Clarendon Press.

———. 1984. *"What Alcibiades Did or What Happened to Him": An Inaugural Lecture.* Durham: University of Durham.

———. 2003. *Ancient Democracy and Modern Ideology.* London: Duckworth.

———, ed. 2004. *Athenian Democracy.* Edinburgh: University of Edinburgh Press.

Rhodes, P. J., and David M. Lewis, eds. 1997. *The Decrees of the Greek States.* Oxford: Clarendon Press.

Ridgway, Brunilde Sismondo. 1997. *Fourth-Century Styles in Greek Sculpture.* Madison: University of Wisconsin Press.

Roberts, Jennifer Tolbert. 1982. *Accountability in Athenian Government.* Madison: University of Wisconsin Press.

———. 1994. *Athens on Trial: The Antidemocratic Tradition in Western Thought.* Princeton, N.J.: Princeton University Press.

———. 1996. "Comparatively Equal: A Constant Surrounded by Flux," 187–202, in *Dēmokratia: A Conversation on Democracies, Ancient and Modern*, edited by Josiah Ober and Charles W. Hedrick. Princeton, N.J.: Princeton University Press.

Robinson, Eric W, ed. 2004. *Ancient Greek Democracy: Readings and Sources.* Oxford: Blackwell.

Roesch, Paul. 1965. *Thespies et la confédération béotienne.* Paris: Editions de Boccard.

Rousset, Denis, and Photios P. Katzouros. 1992. "Une délimitation de frontière en Phocide." *Bulletin de Correspondence Hellénique* 116:197–215.

Rubinstein, L. 1998. "The Political Perception of the *Idiotes*," 125–43, in *Kosmos: Essays in Order, Conflict, and Community in Classical Athens*, edited by Paul Cartledge, Paul Millett, and Sitta von Reden. Cambridge: Cambridge University Press.

———. forthcoming. "Argument from Precedent in the Attic Orators," in *Oxford Readings in Attic Orators: Rhetoric and Law*, edited by Edwin Carawan. Oxford: Oxford University Press.

Sandel, Michael J. 1984. *Liberalism and Its Critics*. Oxford: Blackwell.

———. 1996. *Democracy's Discontent: America in Search of a Public Philosophy*. Cambridge, Mass.: Belknap Press of Harvard University Press.

———. 1998. *Liberalism and the Limits of Justice*. Cambridge: Cambridge Universtiy Press.

Sartre, M. 1979. "Aspects économiques et aspects religieux de la frontière dans les cités grecques." *Ktèma* 4:213–24.

Saxonhouse, Arlene W. 1992. *Fear of Diversity: The Birth of Political Science in Ancient Greek Thought*. Chicago: University of Chicago Press.

———. 1996. *Athenian Democracy: Modern Mythmakers and Ancient Theorists*. Notre Dame, Ind.: University of Notre Dame Press.

Scalia, Antonin. 1997. *A Matter of Interpretation: Federal Courts and the Law— An Essay*. Princeton, N.J.: Princeton University Press.

Seaford, Richard. 1994. *Reciprocity and Ritual: Homer and Tragedy in the Developing City-State*. Oxford: Clarendon Press.

———. 2003. "Tragic Tyranny," 95–116, in *Popular Tyranny: Sovereignty and Its Discontents in Ancient Greece*, edited by Kathryn Morgan. Austin: University of Texas Press.

Searle, John R. 1969. *Speech Acts: An Essay in the Philosophy of Language*. Cambridge: Cambridge University Press.

———. 1995. *The Construction of Social Reality*. New York: Free Press.

Sewell, William. 1999. "The Concept(s) of Culture," 35–61, in *Beyond the Cultural Turn: New Directions in the Study of Society and Culture*, edited by Victoria E. Bonnell and Lynn Avery Hunt. Berkeley and Los Angeles: University of California Press.

Shefton, B. B. 1960. "Some Iconographic Remarks on the Tyrannicides." *American Journal of Archaeology* 64:173–79.

Siewart, P. 1977. "The Ephebic Oath in Fifth-Century Athens." *Journal of Hellenic Studies* 97:102–11.

Simon, Erika, and Max Hirmer. 1976. *Die griechischen Vasen*. Munich: Hirmer.

Skinner, Quentin. 1998. *Liberty Before Liberalism*. Cambridge: Cambridge University Press.

Slaton, Christa Daryl. 1992. *Televote: Expanding Citizen Participation in the Quantum Age*. New York: Praeger.

Sommerstein, Alan H., ed. 1990. *The Comedies of Aristophanes. Vol. 7: Lysistrata*. Warminster Switzerland: Aris & Phillips.

Spinosa, Charles, Fernando Flores, and Hubert L. Dreyfus. 1997. *Disclosing New Worlds: Entrepreneurship, Democratic Action, and the Cultivation of Solidarity*. Cambridge, Mass.: MIT Press.

Stanton, G. R. 1984. "Some Attic Inscriptions." *Annual of the British School at Athens* 79:289–306.

———. 1990. *Athenian Politics, c. 800–500 B.C.: A Sourcebook*. London and New York: Routledge.

———. 1996. "Some Inscriptions in Attic Demes." *Annual of the British School at Athens* 91:341–64.

Stinton, T. C. 1976. "Solon, Fragment 25." *Journal of Hellenic Studies* 96:159–62.

Stout, Jeffrey. 2004. *Democracy and Tradition*. Princeton, N.J.: Princeton University Press.

Strauss, Barry S. 1985. "Ritual, Social Drama and Politics in Classical Athens." *American Journal of Ancient History* 10:67–83.

———. 1994. "The Melting Pot, the Mosaic, and the Agora," 252–64, in *Athenian Political Thought and The Reconstruction of American Democracy*, edited by J. Peter Euben, John Wallach, and Josiah Ober, Ithaca; N.Y.: Cornell University Press.

———. 1996. "The Athenian Trireme, School of Democracy," 313–26, in *Dēmokratia: A Conversation on Democracies, Ancient and Modern*, edited by Josiah Ober and Charles W. Hedrick. Princeton, N.J.: Princeton University Press.

Stupperich, R. 1994. "The Iconography of Athenian State Burials in the Classical Period," 93–101, in *The Archaeology of Athens and Attica under the Democracy*, edited by William D. E. Coulson. Oxford: Oxbow Books.

Sunstein, Cass R., and Richard Allen Epstein. 2001. *The Vote: Bush, Gore, and the Supreme Court*. Chicago: University of Chicago Press.

Svenbro, Jesper. 1988. *Phrasikleia: anthropologie de la lecture en Grèce ancienne*. Paris: La Découverte.

Taylor, Charles et al. 1994. *Multiculturalism: Examining the Politics of Recognition*. Edited by Amy Gutmann. Princeton, N.J.: Princeton University Press.

Taylor, Michael W. 1991. *The Tyrant Slayers: The Heroic Image in Fifth Century B.C. Athenian Art and Politics*. Salem, N.H.: Ayers.

Thompson, Homer A., and R. E. Wycherley. 1972. *The Agora of Athens: The History, Shape, and Uses of an Ancient City Center*. Princeton, N.J.: American School of Classical Studies at Athens.

Thompson, W. E. 1971. "The Deme in Kleisthenes' Reforms." *Symbolae Osloenses* 46:72–79.

Todd, S. C. 1990. "Lady Chatterley's Lover and the Athenian Orators: The Social Composition of the Athenian Jury." *Journal of Hellenic Studies* 110:146–70.

———. 1993. *The Shape of Athenian Law*. Oxford: Clarendon Press.

Too, Yun Lee, ed. 2001a. *Education in Greek and Roman Antiquity*. Leiden: E. J. Brill.

———. 2001b. "Legal Instructions in Classical Athens," 111–32, in *Education in Greek and Roman Antiquity*, edited by Yun Lee Too. Leiden: E. J. Brill.

Traill, John S. 1982. "An Interpretation of Six Rock-Cut Inscriptions in the Attic Demes of Lamptrai," 158–71, in *Studies in Attic Epigraphy, History, and Topography: Presented to Eugene Vanderpool*. Princeton, N.J.: American School of Classical Studies at Athens.

———. 1986. *Demos and Trittys: Epigraphical and Topographical Studies in the Organization of Attica*. Toronto: Victoria College.

Trevett, Jeremy. 1992. *Apollodoros, the Son of Pasion*. Oxford: Clarendon Press.

Urbinati, Nadia. 2002. *Mill on Democracy: From the Athenian Polis to Representative Government*. Chicago: University of Chicago Press.

Vasiliou, I. 1999. "Conditional Irony in the Socratic Dialogues." *Classical Quarterly* 49:456–72.

———. 2002. "Socrates' Reverse Irony." *Classical Quarterly* 52:220–30.

Vermeule, Emily. 1970. "Five Vases from the Grave Precinct of Dexileos." *Jahrbuch des deutschen archäologischen Instituts* 85:94–111.

Vernant, Jean Pierre. 1982. *The Origins of Greek Thought*. Ithaca: Cornell University Press.

Vidal-Naquet, Pierre. 1986. *The Black Hunter: Forms of Thought and Forms of Society in the Greek World*. Baltimore, Ma.: Johns Hopkins University Press.

Villa, Dana Richard. 2001. *Socratic Citizenship*. Princeton, N.J.: Princeton University Press.

Waldron, Jeremy. 1992. "Minority Cultures and the Cosmopolitan Alternative." *University of Michigan Journal of Law Reform* 25:751–93.

———. 2000. "Arendt's Constitutional Politics," 201–19, in *The Cambridge Companion to Hannah Arendt*, edited by Dana Richard Villa. Cambridge: Cambridge University Press.

Wallace, Robert W. 1989. *The Areopagos Council, to 307 B.C.* Baltimore, Md.: Johns Hopkins University Press.

———. 1994. "Private Lives and Public Enemies: Freedom of Thought in Classical Athens," 127–55, in *Athenian Identity and Civic Ideology*, edited by Alan L. Boegehold and Adele C. Scafuro. Baltimore, Md.: Johns Hopkins University Press.

Wallach, John R. 2001. *The Platonic Political Art: A Study of Critical Reason and Democracy*. University Park: Pennsylvania State University Press.

Walzer, Michael. 1988. *The Company of Critics: Social Criticism and Political Commitment in the Twentieth Century*. New York: Basic Books.

Wardy, Robert. 1996. *The Birth of Rhetoric: Gorgias, Plato, and Their Successors*. London: Routledge.

Weingast, Barry R. 1997. "The Political Foundations of Democracy and the Rule of Law." *American Political Science Review* 91:245–63.

Weiss, Roslyn. 1998. *Socrates Dissatisfied: An Analysis of Plato's* Crito. New York: Oxford University Press.

Wenger, Etienne. 1998. *Communities of Practice: Learning, Meaning, and Identity*. Cambridge: University Press.

White, J. B. 1996. "Plato's *Crito*. The Authority of Law and Philosophy," 97–144, in *The Greeks and Us: Essays in Honor of Arthur W. H. Adkins*, edited by Robert B. Louden and Paul Schollmeier. Chicago: University of Chicago Press.

Whitehead, David. 1977. *The Ideology of the Athenian Metic*. Cambridge: Cambridge Philological Society.

———. 1983. "Competitive Outlay and Community Profit: *Philotimia* in Democratic Athens." *Classica et Mediaevalia* 34:55–74.

———. 1986. *The Demes of Attica, 508/7–ca. 250 B.C.: A Political and Social Study*. Princeton, N.J.: Princeton University Press.

———. 1993. "Cardinal Virtues: The Language of Public Approbation in Democratic Athens." *Classica et Mediaevalia* 44:37–75.

Wilson, Peter. 1991. "Demosthenes 21 (*Against Meidias*): Democratic Abuse." *Proceedings of the Cambridge Philological Society* 37:164–95.

———. 2000. *The Athenian Institution of the Khoregia. The Chorus, the City, and the Stage*. Cambridge: Cambridge University Press.

Winkler, John J. 1990. *The Constraints of Desire: The Anthropology of Sex and Gender in Ancient Greece*. New York: Routledge.

Winkler, John J., and Froma I. Zeitlin, eds. 1990. *Nothing to Do with Dionysos?: Athenian Drama in Its Social Context*. Princeton, N.J.: Princeton University Press.

Wohl, Victoria. 2002. *Love among the Ruins: The Erotics of Democracy in Classical Athens*. Princeton, N.J.: Princeton University Press.

Wolpert, Andrew. 2002. *Remembering Defeat: Civil War and Civic Memory in Ancient Athens*. Baltimore, Md.: The Johns Hopkins University Press.

Wright, Robert. 1994. *The Moral Animal: The New Science of Evolutionary Psychology*. New York: Pantheon Books.

Yunis, Harvey. 1996. *Taming Democracy: Models of Political Rhetoric in Classical Athens*. Ithaca, N.Y.: Cornell University Press.

Zakaria, Fareed. 1997. "The Rise of Illiberal Democracy." *Foreign Affairs* 76:23–43.

———. 2003. *The Future of Freedom: Illiberal Democracy at Home and Abroad*. New York: W. W. Norton.

Zaret, David. 2000. *Origins of Democratic Culture: Printing, Petitions, and the Public Sphere in Early-Modern England*. Princeton, N.J.: Princeton University Press.

Ziolkowski, John E. 1981. *Thucydides and the Tradition of Funeral Speeches at Athens*. New York: Arno Press.

Index

Note: Page numbers in *italic* type indicate figures.

to, 77–91; rights applicable to, 74; risks and costs of, 85; societal, 70; as theory, 70–71

The Cultures within Greek Culture (Dougherty and Kurke), 71–73, 78, 87

culture wars, 60

Dahl, Robert, 99
Darwin, Charles, 175–76
Delphic oracle, 164
demes: boundaries of, 206–10; role of, 36–37
democracy: Aristotle on, 111; diversity and, 5–6; liberalism and, 92–97; Mill on, 33, 37, 38n; modern, 5–6; moral authority in, 54–55; revolution and, 62; rights and, 92; social versus technical knowledge in, 33–34; state and group/individual relations in, 6–7; theory versus practice in, 8–9; as tyranny, 231–33; value of, 29. *See also* Athenian democracy
democratic persistence, 8, 22, 224, 236–37
Demophantos, 224–25
Demos crowned by Demokratia, 223
Demosthenes, 113–16, 151–53
Dexileos relief, 241–45, 242
diversity: in Athens, 2–5, 8–9, 12, 25, 87, 89; democracy and, 5–6; in Greece, 88; in poleis, 89; political philosophers' approach to, 4; politics in response to, 78, 89; of subnational groups, 85–88
double-pointed speeches of Isocrates, 245
drama. *See* comedy; tragedy

Ecclesiazusae (Aristophanes), 122, 125
Edmonson, Colin, 241
education. *See* civic education
Electoral College, 30
elites: in Athenian democracy, 83, 98–99; citizenship responsibilities of, 69–70, 84; ethical code of, 137, 139, 144–45; and *hubris*, 113–14. *See also* aristocracy; cavalry; oligarchy
English common law, precedent and, 56
ephēbeia, 154–55, 202
ephebes, 154–55, 196–203
Ephialtes, 23
equality of Athenian citizens, 98–99, 140
Erythrae, 228–30
ethics: Athenian democratic values and,

135–36; cooperative values in, 138; process of democracy and, 146; sophists as teachers of, 144–45; standard Greek, 137, 139, 144–45
Euben, Peter, 88
Eukrates *nomos*, 21–24, 167, 222–25, 223
Eumenides (Aeschylus), 23
Euripides, 82
evolutionary psychology, 175–76
exempla, past actions as moral, 57–60
expertise: moral, 47–48, 50n.16; social versus technical knowledge and, 33–34

face-to-face society, 41
Farenga, Vincent, 216, 222
Fehr, Burkhard, 216
felicity, in communication, 184, 186–87
Finley, M. I., 178
Fisher, N.R.E., 113
Ford, Henry, 62
foreign policy, U.S., 92, 94
freedom of Athenian citizens, 140. *See also* liberties
freedom of speech, 131
French Revolution, 28, 61

Geertz, Clifford, 71
globalization, 84
Godard, Jean-Luc, 62
"going on together," value of, 2–3. *See also* democratic persistence; political community
good: civic education and concept of, 142; cultural diversity as, 80; political community as, 75, 75n.12, 79
Gorgias (Plato), 151, 232–34
Greece: as culture-zone, 76–77; diversity in, 88; mentality of, 102–4; positivist history of, 177–79; standard ethics of, 137, 139, 144–45; thin versus thick coherence of, 71–72; tyrant-killing outside Athens, 227–30

Hampshire, Stuart, 180–81
Hancock, John, 46
Hansen, Mogens H., 157, 158, 164, 166, 168–69, 178–79
Harmodios, 216–22, 225, 227. *See also* Kritios, tyrannicide sculpture group (with Nesiotes)

Pisistratus, 104

Plato: ahistorical politics of, 62; on democracy, 112, 118–19, 144–45, 230–36; on education, 95, 144–45; on ideal political community, 8, 9; on knowledge, 33–34; on legacy of political community, 59n.33; on moral authority, 50n.16; on political regimes, 236; on soul-polis isomorphism, 3–4, 9; on tyranny, 230–36

Platt, Lew, 35

plurality: in Athens, 2–3; in modern democracies, 6. *See also* diversity

Plutarch, 197

poleis: conflict in, 3–4; diversity of, 76–78; inclusion and exclusion in, 85; nation-states compared to, 75n.11

politeia: definition of, 7, 30; and moral authority in Athens, 62, 64–65

political community: as good in itself, 75, 75n.12, 79, 109; value of, 2–3, 5, 44

political theory, discipline of, 72–73

politics: cosmopolitanism and, 69–70, 80–81, 84; culture in relation to, 77–91; thin coherence maintained by, 78, 89

Politics (Aristotle), 108–11, 123

Popular Tyranny (Morgan), 214, 222, 231

positive liberties, 7, 95

positivism, 177–79

postmodern political theory, 7

precedent, moral authority and, 55–57

presidential election of 2000, U.S., 30

property, 98, 102–4, 117

Protagoras (Plato), 34

prytaneis, 39

Pseudo-Aristotle, *The Constitution of the Athenians*, 30, 154, 173–74, 192, 222

Pseudo-Xenophon, *The Constitution of the Athenians*, 30, 107, 111–12, 117, 231

quasi rights: in Athens, 96–97, 106, 111–25; definition of, 93; evidence concerning, 106; *hubris* and, 113–16; slaves/metics and, 111–13, 117–18; women/children and, 118–25

Quillin, James, 174

Raaflaub, Kurt, 222

rational choice theory, 171

relativism, 74

religion: ancient Mediterranean–western Asian, 3n.4; in Athens, 13, 117; non-Greek, 19; slaves/metics and, 117

Republic (Plato): ahistorical politics in, 62; on education, 95, 144–45; on gender in politics, 118–19; ideal political community in, 9; on non-Greek religion, 19; soul-polis isomorphism in, 3–4; on tyranny, 234–36

resident foreigners. *See* metics

revolution: civic education and, 128; democracy and, 62. *See also* French Revolution

Ridgway, Brunilde, 244

rights: ancients versus moderns on, 32, 92; Athenian ethical code and, 136; democracy and, 92; performative maintenance of, 127. *See also* civil rights, U.S.; human rights; quasi rights

Rousseau, Jean-Jacques, 61, 69, 71, 128

rupestral *horoi*, 203–11; authority behind, 205–8; dating of, 205; description of, 204; geographic dispersal of, 205–8

Sandel, Michael, 7

Saxonhouse, Arlene, 4, 88

security of Athenian citizens, 140

Sewell, William, 44n.2, 70–71, 74–77, 89

Shefton, B. B., 221

slavery: Aristotle on, 110; in Athens, 86, 90–91, 111–13, 117–18, 195–96; *hubris* and, 115–16; Solon and, 195–96

Smith, Adam, 127

Smith, Nicholas, 164

Social Contract (Rousseau), 61

social fact, moral authority as, 48–51

social reproduction. *See* Athenian democracy, reproduction through practice of; civic education

social science history, 171–72, 174–77, 181

societal culture, 70

Socrates: on civic education, 133–35, 141; commitment to Athens of, 159–60; on Council of 500, 40n; on legacy of political community, 59n.33, 160; on non-Greek religion, 19; on obedience to law, 24, 123, 152, 157–70; philosophy versus citizenship for, 161–65; Plato's depiction of, 159n; and refusal to escape, 160–61; versus sophists, 159; Thirty Tyrants